W9-CFQ-048

macromedia®

DREAMWEAVER® 8

Training from the Source

Khristine Annwn Page

ADOBE
PRESS

Adobe

Macromedia® Dreamweaver® 8
Training from the Source

Khristine Annwn Page

ADOBE
PRESS

 Adobe Press books are published by:

Peachpit

1249 Eighth Street
Berkeley, CA 94710
510/524-2178
800/283-9444
510/524-2221 (fax)
Find us on the World Wide Web at:
www.peachpit.com
www.adobe.com

To report errors, please send a note to errata@peachpit.com

Copyright © 2006 by Adobe Systems, Inc.

Notice of Rights

All rights reserved. No part of this book may be reproduced or transmitted in any form by any means, electronic, mechanical, photocopying, recording, or otherwise, without the prior written permission of the publisher. For information on getting permission for reprints and excerpts, contact permissions@peachpit.com.

Trademarks

Flash, Dreamweaver and Macromedia are registered trademarks of Adobe Systems, Inc.

Throughout this book, trademarked names are used. Rather than put a trademark symbol in every occurrence of a trademarked name, we state that we are using the names in an editorial fashion only and to the benefit of the trademark owner with no intention of infringement of the trademark.

Notice of Liability

The information in this book is distributed on an "As Is" basis, without warranty. While every precaution has been taken in the preparation of the book, neither the author, Macromedia, Inc., Adobe Systems, Inc. nor the publisher, shall have any liability to any person or entity with respect to any loss or damage caused or alleged to be caused directly or indirectly by the instructions contained in this book or by the computer software and hardware products described in it.

Printed and bound in the United States of America

ISBN 0-321-33626-7

9 8 7 6 5 4 3 2

Credits

Author
Khristine Annwn Page

Macromedia Press Editor
Angela C. Kozlowski

Development Editor
Susan Hobbs

Copy Editor
Nancy Sixsmith

Technical Editors
Demian Holmberg

Dori Smith

Production Coordinator
Becky Winter

Compositors
Rick Gordon, Emerald Valley Graphics

Debbie Roberti, Espresso Graphics

Indexer
Julie Bess, JBIndexing Inc.

Cover Design
George Mattingly, GMD

Dedication

For all of my family, in memory of my grandparents, and with a deep love for Spirit and the Divine, in all its myriad forms.

Bio

Khristine Annwn Page authored *Macromedia Dreamweaver MX 2004 Training from the Source* and *Macromedia Dreamweaver MX Training from the Source* as well as co-authored the *Macromedia Dreamweaver MX 2004 Certified Developer Study Guide* and *Macromedia Dreamweaver 4 Training from the Source*, all published by Peachpit Press and Macromedia Press. She has taught Dreamweaver and Web design classes at San Francisco State University's Multimedia Studies program, and performed Dreamweaver training for the Reuters Digital Vision Fellowship program at Stanford University and numerous independent clients. Khristine is currently Director of Prakasa Ma, a center for art, dance, and yoga in San Jose, California [www.prakasama.com], and the editor/publisher of Crescent Magazine. She also works as a freelance Web developer through NorthWind Studios, a collective of artists and writers [www.northwindstudios.com]. In the past she has worked as a Multimedia Specialist at the San Francisco Exploratorium and as a Senior Web Designer at Ideum, a company devoted to producing Websites for museums, non-profits, and socially responsible companies. Khristine holds a BFA with a Senior Award for Excellence from Rhode Island School of Design [www.risd.edu]. She has received awards from Adobe and her artwork has been shown in galleries in Providence, RI, New York City, and Palo Alto, CA.

Acknowledgments

A great many thanks to Susan Hobbs, Angela Kozlowski, Demian Holmberg, Sue Hove, and the rest of the wonderful people at Peachpit and Macromedia. Many thanks especially to Jayne Hillman and Yoga Sangha [www.yogasangha.com], as well as the rest of the instructors and staff at the studio, for allowing their site to be used as the project for this book. I'd like to express particular thanks to Mary Page, Rick Page, Jill Page, Rich Page, Yayoi Page, Adrienne Renka Page, Jessie Gauld, Russell Reza-Khaliq Gonzaga, Carol Coughlin, Paul and Britta from Avalon Art and Yoga, Katarina, Bhaktisukhini and everyone from DoK, and the rest of my friends and family for all the support, love and encouragement.

Table of Contents

Introduction

Dreamweaver 8 combines powerful visual layout tools with robust text-based HTML editing features for the creation, management, and maintenance of Web sites. It gives beginners immediate access to the tools need for creating Web pages while allowing experienced developers who are familiar with hand-coding to work directly with the code when needed. This flexible program makes advanced techniques accessible and easy to use. The integration of powerful design, code, and interactive features provides a wealth of benefits to both beginners and advanced users.

Prerequisites

This book is intended to familiarize you with the Dreamweaver development environment and focuses on equipping you with the skills needed to lay out and design Web pages. Because it is geared toward beginner and intermediate users who may have little or no previous experience with Dreamweaver, coverage of advanced application building and dynamic Web site creation with the use of databases, server behaviors and Web applications is outside the scope of this book. Those features require knowledge and understanding of dynamic design concepts and of the languages used to create these sites-including ASP, JSP, ColdFusion and more. For those who are interested in learning about the code, Lesson 16 will get you started in the coding environment, demonstrating how to work with Dreamweaver's coding tools and pointing you to resources within the program that will enable you to learn more.

The instructions in this book are designed for Web designers, Web developers, and others interested in creating Web pages. This book assumes that you are a beginner with Dreamweaver, but are familiar with the basic methods of giving commands on a Macintosh or Windows computer, such as choosing items from menus, opening and saving files, and so on.

To get the most out of this book, it is recommended that you have basic familiarity with the Web. A general understanding of standard word processing programs, such as Microsoft Word, is also helpful, although not required.

Finally, the instructions in this book assume that you already have Dreamweaver 8 installed on a Macintosh or Windows computer, and that your computer meets the system requirements listed on page 5. This minimum configuration allows you to run Dreamweaver 8.

Outline

This book steps you through the projects in each lesson, presents the major features and tools in Dreamweaver 8, and guides you toward developing the skills you need to create Web sites. All lessons should take approximately 24–28 hours in length and includes the following lessons:

Lesson 1: Dreamweaver 8 Basics

Lesson 2: Adding Content to a Page

Lesson 3: Creating Links

Elements and Format

Each lesson begins with an overview of the lesson's content and learning objectives. Lessons are divided into individual tasks that help you learn and utilize various aspects of the lesson's topic.

This book is part of the *Training from the Source* series. It contains conceptual information, in-depth material, and step-by-step explanations. In addition, each lesson includes the following special features:

- **Special font for code:** To help you easily identify code within the book, the code has been styled in a `special font` that's unique from the rest of the text.
- **Italic text:** An italic font is used to show text the reader types. As you work your way through the numbered steps, you can see immediately your next typed entry.

- **Tips:** Tips contain shortcuts for carrying out common tasks, and ways you can use the skills you're learning to solve common problems.
- **Notes:** Notes provide additional information pertaining to the task at hand.
- **Appendices:** The Appendices contains a variety of helpful Dreamweaver-related information, from regular expressions to keyboard shortcuts for both PC and Mac.

This course is developed to help you build your skills progressively as you work through each lesson. When you've completed the entire course, you'll have a thorough knowledge of Dreamweaver.

The accompanying CD contains all the files necessary to complete each lesson. Files for each lesson appear in a folder titled with the lesson number. It is strongly suggested that you create a folder on your hard drive and transfer all lesson files to that folder prior to beginning the course.

The lessons in this book assume that the following statements are true:

- You're familiar with using menus, opening and saving files, and so on for either the Windows or Macintosh operating system.
- Dreamweaver 8 is already installed on your machine.
- Your computer meets the system requirements listed in the following section.

Macromedia Training from the Source

Ideal for active learners, the books in the *Training from the Source* series offer hands-on instruction designed to provide you with a solid grounding in the program's fundamentals. If you learn best by doing, this is the series for you. Each *Training from the Source* title contains hours of instruction. They are designed to teach the techniques that you need to create sophisticated professional-level projects. Each book includes a CD-ROM that contains all the files used in the lessons, completed projects for comparison, and more.

Macromedia Authorized Training and Certification

This book is designed to enable you to study at your own pace with content from the source. Other training options exist through the Macromedia Authorized Training Partner program. Get up to speed in a matter of days with task-oriented courses taught by Macromedia Certified Instructors. Or learn on your own with interactive online training from Macromedia University. All these sources of training will prepare you to become a Macromedia Certified Developer.

For more information about authorized training and certification, check out *www.macromedia.com/support/training.*

What You Will Learn

As you work through these lessons, you will develop the skills you need to create and maintain your own Web sites.

By the end of this course, you will be able to do all of the following:

- Open Dreamweaver, create pages, and preview them in browsers
- Format text in different sizes, colors and styles using integrated styles
- Import text from a variety of sources, including text files, Word documents, and spreadsheets
- Insert graphics and control their appearance
- Create and manage email and internal and external inks throughout your site
- Learn how to make changes directly within the HTML code
- Place text and graphics within tables to achiever more control over the layout
- Make use of image rollovers and other interactive elements
- Use the site window to manage your files and folders
- Develop library items to use the same elements quickly and repeatedly
- Create templates to set the look and feel of a site
- Make your pages accessible and redirect visitors according to the browser version they are using
- Insert a background graphics or change the background colors of your pages
- Specify text attributes using cascading style sheets to gain more control over the appearance of text
- Customize and extend Dreamweaver's capabilities to suit your needs

Minimum System Requirements

Windows

- 800 MHz Intel Pentium III processor (or equivalent) and later
- Microsoft Windows 2000, or Windows XP
- 256 MB RAM (1 GB recommended to run more than one Studio 8 product simultaneously)
- 1024 × 768, 16-bit display (32-bit recommended)
- 650 MB available disk space

Macintosh

- 600 MHz PowerPC G3 and later
- Mac OS X 10.3, 10.4
- 256 MB RAM (1 GB recommended to run more than one Studio 8 product simultaneously)
- 1024 × 768, thousands of colors display (millions of colors recommended)
- 300 MB available disk space

1 Dreamweaver 8 Basics

Macromedia Dreamweaver 8 is the tool of choice for many Web developers—it provides the means for both visual design and code editing, combined in an environment that enables you to work with a wide variety of current and evolving technology solutions while addressing the need for accessible and standards-compliant sites. Dreamweaver helps speed production time and provides tools for site management and maintenance. As the industry leader in Web development software, Dreamweaver gives you the tools you need to meet the challenges of creating and maintaining Websites, including constantly changing standards, new technologies, and the ability to meet user needs.

In this lesson, you'll get started by learning the basics of site planning and preparation—vital steps in the development of any Website, whether it is a completely new Web presence or a redesign of an existing site. In the process, you'll become familiar with the site that is used throughout the lessons in this book. The project is a real-world example: a redesign of the Website for Yoga Sangha—a yoga studio located in San Francisco.

You'll then move on to learning the basics of Dreamweaver 8 and become familiar with the program's interface and tools. You'll start to use the basic site-management features

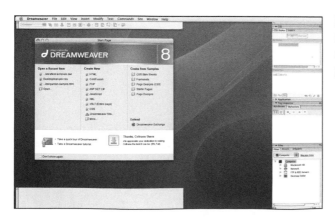

In this lesson, you learn about the Dreamweaver 8 interface while setting up and preparing to develop the site you will use throughout this book.

by establishing a local site on your machine that will contain the pages that you create while developing portions of the Yoga Sangha site.

This lesson teaches you how to work with document settings to create a simple Web page and to open an existing page, as well as how to test your work in different browsers—an essential part of creating functional, accessible Websites. You'll also begin to learn how to customize Dreamweaver to your own workflow and discover how to extend Dreamweaver's functionality.

In the final exercise of this lesson, you'll begin the process of applying the skills and techniques that you learn in this lesson to your own Web projects.

You can find an example of the completed Lesson 1 in the Completed folder inside the Lesson_01_Basics folder on the CD-ROM.

What You Will Learn

In this lesson, you will:

- Become familiar with the Dreamweaver interface
- Customize the Dreamweaver environment
- Explore the planning process
- Set up a new site
- Create and save a new document
- Identify the tools
- Give your page a title
- Specify preview browsers and test your page
- Apply what you've learned to your own site(s)

Approximate Time

This lesson should take approximately one hour to complete.

Lesson Files

Starting Files:

Lesson_01_Basics/resources/client-questionnaire.doc

Completed Project:

Lesson_01_Basics/Completed/yoga.html
Lesson_01_Basics/Completed/yoga-sangha-responses.pdf

Exploring the Workspace

To get started using Dreamweaver, you need to become familiar with the interface and the initial options that are available for your workspace. Windows and Macintosh versions differ slightly.

Windows Users: If this is your first time opening Dreamweaver 8 on a Windows computer, you will be presented with the option to select one of two workspaces: Designer or Coder. For this exercise, you should select the Designer workspace because it will be used throughout this book. The Designer workspace integrates all Dreamweaver-related windows and panels into an environment that is optimized for visually based Website creation—this option is ideal for designers. The Coder workspace is tailored for programmers—those who want to work primarily with HTML and other Web and programming languages. You can access all Dreamweaver features and tools from either workspace. The workspaces simply organize the tools into optimized setups.

You can switch from the Designer workspace to the Coder workspace at any time by choosing Window > Workspace Layout and then selecting your desired workspace.

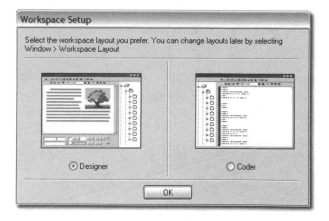

Macintosh Users: The Designer and Coder workspace options described previously are not available on the Macintosh. The Macintosh uses a floating panel system that you can arrange to achieve the same optimized environment as needed.

You'll learn more about customizing the Dreamweaver workspace later in this lesson and throughout the book.

Start Page

Upon opening Dreamweaver 8, you should see the Start page that provides the following:

- Quick links to recent documents
- Options to create a new document from a variety of file types
- Page design samples that can give you a starting point for developing your own sites
- Program resources including a Dreamweaver tour and a tutorial
- A link to the Dreamweaver Exchange that contains resources you can use to extend the program's tools

By default, the Start page appears every time you open Dreamweaver unless you click the Don't show again checkbox.

Note *If the Start page does not appear on startup and you want to view it, you can adjust the display of the Start page in the Dreamweaver Preferences. To do so, choose Dreamweaver > Preferences (Macintosh) or Edit > Preferences (Windows), select General from the Category list, and click the Show Start Page checkbox in the Document options section. A checkmark indicates that the Start page will be displayed when the program is opened; no checkmark indicates that the Start page will not appear.*

When you begin to create new pages or explore other options on the Start page, it will close on its own. Macintosh users can also close this window using the Close button in the upper-left corner of the window.

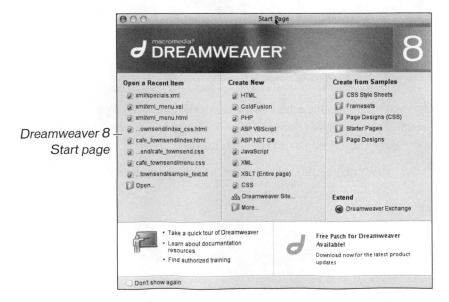

Dreamweaver 8 Start page

Preparing to Develop Your Site

Spending the time to thoroughly address the research and planning stages that are necessary for the creation of a Website is essential. Developing a strategic method with which you can approach development will help you be more efficient, better and more thoroughly develop your ideas, obtain a more comprehensive understanding of the scope of your project, and save time and resources down the road. A good Website should be intuitive and create a positive, unique user experience. The creation of an effective Website starts with tasks that include defining and summarizing the reason and need for the site and analyzing the competition, creating an outline or flowchart, documenting how site features will function and designing the look and feel. In larger companies, these tasks can be delegated to multiple people or departments and the timeframes in which they are completed can overlap significantly. The specific breakdown of this process can vary widely—the core components of Website creation are presented in this book as stages that occur through five phases of development. For the most effective site, all these components should be covered—regardless of whether you are creating your own site, working for a client, or working as part of a team. As you'll learn while working through the lessons, Dreamweaver can help you with many of these tasks—not just those in the production and post-production stages.

Phase 1: Research

Before you start work on any pages, ask yourself or your client questions like the ones presented here. A full version of the Client Questionnaire that was used in the development of the Website you'll be working on, Yoga Sangha, is included on the CD-ROM in the Lesson_01_Basics/resources folder. Throughout this section, you'll find Yoga Sangha's responses to key questions from the questionnaire. Exploring these responses can give you insight into how the Yoga Sangha site was developed and help you to understand how the process described here was the backbone of the site's development. Understanding how this entire process works will help you when creating your own Websites.

- **Who is the audience, why is the site needed, and what do you want the visitors of your site to come away with?** Knowing your audience is vital. Defining a general user profile helps you to effectively reach your target audience. You may have multiple kinds of users; if so, develop a profile for each of them.

  After you know who your audience is, you need to consider which technologies those users are likely to have. What kinds of plug-ins, browsers, and operating systems do the majority of your visitors use? The type of equipment used by your visitors is important to consider when you create a Website that is accessible to your intended audience. For example, you wouldn't want to create a site that uses elements supported by only the most recent and up-to-date browsers if most of your audience uses older machines that can't even run those browsers.

Consider the purpose your site will serve and how each potential user will make use of the site. What does the site need to contain to serve its purpose? Use the visitor profile(s) you created to determine possible scenarios for what visitors would do at your site.

Project Site: Yoga Sangha's Audience

Who is your audience? What are the age ranges and interests of potential students and site visitors?

"We seek to attract students from age 20–60 who are interested in taking yoga or who are trying to improve their health through physical activity."

How will they use the Website and services provided by your company?

"We want them to use the information to choose a class to attend and to discern which workshops they would like to take. We want them to get a first impression of the studio and its offerings that shows our quality, depth, connection, and personable service."

How does Yoga Sangha help students and fit into their lives?

"By offering yoga classes at varying levels of ability all day and during the evening, and by offering workshops on the weekends, which allow students to find a class or workshop that will fit their fitness level and personal schedule."

What are the key reasons students may have for choosing Yoga Sangha?

"Because we're close to where they live, because we offer Anusara yoga, or because their favorite teacher teaches at Yoga Sangha. Plus, at Yoga Sangha they'll learn how to actually practice yoga versus just moving through the poses."

- **What content will be needed for the site?** Identifying and collecting your site assets is an important part of the preparation to design and produce a Website. You need to gather all the content, such as text, graphics, and multimedia elements that will be used on the site. Organizing these assets enables you to create a complete and thorough Website. You can then determine which types of content need to be developed.

Project Site: Yoga Sanhga's Content

List the sections, features, and content that you want to see included on the site. Of this content, what already exists and what will need to be developed?

"We want to see included a studio tour, quarterly news, a quarterly letter from Katchie and Jayne [the studio owners], a map, and directions. These would all need to be developed. We also want to include a quarterly or monthly highlight of a certain nonprofit doing great work in the world, highlights of certain teachers, and whatever other topical information we need to be conveyed, based on future needs. These would also need to be developed."

- **What should the site communicate?** It is essential to know exactly what you want to express to your visitors. If you don't know what you're trying to say, chances are your users won't know, either. Clarify the message of your site. Communication with your visitors is an integral part of maintaining an effective site.

Project Site: Yoga Sangha's Communication Goals

What are the primary objectives for your site?

"Our studio is very community-oriented, ecologically minded, and personal. We would love to more fully convey the Anusara Yoga philosophy, the community focus, and the personal feel and experience of our studio on our Website. We are also part of a new program in which we expect to be a fully Green studio by next year; that is, fully ecologically responsible and sustainable. We want to show how yoga relates with day-to-day life through guest lectures by prominent people in activism, ecological awareness, nutrition, community relations, philosophy, and meditation."

The final part of researching a new Website is to check out the competition. This step is critical, even if the Website you are developing isn't going to be for the public. Because the Web is such a large place, almost any conceivable type of Website has already been created. Understanding who your competition is and how they built their Websites can make all the difference in the world. You may find that your competition's Website is poorly designed, or lacking in features. This can offer you the ability to design a site that stands out, giving you the edge. Or you may discover that the competition's Website is well designed, giving you the incentive to create a better site. Whichever the case, ignoring your competition puts you and the Website you are designing at a disadvantage.

Phase 2: Planning and Structure

The connection between your Website and the audience is dependent in part upon the structure of your site. Clarity and ease-of-use are vital components of a good Website. This important phase of development is the one you'll begin with in this book.

- **Creating the site structure:** Websites rely on structure. A Website with a poor structure can be confusing to navigate, hard to use, and difficult to maintain. To create a site that is clear, communicative, and easy for visitors to use, you need to plan out the structure of the site as well as the hierarchy of files and folders within the site completely—before you begin to build any HTML documents.

Creating a thorough outline of the site as well as a detailed flowchart or storyboard is an important step of the planning process.

More detailed individual page-level flowcharts are often developed at this stage as well to organize the content prior to the design stage in the Phase 3. You'll work on this type of page-level content organization in Lesson 2.

- **Setting up file and folder structure:** It is important to set up a strategy for file management at the beginning of the development process. Keeping different types of media together in individual folders for each file type is a good way of doing this. You might have an HTML folder, an images folder, a Cascading Style Sheets (CSS) folder and a multimedia folder. Using a folder called html_docs to contain only HTML or XHTML files, for instance, will help keep those files organized and easy to find. If the site is very large, you might want to break it down into more manageable portions with a folder for each section and possibly subsections—in which case, there may be folders for the same file types in each section and subsection folder. If you have elements such as graphics that are used site-wide, you might want to create a common folder(s) in the main folder for such files to avoid duplicating the same files in various locations throughout the site. Creating a visual flowchart of the different folder levels can help you in the process of defining the folder hierarchy. A clean, well-structured Website is much easier and more efficient to develop and maintain than one that is disorganized. You'll learn more about site structure and folder hierarchy as they relate to links in Lesson 3. In this book, the file organization is arranged by lesson.

Tip | *In the next exercise, you'll be able to see the structure of the Yoga Sangha project site by looking at the folders and files within the DW8_YogaSangha/ Completed_YogaSangha_SampleSite folder.*

Phase 3: Development—Designing the Site

When designing a Website, you can start by creating thumbnails that show general designs— a quick brainstorming method of getting visual representations of your ideas on paper. Throughout this process, you should continue to take into account the responses to the questions asked in Phase 1 and the results of your research. The second step of developing your design is to fill out more detailed sketches from the best of your initial ideas. Finally, full mockup(s) of how the pages will look can be created for the chosen design. During this design process, there is usually a great deal of communication with the client—you don't want to complete a full mockup for design ideas that are nothing like what your client is expecting. This is the stage at which many of the graphical elements for the site are created—you'll be working on creating page layouts in Lesson 4 and incorporating graphics in your pages in Lesson 5.

Additionally, the process of testing the visual design components to verify that what you're envisioning will work technically in a Web page should be done throughout this stage. Effective Web design relies on creating visual concepts that can be translated to the fully functional technical aspects of a site. The more you learn about what is possible in a Website, the better equipped you'll be to design efficiently for the online medium. You'll learn throughout this book about many technical Web features that Dreamweaver can help you create.

A style guide containing specific details on the look and feel, appearance, colors, and styles to be used throughout the site is usually created at this stage as well.

During the creation of a Website, there is often a considerable amount of overlap of the development phases—work in each of the phases often occurs concurrently. Although you'll address some of the concepts from Phase 2 in the next several lessons, the production stage of Phase 3 is the one in which you'll be working primarily throughout this book's lessons.

Now that you understand what is involved in the preproduction stages of Phases 1 and 2— all of which has already been done for the project site—you're ready to begin working on re-creating portions of the "Yoga Sangha" project site with Dreamweaver. As you work on the project site throughout the book, you'll learn how to implement the site through Dreamweaver by creating the HTML that brings all the research, content, and design together within a successful Website.

Phase 4: Testing

Once you have finished designing your Website, it is important to test it, before you release it to the intended audience. Even the simplest of Websites should be tested in every conceivable way. For example, you should test your Website with as many popular browsers as possible. Although Microsoft Internet Explorer for Windows is the most common browser today, Mozilla Firefox, Opera, and Safari maintain a large enough share of the market to be considered. Even with a browser such as Internet Explorer, there are major differences between versions 5, 5.5, and 6; never mind the differences between the Windows and Macintosh versions. Besides the way that different browsers render your pages, you should also make sure to test every page and link. Dreamweaver 8 can help with these postproduction tasks, as you will see later in Lesson 14.

Phase 5: Maintenance

Many Website developers find that a Website is never done. Adding pages, updating links, modifying content and replacing images are all normal parts of maintaining a Website. Dreamweaver 8 offers a number of features to help make the process of maintaining a Website painless with Library items, templates and other tools. You will learn more about these features in Lessons 13 through 16.

Defining a Local Site

The first step of creating a Website—before you begin to create any individual pages—is to designate or create the folder on your computer that will contain everything within your site. This process is called defining a local site. The designated folder, known as the *local root folder*, sets the boundaries of the local site that resides on your hard disk and mirrors the remote site, which is the actual site on the Web server that your visitors will access. Defining a local site enables you to maintain the same folder hierarchy between the local and remote versions, which is crucial to creating and maintaining a functional site.

The creation of a local site, composed of the local root folder within which you set up the structure of the site's files and folders, prevents your site from storing any site files outside of the local root folder. The files on your hard disk that are outside of the local root folder cannot be transferred to the remote server. This restriction ensures that as you develop your site, you won't access files that aren't available when the site is made available online. Many Dreamweaver features, such as the potential to update all references to a file that may have been moved to a different location in the site, require the definition of a local site to fully function. You should make a practice of always creating and working within local sites. If you don't, you might have problems with links, paths, and file management (Dreamweaver's tools for these features are covered in later lessons of this book).

The development of your site occurs in the local site on your hard disk, in which you build and initially test your pages.

> **Note** *Setting up a site is not required, although it is recommended. Dreamweaver will allow you to quickly edit, connect, and transfer files without setting up a site. You'll learn more about managing your site in Lesson 14.*

1. Copy the DW8_YogaSangha folder from the CD-ROM to your hard disk.

The DW8_YogaSangha folder will become the local root folder of your site. This folder contains all the files and folders for the Yoga Sangha project site that you will re-create portions of as you work through the lessons in this book. When you begin work on your own sites, you will need to create an individual local root folder for each site.

The name of a local root folder can be the name of the respective site or any name you choose. If you develop multiple sites, it is helpful to use names that are descriptive and can be distinguished easily from one another. The name of the local root folder is simply for file management purposes and is not visible to the visitors of the site.

Save your local root folder in a location on your hard disk that is outside the Dreamweaver 8 application folder. If you ever need to reinstall Dreamweaver, your work will be lost if it is located inside the Dreamweaver 8 application folder.

Tip *Suggestions for common locations to store local root folders:*

Macintosh: *Macintosh HD/User Name/Sites/local root folder*
Windows: *MyDocuments\local root folder*

2. On the Dreamweaver Start page, select Dreamweaver Site from the Create New section.

Tip *You can also create a new site by choosing Site > New Site or Site > Manage Sites, clicking the New button, and selecting Site from the pop-up menu. The Site Definition dialog box appears.*

The Site Definition dialog box opens with two tabs: Basic and Advanced. These tabs allow you to choose how you will go through the process of defining a site. The Basic version, which is shown by default when you open the dialog box, walks you step-by-step through the process. The Advanced version gives you a number of additional options and settings to configure, and it does not include the explanatory text descriptions available in Basic view.

For this exercise, click the Basic tab if it is not already selected.

Basic section of the Site Definition dialog box

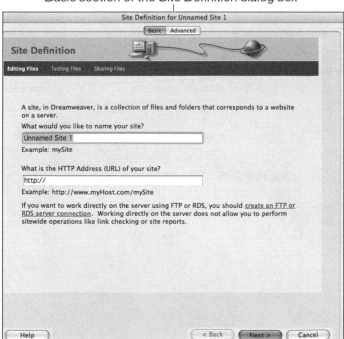

3. In the Basic tab of the Site Definition dialog box, Dreamweaver poses the question, "What would you like to name your site?" Type *Yoga Sangha* in the Site name text field and then click Next.

Yoga Sangha is the name of the project site you are creating. When you create your own sites, the names that you assign should let you easily identify them. Clear and specific site names allow you to immediately distinguish sites by name, making it easier to manage multiple sites. Like the local root folder, the site name is for your reference only in Dreamweaver's list of defined sites and is not visible to users of your site.

You should leave the HTTP Address text field on this screen blank. The HTTP Address—the URL of the online site—is used to define site-root relative links, which are covered in Lesson 3. This item is optional and not necessary for the exercises in this book.

Note *This section of the Basic site setup corresponds to the Site name text field of the Local Info category in the Advanced view. Throughout the course of defining your site, you can switch back and forth between the Basic and Advanced views if you want to see how the Advanced view appears. You'll work with the Advanced view in Lesson 14.*

4. Dreamweaver asks, "Do you want to work with a server technology such as ColdFusion, ASP.NET, ASP, JSP, or PHP?" Click the radio button for the option "No, I do not want to use a server technology." Click Next to advance to the next section.

At this time you are not creating pages that will incorporate databases or other server technologies, so you should select the No option. You can always add this functionality at a later point—any time you need to make changes to your site setup, you can choose Site > Manage Sites, select your site in the list, and click the Edit button.

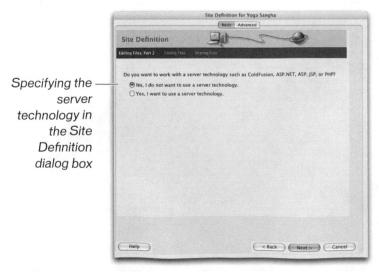

Specifying the server technology in the Site Definition dialog box

Note *This section of the Basic setup corresponds to the Testing Server category in the Advanced View, which gives you additional options that are involved with creating dynamic sites, such as choosing the server model that is used on your remote server.*

5. At the top of this section, Dreamweaver asks, "How do you want to work with your files during development?" Click the option "Edit local copies on my machine, then upload to server when ready (recommended)."

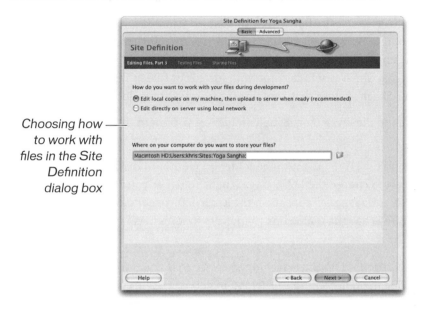

Choosing how to work with files in the Site Definition dialog box

At this time, you will be working with files that are located on your machine—you don't need to have access to a remote server. Editing files that exist on your computer is the most common selection. If you have a remote server, this option means that there are two copies of the files—one copy on your local hard drive and a second copy on your server. This gives you the option to retrieve the original files from the server if necessary—provided that you haven't replaced them by uploading files that were changed locally. Doing production and testing work on your local hard drive prevents unfinished pages from being publicly displayed.

If you were working directly on a server, any changes you might make would be immediately applied to the original files.

6. Also in this section, Dreamweaver asks, "Where on your computer do you want to store your files?" Click the folder icon to the right of the text field and browse to find the **DW8_YogaSangha** folder.

This text field allows you to select the folder on your hard disk within which all the files for the site are stored. This folder is the equivalent of the root folder on the remote site. Dreamweaver needs to define this local root folder to determine the paths for documents, images, and links in your site. You will learn about paths and links in Lesson 3.

The DW8_YogaSangha folder is the folder that you copied from the CD-ROM to your hard disk in Step 1 of this exercise. By default, the text field initially contained the path to a folder called Yoga Sangha. Using that default would create a new folder on your hard disk called Yoga Sangha, which would become your local root folder. Because you need to use the DW8_YogaSangha folder that contains the files, you must locate that folder.

Macintosh Users: Find the DW8_YogaSangha folder on your hard disk, select it, and click Choose.

Windows Users: Find the DW8_YogaSangha folder on your hard disk, select it, and click Open; then click Select to choose the DW8_YogaSangha folder as your local root folder. The text "Select:DW8_YogaSangha" appears in the lower-left corner of the Choose Local Root Folder For Site Yoga Sangha dialog box to indicate that the DW8_YogaSangha folder will be selected.

> **Tip** *Be sure to select the DW8_YogaSangha folder that you copied to your hard disk—not the one residing on the CD-ROM. In some versions of Windows, files copied from a CD are marked read-only; to fix this, select all of the files (Ctrl-A), after copying them, go to Properties (Alt-Enter or right-click on the selected files and click Properties), and uncheck the Read-Only checkbox. Then click Apply, or OK.*

Specifying the local root folder in the Site Definition dialog box

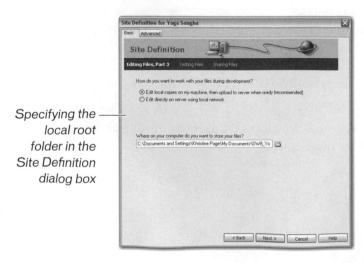

The path to the local root folder, DW8_YogaSangha, is now displayed in the text field and its location is shown in relation to your hard disk.

In this case, however, you need to choose the DW8_YogaSangha folder that already exists (and contains the many files that you need to work with in this book's lessons) as your local root folder.

When you create your own sites, if you do not already have a folder, you might find it useful to allow Dreamweaver to automatically create one for you based on the name you chose for your site.

Understanding the Advanced Site Definition Options

This section of the Basic site setup — in which you are specifying the local root folder — corresponds to the Local root folder text field of the Local Info category in the Advanced view. The Advanced site definition options also allow you to select Refresh Local File List automatically, Enable Cache, specify a Default Images folder, and define the HTTP Address for the site.

The Refresh Local File List option is checked by default, causing Dreamweaver to update the site list whenever you add a new file to the site folder. If you uncheck this option, you need to refresh the local files manually whenever you make changes such as adding or deleting files.

The Enable Cache option is checked by default. Enabling the cache allocates memory to store frequently used site data, improving the speed of linking and site-management tasks. The site cache stores information in your computer's RAM memory making access to features that use the cache quicker. When this option is active, Dreamweaver will continuously update the information stored in the cache as you work. Although it is usually best to leave the cache option on, keep in mind that re-creating the cache can slow operations on extremely large sites.

The Default Images folder allows you to specify the location of images in your site and can reduce the amount of time that it takes to browse for images when inserting them. The use of images is covered in Lesson 5.

The HTTP address, another optional feature, is used to define the URL of your Website. This address is used to verify absolute links. More information on links is covered in Lesson 3.

7. Click Next to advance to the next section. Below the question "How do you connect to your remote server?" choose None from the menu.

Connection options in the Site Definition dialog box

At this time, you are working on a local site; you do not need access to a remote server. More information about connecting to a remote server can be found in Lesson 14.

Note *This section of the Basic setup corresponds to the Remote Info category in the Advanced view, which gives you additional options that are involved in transferring files to a remote server, such as specifying the folder to store files in on the server.*

8. Click Next to advance to the next section. Review the information about the site you just defined and then click the Done button at the bottom of the dialog box.

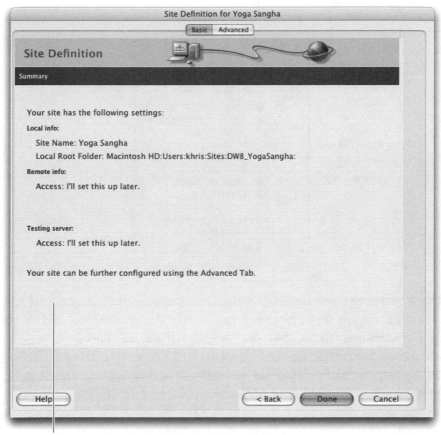

Site summary in the Site Definition dialog box

Because you chose the No options for the Remote Info and Testing Server sections, Dreamweaver displays "Access: I'll set this up later." for both.

When you click Done, Dreamweaver scans the files in the DW8_YogaSangha folder to create the site cache. You may see a dialog box appear briefly as Dreamweaver completes the process of creating the cache for the first time. Creating the cache will take longer on very large sites.

The Files panel now displays the DW8_YogaSangha folder. By default, the Files panel is displayed at the bottom of the panel groups that you'll explore later in this lesson. You'll also learn more about the Files panel in Lesson 14.

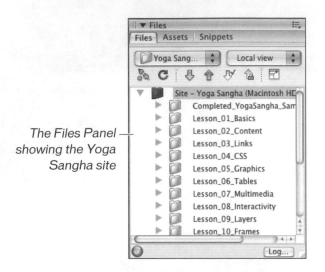

The Files Panel showing the Yoga Sangha site

Note *If you have never defined a site in Dreamweaver, the Files panel displays a hierarchy of folders on your computer and a link to open the Manage Sites dialog box. For Macintosh users, the default selection in the Site panel pop-up menu is Computer, which initially contains Macintosh HD, Network, FTP & RDS Servers, and Desktop folder. For Windows users, the default selection is Desktop, which initially contains My Computer, My Network Places, FTP & RDS Servers, and Desktop items. After you create a site, that site becomes the default selection. If you have more than one site, Dreamweaver displays the most recently used site in the Files panel. The Files panel is located in the Files panel group.*

Creating and Saving a New Page

After your local site is defined, you are ready to start working with and creating Web pages. Whenever you create a new page, the first thing you should do is save the document.

1. Choose File > New. The New Document dialog box appears.

Tip *You can use the keyboard commands Cmd+N (Macintosh) or Ctrl+N (Windows) to open the New Document dialog box. If you want to bypass the New Document dialog box and create a new document immediately whenever using these keyboard commands, choose Dreamweaver > Preferences (Macintosh) or Edit > Preferences (Windows), select New Document from the Category list, and uncheck the Show New Document Dialog on Command+N (Macintosh) or the Show New Document Dialog on Ctrl+N (Windows). This section also provides you with the option to change the default document type as well as the extension and encoding. The lessons in this book assume that you are using the defaults. Clicking the Preferences button at the bottom of the New Document dialog box is another way to open the Preferences dialog box.*

The New Document dialog box opens with two tabs: General and Templates. In this exercise, you are creating a new HTML (Hypertext Markup Language) page. The option to create a new HTML page is located in the Basic category of the General tab. These selections are the defaults and might already be selected for you.

New Document dialog box

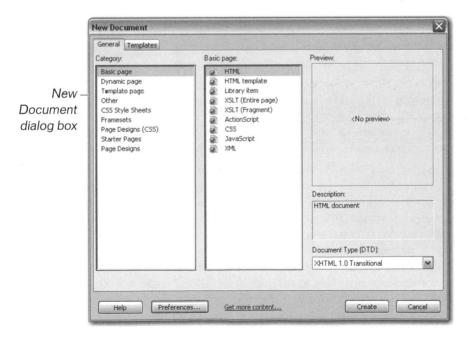

The New Document dialog box also gives you additional options for creating a variety of page types. The Basic Page category offers a number of options in addition to HTML, including CSS (Cascading Style Sheets), JavaScript, and XML. Other available page type categories include Dynamic Pages (that use languages such as ASP, ColdFusion, and PHP) and Page Designs (that you can use as a starting point when creating your own site). You can access specific page types by choosing from the list of categories in the left column of the dialog box that includes Dynamic, Templates, CSS Style Sheets, Framesets, and Page Designs. You won't use any of these additional page types in this exercise, but you should be aware of them. The contents of the middle column of the dialog box change depending upon the category selected in the left column.

Understanding XHTML, XML and Document Type Definitions

Behind the visual appearance of a Web page is code, called a markup language, that is used to produce what a visitor sees in their browser—the markup describes the structure and appearance of a page by labeling elements such as text and images with instructions, in the form of tags and their attributes, as to how those elements should be displayed. Hypertext Markup Language (HTML) is currently one of the most well-known markup languages; however, HTML is limited in nature, particularly in that new features are generally not backward-compatible, and there are a wide number of compatibility issues with HTML for cross-browser use. HTML is an older markup language that is being phased out of use because it doesn't meet current Web standards, nor does it have the potential to evolve to match those standards.

Extensible Hypertext Markup Language (XHTML) replaces and extends the capabilities of HTML by reforming HTML as an Extensible Markup Language (XML) language. XML markup emphasizes and facilitates the separation of structure, content, and presentation by specifying the content and structure of a page, but not the appearance or presentation—the definition of all presentation is handled separately through other means, such as CSS.

The advantages of using XHTML include both backward- and forward-compatibility, operability on alternate Web access devices such as cell phones or handheld computers, and the potential for extensibility. XHTML 1.0 Transitional is a version of XHTML that allows the use of some HTML elements that are deprecated—marked as obsolete by the World Wide Web Consortium (W3C), which develops Web standards to ensure compatibility throughout the industry—and therefore not available in stricter versions of XHTML. Because allowing these deprecated elements enables backward-compatibility through the conversion from HTML to XHTML, XHTML 1.0 Transitional is currently the recommended markup language for Web development.

The use of these languages is defined through the Document Type Definition (DTD). Although invisible to the visitor, the DTD is located at the beginning of the code that comprises the Web page. The DTD declares the syntax of the markup language for the page—that is, it defines how the browser or other Web access device should interpret the page.

Note *By default, Dreamweaver uses XHTML 1.0 Transitional as the Document Type Definition in all new HTML documents unless you select a different type. You can change the DTD of a new document in the New Document dialog box by choosing the desired type from the DTD menu at the bottom of the dialog box. Throughout this book, you should use the default XHTML 1.0 Transitional DTD— do not change the DTD. You can convert between HTML and XHTML by choosing File › Convert and selecting the type to which you want to convert.*

After you click the Create button, a new untitled XHTML document appears, and the Start page closes automatically.

Tip *You can also create a new document directly from the Start page by selecting the file type (such as HTML, as you did in this exercise) from the Create New column. A new document of the type you selected appears, and the Start page closes.*

2. Click the General tab in the New Document dialog box and choose Basic Page in the category list. Choose HTML in the Basic Page list and click the Create button.

3. Choose File › Save and locate the folder html_docs in Lesson_01_Basics, in which you will save this file. Type *yoga.html* in the Save As (Macintosh) or File Name (Windows) field and then click Save.

— Save As dialog box

Don't wait until you have text or graphics on the page to save—save your pages as soon as you open new documents. Provided that your file is saved first, when you import graphics or other media, all the paths that reference where those elements are located in your site will be made properly. If you don't save your document, a path name beginning with file:// is used that describes the location of the element you are inserting relative to your hard disk. If you try to insert an object without first saving the document, Dreamweaver warns you that it needs to use a file:// path name for the element. These file:// paths do not work on remote servers because they describe the location of files specific to your computer.

Tip *You can use the keyboard commands Cmd+S (Macintosh) or Ctrl+S (Windows) to save your document. Always remember to save often so you won't lose a lot of work if your computer crashes for any reason.*

Macintosh Users: Dreamweaver automatically adds the extension .html to the filename of HTML documents in the File Name text field—you must leave this extension or specify a different one for the document to be saved with an extension.

Windows Users: Dreamweaver automatically adds the extension .html to the filename, of HTML documents, when you save if the extension isn't specified in the File Name text field. You can also specify the extension yourself.

Note *Dreamweaver adds the default extension of any file you create. For example, if you create a Cascading Style Sheet file, Dreamweaver will add .css to the filename.*

You should always save your documents with the extension .html. If Dreamweaver is giving you a default of .htm, you can change the default by choosing Dreamweaver > Preferences (Macintosh) or Edit > Preferences (Windows) and selecting the New Document category. The default extension is displayed in a text box. Throughout this book, the extension .html is used in the examples and materials included on the CD-ROM, and the exercises assume that you will be using the default extension.

Tip *The .htm extension is a remnant from the bad old days when Windows could only handle 3 character file extensions. Unless you think that someone with Windows 3.1 is going to be working on this site, there's no reason to ever use the .htm extension as it's generally considered to be unprofessional.*

New documents are given a default name of Untitled-1.html in the Save As text field, with the numbers increasing sequentially for every new document that is created.

Tip *The New Document and Save options are also available on the Standard toolbar, which you can open by choosing View › Toolbars › Standard. Toolbars other than the default document toolbar appear as you add or move them only on the active document; changes are not reflected in other documents.*

File-Naming Conventions

Keep in mind that naming your files for use on a Web server is a little different from naming your files for use on your hard disk. It is helpful to know what operating system the server will be using—the most common systems are Unix, Linux, Windows NT, and Mac OS X. The naming structure is different on Windows from the other *NIX-based operating systems. Unix, for example, is case-sensitive, which means that myfile.html does not equal MYFILE.HTML. Using all lowercase names for your files makes naming files simpler and helps you maintain consistency. You should use only alpha characters (A–Z) and numbers (0–9) to name your files. Here are other important conventions to follow for both filenames and folder names:

- **Spaces.** Don't ever use spaces in filenames. Use the underscore or hyphen characters to simulate a space if you need to separate words. Problems can arise because browsers substitute %20 for spaces.

- **Special characters.** Don't use any special characters, such as ?, %, *, ›, or /. Don't use commas.

- **Numbers.** Avoid beginning your filenames with numbers.

- **Length.** Keep folder names and filenames as short as possible. Remember that the folder name becomes part of the URL you type to get to the page.

Exploring the Tools

Before jumping into further development of any Web pages, you need to become familiar with the variety of tools and panels that make up the Dreamweaver 8 interface and enable you to effectively produce a Website.

1. Move the pointer over the Document window and the document toolbar. Rest the pointer over a button to see its name.

The majority of your design and coding work is done within the Document window. This area is known as the *body* of the page, in which you can insert, modify, and delete the wide variety of elements that make up a Web page. As you work, the Document window displays an approximation of the way your page should appear in a browser. It is an approximation because there are differences in the ways that browsers interpret Web pages.

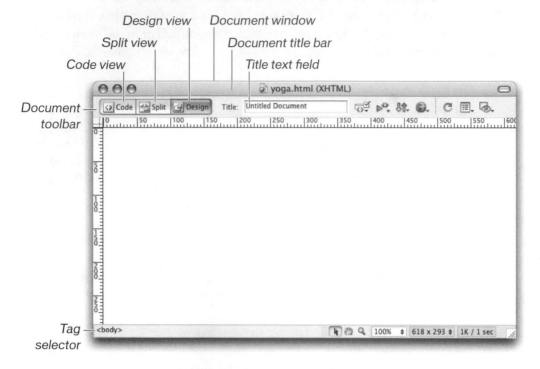

The filename yoga.html (as you saved this page in the previous exercise) is shown on the title bar (On Windows, the filename is shown in a tab at the top of the document window; see the illustration on page 31). By default, this page is initially titled Untitled Document, as shown in the Title text field on the document toolbar. The document toolbar, which can be shown or hidden through View > Toolbars, contains buttons and pop-up menus to provide quick access to common operations. By default, the toolbar is part of the document window. Windows users can double-click or drag the gripper area on the left edge of the toolbar to separate it from the document window, making it become an individual panel.

There are three view modes in Dreamweaver: Design view, Code view, and Split view, which shows both Design view and Code view. The buttons for these modes are located on the left side of the document toolbar. You can see the view mode names by pausing the pointer over the buttons. At this point, the view mode you are using should be Design view. The active button is highlighted, indicating that Dreamweaver is displaying the page in that view mode. You will work with Code view and Split view in Lesson 16. If the Document window is shown split into two panes with code in one pane or a single pane with code, you need to select the Design View icon located on the document toolbar.

In the lower-left corner of the document window is the tag selector. The tag selector always starts from the <body> tag and hierarchically displays HTML tags that apply to the currently selected element. Using the HTML tags that correspond with those elements, the tag selector allows you to move quickly through the hierarchy of code to see what element you are working with and to easily select other elements. Getting used to working with the tag selector will be particularly helpful when you begin using tables in Lesson 6.

Tip *If you can't see the tag selector, try reducing the size of your document window. The tag selector can become hidden beneath the Property inspector.*

You'll become familiar with the many buttons and customizable options in the Document window as you work through the lessons in this book.

2. Make sure that Common is chosen from the pop-up menu at the left end of the Insert bar, then move the pointer over the bar, whose default position is at the top of your screen. Rest the pointer over a button to see its name.

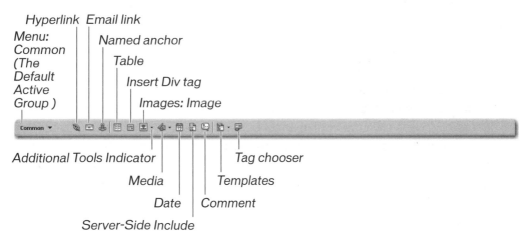

The Insert bar contains many of the objects or elements that you can add to your page, including images, tables, special characters, forms, and HTML. The elements are arranged in eight groups, according to their type: Common, Layout, Forms, Text, HTML, Application, Flash Elements, and Favorites. The name of the active group is displayed on the menu. The Common group is active by default. You can use the pop-up menu to switch to a different group of objects. Many of the individual objects in these groups have their own pop-up menus, indicated by a small black arrow, with additional tools, options and other closely related objects; click the black arrow once to open the pop-up menu. The last option in the Insert bar category pop-up menu is Show As Tabs, which will convert the Insert bar to show tabs at the top of the bar for each category. To switch back to the menu format, choose Show As Menu from the Options menu in the upper-right corner of the Insert bar. Use whichever viewing method—tabs or the menu—that you prefer.

Insert bar with tabs   Options menu button

Note *Throughout this book, the words "objects" and "elements" are used interchangeably. Where possible, "object" is used when referring to the button, and "element" is used for the item after it appears within the Document window.*

To insert an element, you can drag the object's icon from the Insert bar to the location where you want it to appear in the Document window. You can also place the insertion point in your document where the element should appear and then click the object's icon in the panel. When you click the icon, the element appears in the document at the insertion point.

Tip *You can move many of the objects that you use regularly into the Favorites group of the Insert bar by right-clicking (Macintosh users with single-button mice can use Control+click to access the same options) on the bar and choosing Customize Favorites. Select the desired item from the Available Objects menu that appears and click the double arrow button between the Available Objects and Favorite Objects lists. You can use the Up and Down Arrow keys above the Favorite objects list to adjust the order of objects. The dialog box also allows you to remove objects from the Favorites group and add separators between the objects to further organize them.*

3. **Move the pointer over the Property inspector, normally at the bottom of your screen. Rest the pointer over a button to see its name.**

The Property inspector is used to view and modify the attributes of selected text, images, tables and other elements in a document. The Property inspector is contextual—the attributes that it makes available change depending on what is selected in the document window. To expand or collapse the Property inspector, click the expander arrow in the lower-right corner of the panel. If the Property inspector is collapsed, there can be additional properties that are not visible until you expand the panel.

Windows users can also reduce the inspector so that only the name of the panel shows to gain a larger viewing area.

Property inspector

Expand/Reduce

Tip Windows users can also resize the entire area for the Property inspector (and additional panels that later appear in that area) by dragging the arrow button on the horizontal border between the document window and the Property inspector. Clicking the arrow button collapses the entire area; simply click the button again to reopen it. The horizontal border is not part of the Macintosh interface.

Working with Panels and Documents

The majority of Dreamweaver's panels are *docked*—combined in tabbed windows— within panel groups according to their functions. The default panel groups are CSS, Application, Tag Inspector, and Files. You can access panels from within these groups as well as from the Window menu. Panel groups let you quickly hide or access your most frequently used panels. Docking maximizes your screen area while giving you quick access to the panels you need. Each panel group can be expanded to display the active panel plus tabs for the rest of the panels it contains or reduced to show only the name of the group.

If you opened Dreamweaver before beginning this lesson, the panels are placed exactly where they were the last time you quit the program. In the Window menu, a checkmark next to an item indicates that the panel or toolbar is selected and active (visible) in the panel groups.

1. Click the arrow on the CSS panel group title bar to expand the group if it is not already open.

The CSS panel group is located (by default) at the top of the panel groups. When the CSS panel group is expanded, you will see the CSS Styles panel, which you will work with in Lesson 4. In the upper-right corner of the panel you see the Options menu button, which is not visible when the panel group is reduced.

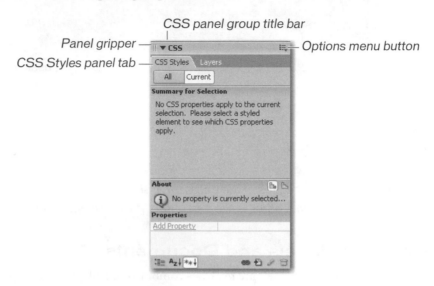

CSS panel group title bar

Panel gripper — — *Options menu button*

CSS Styles panel tab —

In the Window menu, a hidden panel does not have a checkmark next to the panel name. To display a hidden panel, choose the desired panel from the Window menu. If the panel you choose is in a panel group that is not currently available, both the panel and the panel group containing that chosen panel appear. If the group containing the desired panel is visible but reduced, choosing the panel from the Window menu expands the group and displays the selected panel.

Tip *There may be instances in which a panel is hidden beneath another panel or the Document window. Changes in screen resolution can be one cause of this problem. If you are missing a panel and can't bring it up by choosing it from the Window menu, you might need to choose Window > Arrange Panels (Macintosh Only) to reset all open panels to the default positions. Both Macintosh and Windows users can also choose Window > Workspace Layout > Default to restore all tools and panels to their original positions. The Insert bar moves to the upper-left corner of the screen, the Property inspector moves to the bottom of the screen, and all other open panels move to the right of the screen.*

2. Rest the pointer over the bottom of a line that separates two panel groups. When the pointer changes to a vertical two-arrow pointer, click and drag upward or downward to adjust the size of the panels.

As you work, you might need to resize panels to show more information or provide more room for other panels and the Document window.

Tip *Windows users can also resize the width of the entire area for all docked panel groups by dragging the arrow button on the vertical border. Clicking the arrow button collapses the entire docking area; simply click the button again to reopen it.*

The vertical border is not part of the Macintosh interface. Macintosh users can resize the width of docked panel groups by clicking and dragging the resize button at the lower-right corner of the panel groups.

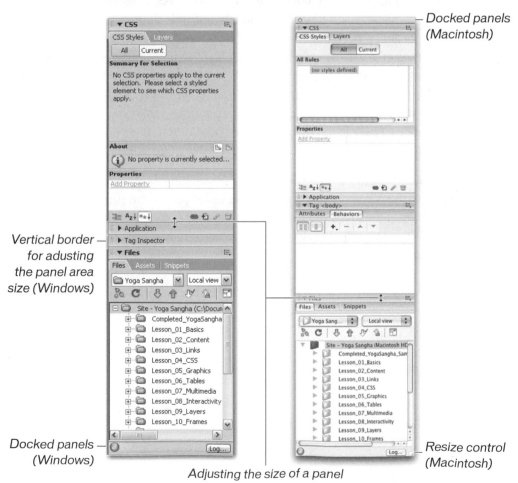

Docked panels (Macintosh)

Vertical border for adusting the panel area size (Windows)

Docked panels (Windows)

Resize control (Macintosh)

Adjusting the size of a panel

After you become familiar with the Dreamweaver panels and tools, you can customize the interface by rearranging panels and reordering panel groups to make the program work with your specific needs. You can save any custom workspace that you create by choosing Window > Workspace Layout > Save Current. The Workspace Layout submenu also offers a workspace for developers who work with two monitors—Dual Screen—as well as the ability to rename or delete saved workspaces through the Manage option.

Note *You can undock any panel group and separate it from the docking area. To undock a panel group, rest the pointer over the panel gripper designated by the dots on the left of the panel group title bar. When the pointer turns to a hand (Macintosh) or a cross-hair with arrows (Windows), click and drag the panel group out of the window and release it. As you drag it outside of the docked panels, you will see a ghost image of the panel group until you release it. You can rename this new window or panel group by clicking the Options menu button and choosing Rename Panel Group from the Options menu. As you drag a panel group back into the docking area with other groups, you see the ghost image of the panel before you release it as well as a thick dark line at the point where the panel group appears. You can also rearrange the order of panel groups by using the grab area to move any of the groups above or below the other groups. If you want to change the organization of panel tabs by moving them into different groups, select a panel by clicking its tab and choose Group (panel name) with from the Options menu.*

The lessons in this book assume that you are using the default configuration of panels in Dreamweaver 8, with no changes to the order or names of panels and panel groups. If you have rearranged any of the tools, you can revert to the default configuration by choosing Window > Workspace Layout > Default (Macintosh) or Window > Workspace and selecting Designer (Windows).

3. **Choose File > New and select HTML from the Basic page category of the General tab.**

A new XHTML document opens with a new tab in the current Document window.

Document window tabs   *Maximize/Restore (Windows only)*

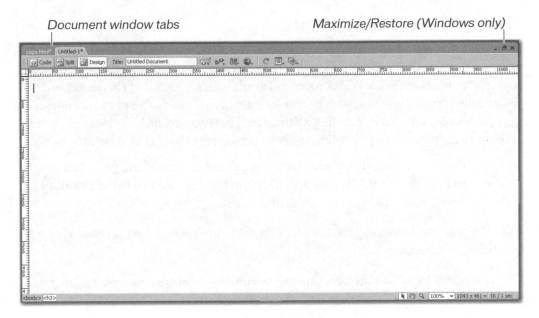

Windows Users: Cascade, Tile Horizontally, and Tile Vertically are three options for viewing documents. If you have more than one Document window open at a time, the Cascade option causes those windows to float, stacked one on top of the other, within the Document window portion of the workspace. The Tile Horizontally option causes the Document windows to appear stacked horizontally. The Tile Vertically option causes the Document windows to appear side by side vertically. These options can be accessed from the Window menu. You can also switch to the Tile view by clicking the maximize button in the upper-right corner of the Document window—not the maximize button for the entire program. Click the Maximize button on a Document window again to switch back to tabs.

Macintosh Users: Cascade, Tile, and Combine As Tabs are the three options for viewing documents. The Cascade option will cause the documents to appear in individual windows that float, stacked one on top of the other. The Tile option will cause the documents to display in individual windows that appear side by side. Combine As Tabs is the default arrangement—new documents will appear in the same window as current documents with tabs for each one. You can open any tabbed document by right-clicking (Windows) or Control+clicking (Macintosh) the corresponding tab and choosing the Move To New Window option.

Giving Your Page a Title

Every HTML document you create needs to have a title. The title is used primarily for document identification. It is displayed in a browser's title bar, indicates the content of a page, and appears as the bookmark name in Favorites lists. You should choose a short informative phrase, beginning with the site name, which is descriptive of the document's purpose. Get into the habit of adding a title to each page you create before you add text or graphics to the page. If you forget, Dreamweaver titles the file Untitled Document by default.

To give a title to your page, click the tab for the yoga.html document and type **Yoga Sangha Project** into the Title text field on the document toolbar. Press Return (Macintosh) or Enter (Windows), or click in the yoga.html document.

Tip *If you don't see the document toolbar with the Title text field, choose View › Toolbars › Document.*

The Title text field initially displays Untitled Document—you are now replacing that placeholder title with a title for a page in the project site.

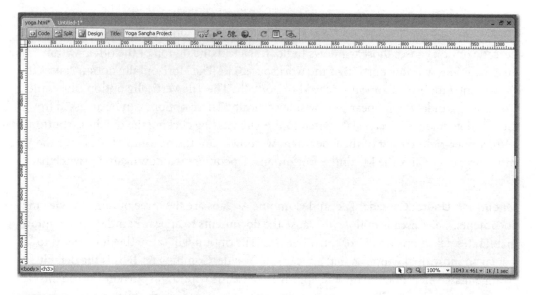

Note *You can also specify the title of your document in the Title text field located in the Title/Encoding category of the Page Properties dialog box. To access the Page Properties dialog box, choose Modify › Page Properties.*

Specifying Preview Browsers

As you develop Web pages, you'll need to continually test how your work appears in different browsers, such as Internet Explorer and Safari. What you see in the Dreamweaver Document window is only an approximation of how the pages will look. Every browser has differences in the way it displays Web pages, and although some of these discrepancies are slight, the differences can sometimes be significant. You might notice differences, even between different versions of the same browser. The more you test your site in multiple browsers and on different operating systems—and make changes to your pages accordingly—the more certain you can be that visitors to the site see your pages as you intended them to appear.

The Preferences in Dreamweaver enable you to specify which browsers you want to use to preview the pages in your site. To speed up the process, you can define a primary and a secondary browser, with a keyboard shortcut for each.

1. Choose File › Preview in Browser › Edit Browser List.

Tip *Alternatively, you can choose Dreamweaver › Preferences (Macintosh) or Edit › Preferences (Windows) and select Preview In Browser in the Category list, located on the left side of the dialog box, to open the same Preview In Browser Preferences dialog box. You can also use the keyboard command Command+U (Macintosh) or Ctrl+U (Windows) to open the Preferences dialog box.*

The Preferences dialog box opens to display the Preview In Browser preferences. Dreamweaver can automatically list one of more of the browsers that are on your computer.

Note *On Windows, Internet Explorer may appear as iexplore or iexplore.exe in the list.*

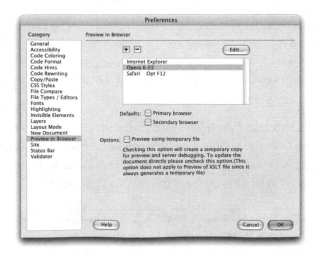

When you click a browser name in the browser list, the checkboxes below the list show whether that browser is the primary or secondary browser. If you have more than two browsers, it leaves both boxes unchecked to show if it is neither.

The Preview Using Temporary File option is unchecked by default for any browsers in the list. Checking this option will cause Dreamweaver to create temporary files when previewing pages in a browser.

2. Click OK to close the dialog box when you are done reviewing the preferences.

You can add, modify, or remove browsers from the list if needed.

- **Adding a Browser:** To add a browser to the list, click the plus (+) button. When the dialog box appears, browse your hard disk to find and choose a browser application. Check the Primary Browser checkbox if you want to launch this browser by pressing Option+F12 (Macintosh) or F12 (Windows) when you preview your pages. Check the Secondary Browser checkbox if you want to preview your documents in this browser by pressing Command+F12 (Macintosh) or Ctrl+F12 (Windows). (You'll be previewing the pages you develop while completing the lessons in this book often, so using these shortcuts can save you time.)

Note *Your function keys must be enabled for the Preview In Browser keyboard shortcuts to work. Function keys are usually enabled by default; if they are not working, check your operating system preferences. If your function keys are performing system functions, you might have to press the Fn key to use the function keys for Dreamweaver—or adjust your system preferences.*

- **Removing a Browser:** To remove a browser from the list, select the browser name in the list and then click the minus (–) button.

Tip *To change a browser choice, select the browser name in the list. Then click Edit and locate a different browser.*

3. Click the yoga.html document tab and press F12 to preview the page in your primary browser.

Tip *You can also choose File > Preview in Browser and select the browser you want to use from the submenu. The document toolbar also contains a Preview/Debug In Browser button; click it to open the pop-up menu and select the browser in which you want to preview your page.*

Preview/Debug in Browser button

The browser defined as the Primary Browser in the Preview In Browser preferences becomes active and displays the yoga.html file in a browser window. Notice the title Yoga Sangha on the title bar of the browser.

At this point, your browser shows a blank page. You are ready to begin inserting content. You'll add text to this file in the next lesson.

Note *Unless you clicked the Don't Show Again checkbox on the Start page earlier in this lesson, the Start page will reappear if you close all open documents.*

4. Save the yoga.html document. Close and do not save the untitled document.

You can leave the yoga.html document open for the next lesson.

Exploring the Basics On Your Own

Now that you learned how to plan a Website, set up a site in Dreamweaver, and worked with both new and existing pages, you're ready to apply these skills and techniques to your own Website(s).

1. Use planning phases and questions to complete the research and develop a Creative Brief for your own site.

As you work through the process, remember to be detailed. Start the process of developing your site by:

- Considering the purpose, goals, and market for your site
- Exploring who the audience is and what their needs are
- Taking stock of content and assets that are already available
- Determining what elements will need to be created
- Developing the site structure
- Setting up the file structure

The Creative Brief is a document in which you organize all the research and work that was done on the site in Phase 1. This can help you coordinate the efforts in later stages while making it easier to stay on track in the development of the site you are creating.

2. Use the Site Definition dialog box to set up your site in Dreamweaver.

Site setup will include the creation of the local root folder in which all your site files will be stored.

3. Use the starter pages and page designs available from the New Document dialog box to create several placeholder pages within your new site.

You can save these pages inside your local root folder as placeholders for future content.

Tip | *You can also access these resources by selecting a category from the Create From Samples section on the Start page.*

As you continue to complete the lessons, you'll learn how to work with the various elements that can be seen in these starter pages, including links, images, and CSS.

Recommended Resources

Book: *Web ReDesign 2.0: Workflow that Works*
by Kelly Goto and Emily Cotler
Published by New Riders. © 2004
ISBN 0-7357-1433-9

This book is a great source of information that can aid you in the process of developing a Website—whether you are creating a new site from scratch or redesigning an existing site. The development process is clearly presented and offers a number of tools and techniques for developing the workflow that will best serve your project—including case studies, forms, checklists and worksheets.

Web: www.macromedia.com/resources/techniques

A Web resource created jointly by Macromedia and Kelly Goto, co-author of *Web ReDesign: Workflow that Works*, this site presents a wide range of articles on each phase of Web development. Additional resources are included in the forums hosted on the site, such as the Production Management Online Forum.

Book: *Don't Make Me Think: A Common Sense Approach to Web Usability (2nd Edition)*
by Steve Krug
Published by New Riders. © 2005
ISBN 0-3213-4475-8

Usability is a key factor in creating successful Websites—it includes attention to ease of use and clarity. Exploring the common-sense aspect of usability concepts for the Web, this book offers methods for examining your site and determining if all portions of that site—navigation, layout, content, and more—are usable for the intended audience.

What You Have Learned

In this lesson, you have:

- Opened Dreamweaver (pages 4–5)
- Learned about the phases of Website development (pages 5–9)
- Prepared to create a Website, set up a local site, and defined the local root folder (pages 10–18)
- Created a new page and saved the document using the proper naming conventions (pages 18–23)
- Familiarized yourself with Dreamweaver's Insert panel; Property inspector; Document window; and other tools, windows, and panels (pages 23–31)
- Given your page a title (page 32)
- Specified preview browsers and used the keyboard shortcut to test your page (pages 33–35)

2 Adding Content to a Page

In this lesson, you'll determine the hierarchy of text-based content to develop the flow of material on a page. This is the next step in creating a Website—developing the structure and hierarchy of content. By establishing the structure and building the framework, you address the core element of the site: content. Specifying the structure using the principles covered in this lesson will help you to create a more flexible, effective, and accessible Website. In the following exercises you'll create the form through which the Website will take shape. You'll do this by determining the order of importance of content—grouping and subdividing the information into distinct areas. These distinctions help give meaning to what the visitor will see and help to create an effective and well-organized site.

This lesson teaches you how to import text that might have been saved in different file formats, how to compensate for receiving material from different operating systems, and how to address multilingual documents. You will also learn how to set basic document

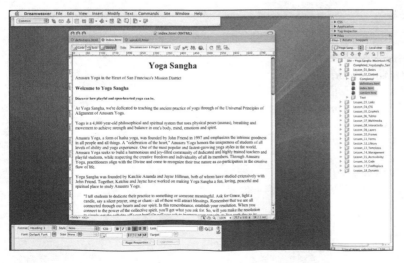

In this lesson, you'll work on the Yoga Sangha project site home page while learning to add content and develop effective page structures by grouping the materials.

properties such as font and text size, how to format text into several different types of lists, and how to include special characters such as copyright symbols.

Formatting text is an important part of making your Web pages easy for visitors to read. Text can be a vital element on your pages; take the time to organize and arrange your material so that users can read through it quickly and easily.

You can find an example of the completed Lesson 2 in the Completed folder inside the Lesson_02_Content folder on the CD-ROM.

What You Will Learn

In this lesson, you will:

- Place text on a page
- Organize content into logical sections
- Position and format text
- Set document defaults for font and color
- Insert special characters and other elements
- Create multilingual documents

Approximate Time

This lesson should take approximately one hour to complete.

Lesson Files

Starting Files:

Lesson_02_Content/index.html
Lesson_02_Content/definitions.html
Lesson_02_Content/sanskrit.html
Lesson_02_Content/Text/home_mac.txt
Lesson_02_Content/Text/home_win.txt
Lesson_02_Content/Text/definitions_mac.txt
Lesson_02_Content/Text/definitions_win.txt
Lesson_02_Content/Text/sanskrit_terms.rtf

Completed Project:

Lesson_02_Content/Completed/index.html
Lesson_02_Content/Completed/definitions.html
Lesson_02_Content/Completed/sanskrit.html

Importing Text

You can add text to a page in a variety of ways, including:

- Typing into the Macromedia Dreamweaver Document window.

- Copying and pasting from another application. You can open both Dreamweaver and the application from which you want to obtain content and then copy and paste (or select and drag the text or desired element) into Dreamweaver.

- Opening an HTML document. You can create HTML documents from a variety of applications, including word-processing programs such as Microsoft Word. To save a Microsoft Word document as HTML, open the document in Word and choose File > Save as Web Page. There are a number of erroneous coding issues with the HTML generated by Word. These problems and their solutions are covered in Lesson 16.

- Opening text files directly in Dreamweaver. You can use Dreamweaver to open files that were created in word-processing or page-layout applications, provided that those files were saved as *ASCII* (American Standard Code for Information Interchange) text files. Text (.txt) files always open in a new window using the Code view in Dreamweaver. After opening a text file in Dreamweaver, you can copy and paste the text you need into another document.

Working with ASCII Files

Simple formatting, such as paragraphs and line breaks, can be retained when importing text from ASCII text files, but to properly preserve the line formats you need to account for the differences between the ASCII format on different platforms. Files created in Windows use an invisible control character called a line feed (LF) to indicate a new line within the text, as well as carriage returns (CRs). Macintosh computers do not use the line-feed character—only CRs. Unix uses only the LF character.

To import text properly from ASCII files and retain the line break formatting, you need to change the Dreamweaver Line Break Type preferences to match the operating system on which the text files you want to import were created.

Edit the preferences by choosing Dreamweaver › Preferences (Macintosh) or Edit › Preferences (Windows) to display the Preferences dialog box and select Code Format in the Category list. From the Line Break Type pop-up menu, select the line break type—each type is shown with the corresponding operating system, so you can pick the one on which the text file was created. In the Line Break Type menu, your choices are CR LF (Windows), CR (Macintosh), and LF (Unix).

- For Macintosh users, the default is CR (Macintosh).
- For Windows users, the default is CR LF (Windows).

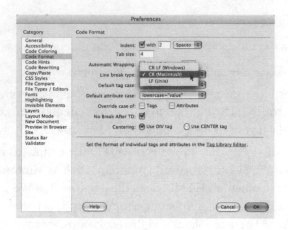

1. Use Dreamweaver to open Lesson_02_Content/Text/home_mac.txt (Macintosh) or home_win.txt (Windows); then select and copy all of the text. Open the Lesson_02_Content/index.html file, make sure the document is displayed in Design view, position the insertion point at the top of the document, and paste the copied text.

Note *For this exercise, choose the document that was created on the same operating system that you are using. You can experiment with importing text files from different platforms by opening the version of this document that was created on the other platform; home_mac.txt was created on a Macintosh computer while home_win.txt was created on a Windows computer. If you choose to experiment on your own with this additional file, remember that you will need to adjust the Line Break Type preferences accordingly, as described in the Working With ASCII Files side bar at the beginning of this exercise.*

The index.html document is an XHTML document similar to the one you created in Lesson 1. For additional practice with using Dreamweaver's tools, you can create a new document in the Lesson_02_Content folder and title it, using the skills learned in the previous lesson. You'll need to save it with a different name because you can't have two documents with the same name in the same folder.

You can use the Edit menu to copy and paste the text (choose Edit > Copy and/or Edit > Paste); or you can use the familiar keyboard commands Cmd+C (Macintosh) or Ctrl+C (Windows) to copy, and Cmd+V (Macintosh) or Ctrl+V (Windows) to paste.

2. Save the index.html file and close the home_mac.txt or home_win.txt file.

You can leave the index.html document open for the next exercise.

Identifying Content Structure

Setting up the document hierarchy by defining the order of page content is an important step in the process of developing your site. In this exercise, and throughout this lesson, you'll be defining the architecture of the material through a number of HTML formatting options, also known as *structural markup*. The correct way to use this kind of markup is to organize and structure content—not for the visual styling of material. HTML formatting is extremely limited in terms of design—you don't have a great deal of control over size, spacing, and alignment because the options are intended for describing document hierarchy, not to create the graphic appearance. You'll work on visual treatments and adjustments to the look of the content in later lessons. It is necessary to develop the structure, as you will begin doing in this exercise, before getting into the aesthetic details.

Note *For specific control over the appearance, you need to use Cascading Style Sheets (CSS) to define the look and placement of elements on your page. CSS will be covered in Lesson 4.*

1. In the index.html Document window, place the cursor in the text Yoga Sangha located at the top of the page.

This text is the primary title for this page.

2. From the Format pop-up menu in the Property inspector, choose Heading 1.

You defined the text format as a Level 1 heading. The text has been formatted as a *block-level element*. All options chosen from the Format menu apply to an entire block—a heading or any other type of block-level formatting cannot be applied to a single word or to a portion of a block. As a result, you don't have to select the text to apply a heading—all text contained in the text block automatically uses the formatting you select from the Format menu.

Other block-level elements include paragraphs, lists, horizontal rules, and the alignment options available in the Property inspector. You'll learn how to work with these formatting tools throughout this lesson.

Headings are displayed in larger or bolder fonts than normal body text. HTML has six levels of headings, numbered 1 through 6. Heading 1 has the largest font size; Heading 6 has the smallest. Tagging a text block as a heading automatically generates a space around the heading, which varies according to the heading you select. You can't control this spacing unless you use CSS to control formatting.

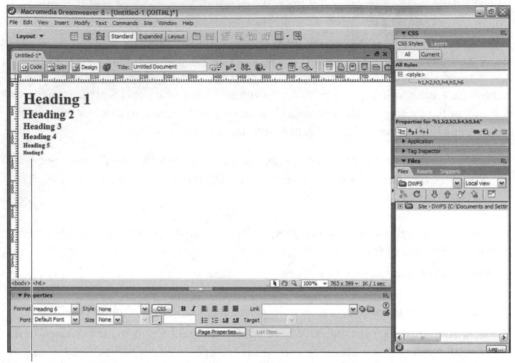

Display of Headings 1 through 6

Headings can be useful for splitting up your content into sections and calling attention to certain portions of the page. Users generally scan Web pages quickly and don't read everything. Taking the ways in which users interact with the Web into account while designing your site helps you develop pages that are much easier for visitors to use. Formatting your text with headings and the other techniques used throughout the rest of this lesson enable you to differentiate between your content and create a clear hierarchy.

Note *In many documents, the first heading on the page is identical in content to the title. In multiple-part documents, the text of the first heading should be related information, such as a chapter title. The title you set for the entire page should identify the document in a wider context (including both the book title and the chapter title, for example).*

3. Use the Format menu in the Property inspector to set the rest of the document headings. The following lines should use Heading 5:

Discover how playful and open-hearted yoga can be.

Intro to Anusara Workshop With Sierra

Anusara Yoga Immersion With Katchie Ananda and Jayne Hillman

The following lines should use Heading 3:

Welcome to Yoga Sangha

Announcements (News, Upcoming Events, etc.)

Feature: The Eight Limbs of Yoga

Schedule

Contact Us

Your document will now be formatted with all the appropriate headers, and should look like the following example.

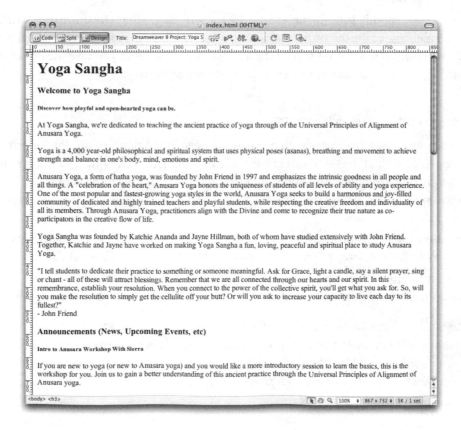

4. Place the cursor at the end of the first line of the document and press Return (Macintosh) or Enter (Windows).

You have just created another line below the Yoga Sangha title—this line is part of a new text block. By default, the new text block is formatted as a paragraph. Each new paragraph is its own text block.

5. Type *Anusara Yoga in the Heart of San Francisco's Mission District*.

The paragraph format is generally used for regular body text and it is set apart from other text blocks by a certain amount of spacing: A blank line separates the new text block from the previous one. You can't control this spacing unless you use CSS to control the formatting.

> **Note** *You can select Paragraph from the Format menu in the Property inspector, or use the keyboard shortcut Cmd+Shift+P (Macintosh) or Ctrl+Shift+P (Windows) to set the formatting of a text block to a paragraph.*

6. Save the file.

Whenever you modify your document, notice the asterisk (*) that Dreamweaver inserts near the filename at the top of the Document window. This asterisk indicates that the file has been modified but not yet saved. The asterisk disappears after you save the document. Be sure to save your documents often to prevent the loss of work.

Creating Line Breaks

If you want to create a new line with no space between it and the previous line of text (a single line break in the text), you can use a line break. This technique is useful for an address line; for example, when you want a new line for each line in the address without the extra spacing that paragraphs create.

1. Position the insertion point in the Intro To Anusara Workshop heading, just before With Sierra. Press Shift+Return (Macintosh) or Shift+Enter (Windows).

The text after the insertion point moves to the next line. A line break, not a new paragraph, has been created, so no additional spacing appears between the two lines.

> **Note** *If you use two line breaks, you can simulate the appearance of a new paragraph; however, because you are not actually creating a new paragraph, you might have difficulty when you try to apply formatting styles to text that has two line breaks instead of a single paragraph return.*

![C:\DWFS\pandbr.html (XHTML) window showing text with paragraph spacing, line break, and two line breaks examples]

Paragraph spacing

Line break

Two line breaks

2. Place line breaks in the following text, as follows:

Anusara Yoga Immersion *(Insert Line Break)*
With Katchie Ananda and Jayne Hillman

3030-A 16th St. *(Insert Line Break)*
(between Mission and Valencia) *(Insert Line Break)*
San Francisco, CA 94103

Email: info@yogasangha.com *(Insert Line Break)*
Phone: 415-934-0000

You can also insert a line break by choosing Insert > HTML > Special Characters > Line Break or by selecting the Text category in the Insert bar, clicking the Characters pop-up menu, and selecting Line Break. The line break character icon shown in the Insert bar is BR because the HTML tag for a line break is <br>, and the XHTML tag for a line break is <br />. You'll learn more about working with these and other tags in Lesson 16.

The Characters pop-up menu in the Text category of the Insert bar

Inserting a Nonbreaking Space

HTML distinguishes a single standard space—multiple spaces are not recognized. A special character called a *nonbreaking space* can be used when you need to create a space between two words that should not be split as a result of a text wrap. A nonbreaking space will prevent a line break from occurring at the point where it is inserted—the content before and after the special space will be constrained to the same line. The location where the line break happens in a block of text as a result of text wrap on a Web page can vary greatly depending on many factors, including font size and the size of the visitor's browser window. Using a regular space between "Yoga" and "Sangha," for instance, might result in the word "Yoga" appearing at the end of a line and the word "Sangha" appearing at the beginning of the next line. Using the nonbreaking space would force the browser to keep these two words together.

The nonbreaking space has been used to create the effect of multiple spaces because you can insert more than one space consecutively. You can also insert nonbreaking spaces at the beginning of a line of text, whereas you can't begin a line with a standard space. However, it is best to use other methods to control the layout such as creating first line indents with CSS. Nonbreaking spaces are best used any time you need to insert a space between characters, words, or other elements that should not be separated, such as mathematical equations, names and their suffixes, and dates.

1. In the index.html document, position the insertion point between the words Anusara and Yoga at the end of the first line below the Discover how playful and open-hearted yoga can be header.

If you press the spacebar more than once, there is no change in the amount of space between the words, and only a single space remains. Multiple spaces are not recognized.

Insertion point of the nonbreaking space

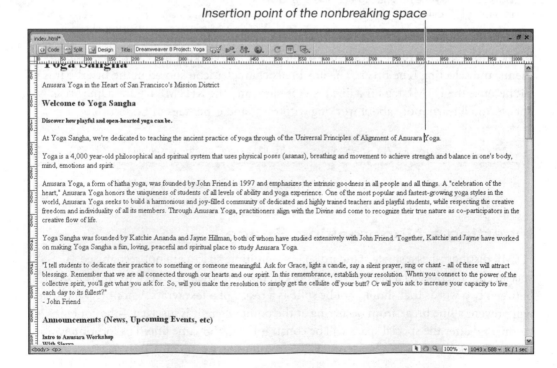

2. Delete the existing space, and then press Option+Spacebar (Macintosh) or Crtl+Shift+Spacebar (Windows) once.

Tip *You can also insert a nonbreaking space by choosing Insert > HTML > Special Characters > Non-Breaking Space or by selecting the Text category in the Insert bar, clicking the Characters menu, and selecting Non-Breaking Space.*

The spacing between the words will increase each time you insert a nonbreaking space.

Note *You can allow for multiple spaces when you type by changing the preferences. Choose Dreamweaver > Preferences (Macintosh) or Edit > Preferences (Windows) and select the General category. Check the box next to Allow Multiple Consecutive Spaces. With this option enabled, Dreamweaver uses nonbreaking spaces whenever you hit the Spacebar more than once. Use this option with care because CSS is a better method of controlling spacing and layout.*

3. Preview index.html in a browser. Expand and reduce the size of the browser window to make the line break occur where the split between the words Anusara and Yoga would appear.

Notice how the words are kept to the same line—the break occurs either before or after, but not where the nonbreaking space is located.

Note *Previewing Dreamweaver documents in browsers was covered in Lesson 1.*

Aligning Text

There are five basic alignment options available: Default (No Alignment Specified), Align Left, Align Center, Align Right, and Justify. Default is usually (depending on the browser defaults) the same as Align Left. These options specify the horizontal alignment of an element in relation to the *container*, which is an item that encloses other elements, such as an entire page or a paragraph.

In index.html, position the insertion point in the Yoga Sangha header at the top of the page Click the Align Center button in the Property inspector.

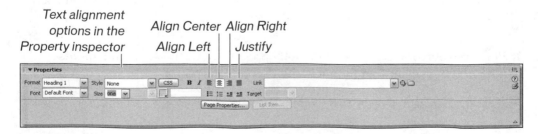

Text alignment options in the Property inspector

Align Left

Align Center Align Right

Justify

The heading is now centered. Any paragraph formatting that you apply to a text block, such as headings or alignments, affects everything contained within that paragraph.

Best Coding Practice: Deprecation of the Align Attribute

As of HTML 4.01 the align attribute has been deprecated—meaning it is marked for deletion by the W3C. The align attribute appears in the tag of the corresponding block element in the following manner:

```
<h1 align="center">Yoga Sangha</h1>
```

Likewise, specifying alignment directly in a div (the `<div>` tag is a type of structural markup, often used in conjunction with CSS, which is used to define sections of a document)is also deprecated, as shown in the following example:

```
<div align="right">
```

The best way to align elements, such as text and graphics, in your pages is through the use of CSS. Whenever possible, use CSS—and avoid using the four alignment options that are available in the Property inspector because they use the align attribute—to create the most efficient pages that are up to current standards.

Using CSS is covered in Lesson 4; working with code is covered in Lesson 16.

Identifying Quotes

There are two options in the Property inspector—called Text Outdent and Text Indent—whose names might be misleading at first glance. They should not be used as a method of indenting text but rather to signify a quoted passage of text. They function by enclosing a block of text in what is called a *blockquote*. A blockquote is a block-level element that indicates the text it contains is a quote—the default appearance of which is indenting the text on both sides, hence the name Text Indent. It is usually reserved for long passages of text that have been quoted. The blockquote does not place opening and closing quotation marks around the quote—you'll need to add these in the text itself.

1. Place the cursor inside the quote that appears above the Announcements header and then click Text Indent in the Property inspector.

Tip   *You can also choose Text > Indent to apply a blockquote and therefore indent the selected text.*

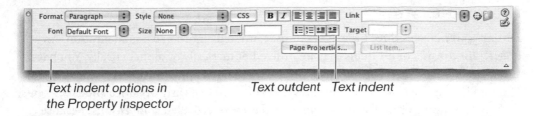

Text indent options in
the Property inspector

Text outdent   Text indent

The paragraph now appears indented on both the left and right margins. Blockquotes are applied to entire paragraphs. The only way to control the amount of this indentation is by creating a CSS style for the blockquote element—applying the blockquote without CSS will use the default spacing that is determined by the browser and that can differ from browser to browser.

Tip *If nearby paragraphs become indented as well, check to see whether you are using paragraphs or two line breaks. To be certain you are using a paragraph return, place the pointer at the beginning of the paragraph you want to indent. Press Delete (Macintosh) or Backspace (Windows) until you reach the end of the preceding paragraph, and press Return (Macintosh) or Enter (Windows) to create a new paragraph.*

If you want to indent text that isn't a quote to set it apart from standard body text on the page or if you want to indent only the first line of a paragraph, you should use CSS (covered in Lesson 4).

2. **Click the Text Outdent button in the Property inspector or choose Text ›**
Outdent to remove a blockquote.

Note *In XHTML, blockquotes must contain block-level elements such as paragraphs—not just text. To meet this requirement, Dreamweaver will automatically maintain the paragraph formatting around the original element in XHTML documents.*

There are a number of additional attributes that can be applied to blockquotes, including cite, which is used to specify the URL source of the quote, lang, which indicates what language the quote is in, and title, which is used to display a tooltip—a short message that will give the user additional information by displaying the message when the mouse rolls over the blockquote. These attributes can also be applied to a number of other tags. You can add such attributes using Dreamweaver's coding tools that are covered in Lesson 16.

Making Lists

Dreamweaver creates three basic types of lists: ordered, unordered, and definition. An *ordered list* consists of list items that are ordered numerically or alphabetically. You have the option of using Arabic or Roman numerals as well as upper- or lowercase letters. Ordered lists are ideal for situations in which you need to clearly organize and label items, such as presenting a list of steps. An *unordered list* is often called a *bulleted list* because each list item has a bullet in front of it. The bullet symbol that Dreamweaver displays by default can be changed to a disc, a circle, or a square. Unordered lists are good for presenting information in which each item needs to be differentiated, but where labeling with numbers or letters is unnecessary, such as a list of food types. *Definition lists* are composed of terms and their definitions; they will be explored in the next exercise.

In all list types, each item in the list needs to be contained in its own paragraph for the list to be correctly formatted.

In this exercise, you'll make two lists: one ordered and one unordered. You then tweak the list styles by using the List Properties dialog box. You'll work with a definition list later in this lesson.

1. In index.html, select the text starting with *yama (restraints or moral codes)* and ending with *samadhi (meditative absorption)*. Click the Ordered List button in the Property inspector.

The selected text is now formatted as a numbered list.

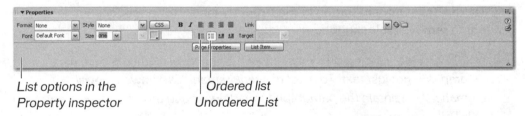

List options in the
Property inspector

Ordered list
Unordered List

There are a number of options available for lists. You can change the numbering scheme of ordered lists by modifying the list's properties, as you'll do in the next few steps with an unordered list.

When modifying an ordered list, the ordered list type is known as a Numbered List in the List type pop-up menu of the List Properties dialog box.

2. Select the days and their respective times listed under the Schedule heading. Click the Unordered List button in the Property inspector.

> **Tip** *You can also choose Text › List › Unordered List to format the selected text as an unordered list.*

The selected text is formatted as a bulleted list.

You can change the default bullet symbol of unordered lists by modifying the list's properties, which will be described in more detail below. The appearance of bullet symbols might vary from browser to browser, and all lists use a set amount of spacing that will vary from browser to browser. You have limited options regarding the appearance of numbers/letters, bullets and list spacing—for more control over list appearances, you can make use of style sheets, which are covered in Lesson 4.

When modifying an unordered list, the unordered list type is known as a Bulleted List in the List type pop-up menu in the List Properties dialog box.

> **Tip** *To remove the list formatting or switch to a different type of list, select the entire list and click the corresponding list button in the Property inspector to remove the list formatting (the Ordered List icon if it is an ordered list or the Numbered List icon if it is a numbered list) or the opposite list type to switch to that type of list.*

3. Place the insertion point at the end of the last line in the bulleted list and then press Return (Macintosh) or Enter (Windows). Type Sunday.

When you add text to a list, you need to use a regular paragraph return to create a new text block for the additional item. Every item in a list must be in a separate paragraph.

> **Tip** *Pressing Return (Macintosh) or Enter (Windows) twice exits the list mode and begins a default paragraph.*

4. Press Shift+Return (Macintosh) or Shift+Enter (Windows) to create a line break, and then type *9-10:30am*. Insert another line break and type *11am-12:30pm*. Insert a third line break and type *6:15-7:45pm*.

If you need to create one or more new lines within the same item you can use line breaks, as you've done in this step.

Your document should appear similar to the following example.

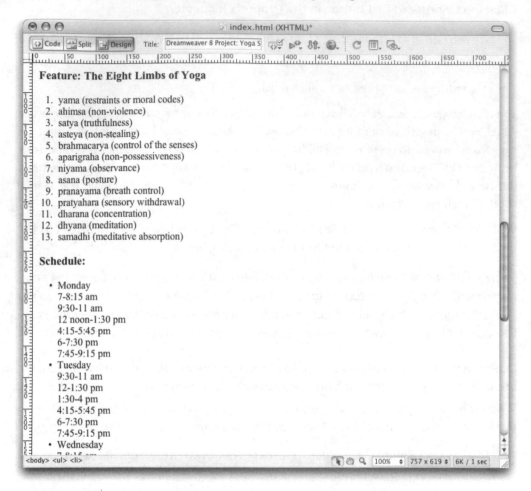

5. Click any line in the bulleted list and then click the List Item button in the Property inspector.

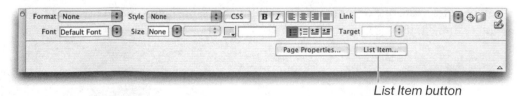

List Item button

If you select the whole list, the List Item button will be dimmed and unavailable. If the List Item button is not visible, click the expander arrow in the lower-right corner of the Property inspector.

Tip *With the cursor in the list, you can choose Text > List > Properties to open the same List Properties dialog box.*

The List Properties dialog box opens. In the List Properties dialog box that opens you can choose the List Type as well as the style you want from the Style pop-up menu. The options in the Style menu will vary depending on whether the list is Ordered or Unordered.

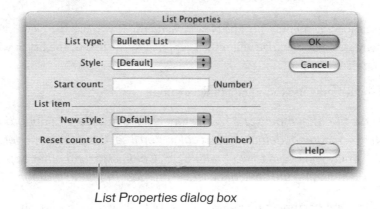

List Properties dialog box

The List item area at the bottom of the List Properties dialog box contains a New style menu that you can use to change the look of a single item or several items in a list, instead of changing the organization and look of the whole list. Also available in this area is the Reset count to text field, which enables you to change the count of the list beginning with the line in which the insertion point is placed.

Note *The List type menu in the List Properties dialog box contains two additional list types: Menu and Directory. These are older variations in the Bulleted list; both are similar in purpose to unordered lists and are typically displayed exactly the same as unordered lists by most browsers. It is generally recommended that you use the Bulleted list option for all unordered lists.*

6. From the Style menu, choose Square. Click OK.

Style menu options in the List Properties dialog box

Be sure to use the Style menu—not the New style menu. If you use the New style menu in the List item area, your change will only be applied to the line of the list in which your insertion point is located.

All items in the list now use the square bullet symbol.

Note *The color of numbers and bullets that is used in ordered or unordered lists is based in the document default for text color. You'll set the document defaults in the Lesson 4 when you begin to work with CSS. Color, size, and other appearance attributes—including the style of bullets—are best modified through CSS.*

Leave the index.html document open—you'll return to it later in this lesson.

Making Definition Lists

A definition list consists of a series of terms and their definitions. The word or term to be defined is left-aligned; the definition is indented and placed on the next line. There are no leading characters as there are in ordered and unordered lists.

1. Open the definitions.html document and select the text starting with the line *Hatha Yoga* and continuing through the end of the document. Choose Text > List > Definition List.

Note *For additional practice, you can create a new document, save it in the Lesson_02_Content folder, give it a title, and import the text from the definitions.txt document located in the Text folder. The definitions.txt file was created on a Macintosh. You might also want to apply a heading to the title Yoga at the top of the document.*

The terms are now at the left margin, and their indented definitions are on succeeding lines.

Your definition list should look like the following example.

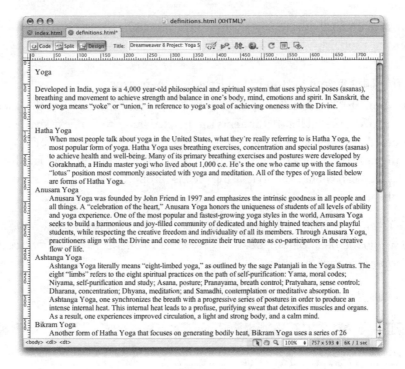

2. Save both the definitions.html and index.html files, and preview them in the browser.

Now that you have put work into creating and formatting all these lists, it's a good time to save your documents. Leave both documents open to work with through the rest of this lesson.

Nesting Lists

You can create *nested lists*, which are lists within lists. Nested lists can be the same type of list as the parent list or they can be a different type of list. An ordered list can be placed within a definition list, for example. By default, bullets are displayed as filled circles, open circles, and squares (in that order) as you nest the lists. Dreamweaver calls the bullet types bullet, circle, and square. The corresponding HTML terminology is disc, circle, and square.

Some browsers display open square bullets. Netscape 4.7 for the Macintosh displays open squares, for example, but Internet Explorer 5.0 for the Macintosh displays filled squares. In Windows, the squares are filled.

1. In the index.html document, select the lines starting with *ahimsa* **through** *aparigrapha.*

These items fall under the category of yama in the preceding line, so you'll nest these items to create a sub list.

2. Click the Text Indent button in the Property inspector.

In this situation, the Text Indent button does not apply the blockquote to the selected text. Instead, it created a nested list that indents the selected items to the next level. When you nest an ordered list, the nested items will start over in the count. In an unordered list, the bullets in the nested list will appear in a different style from those in the main list such as open circles. You can change the style using the List Properties dialog box, as you did earlier for the main list.

Note *To change an item from a nested item to a regular list, position the insertion point within the nested item, but don't select it. Click the Text Outdent button in the Property inspector.*

Your nested list should look like the following example.

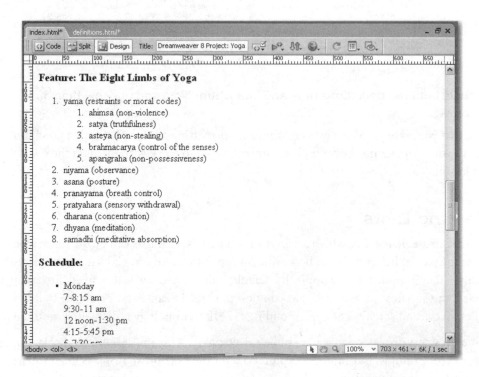

Just as when you indent text, you can't control or adjust the spacing of outdented text, lists, or nested lists.

Note *If an extra blank line appears between the last item in the nested list and the following item in the main list, there might be a line break which you can get rid of by placing the insertion point in the blank line and pressing Delete (Macintosh) or Backspace (Windows). The last character in the last line of the nested list can be deleted when you do this—simply retype that character.*

Inline Character Formatting

Inline formatting is applied directly to content at an individual point—this type of formatting is text-level markup that is also known as a phrase elements. A phrase element specifies information about the structure and specific usage of text fragments to provide context rather than the structure of a larger section of the document, as is the case with block level elements. You can apply a few formatting options to the text you create in Dreamweaver to emphasize certain points, words, or phrases. The two most common options to set are bold and italic.

1. In definitions.html, select the first term at the top of the list *Hatha Yoga*.

You will apply bold formatting to the selected text.

2. Click the Bold button in the Property inspector.

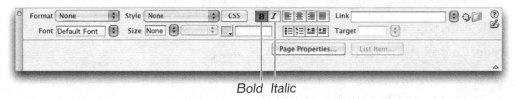

Bold Italic

You can also choose Text > Style > Bold or click the Bold button in the Text category of the Insert bar to apply the bold format to the selected text. The keyboard shortcuts are Cmd+B (Macintosh) and Ctrl+B (Windows).

If your preferences are set to do so, when you use the Property inspector to apply bold formatting, Dreamweaver wraps the `<strong>` and `</strong>` tags around the selected text. Similarly, when you apply italic formatting, Dreamweaver wraps the `<em>` and `</em>` tags (*em* indicates emphasis) around the selected text. Dreamweaver uses strong and emphasis tags, which are referred to as logical markup because they affect content in both conceptual and visual appearance, instead of bold and italic tags (`<b>`, `<i>`), which are referred to as physical markup because they affect only visual appearance. Logical markup is more flexible and accessible to a wider audience—it represents the function of the text portion as opposed to giving presentational information, which is best done through CSS.

Italic formatting is applied in the same way—simply use the Italic button in the Property inspector.

Other formatting options include Underline, which provides a line beneath the text; Teletype, which renders text in a monospaced font; and Strikethrough, which displays text with a line through the center.

> **Note** *Be careful of using the underline formatting on your Web pages. One of the most common ways a link is designated on a Web page is with an underline. Using the underline style for text other than links can potentially confuse your visitors. There are other ways that you can differentiate text including size, color, and spacing—all of which you'll learn to use in Lesson 4. Recognizing and applying standard Web practices will make your site clearer and more readily accessible to viewers. Avoid using styles or elements in ways that can cause them to be easily confused with other uses and meanings.*

3. Repeat the bold formatting on each of the remaining terms in the definition list.

Many times, you might need to repeat the most recent action, such as the formatting you set on another paragraph or other selected text. The Redo command reduces that task to a simple keystroke. The first two items listed in the Edit menu are the Undo and Redo commands. You'll want to remember their keyboard shortcuts:

Undo: Cmd+Z (Macintosh) and Ctrl+Z (Windows)

Redo: Cmd+Y (Macintosh) and Ctrl+Y (Windows)

> **Note** *You can use the History panel to speed up actions that you repeat often. To access the History panel, choose Window › History. You can select a series of actions in the panel and click the Save Selected Steps As Command button in the lower-right corner of the panel or by choosing Save As Command from the context menu in the upper-right corner of the panel. If you want a quick way to insert often-used bits of code, you should use Snippets (covered in Lesson 16).*

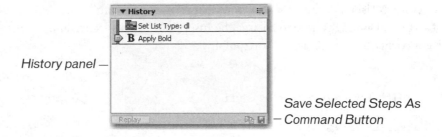

History panel —

Save Selected Steps As
— Command Button

You can save and close the definitions.html document.

Adding Special Characters

As you work in Dreamweaver, you will sometimes need to use characters that you can't access directly from the keyboard. These special characters have specific HTML codes or alternative keyboard commands that might be difficult to remember.

1. In index.html, place the insertion point at the beginning of the last paragraph, just in front of *2005 Yoga Sangha*.

Web pages often have footers with copyright information at the bottom. These footers also tend to contain text links to the main sections of the site for navigation and accessibility purposes. Footers sometimes contain contact information as well.

2. Choose the Text category from the Insert bar. Click the Characters menu and click the © (copyright) character to insert it.

The Characters menu can be accessed by clicking the black arrow to the right of the icon.

The © (copyright) character is inserted in the new line when you click the icon in the characters menu.

Like other menus in the Insert bar, the icon that represents the Characters menu will change based on what item was last selected in the menu.

Note *You might receive a warning that special characters might not appear in all browsers depending on the encoding of your document. Changing the encoding is discussed in the next exercise.*

Macintosh Users: If you do not see the Characters icon/menu in the Text category of the Insert bar, you might need to enlarge the Insert bar. To do so, click and drag the lower-right corner to extend the bar horizontally.

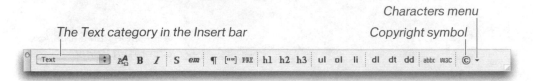

The Text category in the Insert bar

Characters menu

Copyright symbol

Note *Although the Characters menu in the Text category of the Insert bar gives you quick access to many of the most common characters you might need, it doesn't provide an all-encompassing list. If the character you want to use isn't available in the Characters menu, you can still find it by clicking the Other Characters option at the bottom of the menu or by choosing Insert > HTML > Special Characters > Other. When you select a character in the Insert Other Character dialog box, the corresponding HTML code appears in the text field at the upper-left corner of the dialog box. After you click the character that you want to use, click OK.*

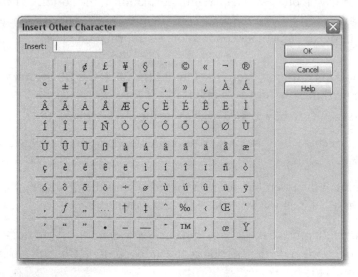

Leave the index.html document open.

Creating Multilingual Documents

To create multilingual documents that make use of alphabets with characters that differ from the one you use primarily, you'll need to adjust the encoding of each page and know which character set(s) is needed for your page. A character set is a group of characters that have been combined for a specific purpose, such as characters that make up an alphabet. An encoding system is the method by which the characters in such a set have been mapped to the bytes of data that represent them.

1. Open sanskrit.html from the Lesson_02_Content folder. Choose Modify › Page Properties and select the Title/Encoding category. From the Encoding pop-up menu, select Unicode 4.0 UTF-8 (Macintosh) or Unicode (UTF-8) (Windows). Click OK to close the dialog box.

You can leave the rest of the dialog options set to their defaults.

Note *You might receive a warning dialog box informing you that the selected encoding does not have all the characters that were using in the original encoding. Click Apply to confirm and apply the new encoding.*

The Title/Encoding options in the Page Properties dialog box

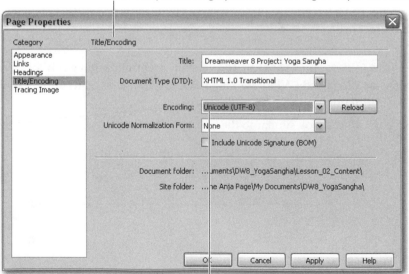

Selecting the encoding type

The default encoding used in Dreamweaver is Western ISO (Latin 1), which covers most West European languages. (*ISO* stands for the International Standards Organization.)

Note *The Western ISO (Latin 1) encoding, also known as ISO-8859-1 (Latin 1), might not be the default for international versions of Dreamweaver.*

Unicode is a universal character set that is inclusive of the majority of characters in a large number of languages. It is intended to act as a superset of most other character sets by allowing a single document to contain characters from many diverse languages—it is both multilingual and multiplatform. You can use the UTF-8 (Unicode Transformation Format 8) encoding to display characters from multiple alphabets. It is ASCII-compatible, which is the format commonly used in .txt documents, as you learned earlier in this lesson. UTF-8 is supported by Windows 2000 and Macintosh OS X—although you might still need to provide a link to download a Unicode font(s) and/or specify particular unicode fonts. Older browsers and older operating systems might not support UTF-8.

You might need to use the UTF-8 encoding if you need to use characters that are not in Western Latin alphabet (or vice versa, depending on the language you use), such as making use of the Japanese Katakana alphabet (foreign words) and/or the Hiragana alphabet (Japanese words). You might want to use characters from other alphabets in your documents if your company has a multilingual environment or offers services in more than one language.

In this exercise, you'll learn to do this by working with Sanskrit words using the Devanagari alphabet.

2. **In the Text folder, open sanskrit_terms.rtf in an application such as TextEdit (Macintosh) or WordPad (Windows), select everything, copy it, and paste it into the sanskrit.html document.**

Your document should look similar to the example shown here.

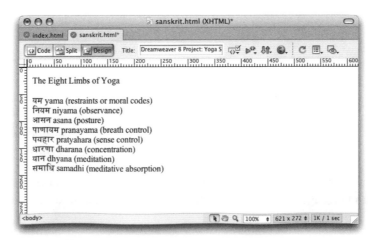

To import text that uses characters from other alphabets, you'll need to either copy it from another document, as you've done in this exercise, or create it yourself through the use of language kits that give you access to other character sets through either input menus or directly from the keyboard.

Macintosh OS X provides support for a wide number of languages. You can modify your current settings and access the different languages through the International section of the System Preferences. The Input menu allows you to select the way in which you want to work with different characters—such as through the keyboard or an input palette.

Windows 2000 and later versions of Windows support multiple languages through Unicode.

3. Save the sanskrit.html document and preview it in a browser.

You might want to test the page in multiple browsers—not all support the use of Unicode.

> **Note** An alternative method of displaying content in other languages and alphabets is to use graphics. Images however, can make modifications occur much more slowly—text has the benefit of being updatable quickly and easily directly in Dreamweaver. Text is more accessible, flexible, and portable than images.

You can close the sanskrit.html document.

Adding Horizontal Rules

A *horizontal rule* is a line that goes across the page and provides a visual division between sections of your content. It can be useful when identifying the structure of a document and provides clear designations for each portion of material. In this exercise, you will add a horizontal rule above the copyright information.

Place the insertion point just in front of the copyright character you inserted earlier near the bottom of the index.html document. From the HTML category in the Insert bar, click the Horizontal Rule button.

Horizontal rule

> **Tip** If the Insert bar is not visible, choose Window > Insert. You can also click in the document and choose Insert > HTML > Horizontal Rule.

After you insert the horizontal rule, it is selected in the Document window. It is placed just above the copyright information, which drops down to a line below the horizontal rule. The horizontal rule has a set amount of space above and below the line; you can't control the amount of spacing unless you use CSS.

The Property inspector will show the attributes of the horizontal rule when it is selected. Options include specifying an ID, width and height, pixel and percentage units of measurement, shading, horizontal alignment, and the ability to apply CSS through the Class menu.

The Horizontal Rule attributes in the Property inspector

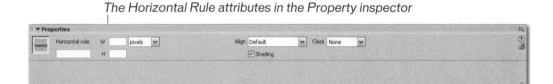

The size and alignment options available in the Property inspector use tags that are deprecated in HTML 4.0 and beyond. It's better to use CSS to control the appearance, as you will learn in Lesson 4.

Note *Although the color of the horizontal rule might still appear as the default gray in Dreamweaver—even when you have modified it through the use of CSS—you should see properties applied for the horizontal rule with CSS in the browser.*

Adding a Date Automatically

Sometimes, you might need to keep track of the date you last modified a page on your site or you might want your visitors to see when the information on your page was last updated. Dreamweaver lets you place a date and time on your pages to track this information. Dreamweaver can update the date and time automatically every time you save the page using Dreamweaver, so you don't have to do it manually.

Note *This date is not a dynamic date that changes according to the date and/or time a user accesses the page. This date simply tells your users when your pages have been updated. Dynamic dates that display the current date and/or time are often generated with JavaScript. You can learn more about JavaScript in Lesson 8.*

1. Place the insertion point at the end of the copyright information paragraph, insert a line break and enter *Updated:.*

This information is often shown in the upper-right corner of news sites or displayed at the bottom of a page on other informational sites.

2. Select the Common category in the Insert bar and click the Date button to place the current date on the page.

Tip You can also choose Insert › Date to open the Insert Date dialog box.

Date

The Insert Date dialog box opens.

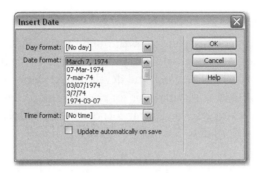

3. From the Day format menu, choose the *Thursday* option. From the Date format menu, choose *March 7, 1974*. From the Time format menu, choose *10:18 PM*. Check the Update Automatically On Save checkbox to update the date on your page each time you save your document. Click OK.

The current day, date, and time are displayed, and this information changes every time you save the document. Thursday is used as an example in the Insert Date dialog box of how the day will appear in your document. The date and time are also examples.

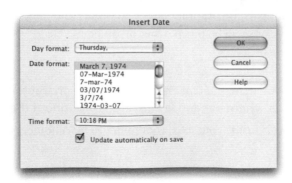

Note *If the date is set to update automatically, you can change the format at any point after inserting the date. To change the date format, click the date in your document and click Edit Date Format in the Property inspector. The Insert Date dialog box opens. Make the appropriate changes and then click OK. Your changes are applied to the document. The format of dates that do not update automatically can't be edited through the dialog box—to update such dates, you will have to delete and reinsert the date or change the text yourself in the Document window.*

You can save, preview, and close the index.html document.

Formatting Content On Your Own

Now that you learned to structure your pages through the use of formatting techniques that can help organize and prioritize content, you're ready to apply those skills to your own pages. You'll need to use the research and development work that you created in the On Your Own section of Lesson 1 as the basis for creating the content for your site. After you have the text for your site, you can start incorporating the material into pages that you create in Dreamweaver, as described in the following steps.

1. Create as many separate HTML pages as needed and import the corresponding content into them.

Use the site structure that you developed at the end of Lesson 1 as a guide for determining how many pages need to be created, where they should reside in the file structure, and what content should go on each page.

2. Apply headings to give structure to each page, and include line breaks, paragraphs, and nonbreaking spaces as needed.

Using combinations of paragraphs and different heading levels will help you define the sections of your documents. Incorporating presentational and design elements that you'll learn to use in later lessons will be much easier if you have a clearly defined structure in each of your documents.

3. Incorporate quotes, lists, special characters, inline character formatting, and multilingual elements where needed, as covered throughout the lesson.

You can save these pages inside your local root folder as placeholders for future content.

What You Have Learned

In this lesson, you have:

- Learned how to set text preferences and import text in different ways (pages 41–42)
- Structured text by using combinations of headings and paragraphs (pages 43–46)
- Incorporated line breaks and nonbreaking spaces to control the flow of content (pages 46–49)
- Used the Text Indent tool to properly designate quoted material (pages 49–52)
- Created three list types and modified their properties (pages 52–59)
- Applied inline character formatting of bold and italic to selected content (pages 59–61)
- Added special characters to the page (pages 61–62)
- Worked with multilingual content to include characters from other character sets (pages 63–66)
- Added a date to the page and set it to update every time the page is saved (pages 66–68)

3 Creating Links

The power of Websites as a unique medium comes from their capability to connect text and images with other documents through links that are not sequential or linear. The browser can highlight these regions (usually with color or underlines) to indicate that they are links.

A link in HTML has two parts: the name and path (or Uniform Resource Locator, URL) of the file to which you want to link and the text or graphic that serves as the clickable area. When the user clicks a link, the browser loads the linked document. In some browsers, the path of the link is displayed in the status area of the browser window (located in the lower-left part of the window) when the pointer is positioned over the link. Links can direct the user to other HTML files, images and other media, and downloadable files — you'll work with text-based links in this lesson and continue to apply what you learn to other media as you progress through other lessons.

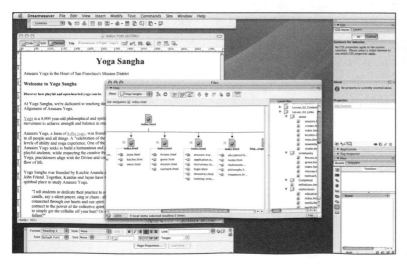

In this lesson, you'll create a functional test site that includes placeholders for the entire Yoga Sangha project site with navigational links.

In this lesson, you'll develop the initial framework of the site structure by developing placeholders for the pages in the Yoga Sangha project site. You'll link these pages together using Dreamweaver's visual site-mapping tools to create a working test site. Creating this kind of framework through pages and links in a bare but functional version of the site can help you test the navigation that you have developed. Testing the proposed site structure before creating the design will help you catch fundamental problems at the beginning of development, enabling you to address them more efficiently.

To see an example of the finished pages, view the files in the Lesson_03_Links/Completed folder.

What You Will Learn

In this lesson, you will:

- Specify link colors according to the link state
- Create links in text to other documents
- Use anchors to jump to different parts of the page
- Create e-mail links

Approximate Time

This lesson should take about two hours to complete.

Lesson Files

Starting Files:

Lesson_03_Links/index.html
Lesson_03_Links/definitions.html
Lesson_03_Links/sanskrit.html

Completed Project:

Lesson_03_Links/Completed/…all files

Specifying Link Color and Format

You can specify the default color of text links on your page. Choosing a link color that stands out from the regular body text in the document enables viewers to spot the links easily. The default link properties for your document are specified through the Page Properties dialog box.

If you don't specify link colors, the browser defaults will be used when the page displays in the user's browser. These defaults can vary depending on the browser.

When you begin working on the appearance of your site, it is best to take the color scheme of the site as a whole into account. When you decide on the site-wide styles and colors, you can change the link colors so that they will be consistent with the colors used elsewhere in your pages. The colors you select should contrast (but not clash) with the background and other elements so the links can be read clearly.

Note *Dreamweaver can control the appearance of links through the use of Cascading Style Sheets (CSS) to set color, font face, and font size properties that apply only to links. A CSS link style is known as a **pseudoclass**, which is a type of style that is created with parameters that it be applied only under specific circumstances. CSS is covered in Lesson 4.*

1. Open the index.html document, located in the Lesson_03_Links folder. Choose Modify › Page Properties (Cmd-J/Ctrl-J) and then select the Links category.

For this exercise, you should leave the Link font option on the default selection (Same as page font). With this setting, the links on your page inherit the properties of the styles that you'll set for your document in the next lesson.

Note *If you apply a CSS style for the text in which a link is located—as you'll do in the next lesson—the link inherits the properties of that style instead of the default document styles.*

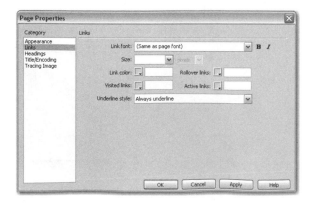

There are different states of a link, such as links that haven't been clicked and those that have. You can specify appearance attributes for each state of a link. You have the option to define colors for up to four different link states based on a user's actions.

- **Link Color:** The initial color of a link, prior to the link being clicked. The standard default browser color for a link is blue.

- **Visited Links:** The color that a link changes to when a user clicks the link. The standard default browser color for a visited link is purple.

- **Rollover Links:** The color to which a link changes as a user pauses the pointer over the link. This serves as an additional indicator that the item is clickable. No rollover is used if this is left blank.

- **Active Links:** The color of the link when the mouse is being pressed. Active links can serve as an interactive indicator to the visitor that the link is being clicked, although as a result of the growing speed with which users access the Web, the Active link is no longer as prominent as it used to be. No active color is used if it is left blank.

Note *CSS link styles control the link tag (<a>) with specific attributes for the different states that can be applied to it. The different states of the <a> tag are activated when a user performs an action such as clicking the link. The states are defined through the following CSS selectors: a:link for the link color; a:visited for visited links; a:hover for rollover links; and a:active for active links.*

2. Use the text fields next to the color boxes to select the colors for your links by entering *#FF3300* for the Link color, *#FF9900* for the Rollover Links color, *#993300* for the Visited Links color, and *#FFCC00* for the Active Links color.

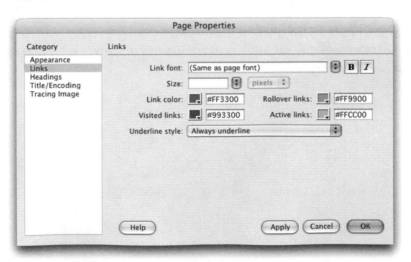

When you know the *hexadecimal* values—codes that are used on the Web to represent colors—of the colors you want to use, you can enter the numbers directly in the link color text fields. Dreamweaver automatically fills in the color box with the matching color swatch. You can also click the color box located just to the left of the text field to bring up a palette with a variety of color swatches. If you choose a color swatch from the palette, Dreamweaver automatically fills in the text field with the equivalent hexadecimal value, which displays at the top of the palette as you roll over the color swatches. When using the color palette, the mouse will turn into a color picker, which you can use to select any color visible on the screen by rolling over the desired area and clicking to select the color. This method allows you to easily match existing colors from other documents, images, and media.

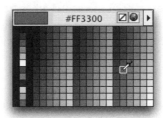

Note For more colors, click the arrow located in the upper-right corner of the color pop-up window and choose another color palette type from the pop-up menu. Keep in mind that other palettes are not limited to cross-platform, Web-safe colors. Web-safe colors are a set of 216 colors that are the same on both Macintosh and Windows operating systems. Although the color choices in this palette are extremely limited, using Web-safe colors ensures that users with systems that use 256 colors—much less common now that many people have video cards capable of millions of colors—can see your pages with the intended colors. Alternative Web access devices such as PDAs still use a limited number of colors, so you might want to use Web-safe colors if you are developing sites that are intended to be accessible by such devices. This factor is one example of why it is important to spend the time to research the audience of your site—as you learned in Lesson 1—and to determine the most common systems and configurations the majority of that audience is likely to have.

Understanding Hexadecimal Color Codes

Colors are defined in hexadecimal code using RGB: red, green, and blue. Hexadecimal is a base-16 numbering system that uses 0 through 9 and A through F. In the six-digit code used in HTML to describe color, the first two digits represent red, the second two digits represent green, and the last two digits represent blue. For example, #00FF00 has no red, a bright green, and no blue; #000000 has no red, no green, and no blue—it is black. Conversely, #FFFFFF signifies the maximum levels of red, green and blue, which combine to display white on your screen. Remember that computer screens use light to render the colors that you see. The color properties of light (which is based on an additive system, in which all colors combine to make white) are much different from the properties of pigment used in print media (which is based on a subtractive system, in which all colors combine to make black). The number sign (#), also known as a pound sign, indicates that what follows is a hexadecimal value and not a named color (such as black, white, red, and so on).

Although Dreamweaver will accept values entered without the number sign, it is best to include it. When you use the color box to select a swatch, notice that the number sign is included.

Consider the standard link colors, listed for each link state in Step 1 of this exercise, when you select the colors for your link. It might be confusing for visitors if, for example, you decide to use a purple similar to the standard visited link color as your regular (not yet clicked) link color. Taking what have become standard Web conventions into consideration and understanding your viewers' expectations are important when designing your site.

The last option in the Links section of the Page Properties dialog box is the definition of the Underline style to be used on your page. For this exercise, you should leave the menu selection on the default: Always Underline. The other options in this menu are Never Underline, Show Underline Only On Rollover, and Hide Underline On Rollover. You can use the Never Underline option to remove the default underline that appears on all links, but remember to consider the expectations of your visitors when creating Websites. Many users have become accustomed to the conventional underlined appearance of links. If you remove the underlines, your users might overlook the links and miss the information. Conversely, if you underline other words in your text, users might try to click them, expecting links.

3. Click OK to close the Page Properties dialog box and then save the index.html file.

The default link colors for your page are now the colors you specified. You will see these colors in use as you begin to create links in the next exercise.

Keep the document index.html open to work with in the following exercises.

Creating Hypertext Links

Hypertext links give you the ability to direct the visitor to documents within your Website or to any other location on the Web. Links made within the same site are called *relative links*, which can connect to files in any number of locations within the folder structure of a single site. There are a variety of ways to create such a link. The following exercise demonstrates these methods.

Remember that it is important to save new documents before you create any links. Saving a file tells Dreamweaver where your document is and enables it to determine the link paths. Dreamweaver needs to determine the location of the linked file in relation to the file in which you are putting the link. If you try to create a link without saving your document for the first time, these paths begin with file:// and they do not work on remote sites because they are relative to your hard disk—not to the file in which the link is contained. Although Dreamweaver automatically updates the links when you save a file, it is better to avoid the chance of problematic paths that could cause problems.

1. In the index.html document, select the word *Yoga* at the beginning of the line *Yoga is a 4,000 year-old...*

This line is located in the Welcome to Yoga Sangha section in the beginning of the document.

You will create a link from this term to the page with definitions of different styles of yoga.

Note   *The starting files in this lesson are copies of the files you've been working with in previous lessons. The completed versions are provided here for your convenience—they have been created using the techniques you learned so far in this book.*

When creating sites, choose the language that you use to indicate links carefully. Avoid using the phrase "click here" because it is unclear and can cause multiple problems including navigational difficulties. For example, visitors with vision disabilities might not be able to distinguish between multiple links that use "click here"—especially if they are using an audio browser—they might have a particularly hard time navigating as a result. In addition, when users skim pages looking for links of interest, they usually watch for the underlines that indicate links. Seeing "click here" instead of a clear description can make this process more difficult. Always be specific when creating phrases that contain links. For example, when directing readers to a document in which they can learn about the different styles of yoga, you might want to use "learn more about different Yoga styles" (where "Yoga styles" is linked) in which the actual link is more descriptive and informative instead of "click here to learn more about Yoga styles" (where "click here" is linked).

2. In the Property inspector, click the Browse For File button to the right of the Link text field.

Link text field   *Browse for File button*

The Select File dialog box opens.

3. Select the definitions.html file in the Lesson_03_Links folder, and click Choose (Macintosh) or OK (Windows).

The filename definitions.html appears in the Link text field, and the text you selected in the index.html document is now marked as a link. This link is underlined and appears in the color you selected for links in the first exercise of this lesson.

> **Note** *You can easily override the page's default link color for individual links by selecting the text that is linked and choosing a color from the Property inspector. Dreamweaver automatically creates a new CSS style for that color. With this method, the CSS style created by Dreamweaver is an internal style, which you'll learn more about in Lesson 4.*

This link is an example of a document-relative path, which is the best option to use for local links in most Websites and is the type that is used throughout this book. A document-relative path omits the part of the absolute URL that is the same for the current document and the linked document; therefore it uses only the portion of the path that differs. An absolute URL is one that gives the entire Web address of a site or resource, such as http://www.yogasangha.com. The path to the linked document is determined in relation to the location of the document in which the link is contained as the starting point. A path to a file in the same folder, for example, is expressed as name_of_file.html. A path to a file in a subfolder would look like this: name_of_folder/name_of_file.html.

On the other hand, a *site root-relative path* is determined in relation to the root folder of the site as the starting point and is not based on where the current document is located. The linked document is specified according to its location within the structure of the site.

4. **In the Feature: The Eight Limbs of Yoga section, place the cursor at the end of the line for item 8 in the numbered list. Press Return (Macintosh) or Enter (Windows) twice and type** *See the Sanskrit text for the Eight Limbs.* **Repeat Steps 1 through 3 to link the word Sanskrit to the sanskrit.html file in the Lesson_03_Links folder.**

> **Note** *As you learned in Lesson 2, it is necessary to press Return or Enter twice to exit a list; using just one paragraph return would create a new item in the list.*

When you know the names and locations of the files to which you need to link, you can type their paths directly into the Link text box instead of browsing to find them; however, letting Dreamweaver create the paths will reduce the chance of typos.

> **Tip** *If you need to use the same links multiple times in the same session — a session being the time in which you've had Dreamweaver open until the time when you quit the program — you can save time by choosing recently used links from the pop-up menu to the right of the Link text field on the Property inspector.*

Editing the destination of a link is a simple process: Click anywhere inside an existing link and make the desired changes to the value in the link text field on the Property inspector by changing the path in the text field or clicking the Browse for File icon. You do not need to select the entire link because Dreamweaver automatically prevents links from becoming nested within each other—a link can't be placed inside of another link. Text that you choose to apply a link to is defined by the HTML tags that surround or contain it; therefore, any change you make to the link is automatically applied to all the text contained within the link (between the opening and closing portions of the <a> tag that denotes links of all types). You'll learn more about HTML tags in Lesson 16.

5. Select the text *www.yogasangha.com* near the very bottom of the document. Type *http://www.yogasangha.com* into the link text field on the Property inspector and press Return (Macintosh) or Enter (Windows) to apply the link.

You created an absolute link that will direct users to a site outside of the project site.

6. Save the index.html file and preview it in the browser. Close the index.html file.

The three links you just created should take you to their corresponding pages. Always test your links to be sure they go to the correct locations!

If the Start page appears, you can close it.

> **Tip** *You can preview your document in the browser by pressing F12 to open a window of the primary browser that you defined in Lesson 1. You might need to use a modifier key if your function keys are enabled for system operations.*

Understanding Links and File Structure

The links that you create depend on the file and folder structure of your site. It is good to understand how the paths work when creating links. The following illustration is an example of a possible site structure.

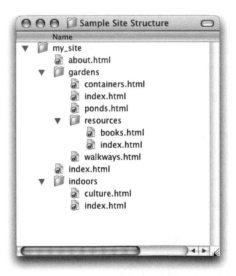

When you create a link to any document that exists outside the folder in which the current document is located, the path for the link will include the characters ../ preceding the filename. ../ is a command that tells the browser to go up one folder level from the current location. Each instance of ../ indicates moving up one folder level; you might have something similar to ../../filename.html to link to a document that is located two folder levels above the current directory. For instance, in the previous example, the path of a link from the books.html page to the about.html page would be ../../about.html. In Dreamweaver, you do not need to use the ../ characters unless you are inserting links by typing them directly into the link text field. If you are not sure of the proper path, you should browse to select the desired file. Dreamweaver will determine the appropriate path for you.

You'll also notice that there are multiple index.html files in the preceding sample site structure. The filename *index* is a standard name for the default file of a folder or directory on many servers. These default files do not need to be specified in the URL. The visitor is automatically taken to the default file of a folder if no file is specified. In the previous example, a user could simply type the domain name followed by **/gardens** to get to the index page inside of the gardens folder. The filename index.html is the most common, but other names for default files include default.html and home.html. Many types of extensions can be used, but your server might need to be configured to recognize index files with extensions other than .html or .htm. Check with your server or host to find out how it is configured.

When you link to a document that exists in the same folder as the current document, the path for the link will be the name of the linked document. When you link to a document that exists in a folder inside the one in which the current document is located, the path for the link includes *foldername/* preceding the filename. foldername/ tells the browser to look in the specified folder, and that folder is located inside of the current directory.

As you develop your site, you might find it necessary to move files or even entire folders to different locations. Using the preceding example, suppose you move containers.html into the indoors folder. Any links or other paths that are included in the containers.html document need to be updated, as do any links from other files to that document. If those paths are not updated, the paths are "broken," meaning that links and images no longer work. As you move files, Dreamweaver automatically updates the paths for all links, images, and other media in your site as long as you make all changes within the Dreamweaver Files panel. If you make any changes outside of Dreamweaver, such as through Mac OS X's Finder or Windows Explorer, Dreamweaver has no way to track or maintain your files.

Tip | *Macintosh users can Command+click on the filename in the title bar of the document to view the hierarchy of folders from the hard disk to the file.*

Adding New Folders and Files to a Site

To create the initial framework of the site structure through the development of linked placeholder pages in the Yoga Sangha project site, you'll need to create a number of new pages and folders. This can be done quickly and easily from the Files panel, which enables you to set up a site's file and folder structure. You can immediately create pages that act as placeholders and add content to them at a later time.

1. Click the Expand button on the Files panel toolbar in the Files panel.

Tip *If the Files panel is not visible in the panels, you might need to choose Window › Files.*

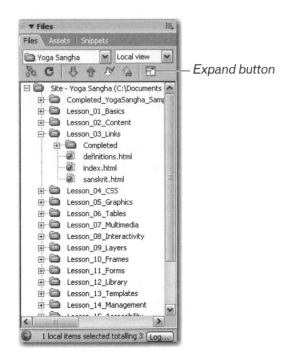

— Expand button

Expand to show local and remote sites.

The Expand button is located on the right side of the toolbar, above the list of files. You'll learn more about the other options and tools on the Files panel in Lesson 14.

2. On the expanded Files panel, verify that Yoga Sangha is selected in the Show menu. Open the Lesson_03_Links folder shown in the Local Files column by clicking the arrow (Macintosh) or plus icon (Windows).

Note *The Show menu is only visible in Windows if you are in a site. If you are viewing just a drive (such as F:) you only get the Manage Sites link.*

The Local Files column is located on the right side of the expanded Files panel. The Remote Site column on the left side of the panel does not contain any files because you haven't defined a remote site. You'll learn more about doing so in Lesson 14.

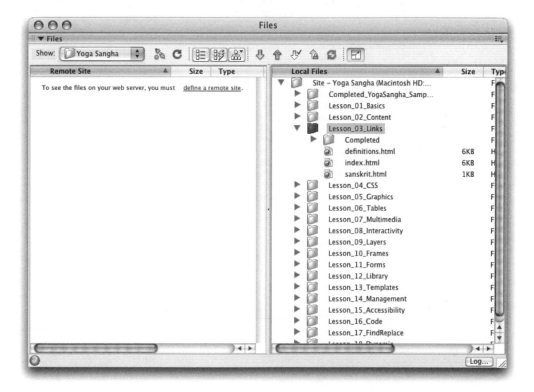

Tip *You can adjust the amount of space within which the files are displayed by moving the bar that separates the two sides of the expanded Files panel.*

3. Right-click (Windows) or Control-click (Macintosh) the Lesson_03_Links folder.

Tip *You might want to collapse other lesson folders if any are open to give yourself more room in the Files panel and make it quicker to scroll through the contents of the site.*

A context menu opens, displaying a variety of options. The options available through this menu vary, depending upon what is selected. The context menu is a quick way to access many of Dreamweaver's functions and can help speed up your production.

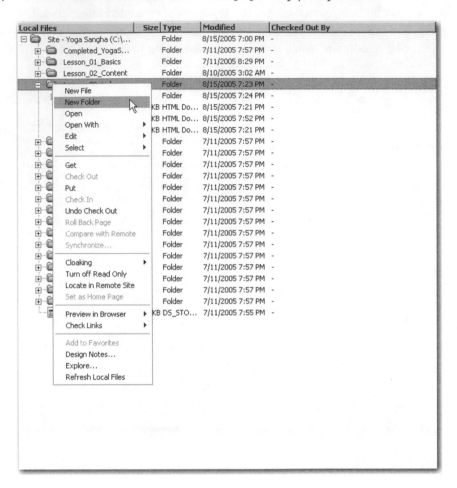

4. Choose New Folder from the context menu.

A new untitled folder is added within the Lesson_03_Links folder. Because you just created the new folder, the name is highlighted and displayed with a heavy line around the text field to indicate that you can name the folder.

5. Type *about* and then press Return (Macintosh) or Enter (Windows) to name the new folder.

The new folder displays the name you have just given it.

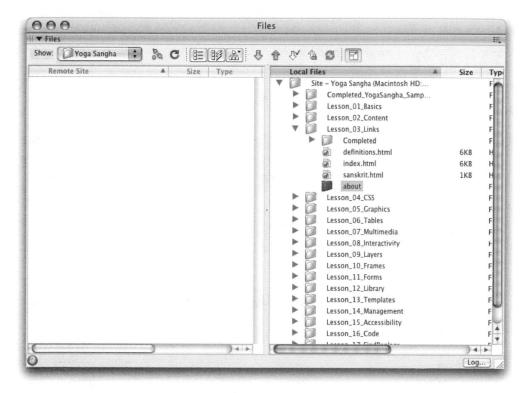

Tip *Clicking elsewhere in the Files panel causes the name to become deselected. If that happens and you still need to name the folder, you need to click the name of the folder, pause, and then click it again. Selecting the title allows you to edit it. Don't double-click; doing so will cause the folder to open.*

6. Right-click (Windows) or Control-click (Macintosh) the about folder you just created inside the Lesson_03_Links folder in the Files panel.

You are clicking the folder in which you will create a new file in the next step.

The context menu opens.

Note *If you mistakenly create a new file in the wrong folder, you can delete it using the context menu by choosing Edit > Delete. Windows users can also use the menus along the top of the Files panel as well as the context menu.*

7. **Choose New File from the context menu.**

A new unnamed document is created in the about folder. The name field is highlighted, indicating that you need to type a name for this document.

8. **Name the new file** *studio.html*.

Note *When you create new folders in the Files panel, those folders will not open unless there are files within them. You might need to open the folder before being able to name the file. Press Return (Macintosh) or Enter (Windows) to apply the filename change.*

Don't forget to keep the .html extension in the filename. All documents that you create in a site must have the appropriate extension for their document type so browsers can recognize them.

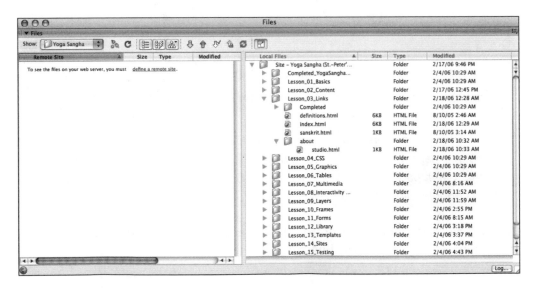

Tip *If your filenames are too long for the Local Files column, they might appear to be cut off, which is just a result of the limited space for display in the Files panel. You can see the full filename by pausing the pointer over the file and waiting for the name to pop up or by adjusting the positions of the columns. Click and drag the vertical lines separating the column titles to adjust them.*

9. **Repeating Steps 6 through 8, add the following files inside the about folder:** *contact.html, newsletter.html, news.html, location.html, anusara.html,* **and** *index.html.*

There should now be seven XHTML files in the **about** folder. Remember, XHTML files still use the .html extension.

As you learned earlier in this lesson, each folder can contain its own index.html file. Using an index.html file ensures that if a visitor enters only the folder name such as **www.yogasangha.com/about**, the index.html file will be displayed.

Note *The most common name for a directory's default document is index.html; however, depending on the Web server being used in your environment, it could be any number of others (default.html, index.cfm, index.jsp, or index.asp just to name a few).*

10. **Repeating Steps 3 through 8, create the following folders and the subsequent files those folders need to contain:**

Folder name	Files
schedule	faq.html, events.html, download-schedule.html, index.html
teachers	jayne.html, katchie.html, sierra.html, index.html
community	outreach.html, mission.html, green.html, forums.html, index.html
training	anusara-training.html, instructors.html, training-schedule.html, application.html, resources.html, login.html, index.html
explorations	philosophy.html, sequences.html, meditations.html, media.html, educational.html, index.html

You've now finished creating placeholders for each page in the Yoga Sangha project site, and you're ready to start linking them together. The folders and files in the Files panel should now look like the following example.

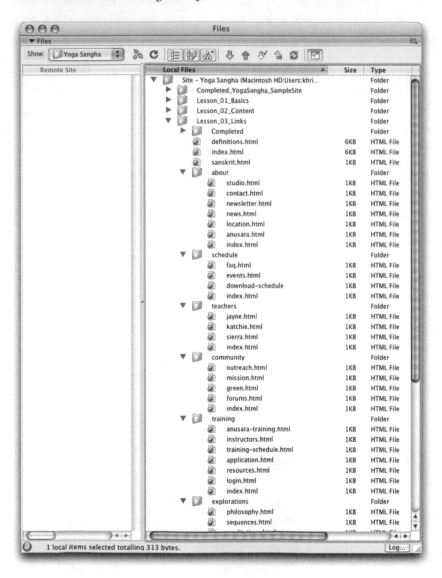

Creating a Site Map

A *site map* gives you a visual representation of a selected portion of your site. It does not display all the pages in your site; rather, it starts with a page that has been defined as the home page and shows you all pages that the home page links to. It continues down the hierarchy of links until it reaches a dead-end page—one with no links. If you have "orphaned" pages that cannot be reached through direct paths from the home page, they do not display in the site map.

1. In the Files panel, Right-click (Windows) or Control-click (Macintosh) the index.html file located in the Lesson_03_Links folder and choose Set as Home Page from the context menu.

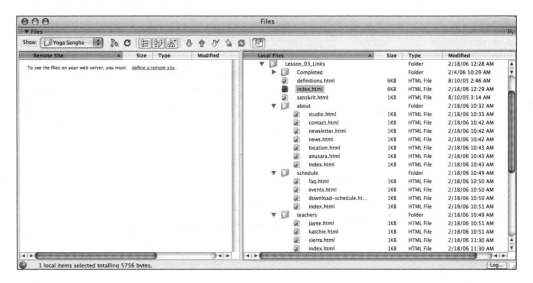

You're selecting the top-level index page in the Lesson_03_Links folder as the home page—the main page of the project site.

You will not see the result of this command until you enable the site map. Now that you have defined the home page, you can switch to the site map view. A home page must be created to give the site map a starting point.

2. Click the Site Map button on the toolbar and choose Map Only from the menu that appears.

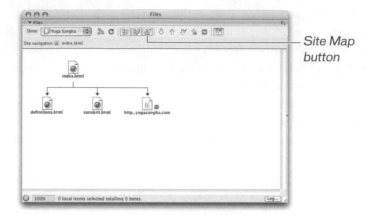

Site Map button

Note *The Site Map button also works as a menu—if you click and hold, a menu will appear through which you can select the Map Only view or the Map and Files view. If you resize the Files panel while in Map Only view, you might see the files portion of the window appear.*

At this point, you should see a map with the index.html, definitions.html, and sanskrit.html documents, and an external link icon representing the yogasangha.com link.

The site map is a graphical representation of your site; the home page, index.html, is displayed at the top level of the site map. A link from one page to another is indicated by a line that is drawn from the file containing the link to every page that it links to. Arrowheads at the ends of this line point to each linked page.

The new files you created in the previous exercise are not displayed in the map because the index.html page does not contain any links to those files—and neither do the files that index.html links to. In the next exercise, you'll start creating those links, and the files will start showing up on the map.

Tip *With the Files panel in its expanded view, you can adjust the Map view by choosing View ‹ Site Map Options ‹ Layout from the Files panel menu (Windows) or from the Files panel Options menu (Macintosh). The Site Definition dialog box opens. To display the Site Map Layout options, click the Advanced tab. By default, Dreamweaver displays the site map horizontally. You can change the number of columns and the column width to make the site map fit a single page for easier viewing—you might want to do this if the home page has many links and there isn't enough room on the site map to show all the pages.*

Working with Links in Site Map View

You can add or delete links through the Files panel site map.

Note *You can control which files display in the site map by choosing to show or hide individual linked files. Hiding files will cause them to be hidden only in the Map view—they will still be visible in the Local Files list. You can also make changes to the files by adding or deleting links. To hide or show a linked file, right-click (Windows) or Control-click (Macintosh) the link you want to modify and choose Show/Hide Link. You can choose View › Show Hidden Files from the Files panel menu (Windows) or from the Files panel Options menu (Macintosh) to reveal all hidden files. The filename will be italicized to indicate that it is a hidden link—you can then right-click (Windows) or Control-click (Macintosh) the hidden files and choose Show/Hide Link.*

1. Choose Map and Files from the Site Map menu. Select the icon for the index.html file in the Map view pane, click the Point To File icon, and drag the Point To File icon to the icon for the index.html file in the about folder. Release the mouse button when the index.html file becomes highlighted.

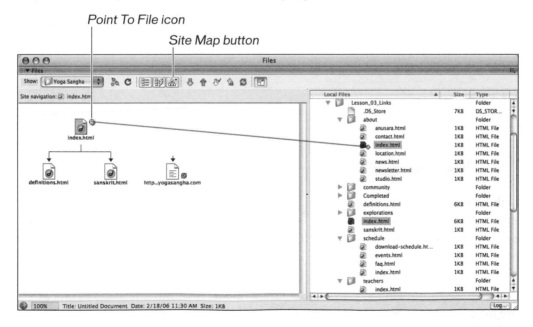

Point To File icon

Site Map button

As you drag, the pointer becomes an arrow and a Point To File icon. A blue line is drawn as you drag from the top-level index.html file to the index.html file that is contained in the about folder. When you release the pointer, the index.html file located in the about folder shows up in the Site Map view. The link has been inserted into the top-level index.html document. If you open the top-level index.html, document you will see the link.

Tip   *You can also add, remove, and change links by using the Site > Site Map View submenu, accessible through the Files panel menu (Windows) or through the Options menu on the right top side of the Files panel (Macintosh).*

2. Repeat Step 1 to create links from the top-level index.html file to the remaining index.html files in the following folders: schedule, teachers, community, training, and explorations.

Pausing over a file displayed in the map will show a tooltip displaying the name and location of the file. Selecting a file in the map view will highlight the same folder in the Files view, and vice versa.

In this step, you linked the main page of the site, index.html, to main pages of each section—the index.html files that are located in each of the folders.

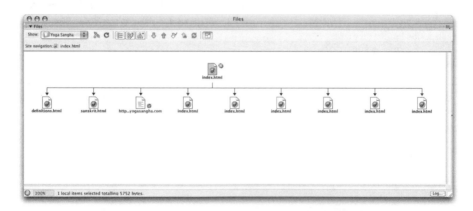

Links made this way will appear on the same line—one after the other—beneath any pre-existing content in the document and will use the name of the file for the text of the link on the page. In this case, the filename index.html is not very descriptive so you'll apply the links to the navigation area in the next step.

3. Open index.html in the Lesson_03_Links folder. Select the first index link at the bottom of the page. Then select the text in the Link field in the Property inspector. Select the word About in the list of sections just above the copyright information and paste the copied link into the Link field in the Property inspector.

In this lesson, you're creating the main navigational links at the bottom of the page in the index.html document. In a fully functional site, you would repeat this set of links in each document. Maintaining consistent navigational links throughout a site—in the same place on each page—makes it easier for visitors to browse a site. In later lessons, you'll create the main navigation system that will be used at the top of all pages in the project site.

4. **Repeat Step 3 for the corresponding links and sections for the Schedule, Teachers, Community, Training, and Explorations sections. Delete the line of index links at the bottom of the page, save and close the file.**

Be sure to look at the link location in the link text field on the Property inspector as you copy the links to apply the correct index link to the corresponding section—if you closed Dreamweaver at any time between creating the folders earlier in this lesson and this exercise, the Files panel might have refreshed into alphabetical order. Therefore, the index links might not be in the same order as the list of sections.

The navigational links are now clear about the location to which they will take the visitor.

If the Start page opens, you can close it.

5. **Repeat Step 1 to create links from the index.html file in the schedule folder to all the other documents in the schedule folder.**

In this step, you linked the main page of the schedule section, schedule/index.html, to the rest of the pages of the schedule section.

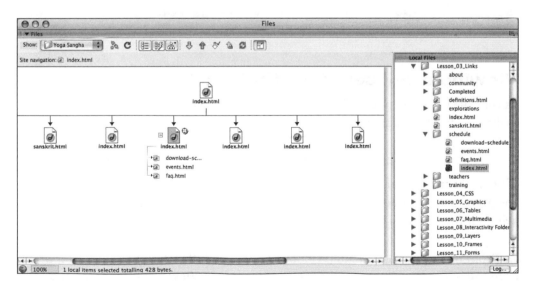

Pages that contain links are displayed on the site map with a plus (+) or minus (-) sign just to the left of the file. Clicking the plus sign displays a list of the links contained in the document, each with its own plus sign. Broken links (those that don't work) are displayed in red type. External links, such as e-mail links and URLs, are blue and are indicated with a small globe.

6. Repeat Step 5 for the files in the remaining folders: about, teachers, community, training, and explorations.

You now have a test site with many of the links that will allow you to browse through the site and test the navigation and site structure. To complete this test site, you'll need to add links from each index.html file in the six folders to the top-level index file, as well as adding links from each page in a folder to the index.html file in the same folder. After doing so, your site map would look like the following example.

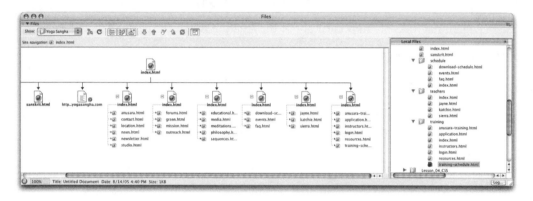

Viewing a Subset of the Entire Site

As your site becomes larger and more complex, the site map might become too big to see in the Files panel. You can refine the view to show just a selected page and its links.

1. In the Files panel site map, select the index.html page inside the about folder.

Viewing the index.html document from the about folder as a subset will let you focus on any pages that can be accessed with about/index.html as the starting point—this can be helpful if you have a large site.

2. From the Files panel menu (Windows) or through the Options menu on the right top side of the Files panel (Macintosh), choose View > Site Map Options > View as Root.

Tip *Alternatively, you can set the View as Root option by right-clicking or Control-clicking the file to access the context menu from which you can choose the View As Root option.*

The site map changes to show the about/index.html page as the root (the top level of the map view) along with its links (the second level). Below the Files toolbar is a gray bar displaying the hierarchy of the site, beginning with the file you set as the home page and ending with the file that you chose to view as the root of the site. In this exercise, you should see index.html > index.html. You might see a red arrow just after the index.html file on this bar if there is not enough room to display the full file path.

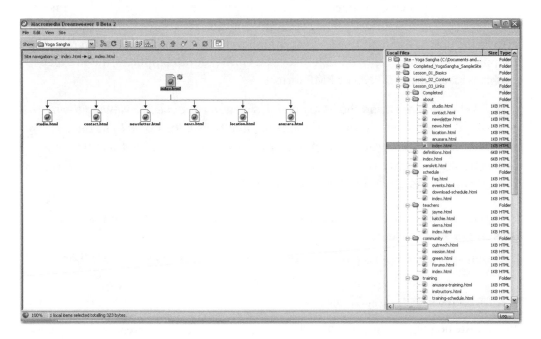

Note *This structural site navigation works the same way as breadcrumb navigation, which is used on many sites. Breadcrumbs show the visitor the hierarchical path from the main page of the site to the page they are on. They usually appear near the top of the page. Each part of the site listed in the breadcrumb path is normally linked to that section. For example, the breadcrumb navigation for the anusara.html page in the about folder would be Main › About › Anusara. In this example, the text Main would be linked to the top-level index.html page, and About would be the index.html file in the about folder, which is linked to the anusara.html page. Anusara is not linked—it is at the end of the breadcrumbs, which indicates to the visitor that the page being viewed is the Anusara page.*

3. Click the Dreamweaver file icon to the left of the first index.html listed on the Site Navigation bar.

The site root is returned to your home page—the top-level index.html page in the Yoga Sangha project site.

Saving the Site Map

1. From the Files panel menu (Windows) or through the panel Options menu on the right top side of the Files panel (Macintosh), choose File > Save Site Map.

The Save Site Map dialog box opens so you can save the site map as a graphic. At times, you might need to share the site map with people outside Dreamweaver. The option to save the site map as a graphic makes it easier to show that site map to others. On Macintosh computers, the graphic is saved in PICT format. On Windows computers, the site-map graphic is saved in either PNG or BMP format.

> Tip   *When you are using the Map and Files view, as opposed to viewing the map only, you cannot access all of the site map functions if the Local Files pane is active. If Save Site Map is grayed-out, go back to the Files panel and click the empty white space of the site-map pane to make sure it is active. Then go back and choose the Save Site Map command again.*

2. In the File name text box, type *project_yoga* and save the file into the Lesson_03_Links folder.

The site map is saved as a graphic that can be printed or viewed in an image editor.

Targeting Links

Whenever a user clicks a link, the linked page usually replaces the current browser page. This is the standard link function, which has been used for all links in this lesson up until this point. The instruction to a browser regarding where the link will appear is known as the *target*. There are a number of different targets that you can use with your links. At times, you might want to display the new browser page in a different window. If you link to a site outside your site, for example, you might be leading users out of your site if the new site replaces yours in the browser window. If users haven't bookmarked your URL, they might not remember how to return to your site. When an outside link opens a new browser window, the original page remains in the first window.

1. Open the index.html document in the Lesson_03_Links folder and select the link to the Yoga Sangha Website. From the Property inspector's Target menu, choose _blank.

You created the link to the Yoga Sangha Website near the bottom of the page in the second exercise of this lesson.

Notice the six index links at the bottom of the document—these are the links you created earlier in this lesson to the index.html files inside the six folders.

Dreamweaver provides you with a number of target options to change where the linked page is to be displayed. Targets other than _blank are used with frames. You will learn about frames in Lesson 10. The possible targets are as follows:

- **_blank:** Loads the linked document into a new unnamed browser window.
- **_parent:** Loads the linked document into the parent frameset or window of the frame that contains the link.
- **_self:** Loads the linked document into the same frame or window as the link. This target is the same as the default, so you usually don't have to specify it.
- **_top:** Loads the linked document into the full browser window, thereby removing all frames.

2. Save the file and preview it in the browser.

When you click the yogasangha.com link, the linked page opens in a new browser window. You can close this file.

> **Tip** *Be careful when using link targets to open new browser windows. Multiple windows might annoy or confuse your visitors. Each new window can increase the RAM requirements on the user's computer—with the amount of memory that most computers have these days, this is not so much of an issue, although it might be if a significant portion of your audience uses older machines.*

Inserting and Linking to Named Anchors

When a document is long or has many sections, you might need to create a series of links that will jump the user to specific places within the document. This technique eliminates the need for the viewer to scroll through long passages of text. A *named anchor* marks the place in the page to which a link jumps. In this exercise, you insert and link to a named anchor. You will also learn another method of selecting link files—using the Point To File icon.

1. Open definitions.html from the Lesson_03_Links folder. Choose Modify > Page Properties and select the Links category of the Page Properties dialog box. Set the same default link colors that you used for the index.html document in this lesson's first exercise. Click OK.

Recall that the link color's hexadecimal value was #FF3300, the rollover link color was #FF9900, the visited-link value was #993300, and the active link color was #FFCC00.

Tip *Keep your link colors the same throughout your site. Randomly changing link colors can be confusing for visitors.*

This file contains a large amount of text that requires the visitor to scroll to see the entire document.

2. Position the insertion point in front of the term Vinyasa Yoga at the bottom of the document. Click the Named Anchor button in the Common category of the Insert bar.

Named Anchor

The Named Anchor dialog box opens.

Tip *You can also insert a named anchor by choosing Insert > Named Anchor, or by using the keyboard commands Option+Command+A (Macintosh) or Ctrl+Alt+A (Windows).*

3. Type *vinyasa* in the Anchor name text field; then click OK.

Don't use spaces, punctuation, or special characters (such as copyright symbols, number signs, and so on) in the name. There should never be more than one named anchor with the same name in the same document; otherwise, the browser cannot jump the user to the correct named anchor.

A yellow icon appears on the page to represent the named anchor. The icon might be selected when it first appears on the page—selected anchor icons are blue. This icon is an invisible element that doesn't appear in the browser.

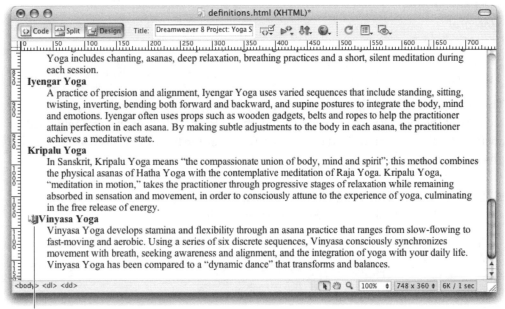

Named Anchor Icon

Tip *If you can't see the Named Anchor icon, make sure that the Invisible Elements option is turned on by choosing View > Visual Aids > Invisible Elements. When you insert a named anchor, a dialog box might open to warn you that you won't see the anchor unless the Invisible Elements option is turned on. Named anchors must also be checked in the Invisible Elements category of the Preferences. You can determine which options have been turned on by choosing Edit > Preferences and selecting the Invisible Elements category. The Named Anchors box should be checked. The lessons in this book assume that you are using the default configuration.*

4. Place the cursor at the end of the paragraph describing yoga at the top of the page. Press Return and type *There are many styles of yoga, including:*. Press Return (Macintosh) or Enter (Windows) and type the following terms, with a line break between each:

Hatha
Anusara
Ashtanga
Bikram
Dynamic Hatha
Integral
Iyengar
Kripalu
Vinyasa

This text will act as a navigational element by jumping the user to the corresponding sections of the page. Each term will be a link that references the corresponding named anchor, like the one you created for Vinyasa Yoga near the bottom of this page in the preceding steps.

5. Select the text *Vinyasa* from the new list of yoga styles you just created. Type *#vinyasa* into the Link text field on the Property inspector.

The number sign (#) is required to tell the browser that this link is internal—it takes the user to a location on the same page.

Make sure that the name you type after the number sign is exactly the same as the anchor name. You should follow the naming guidelines from Lesson 1 when you name your anchors. Named anchors are case-sensitive, even though many browsers accommodate a case change. For example, if you name your anchor **vinyasa** and then type **#Vinyasa** in the Link text field, your link might not work consistently in all browsers.

The text Vinyasa, located in the list of yoga styles, is now linked to the Vinyasa term and definition near the bottom of the page. Now you will repeat the process for Kripalu.

6. Add another named anchor before the Kripalu term near the bottom of the document and name it *kripalu*.

You have created a second anchor.

Tip | *If the anchor is inserted in the wrong place, you can drag it to a new position.*

7. Select the word Kripalu in the list of yoga styles at the top of the document. Drag the Point to File icon (located next to the Link text field in the Property inspector) to the kripalu-named anchor you just made. Release the mouse button when the pointer is directly over the named anchor.

When you first click the Point to File tool, the Link text field initially contains instructional text that will be replaced with the link that you choose. After you roll over the named anchor, #kripalu will appear in the Link text field. Using the Point to File icon to create links might help prevent typing errors.

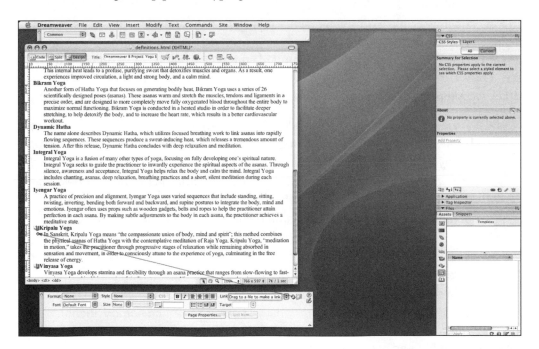

Note | *You can also use the Point to File icon to link to other files in your site if the Files panel is open. With the text or graphic selected that you want to link, click the Point to File icon and drag it over the Files panel. The Files panel comes to the front if it is behind the Document window or other panels, and you can continue to drag the mouse until you have the pointer directly over the file you want to link to.*

8. Insert named anchors and links to them for the remaining navigational terms you created at the beginning of the document. For the anchor names, type *hatha*, *anusara*, *ashtanga*, *bikram*, *dynamic*, *integral*, and *iyengar* for their respective yoga types.

You can edit the names of any anchors you create by clicking the named anchor. The Property inspector changes to show that a named anchor is selected. You can change the name in the Property inspector's Name text field.

9. Insert a named anchor at the very top of the page in front of the text Yoga and name it *top*. Create a new line at the bottom of the page, type *Back to Top* and link it to #top using the Link text field on the Property inspector.

> **Tip** | *Remember to use two paragraph returns to escape the definition list and create the new line.*

In long documents, it is a common practice to include links at the end of every section to a named anchor at the top of the page or to a navigational table of contents. This common anchor is usually called #top. When you provide this type of a link, users don't need to scroll back up to the top of the page if they want to continue using those links to jump to other sections. Any number of links on the page can reference the same named anchor.

> **Note** | *Viewing problems, such as a link to a named anchor jumping to the wrong area or simply not working, might occur if that named anchor is located inside of a link. To avoid this problem, any attempts to move or insert a named anchor inside of a link causes Dreamweaver to automatically end the link just before the named anchor and create a second link to the same destination immediately after the named anchor (which ends at the same point where the original link ended). In these cases, the named anchor is actually sandwiched between two separate links that have an identical value. As a result, placing the cursor at the beginning of the linked text and making a change to the link value changes only the first instance of the link; you need to remember to duplicate any changes that you make to the second instance of the link that occurs after the named anchor.*

10. Save the file and preview it in the browser.

The navigational terms at the top of the page now link to their corresponding sections. You can close the definitions.html file.

Tip *Named anchors might not work as expected if they are placed inside tables or layers. For best results, keep named anchors outside of tables and layers. You'll learn to create tables in Lesson 6 and layers in Lesson 9.*

In the following step, you will continue learn how to link to a particular section of another document using a named anchor.

11. Open the top-level index.html file in the Lesson_03_links folder. In the paragraph beginning with *Anusara Yoga, a form of hatha yoga...* select the words *hatha yoga*. Type *definitions.html#hatha* in the Property inspector's Link text field.

Be sure to replace the original number sign (#) in the Link text field with the link you have typed in.

In the previous steps, you created a named anchor at the hatha section of the definitions.html file. Now you are making a link in index.html point directly to the hatha section in definitions.html—instead of linking to the top of the page as it would if you had used definitions.html as the link. You can preview index.html in the browser and test this new link.

The use of anchors to link to specific portions of other pages helps your site to be more functional, directing your viewers to what they are looking for immediately and reducing the amount of time they have to spend scrolling through long documents. The more functional and easy to use your site is, the more likely it is that you will have new and repeat visitors.

Note *You can also create links that include named anchors to other pages using the Point to File tool, which you used in the previous steps to create links within the same document. For example, with both index.html and definitions.html open in separate windows, you can select a link in index.html, click the Point to File icon to the right of the Link text field, and point to the desired named anchor in definitions.html.*

Leave the index.html document open for the next exercise.

Inserting E-mail Links

Providing a linked e-mail address makes it easy for your visitors to contact you from a Web page. You should always include some method of contact that allows visitors to correspond or interact with someone in your organization.

There are two ways to insert an e-mail link in Dreamweaver. You can either insert both the text and the e-mail address for the link at the same time, or you can add a link to text that already exists on the page. You'll learn to do both in this exercise.

1. In index.html click at the end of the date at the bottom of the document, press the spacebar, and type *by* followed by another space.

You will insert an e-mail link here, in the next step.

2. Click the Email Link button in the Common category of the Insert bar or choose Insert > Email Link.

Email Link

The Email Link dialog box appears, displaying options for text and e-mail.

Note *The Insert bar should be open by default. If it is not visible, choose Window > Insert to open the Insert bar or Window > Arrange Panels to reset the panels, inspectors, and bars to their default positions.*

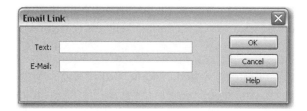

3. In the Text text field, enter your name. In the Email text field, enter your e-mail address; then click OK.

The text appears on the page as a link. The Property inspector shows "mailto:" followed by the e-mail address in the Link text field when you place the insertion point within the link.

If you select text that is already on the page and then open the Insert Email Link dialog box, the selected text appears in the Text text field.

Contact information commonly appears at the bottom of a page, often near copyright information.

You can also create e-mail links by typing **mailto:** immediately followed by your e-mail address in the Link text field on the Property inspector—when doing so, make sure that you type the colon and do not leave a space between the colon and your e-mail address.

You can save and close the index.html file.

Working with Links On Your Own

As you learned through this lesson, creating a test site with navigational links allows you to click through the site and see what about the way the visitor moves through the site is or isn't working. Testing the navigation at this stage offers you the opportunity to make adjustments before you do a great deal of development. In this exercise you'll create a test site for your own site.

1. Using the file structure that you developed for your site in Lesson 1 as a guide, create the section folders and page placeholders for your site.

Setting up the section folders and placeholder files is the first step in creating the test site. Using the expanded Files panel to add these new folders and files to your site is a quick method of creating a number of new files.

2. Develop a system of links on the placeholder pages of your site using the skills and techniques you learned earlier in this lesson.

Using the Site Map view of the Files panel allows you to create links between the pages in your site without having to open each individual file.

Don't apply any link colors to your new pages—you'll learn to control the link colors used in your documents through one file for the entire site in the next lesson.

3. Use the outline of content that you developed in Lesson 1 to insert text-based content into your pages.

You can use outlines or lists of the content that will appear on each page or you can insert the content itself into the pages. Although you'll continue to add and modify the content in your site throughout the different developmental phases, inserting content now can help you see what you've got, what's missing, and how the content is flowing and working throughout the site.

You can target links, insert named anchors and links to them, and create e-mail links if needed. You'll continue to work with links throughout the development of your site—you don't need to complete it all now.

4. Preview your home page in a browser and test the navigation and site structure you developed by clicking through your test site.

Try to imagine how the visitor might use your site—what are potential paths that they might take through the site? Make any changes as needed.

What You Have Learned

In this lesson, you have:

- Specified the default colors of links, visited links, and active links (pages 73–77)
- Created text links to pages within the project site as well a link to an outside site (pages 77–81)
- Created section folders and placeholder files (pages 82–88)
- Learned to use the Files panel and site map to create and view links (pages 89–96)
- Targeted a link to open in a new window (pages 96–97)
- Inserted named anchors for each section of a document and linked the corresponding titles of those sections to each named anchor (pages 98–103)
- Learned to create e-mail links automatically using the Insert bar and manually using the Property inspector's Link text field (pages 104–106)

4 Developing Style Sheets

Cascading Style Sheets (CSS) enable you to define how a variety of elements, such as text and images, display on your Web pages. The term *cascading* refers to the ordered sequence and precedence of styles. A *style* is a group of formatting attributes, identified by a single name, which tells the browser how to display an element. CSS styles in HTML documents give you a great deal of control over formatting, appearance, and layout. The advantage of using styles is that when you make a change to an attribute of the

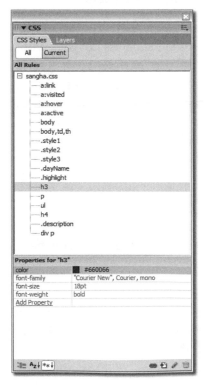

In this lesson, you will use CSS to apply a variety of format options to text using the three types of styles provided in Dreamweaver: class styles, tag styles, and advanced custom styles.

style, all the elements controlled by that style are automatically updated—in a single document or site-wide, depending on how you created the style. Adjustments can be made on a wide variety of settings, ranging from standard attributes—such as font, size, and color of text—to advanced attributes available only through CSS—such as the space between lines of text (*leading*, also known as line height).

Using style sheets, you can, for example, create a paragraph with a half-inch margin, 20 points between the lines, and the text displayed in a 12-point font. This would not be possible without the use of CSS, which is supported by 4.0 or later browsers. Earlier browsers ignored CSS, although Internet Explorer 3.0 recognized some style attributes. The best results are achieved with 5.0 and higher browsers, which support a wider range of features.

You can use an internal style—one that is stored inside the document—when you need to format a single page. You can use an external style sheet—one that is stored outside of the Web page and linked by the current page—when you need to control the appearance of several documents at once to keep the same style of text formatting on multiple pages. In such cases, it is ideal to keep the treatments of text and page layout consistent throughout your site because drastic changes in appearance might give viewers the impression that they have landed on another site.

Another advantage to using style sheets is the ability to keep the content of your Web pages separate from the formatting. Ultimately, this means that you have more precise control over the appearance of your content. Inserting content into your Website will become a quicker and less-complicated process as a result. Isolating the content in this manner makes the process of updating and maintaining the site far simpler. Controlling the formatting of Web pages through style sheets allows you to create pages that are more compatible across different platforms and browsers.

In this lesson, you'll learn to create basic style sheets with styles that affect the appearance of text. In the process, you'll learn about the properties of CSS and gain an understanding of how it works. You'll then apply this understanding by creating a basic CSS-based layout. Throughout the rest of the lessons in this book, you'll continue to build on these skills by learning additional CSS techniques, applying styles to elements other than text, such as graphics in Lesson 5.

To see examples of the finished pages for this lesson, open index.html and sangha.css from the Lesson_04_CSS/Completed folder and index.html from the Lesson_04_CSS/Completed/about folder.

What You Will Learn

In this lesson, you will:

- Set the background color of a page
- Apply text attributes including font, color, and size
- Create an external style sheet
- Add styles to an existing style sheet
- Edit a style
- Create a custom style
- Link to an external style sheet
- Create an internal style
- Convert internal styles to external styles
- Create a basic page layout

Approximate Time

This lesson should take about three hours to complete.

Lesson Files

Starting Files:

Lesson_04_CSS/index.html
Lesson_04_CSS/about/index.html
Lesson_04_CSS/Text/about.txt

Completed Project:

Lesson_04_CSS/Completed/index.html
Lesson_04_CSS/Completed/about/index.html
Lesson_04_CSS/Completed/sangha.css

Specifying a Background Color

In Dreamweaver, you can easily change the background color of a page using a palette like the one you used in Lesson 3 when you defined link colors. In this exercise, you'll access the color palette from the Page Properties dialog box to change the background color for the index.html document.

1. Open index.html from the Lesson_04_CSS folder. Choose Modify > Page Properties and select Appearance from the Category list.

Tip *You can use the keyboard commands Cmd+J (Macintosh) or Ctrl+J (Windows) to open the Page Properties dialog box.*

In the Appearance screen of the Page Properties dialog box, you'll see that no defaults have been defined for this page, even though white is the default background color for the Document window in Dreamweaver. If you do not define a background color, the page will be displayed using the browser default (usually white) when a visitor views the page. Because the browser default can vary from browser to browser, it is recommended that you always define the background color of the page.

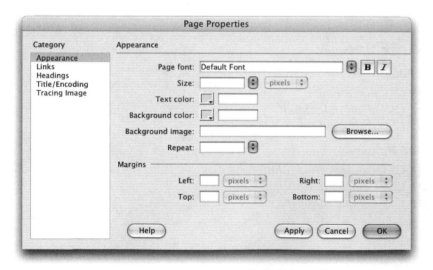

2. Click the color box for the Background Color option. Click the pale yellow swatch that displays the hexadecimal code #FFFFCC.

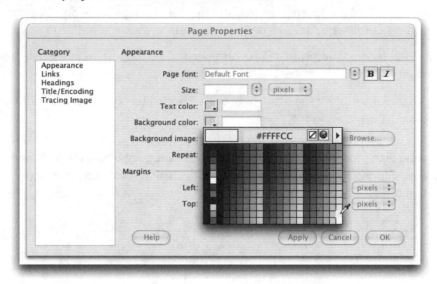

The pale yellow color #FFFFCC is now selected as the background color for your page. You can also type the hexadecimal code directly into the text field next to the color box to change the color.

3. Click Apply to view the new background color without closing the Page Properties dialog box.

The background color of your page is now the light yellow color that you selected in the Page Properties dialog box.

Leave the Page Properties dialog box open for the next exercise.

Changing the Font

To make your page more interesting and easier to read, you can change the fonts that are used to display text. Although a great deal of information is available concerning how type is used for print media, not all of that knowledge translates to the Web.

Generally, sans-serif fonts are easier to read than serif fonts on computer screens. Typically, serif fonts are used in print media because the serifs (the small strokes or flares on the ends of the lines) make characters easier to recognize. On a computer screen, however, those same serifs can actually make it more difficult to discern letter forms, particularly when large amounts of text are involved or when the text in question uses a relatively small font size. It is also important to consider that the way type flows on a page can vary from browser to browser, and from computer to computer.

To define font options, Dreamweaver uses integrated CSS styles instead of the older method of using font tag attributes.

You can change the font for the entire page or for selected text on the page, as you will see in the following exercise.

1. From the Page font menu in the Appearance category of the Page Properties dialog box, choose Arial, Helvetica, sans-serif. Click OK to close the Page Properties dialog box.

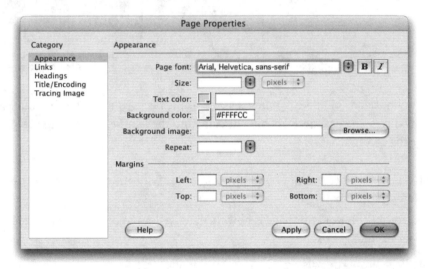

All the text on the page is now formatted in one of the fonts in the list you selected: Arial, Helvetica, sans-serif. Any additional text that you might add to the page in the future will be formatted in the same font.

Note *The Page Properties dialog box generates an internal CSS style to redefine a set of tags (body, td, th) with the font attribute. External CSS styles are covered later in this lesson.*

The font combinations that are listed in the Page font menu of the Appearance category on the Page Properties dialog box instruct the browser to display the text using a font in the selected group, depending on which fonts are installed on the visitors' computers. If the first option in the font group is not available, the browser attempts to use the second font option. If the second font is not available, it uses the third one. If none of the fonts in the combination is available on the user's computer, the text is displayed in the browser's default font.

2. Select the text *Anusara Yoga in the Heart of San Francisco's Mission District* near the top of the page. From the Property inspector's Font menu, choose Courier New, Courier, monospace.

The font set you chose for the tag line overrides the default font set that was specified for the page. The font combinations available to choose from in the Font menu on the Property inspector are the same as the font combinations that were listed in the Page Font menu of the Appearance category on the Page Properties dialog box.

> **Tip** *A number of formatting options can be applied directly in the Document window to selected text if you right-click (Windows) or Ctrl-click (Macintosh) to access the context menu.*

For visitors to your site to see the text displayed in the fonts that you chose, those fonts must be installed on their computers. Don't assume that all fonts are loaded on everyone's computer. Any fonts not included with the basic operating system are potentially not on your visitors' machines. In addition, the availability of fonts is not the same on the Macintosh as it is on Windows. The fonts specified in Dreamweaver's default font sets are generally available on most computers, both Macintosh and Windows.

> **Note** *If you want to use a special font that might not be installed on a visitor's computer, it is recommended that you create a graphic to use in place of the text. This technique is often used for headers, titles, and so on. Graphics are not recommended for large amounts of text because they restrict accessibility and can make updating content more difficult.*

The font combinations (such as Arial, Helvetica, sans-serif) are useful, but they might not always include the specific fonts you want to use. You can change a font combination by choosing Edit Font List from the Property inspector's Font menu or by choosing Text > Font > Edit Font List to display the Edit Font List dialog box.

Using the Font List dialog box, you can make a number of changes to font sets:

- **To add fonts to an existing combination:** Select the font combination you want to modify in the Font list and select the font you want to add in the Available fonts list; then click the left directional button located between the Chosen fonts list and the Available fonts list to add the font to the Chosen fonts list.

- **To remove fonts from an existing combination:** Select the font combination you want to modify and select the font you want to remove from the Chosen fonts list; then click the right directional button located between the Chosen Fonts list and the Available Fonts list to remove the font from the Chosen fonts list.

- **To add a font combination:** Select the Add fonts in list below choice in the Font list. For additional font combinations, click the plus sign (+) button in the upper-left corner of the dialog box and then select the new Add fonts in list below choice from the Font list.

- **To remove a font combination:** Select the font combination you want to remove from the Font list and click the minus sign (–) button in the upper-left corner of the dialog box.

- **To add a font that is not installed on your system:** Type the font name in the text field below the Available fonts list and click the directional arrow to add it to the combination. Adding a font that is not installed on your system is useful; you can specify a Windows-only font when you are authoring on a Macintosh, for example. Be sure to use the exact font name.

- **To change the order of the font combinations:** Select a font combination and click the directional arrow buttons in the upper-right corner of the dialog box.

The Available fonts list in the Edit Font List dialog box contains the fonts that are installed on your computer.

3. Save the file and preview it in the browser.

The text now displays with the fonts you selected in your browser, depending on which fonts are installed on your computer.

Tip *You can remove font settings on a page and return selected type to its default setting by first selecting the text that uses the font you want to remove. In the Property inspector, choose Default Font from the Font menu or choose Text › Font › Default Font.*

Changing the Font Size

Dreamweaver has a variety of preset font sizes, including numeric values at set intervals ranging from 9 to 36, relative values ranging from xx-small to xx-large, and options for smaller and larger. All these options use CSS to define text size. Using Dreamweaver, you can achieve a great deal of control over the text on your pages through the use of these integrated CSS features. You'll learn about more advanced CSS functionality later in this lesson.

Best Coding Practice: Deprecation of the Font Tag

In HTML 4.01 the font tag (a tag that defines the properties of text) has been *deprecated*—removed from the standard—although it is still supported by browsers at this time. The font tag wraps around text in the following manner, with opening and closing tags:

```
<font face="Arial, Helvetica, sans-serif">Yoga Sangha</font>
```

Attributes of the font tag offer a bare minimum of control over text appearance, whereas the use of CSS allows Web developers to control text with much greater precision. Dreamweaver recognizes and supports the font tag by providing tools to use them when necessary–such as when dealing with legacy pages.

Whenever possible, use CSS—and avoid using the font tag—to create efficient pages that are up to current standards.

Note *There is a dramatic difference between font sizes on a Macintosh and on Windows. Macintosh computers display text approximately 25 percent smaller than the same text on Windows computers—text on a Macintosh computer is three-quarters the size of text on Windows. Users can also change the font size, which might affect your page design. Test and design your pages accordingly, taking these potential variations into account for a flexible Website that will function correctly for the widest possible range of visitors.*

Select the paragraph beginning with At Yoga Sangha, we're dedicated… near the top of the page. From the Property inspector's Size menu, choose 12. Leave the measurement unit at the default: pixels.

Tip *You can also set a default text size for the document in the Appearance section of the Page Properties dialog box.*

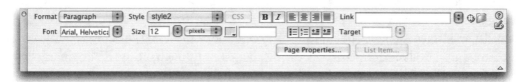

The text size of the paragraph decreases slightly and appears somewhat smaller than the rest of the text on the page that has not yet been formatted with a size. You can type a value into the Size menu or select one of the preset choices.

Every time you choose an attribute—or a combination of attributes—such as a size that's used for the first time on your page, Dreamweaver creates a new style that is listed in the Style menu on the Property inspector. All subsequent text that is defined at the same size will use the same style. New styles are created for each unique combination of font face, size, and color formatting. These styles have generic names that are generated automatically in a numeric order: style1, style2, and so on. You can rename an active style—the one that displays in the Style menu on the Property inspector—by clicking the Style menu and choosing Rename. You can make a style active by placing the cursor within text that uses that style.

If no size is specified for the selected text, None is displayed in the Size menu. Browsers display text that has no size definition at the default size that is equal to the value 14 in the Size menu (although it might vary from browser to browser and/or on user preferences that visitors set within their browsers).

The numeric font size options that are available in the Size menu might be familiar to you because they are similar to the standard sizes that can be found in word-processing programs.

Note *If you want to remove font size settings and switch back to the default setting, first select the text that you want to change in the Property inspector and then choose None from the Style menu or choose Text > CSS Styles > None.*

Font Size Comparison:
The Font Tag versus CSS

As a Web developer, you might have to work with pages that use the outdated `<font>` tag—for this reason you should be familiar with the sizes and options. You might need to convert to CSS by removing all instances of the `<font>` tag and creating CSS styles. You can easily strip the `<font>` tag from a site using the Find and Replace feature, which you'll learn about in Lesson 17. The following table compares the values that are now available in the Property inspector Size menu to the older `<font>` tag size options.

Font Tag Sizes	Numeric Values*	Relative Values in the Size menu (CSS-based)	Absolute Values in the Size menu (CSS-based)
		9	
-2	1	10	xx-small
-1	2	12	x-small / smaller
None (default)	3	14	small
+1	4	18	medium / larger
+2	5	24	large
+3	6		x-large
		36**	
+4	7		xx-large

Using the default setting, pixels, in the measurement menu
**This numeric value is slightly larger than x-large (6), and slightly smaller than xx-large (7).*

The HTML `<font>` tag defines text in sizes that are absolute (1 to 7) or relative (+1 to +7 and -1 to -7). Selecting an absolute number (1 is smallest, 7 is largest) sets the size. The default base size for text in a browser is 3. Picking a positive or negative number makes the font size relative to the base size of the font. The base The positive number +1, for example, makes the font size one size larger than the base size. If you choose +3 for the font size, you are effectively changing the size to 6 (3 + 3). The largest size for the font is 7, and the smallest is 1. Any HTML font size larger than 7 displays as 7; for example, if you set the font size to +6, 3 + 6 is larger than 7, but the font still displays only at the 7 size. These are limitations of the HTML `<font>` tag and do not affect CSS, which is a far more flexible and versatile method for defining text specifications.

Specifying Font Color

When you change the background color of a page, as you did in the first exercise of this lesson, you might also need to change the color of the text to avoid viewing problems. Black text doesn't display on a black background, for example. When choosing a color scheme for your document, try to select combinations of colors that work well together and have enough contrast between them. Colors that are too similar to each other can be very hard to view, as can complementary colors, especially on a computer screen. In the following steps, you'll change the default font color in the index.html document.

1. Choose Modify › Page Properties and verify that Appearance is selected in the Category list.

The Appearance section of the Page Properties dialog box provides a number of options that will allow you to adjust a wide variety of document settings.

2. Click the color box for the Text color option.

A color palette pops up, similar to the one that you used to pick the background color for the document earlier in this lesson.

3. Select the dark reddish-black color with the hexadecimal code #330000 and then click OK.

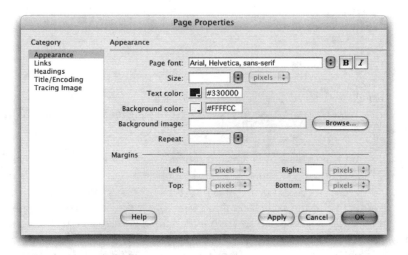

You can either type the hexadecimal color code into the text field or you can click to select the color from the swatches. After you click OK, the Page Properties dialog box closes, and you return to the document.

Note *You can access an additional Colors dialog box by choosing Text > Color. Hexadecimal color codes can also be typed directly into the color text field, alongside the Text Color picker on the Property inspector.*

4. Select the text *Welcome to Yoga Sangha*. Click the Text Color box in the Property inspector and choose a medium orange color (#FFCC33).

Similar to font face and size options, font color is defined in Dreamweaver through CSS styles. By applying a color, you have created a new style. You can see the name of the style listed in the Style menu on the Property inspector. The number of your style might differ from those shown in the examples if you have created any additional styles by experimenting with font face, size, or color attributes. If you apply font, size, or color options to text that already has a style, the new attributes will added to the older style if the selected text is the only instance of that style. If there are other instances of the style or if you are applying new attributes to only a portion of the previously styled text, Dreamweaver will create a new style.

As you style text, it is a good idea to keep your styles organized—try not to randomly apply text attributes because Dreamweaver will create new styles for each new combination. Instead, think about creating a system of organized styles that inherit attributes as needed. You'll learn more about inheritance later in this lesson.

Note *You can keep track of the hexadecimal colors used in your sites through the Assets panel, which is located in the Files panel group. You can also open the Assets panel by choosing Window › Assets. To access the color assets, click the Colors icon in the left column of the Assets panel. Radio buttons across the top of the Assets panel give you two options for viewing colors: Site and Favorites. Clicking the Site list radio button shows the colors that have already been used within the Yoga Sangha project site or your current active site. You won't see colors in the list if you haven't used any colors in your site. If you have defined colors, but do not see them listed, click the Refresh Site List button in the lower-right corner of the panel. You will see colors in this list that you have not yet used because there are colors used throughout documents in other lesson folders in the Lights of the Coast project site. To ensure that the colors you use are consistent across your site, you can save commonly used colors in the Assets panel as Favorites. To save a favorite color, select the desired color from the Site list and click the Add to Favorites button in the lower-right corner of the Assets panel. Dreamweaver displays a dialog box that informs you that the color has been added to your favorites. You need to click the Favorites radio button at the top of the Assets panel to see the favorites list. You'll work with the Assets panel to manage graphics in Lesson 5.*

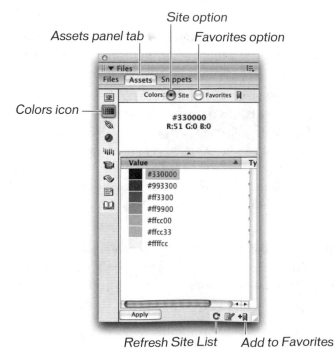

Site option

Assets panel tab

Favorites option

Colors icon

Refresh Site List   Add to Favorites

Understanding Styles

At this point, you've used a number of CSS styles in this lesson's previous exercises. At the beginning of this lesson you began to format text with font face, size, and color attributes using the Property inspector while Dreamweaver creates the corresponding CSS styles. You've seen how each time you create a new combination of attributes in a page, Dreamweaver creates a new style, which is then listed in the Style menu on the Property inspector. By now, you have also worked with a variety of Page Properties including background color and colors for the different states of links in Lesson 3 and default font settings in the beginning of this lesson; all these attributes are controlled by CSS styles in Dreamweaver.

In this exercise, you'll learn more about what a style sheet is and how it works.

1. In the index.html document, click the Split button on the upper-left portion of the document toolbar.

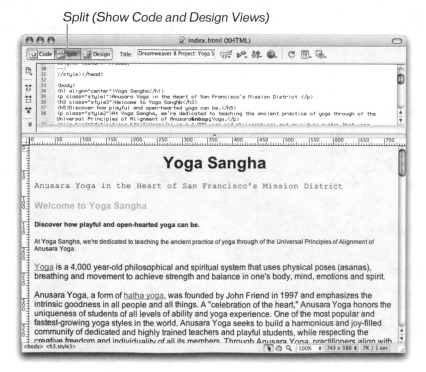

Split (Show Code and Design Views)

You now see a split view in the Document window that shows both the Design view that you've been working with thus far in the lessons, and the corresponding code. You'll work more with this view in Lesson 16. By default, the Code view is shown in the top portion of the Document window, and the Design view is shown in the lower portion.

Note *You can adjust the size of these views by placing the cursor over the bar that separates these two views. The pointer will turn into a double arrow, and you can click and drag the bar as needed.*

2. Scroll upward in the Code view until you see the following:

```
<style type="text/css">
<!—
a:link {
   color: #FF3300;
}
```

This code marks the beginning of a style sheet that contains all the information for the styles used in this page. It is known as an *internal style sheet* because it is embedded into the document. All styles that have been created in previous lessons using the Property inspector and the Page Properties dialog box have been internal styles. Dreamweaver 8 automatically creates those styles whenever you define text formatting or page properties.

CSS styles and style sheet attachments are placed between the <head> and </head> tags of the document.

In CSS, a *style sheet* is a group of styles. A *style* (often referred to as a *rule*) is a set of properties that defines and controls the appearance of an element. In the code for index.html, the style sheet is everything contained between <style type="text/css"> (which defines the style sheet) and </style> (which ends the style sheet). The code a:link { color: #FF3300; } represents a single style (or rule). Further down in the style sheet you'll see the following code, which was created when you set the background color of the page:

```
body {
   background-color: #FFFFCC;
}
```

Rules are composed of selectors and declarations. A *selector* is the element that is being defined. A *declaration* is the combination of properties and their values. The *properties* are the attributes of the element that control the appearance, and the *value* is the quantity or format that is specified. The structure of a style is selector { property: value }, and property: value is the declaration.

For example, in the following style, the element being defined is the selector "body":

```
body { background-color: #FFFFCC }
```

The declaration { background-color: #FFFFCC } is the combination of properties and values. The attribute of the background element that is being specified is the property of "background-color." The value that defines the color is #FFCCCC.

Working With Internal Styles

Internal styles are those that are defined and used only in the current document. If you need to create style definitions for only one page in your site, you can use internal styles. If you want your site to have a cohesive look across multiple pages, you should use an external style sheet and link that style sheet to each document that you want to use that look.

Tip *Using external style sheets is recommended whenever possible. External styles are beneficial because they enable you to use styles in other documents. Additionally, because the formatting code for external styles is contained in a common external document, the pages that use that style sheet do not have to continually reload the formatting information; this causes less code to be used, so the pages download more quickly. It also makes styles easier to update because they are all in one place. You learn to create external styles later in this lesson.*

All the styles you created so far are internal styles. The style sheet that you looked at in the previous exercise is an internal style sheet—one that is contained entirely within the index.html document.

1. Open the CSS Styles panel located in the CSS panel group, and click the All button at the top of the panel.

Tip *If the CSS Styles panel isn't open, you can access it by choosing Window › CSS Styles.*

The CSS Styles panel displays a list of the styles that were created when you defined the page properties.

 **Tip** *You might need to expand the <style> group at the top of the CSS Styles panel to see the list of all internal styles.*

2. **Click New CSS Rule icon at the bottom of the CSS Styles panel.**

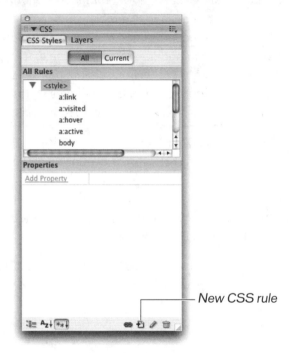

New CSS rule

The New CSS Rule dialog box opens.

Tip *You can also open this dialog box by choosing Text > CSS Styles > New.*

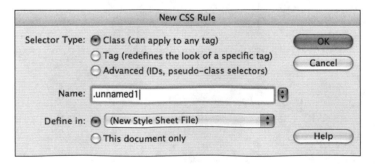

There are three different selector types (kinds of elements defined by styles) that you can use in Dreamweaver:

- **Class:** This type of selector allows you to create classes that are not tied to any particular elements. You can apply a single class to many different elements. Classes are indicated by their initial period.
- **Tag:** This type of selector allows you to specify an HTML tag as the element that will be redefined by the style. The default appearance of the tag becomes modified by the style.
- **Advanced:** This type of selector allows you to create styles that are used for specific tag combinations (contextual selectors). This selector type also enables you to create IDs, which are similar to classes with one major exception: They can only be used once per page as a way of defining or uniquely identifying a particular element. Because of their unique nature, IDs are often used for scripting purposes and are indicated by #.

3. Select *Class* from the Selector Type area of the New CSS Rule dialog box.

The text field becomes a Name text field for creating a custom style.

Dreamweaver assigns generic names automatically in a numeric order: .unnamed1, .unnamed2, and so on. These names are not very descriptive and they can be especially unhelpful when you are creating multiple classes. It's best to get in the habit of giving your styles short names that are descriptive of their purposes.

4. Type *.dayName* in the Name text field for the name of your class.

A period before the name is required. If you delete the period, Dreamweaver automatically includes it at the beginning of the name, even if it isn't shown.

Getting into the habit of assigning names based on the function of the style rather than a description of style's appearance attributes is best—functionally descriptive names are more accessible, especially for speech based browsers.

5. Select *This document only* in the Define in area and then click OK.

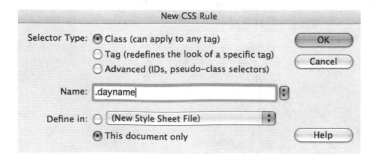

The document only option specifies that you are creating a new internal style. The CSS Rule definition for .dayName dialog box opens.

6. In the Type category of the CSS Rule Definition dialog box, set the size to 12 pixels, the Weight to bold, the Variant to small-caps and the color to black (#000000). Leave all other options undefined and click OK.

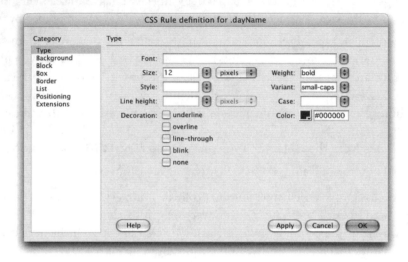

You see the class you just created displayed in the list of styles on the CSS Styles panel.

Because you just created the .dayName rule, it will now be automatically selected in the All Rules list on the top portion of the CSS Styles panel. In the lower half of the panel is a list of the properties for the selected rule—properties are listed in the left column, and their values are listed in the right column. By default, the properties are displayed in the Show Only Set Properties mode, which lists only the properties for which values have been defined. There are two additional viewing modes for the properties: Show List View and Show Category View. Show List View displays the entire list of attributes, whereas Show Category View shows the list of attributes organized into the same categories that were available in the CSS Rule Definition dialog box.

There are a number of ways to edit the rule selected in the CSS Styles panel:

- **Modify the values of existing properties.** You can modify the property values directly in the properties list by clicking the value to access corresponding menus.

- **Add a new property and value.** When viewing the properties list in Show Only Set Properties mode, you can click the Add property link at the bottom of the list to access a menu from which you can select a new property. When viewing the properties list in either Show Category View or Show List View, you can add a value to a listed property by clicking in the value field for the desired property.

- **Use the dialog box to edit the rule.** You can click the Edit Style button at the bottom of the panel to open the CSS Rule definition dialog box.

Classes give you specific control over the formatting of your document. You can apply them the same way you apply styles in a word processor: by selecting the text and then applying the style. You can apply this style to text blocks or to individual words within blocks of text.

In the next steps, you'll apply the dayName class to certain items in the bulleted list.

7. Select the word *Monday* in the Schedule list in the index.html document. Choose dayName from the Style menu on the Property inspector to apply the style. Continue to apply the dayName to the rest of the days in the list.

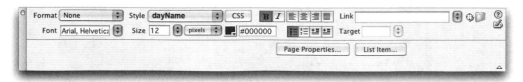

The selected text changes to reflect the dayName class.

You might notice after applying the style, that the selected word in the Code view is preceded by `<span class="dayName">`; span defines the selection of elements while class specifies which style is applied to the text enclosed by <span> (the opening tag) and </span> (the closing tag). The <span> tag is an inline element that defines items such as several words within a larger text block. It is similar to the <div> tag, which is a block-level element that defines entire blocks, similar to a paragraph.

Note *If you want to remove the style formatting from text, place the insertion point within the text and choose None from the Style menu on the Property inspector. The style and its formatting are removed from the text, although the style will remain in the style sheet.*

8. Click the New CSS Style button on the CSS Styles panel. Set the Selector Type to Class, type *.highlight* in the Name text field, and choose This Document Only in the Define In area. Click OK.

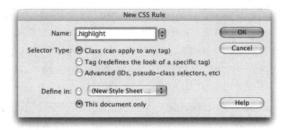

The CSS Rule Definition for .highlight dialog box appears.

9. In the CSS Rule Definition dialog box, choose Background from the Category list on the left.

The CSS Rule Definition dialog box changes to display background options.

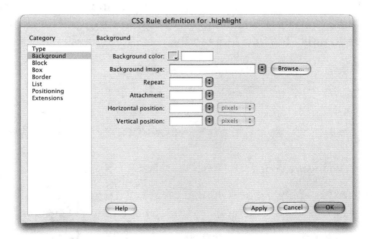

10. Set the Background Color to white (#FFFFFF) and click OK.

The highlight class you just created appears in the rule list on the CSS Styles panel and is available in the Style menu on the Property inspector.

11. In the Announcements section, select the first event title, *Intro to Anusara Workshop*, and apply the highlight style using the Style menu on the Property inspector.

The text now appears to be highlighted with white. The new styles you created in this exercise, dayName and highlight, display in the Style menu with visual representations—just like the styles that Dreamweaver created when you used Property inspector to set text properties earlier in this lesson.

Note To delete an internal rule from the embedded style sheet, you can use the CSS Styles panel to select the rule you want to remove and click the Delete CSS Rule icon on the lower-right corner of the panel. The style will be removed from the style sheet. Because that style definition then no longer exists, any text that the style was applied to will not show the attributes defined by the deleted style. However, you should remember that deleting a style from the CSS Styles panel is not the same as removing a style from text by choosing None in the Style menu on the Property inspector—if a style is deleted from the style sheet the references to the deleted style which are inserted into the code whenever you apply a style will remain in the document. If you also need to remove the references, you can do so quickly with Find & Replace, which is covered is Lesson 17. You can also delete properties from rules by selecting a single property in the properties list and clicking the Delete CSS property icon.

You can save the index.html file and leave it open for the next exercise.

Converting Internal Styles to External Styles

Style sheets can be stored externally and linked to one or more documents. An *external style sheet* is a file that contains only CSS specifications. You can use external style sheets with multiple Web pages to ensure consistency from page to page.

If you have a document with internal styles and you decide you want to use those styles in other pages, you can easily export those styles to an external style sheet.

1. In the index.html document, choose File › Export › CSS Styles.

The Export Styles As CSS File dialog box opens.

2. In the Save As text field, name your style sheet *sangha.css*. Save the file in the Lesson_04_CSS folder.

> **Tip** *You don't have to add the extension .css; it's appended to the document automatically upon saving if you don't include it.*

An external style sheet is created that contains all of the internal styles existing in the index.html document—including those that define the page properties as well as the dayName style and the highlight style.

> **Note** *When you export styles, only internal styles are included in the new document. If there is an external style sheet attached to the document from which you are exporting internal styles, the styles in that external style sheet are not included in the new style sheet.*

If you want to use the external style sheet in the document from which you converted internal styles, you should remove the internal style sheet before linking the style sheet, which you will learn to do in the next exercise. Although Dreamweaver enables you to attach an external style sheet with styles that use the same names as those contained in an internal style sheet, you should delete the internal styles to avoid conflict, reduce the amount of code in your HTML document, and reduce the possibility of errors and confusion.

To remove the internal style sheet, scroll up to the top of the list of rules on the CSS Styles panel. Select the internal style sheet which is represented by `<style>`, which contains all the rules that you've been working with in this lesson. With `<style>` selected, click the trash icon on the bottom of the CSS Styles panel: the Delete Embedded Style Sheet button. You might have noticed that this button is contextual—it changes based on what is selected, whether that is a property, a rule, or an entire style sheet.

You can close the index.html document.

Linking to an Existing External Style Sheet

You now have an external style sheet with multiple style definitions. Because it is external, you can use this file with other documents by linking it to the Web pages in which you want the style definitions to be applied or made available to. You will need to manually apply any classes to the appropriate paragraphs or selected text. Later in this lesson you'll learn to develop styles that redefine HTML tags as well as create contextual selectors—both style types will be applied automatically to all documents that have the style sheet attached.

Note *IDs, which can be created using the CSS Selector Styles type, are not automatically applied to documents when external style sheets are attached.*

1. Open the index.html file from the Lesson_04_CSS/about folder.

Note *Text content has been added to this page and formatted using the techniques that you learned in the previous lessons. For additional practice, you can import the text content from the about.txt document in the Lesson_04_CSS/Text folder and format it to match the document you're using in this exercise.*

This page has no internal or external styles.

In the following steps, you will link this document to the external style sheet that you created in the previous exercise from the internal styles in the index.html document. This linking will ensure that the text formatting is consistent between both pages.

Note *For the formatting to remain consistent as you continue to develop styles you would need to remove the internal styles from the definitions.html document and follow the steps in this exercise to attach the external style sheet. Using external style sheets will ensure that all documents linked to those style sheets will continually reflect any modifications to the styles that those external style sheets contain. You can leave the definitions.html document as-is for this lesson or work with it as suggested here for additional practice.*

2. Click the Attach Style Sheet icon located at the lower-right of the CSS Styles panel.

Attach style sheet

The Attach External Style Sheet dialog box opens.

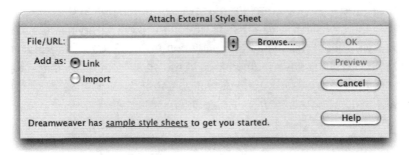

Note *Dreamweaver includes a number of predesigned CSS you can use in your own Websites. To use one of these style sheets, click the sample style sheets link at the bottom of the Attach External Style Sheet dialog box. Select the style sheet you want to use from the Sample Style Sheets dialog box and click OK. You can use these style sheets as-is or use them as a starting point to develop your own. Clicking Cancel from the Sample Style Sheets dialog box returns you to the Attach External Style Sheet dialog box.*

If you are proficient in writing HTML and know how to write CSS, you can create a CSS page from scratch by choosing File › New and selecting the CSS document type from the Basic Page category on the General tab. A new document opens, in which Code view is the only available viewing mode.

For more information about CSS, choose O'REILLY CSS Reference from the Book menu on the Reference panel located in the Code panel group to learn more about CSS elements. Use the Style menu to choose CSS terms and read their descriptions. You'll work with the Reference panel more in Lesson 15.

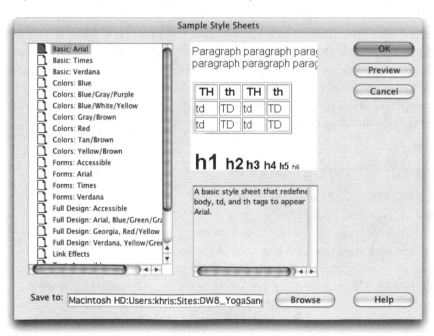

3. Click Browse and locate the sangha.css file that you created at the beginning of this lesson. Select the style sheet by clicking Choose (Macintosh) or OK (Windows) on the Select Style Sheet File dialog box. Verify that the Link option is selected from the Add As section of the Attach External Style Sheet dialog box and click OK.

The external style sheet sangha.css is now linked to the index.html document. The page now reflects the formatting attributes that are specified in the external style sheet. You'll immediately see the effects—the link colors will become the same as those that you set in Lesson 3, the background color will switch to the pale yellow that you set earlier in this lesson, and the default page font will switch to the font that you selected, also earlier in this lesson.

The Link option was selected by default because is the first time that you are attaching a style sheet to the index.html document. The Import option for attaching a style sheet does not work in Netscape Navigator 4.x; that browser ignores any style sheets that are attached using Import. Given the cascading nature of style sheets, the second style sheet has priority and overrides any conflicting styles in the first sheet. Likewise, a third style sheet overrides any conflicts in the first and second sheets. The process of using multiple style sheets is known as *cascading*.

A technique often used in consideration of Netscape 4.x users is to place all styles that are not compatible with that browser into subsequent style sheets that use the Import option. That way, Netscape 4.x uses only the styles in the first style sheet; it is not affected by styles that might conflict or cause errors because it ignores style sheets linked with the Import option. Imported styles contained within subsequent style sheets can then override those created for older browsers in the first sheet.

Creating External Styles

Although you can easily change a variety of formatting attributes such as font face, size, and color in individual documents, external styles can expand your options and make it easy to apply those same styles to other documents within your site. Rather than re-creating your styles in each page in which you want to use them, you can use an external style sheet to store all your styles, making those styles accessible to any document to which the style sheet is attached. This can speed up the formatting process greatly.

In this exercise, you'll create a new style in the sangha.css external style sheet by redefining an HTML tag. By redefining the Heading 3 (<h3>) HTML tag in this exercise, you tell the browser that any text using the <h3> tag should be displayed with the formatting you specify. This is useful because it allows you to alter the basic Heading 3 format so that all text that uses the Heading 3 format is formatted with the style attributes you specified.

1. Click the New CSS Rule icon on the CSS Styles panel. In the Selector Type area, select Tag. Use the Tag menu to select h3.

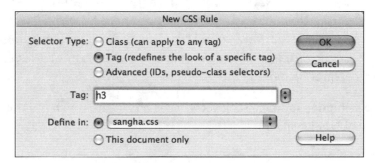

In this exercise, you make a style for the format Heading 3. In HTML, the corresponding tag is <h3>. Tags are specified in the New CSS Style dialog box without the brackets that surround them in the code. The heading near the top of the document is formatted as a Heading 3 and will take on the attributes you specify in the next step.

Note *When you are creating a style that redefines an existing HTML tag, it is helpful to place the insertion point within text on the page that uses the same tag or select that tag in the tag selector before you create the style. Dreamweaver then automatically associates the HTML tag with the style that will be created as long as the tag selector type is the default selection—the default selector type is whichever type was last used. If the tag selector type is not the default, you can select it, click Cancel on the New CSS Rule dialog box, and click New CSS Rule again—tag will be selected when the dialog box reopens. Selecting the tag prior to opening the New CSS Rule dialog box can be helpful if you are not familiar with HTML. For example, you could click in the heading and select the <h3> tag and then click the New CSS Rule icon on the CSS Styles panel. If Tag is selected in the Selector Type area, the <h3> tag is displayed as h3 in the Tag text field.*

2. From the Define In area, select the menu option and choose sangha.css from the menu. Click OK.

Because this is the only style sheet that is linked to the current document, (New Style Sheet File) and sangha.css are the only options in the menu. For documents that do not have any external style sheets attached, the only option in this menu would be (New Style Sheet File).

Note *You can create a new external style sheet while creating a new style by selecting (New Style Sheet File) in the menu option in the Define In area of the New CSS Rule dialog box. When you create a new external style sheet for a rule, the style sheet is automatically linked to the document for which it was created. You should save any such new external style sheets with the .css extension. To keep the file structure clean and organized, some sites keep all external styles sheets in a central location.*

The CSS Rule Definition for h3 in sangha.css dialog box opens, which you use to define the formatting of Heading 3 tags.

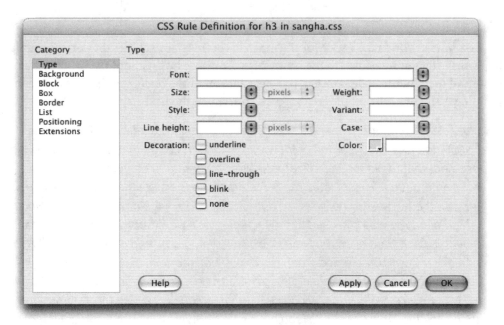

The CSS Rule Definition dialog box always displays the selector of the style—the element that is being modified—and the name of the style sheet that it is being defined in. In this case, the selector is h3 and the style sheet is sangha.css.

3. In the Type category, select **18** from the Size menu and change the measurement to points. From the Font menu, choose **Courier New, Courier, monospace**. Change the color to **#660066**. Select bold from the Weight menu and click **OK**.

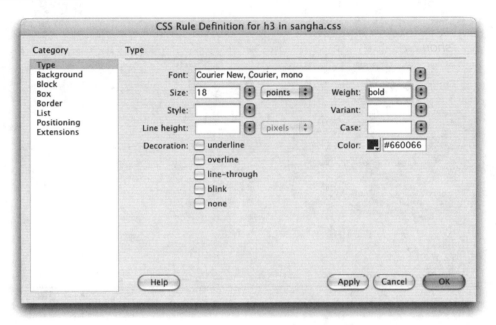

You can also open the sangha.css file to make changes directly to the CSS code.

When you click OK to close the CSS Rule Definition dialog box, the sangha.css file automatically opens in a new tab in the Document window. CSS files are displayed in Code view, which you will work with more in Lesson 16. If you make changes to the style sheet such as creating, editing or deleting styles, be sure to save the CSS document before closing it. If you close it without saving, you will lose any changes that you might have made. You might want to periodically save your CSS document as well as your HTML document while you are working.

```
1    a:link {
2        color: #FF3300;
3    }
4    a:visited {
5        color: #993300;
6    }
7    a:hover {
8        color: #FF9900;
9    }
10   a:active {
11       color: #FFCC00;
12   }
13   body {
14       background-color: #FFFFCC;
15   }
16   body, td, th {
17       font-family: Arial, Helvetica, sans-serif;
18       color: #330000;
19   }
20   .style1 {font-family: "Courier New", Courier, mono}
21   .style2 {font-size: 12px}
22   .style3 {color: #FFCC33}
23   .dayName {
24       font-size: 12px;
25       font-weight: bold;
26       font-variant: small-caps;
27       color: #000000;
28   }
29   .highlight {
30       background-color: #FFFFFF;
31   }
32   h3 {
33       font-family: "Courier New", Courier, mono;
34       font-size: 18pt;
35       font-weight: bold;
36       color: #660066;
37   }
38
```

Note *You can use the Dreamweaver Preferences to adjust how you work with CSS. The CSS Styles category allows you to choose to open CSS files when they are modified—this option is on by default. You should leave this option selected for this lesson. Also included in this section of the Preferences are shorthand options that affect the way CSS is written by Dreamweaver.*

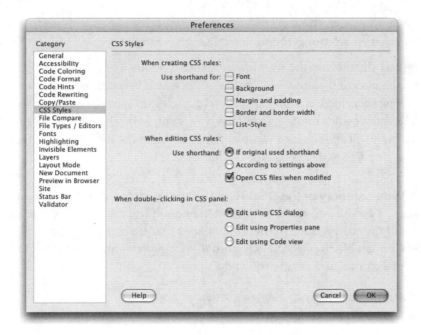

Redefined HTML tag styles are applied automatically to any content contained by the redefined tags in the document(s) to which the style sheet applies. The style you created is now reflected in text that uses the heading 3 format.

4. Place the insertion point within the first paragraph beginning with *Yoga Sangha's inspiration is emerging....*

The tag selector at the lower left of the Document window displays the HTML tag <p>, indicating that the insertion point is within the paragraph. The <p> tag defines a paragraph.

5. Click New CSS Rule icon on the CSS Styles panel. The Tag text field should display p, Tag should be selected in the Selector Type section, and the Define In section should show sangha.css selected in the menu. Make any changes necessary to match these values and then click OK.

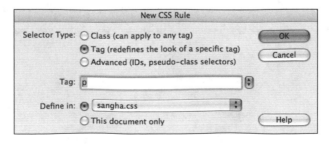

The new style you are creating will redefine the way text formatted with paragraph tags should appear—the selector is p, and the style sheet is sangha.css.

The dialog box should have the <p> tag automatically selected in the Tag text field because you placed the insertion point within a paragraph, which uses the <p> tag, before choosing to create a new CSS rule. Because you used the tag selector Type the last time you used the New CSS Rule dialog box in this lesson, that type is automatically selected. If you close Dreamweaver, it will revert back to automatically selecting the Class Selector Type upon opening the New CSS Style dialog box.

6. In the Type category of the **CSS Rule Definition** dialog box, leave the Font menu blank. Type *12* into the Size text field and set the measurement to pixels in the Size unit menu. Type *20* in the Line Height text field and set the measurement to pixels. Choose black (#000000) from the Color area and then click **OK** to close the dialog box and create the style.

Tip *You can click Apply to see your selections appear on the page while the dialog box is still open. If you want to make changes based on how the text appears, you can do so before closing the dialog box.*

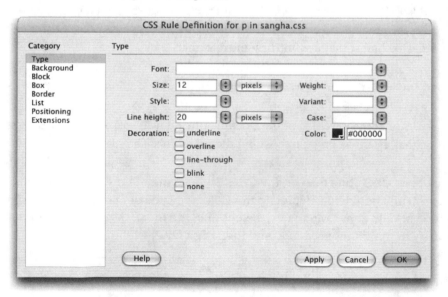

Any text that is contained within paragraph tags in the document will now appear with the formatting for the attributes that you defined in the external style sheet. The style sheet does not affect any text that has a different format applied to it, headings, or lists.

Resolution and Units of Measurement on the Web

Pixels are a unit of measurement for defining text size in Web pages. Points are derived from print-based media and so are only a good choice for pages that are intended for printing. Pixels originate from digital media and describe a unit of measurement based on screen resolution. Consequently, pixels tend to translate more consistently from browser to browser and platform to platform than points. Small text that is readable on a Windows computer can be completely illegible on a Macintosh — a situation that occurs most often when developers use points to define text size.

There are several other measurement options available, including relative sizes that you learned about in Lesson 2 (choices of small, medium, large, and so on in the size menu on the Property inspector) in comparison with absolute values (defined numerically), which require the selection of a unit of measurement. Inches, centimeters, and millimeters are the other print-based units available. Picas (one pica is 12 points), ems, exes, and percents are other units of measurement. The percentage option relies on the size defined by the parent element or tag and therefore depends on inheriting a size attribute from either a previous style or the browser default. You learn more about style precedence and inheritance later in this lesson.

Although relative sizes, ems and percentages are usually recommended over pixels, points or other print-based units of measurement, the most important thing is to check your Web pages on different platforms and see how your text appears on both Macintosh and Windows computers.

7. Place the insertion point in the first line of the list that begins with *is a form of Hatha yoga*. In the tag selector, click <ul>.

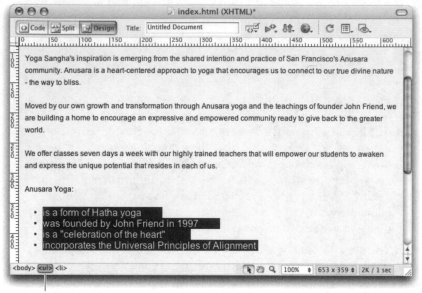

Tag selector

This procedure selects the list tag that controls the formatting of the text. By selecting the <ul> tag (which applies to the entire list), you apply the formatting to both the list bullet and the list item at the same time. You will also see the <li> tag (which applies only to an individual item in the list) in the tag selector.

8. Click New CSS Rule on the CSS Styles panel. Verify that tag is selected in the Selector Type area, that ul is displayed in the Tag text field, and that the style will be created in the sangha.css style sheet. Click OK and use the CSS Rule Definition dialog box to set the size to 12 pixels, the weight to bold, and the color to #333333. Click OK.

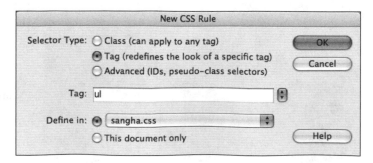

The ul style overrides the settings that you specified for the default body text color (black). You learn more about how to determine which styles are given priority later in this lesson.

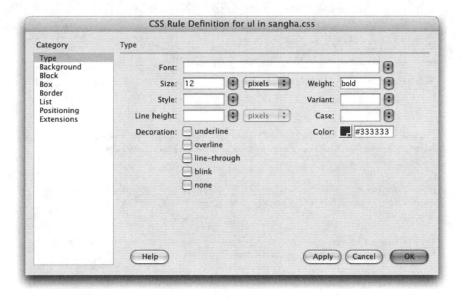

9. In the Document window, click in the heading Anusara Yoga:, located just above the bulleted list. Select the <h4> tag in the tag selector, and click New CSS Rule on the CSS Styles panel. In the New CSS Rule dialog box, verify that the Tag field displays <h4>, the Selector Type is Tag, and the style will be defined in sangha.css; then click OK. In the CSS Rule Definition dialog box, set the font to Courier New, Courier, mono and set the size to 16 pixels. Click OK.

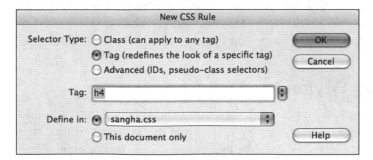

This subheading is set to the Heading 4 format. You can see the <h4> tag displayed in the tag selector at the lower left of the Document window, and you can also see Heading 4 displayed in the Format menu on the Property inspector.

At this point, your document should look similar to the example shown here.

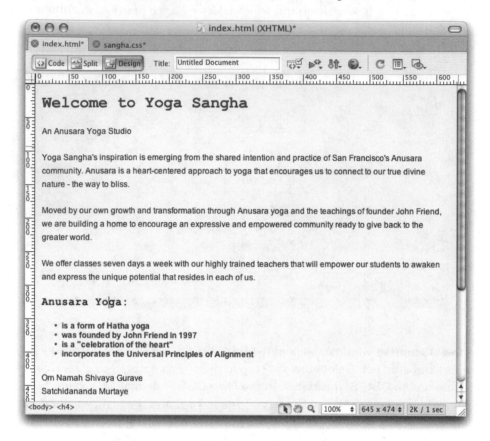

Leave the index.html file open for the next exercise. Save both the index.html and sangha.css documents. Remember that the sangha.css document opened in a new tab automatically when you began to edit the style sheet earlier in this lesson.

Creating Styles for Tag Combinations

You've used two selector types so far: class and tag. The third option in the New CSS Rule dialog box is the Advanced selector type, which enables you to create a variety of advanced styles, including contextual selectors that can be used to format combinations of tags—combinations being the circumstance in which tags appear within other tags.

In this exercise, you'll specify a different format for text paragraphs with an alignment. Because you already created a style for the <p> tag, the paragraphs in the document currently reflect that formatting.

1. Place the cursor in the first paragraph located at the top of the document, just below the An Anusara Yoga Studio line. Use the tag selector to select the <p> tag.

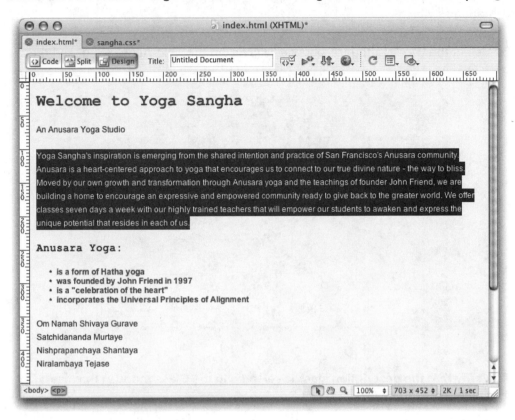

The entire paragraph becomes selected.

The tag selector at the lower left of the Document window shows the hierarchy of the code. You'll create a tag combination that includes the paragraph block in the following steps.

2. Click Insert Div Tag on the Insert bar. Choose Wrap Around Selection in the Insert menu and click the New CSS Style button. Select the Class selector type, type *.description* into the name text field, and choose sangha.css in the Define in area; then click OK.

Insert Div Tag

You're now creating a style, description, that will apply to this particular <div> tag. In the following step, you'll use the CSS Rule Definition dialog box to define the attributes of the description style.

3. Select the Block category, choose *justify* from the Text Align menu, and then click OK.

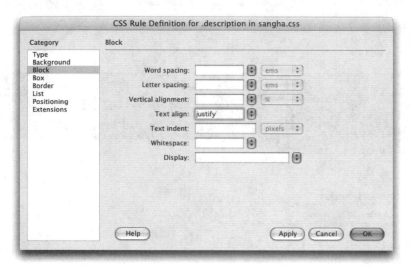

4. Verify that the description class is selected in the Class menu in the Insert Div Tag dialog box. Click OK.

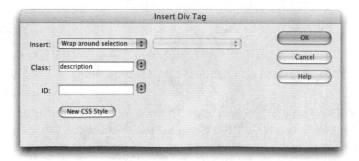

The paragraph is now contained within a div, which is represented in the Document window by dotted outlines—this is a Dreamweaver visual aid that will not be visible in the browser. Rolling the mouse pointer over the dotted lines will cause them to become solid red lines, indicating that you can select the div.

Tip *If you do not see the outlines, you can select View › Visual Aids › CSS Layout Outlines.*

If you insert a div without selecting something for it to wrap around, such as the <p> tag as in this exercise, the div will be inserted with the placeholder text **Content for class "name of class" Goes Here**.

5. **Place the cursor in the paragraph located inside the div.**

In this case, <div.description><p> is shown in the tag selector. In the following steps, you'll create a style to specify tag combinations, which will allow you to create a different style for the paragraph inside the table.

6. **Click New CSS Rule on the CSS Styles panel. Select** *Advanced* **in the Selector Type area and enter** *div p* **in the Selector text field. Select** *sangha.css* **in the Define In area and click OK.**

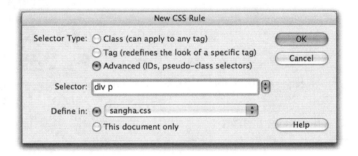

The div p typed in the Selector text field represents the div tag and the paragraph tag inside it. Whenever this specific combination of tags appears in a document linked to the sangha.css style sheet, the formatting you will choose in the following steps will be applied. By using div p, you specify that only paragraphs contained within a div will be affected.

Note *The Selector menu lists the four states applicable to links: a:link, a:visited, a:hover (not supported by older browsers), and a:active. This type of CSS Selector is known as a pseudo-class.*

The CSS Rule Definition dialog box opens.

7. Select the Block category from the Category list. Type *15* into the Text Indent text field, select pixels as the unit of measurement, and click OK.

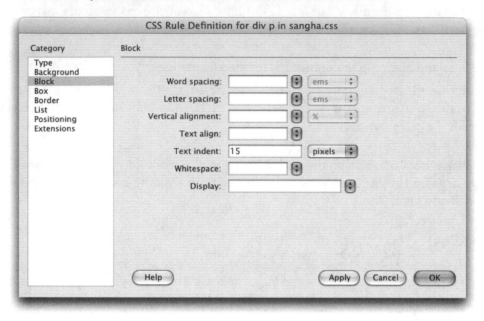

Your changes are reflected in the text.

8. Save your changes to the index.html and sangha.css documents and preview index.html in a browser.

> Tip *Because the external style sheet is not automatically saved, you must save it before previewing your page in the browser. If you do not save it before you preview, Dreamweaver will prompt you to do so.*

Because contextual selectors allow you to format tags that appear in sequence with other tags, the changes you made for the paragraph in the div do not affect the other paragraphs on the page.

Editing an Existing Style

One of the major advantages of using external style sheets is the ability to edit styles with ease and speed. Because changes are made only in the style sheets and not in the individual Web pages, you do not have to duplicate your modifications across a large number of documents. With external styles, formatting is not kept in the HTML document (such as index.html)—the only style information included is a reference that specifies which style should be used in the case of classes. Web pages tell the browser which external style sheets to use for instructions on how to display the formatting. The styles are applied to the elements by the browser at the time that a file is seen by a visitor, as you can see in the following illustration.

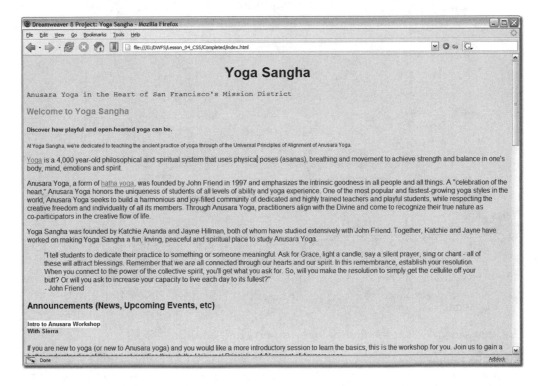

Any modifications are automatically reflected in every page that is attached to the edited style sheet at the time that it is viewed. Because formatting values are contained in the style sheet (sangha.css, for example), those values need to be modified in only that one location to affect all pages linked to the style sheet. This is useful because the appearance of an element such as text can be changed in several pages or even an entire site very quickly.

In this exercise, you'll edit a style in the sangha.css external style sheet.

1. Select p from the list of **All Rules** in the top portion of the **CSS Styles** panel.

The styles you create in the external style sheet sangha.css appear in the list on the CSS Styles panel.

When you select p from the CSS Styles panel, the CSS Properties segment of the CSS Styles panel indicates that the p style is currently selected and displays the properties that have been defined for that style—color, font-size, and line-height are the properties in this case. Each property shows the specific attributes that have been defined in the style.

2. Click the value for the line-height property and change it to *18*.

Changing properties and their values directly in the CSS Styles panel is a quick way to modify styles. Clicking the name of the property (in the left column) selects that property. Clicking the value (in the right column) allows you to change that value. For example, you can access a menu with the available font groups by clicking the name of the font, and you can access the color picker by clicking the color square.

Your changes are applied to the document. The space between each line of text is now slightly smaller. Text that uses the <p> tag in any other documents that are linked to this style sheet will be formatted automatically when viewed in Dreamweaver or a browser according to the modifications you just made.

Clicking the Add Property link at the bottom of the Properties list will allow you to select a new property to add to the rule.

Tip *You can also edit styles by selecting the desired style and clicking the Edit Style icon on the bottom of the CSS Styles panel. The CSS Rule Definition dialog box opens—the same dialog box you used in the previous exercises to create the styles.*

Save and leave open both index.html and sangha.css.

Working with Style Precedence

When more than one style applies to the same element, the browser displays the attributes of each style in combination with the other styles—and those styles might conflict with each other. In case of such a conflict, the precedence of styles is determined by the cascading nature of CSS. Understanding how to manage and order your styles can help you to avoid unexpected results.

CSS is applied cumulatively; that is, each style builds upon other styles if they apply to the same element in an ordered sequence according to the following rules of origin, specificity, and order.

Origin

The *origin*, which is the source of a style, is evaluated first. The sequence of style origins is as follows, beginning with the lowest priority—what the browser uses first:

- Browser defaults (lowest priority)
- Styles created by the user
- Styles specified by the Web page (highest priority)

This means that browsers use their default formatting specifications unless there is a style sheet that overrides those defaults. A user-specified style sheet overrides browser defaults, whereas styles specified by the Web page override user-specified styles.

1. Windows users: open the Internet Explorer browser, choose Tools › Internet Options, select the General tab, and click the Accessibility button near the bottom of the dialog box. Mac OS X users: open the Safari browser, choose Safari › Preferences, select the Advanced category, and use the Style Sheet pop-up menu to choose your own previously-created style sheet.

Tip *If you do not have Explorer or Safari installed on your computer, you can use any Web browser to complete this step. The exact location and title of the section in which a user style sheet is specified might vary from browser to browser and from version to version. As a Web developer, it is recommended that you become familiar with a variety of browsers, so you might want to repeat this step for other browsers. If you can't find the option for specifying a style sheet, try looking in the browser program's help or documentation.*

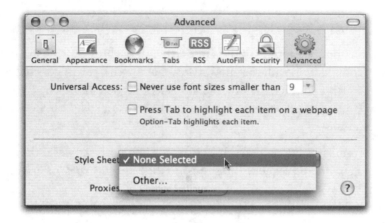

Visitors have the option to instruct browsers to apply style sheets of their choosing to the pages they visit. This option can provide greater accessibility by allowing users to adjust the appearance of Web pages through a style sheet that is optimized for their needs. This is an important option for users who might have visual disabilities. For instance, if a user has a hard time distinguishing small text against backgrounds that don't contrast well, that user can specify a style sheet with large text and a color combination with a dramatic contrast such as black text on a white background. Although this option is available, the majority of your visitors will most likely have no style sheet specified, so it is still important to consider the accessibility of your design when developing a site. Keep in mind the fact that some users might not know this option exists—don't rely on your visitors to make your site viewable. The more work they have to do to see your site, the less likely that they'll stick around to view the content. Design with the experiences of your audience in mind and aim to present sites as complete, seamless, and as easy to use as possible for the best results (more visitors!).

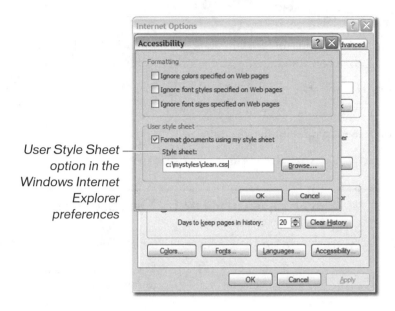

User Style Sheet option in the Windows Internet Explorer preferences

If there are conflicting styles between a style sheet specified by the user and one specified by the Web page, the one specified by the Web page will be used. If a style sheet specified by a user defines the default font face as Verdana, and a style sheet specified by the Web page defines the default font color as green, the default text style will be both Verdana and green. This cumulative effect is known as *inheritance*.

You can close the browser Preferences (Macintosh) or Tools (Windows).

CSS Weight Declaration

Styles can also be modified by the *weight* declaration, a method of establishing priority that is primarily intended to give the user an option for control over the style precedence. To increase the weight of a style, `!important` is included at the end of the style declaration, after the attribute values. Any style defined with `!important` in a style sheet specified by the user will override conflicting styles specified by the Web page—regardless of whether the styles defined by the Web page use the `!important` modifier. Older CSS standards allowed styles containing `!important` and originating from the Web page to override user-specified styles containing `!important`. The change to give user-specified styles containing the `!important` declaration priority is intended to give users control over styles—this can be important for visitors who need to view pages in certain ways. Use the modifier with discretion and consider whether it is truly necessary. A style using the `!important` modifier would appear as follows: `body { color: #339900 !important }`.

Understanding Specificity

The precedence of style types depends on a system that determines which style is the most specific. Style *specificity* is based on values in the format of abc as follows:

- a is the number of IDs in the style
- b is the number of attributes that are defined by the style
- c is the number of element names in the selector.

Styles with higher specificity values are given priority over styles with lower values.

Examples of How Specificity Is Determined

Sample Styles	Style Type	a	b	c	Specificity	(abc) Value
`p { color: #000000 }`	Tag	0	1	1	11	This style specifies that text contained within paragraph blocks will be black.
`div p { font-size: 22px }`	Advanced	0	1	2	12	(Contextual Selector) This style specifies that text contained within a paragraph block(s) that is contained within a div will be 22 pixels.
`h5 { font-family: Verdana, Arial, Helvetica, sans-serif; font-size 18px }`	Tag	0	2	1	21	This style specifies that text formatted as a Heading 5 will be displayed in Verdana, Arial, Helvetica, sans-serif at a size of 18 pixels.
`.quote { font-style: normal; font-weight: bold; color: #0033CC }`	Class	0	3	0	30	This style specifies that text to which the .quote style is applied will use the normal font style, be bold, and use a dark blue color (#0033CC)
`#left { font-size: 22px; color: #000000 }`	Advanced (ID and Contextual Selector)	1	2	0	120	This style specifies that the text marked with the unique ID left will be 22 pixels and black.

2. Switch to the sangha.css style sheet in Dreamweaver. Calculate the specificity values for the following styles: the <h4> tag, the highlight class, and the <ul> tag.

After you have calculated the values, you can compare them with the values listed at the end of this step.

The following figure is how your current style sheet should appear. The specificity values listed below the example of how specificity determines the order of styles are calculated based on the style sheet you see here.

```
10   a:active {
11        color: #FFCC00;
12   }
13   body {
14        background-color: #FFFFCC;
15   }
16   body, td, th {
17        font-family: Arial, Helvetica, sans-serif;
18        color: #330000;
19   }
20   .style1 {font-family: "Courier New", Courier, mono}
21   .style2 {font-size: 12px}
22   .style3 {color: #FFCC33}
23   .dayName {
24        font-size: 12px;
25        font-weight: bold;
26        font-variant: small-caps;
27        color: #000000;
28   }
29   .highlight {
30        background-color: #FFFFFF;
31   }
32   h3 {
33        font-family: "Courier New", Courier, mono;
34        font-size: 18pt;
35        font-weight: bold;
36        color: #660066;
37   }
38   p {
39        font-size: 12px;
40        line-height: 18px;
41        color: #000000;
42   }
43   ul {
44        font-size: 12px;
45        font-weight: bold;
46        color: #333333;
47   }
48   h4 {
49        font-family: "Courier New", Courier, mono;
50        font-size: 16px;
51   }
52   .description {
53        text-align: justify;
54   }
55   div p {
56        text-indent: 15px;
57   }
58
```

Here's an example of how specificity determines the order of styles: The Heading 3 tag style that you created earlier in this lesson overrides the font defined by the style that was created when you set the default font to Arial, Helvetica, sans-serif in the Page Properties dialog box at the beginning of this lesson. Although the style that was created was initially an internal style, it was exported along with the other internal styles from the top-level index.html document to create the external sangha.css style sheet. The <h3> tag style has a higher specificity value (41—four attributes and one selector) than the default text style (23—two attributes and three selectors). The default text style appears in the CSS document as: body, td, th { font-family: Arial, Helvetica, sans-serif; color: #000000 }; the heading 3 style appears as h3 {font-family: "Courier New", Courier, mono; font-size: 18pt; font-weight: bold; color: #660066;}

Notice the commas separating the selectors in the style defining default text color: body, td, th. These commas indicate that this style is not a tag combination similar to the one you created earlier for div p; instead this style defines a number of selectors as a group. It is more efficient to group selectors when their attributes will be identical, as opposed to creating three separate styles.

In the sangha.css style sheet, the specificity values you calculated in this step should be:

- h4 (Tag): a = 0, b = 2, c = 1 (for a value of 21)

  There are no IDs (a) in this style; there are two attributes (b) of font-family and font-size; and there is one selector (c), h4.

- highlight (Class): a = 0, b = 1, c = 0 (for a value of 10)

  There are no IDs (a) in this style; there is one attribute (b) of background-color; and there are no selectors (c).

- ul (Tag): a = 0, b = 3, c = 1 (for a value of 31)

  There are no IDs (a) in this style; there are three attributes (b) of font-size, weight, and color; and there is one selector (c), ul.

Note *CSS specificity uses a large arbitrary number base to calculate the values of styles—it does not use base 10 because styles can potentially have more than 9 IDs, attributes, or elements. Suppose that a style has no IDs, 14 attributes, and 5 elements. In base 10 such a style would use a = 0, b = 14, and c = 5, so the value would be 145. In a numbering system with a large base, a = 0, b = E, and c = 5, so the value is E5. This is important because a style with one ID, one attribute, and zero elements would have a value of 110 in both base 10 and a numbering system with a larger base. In base 10, the first style with a value of 145 would override the second style with a value of 110. However, in a numbering system with a larger base the second style with a value of 110 would override the first style with a value of E5, which is the correct order of specificity.*

Understanding Order

The *order* of styles, which concerns where styles are located, is as follows, beginning with the lowest:

- Browser defaults (the formatting that is farthest away from the text; lowest priority)
- External CSS styles
- Internal CSS styles
- Inline CSS Styles
- Local HTML formatting (the formatting that is closest to the text; highest priority— overrides any options set in the styles above if there are conflicts)

Best Coding Practice: Avoid Inline Styles and Local Formatting

An inline style is an instance of a style that is placed directly in the code. The use of inline styles is generally not recommended. `<h1 style="color: #333333; font-family: Verdana, Arial, Helvetica, sans-serif">` is an example of an inline style. Inline styles are defined within the content of the document and do not use any style sheet information at the top of the document (as internal styles do) or in a separate style sheet (as external styles do). Internal and external style sheets are significantly more powerful because inline styles merge content with formatting and because they are single instances of a style definition that can't be used elsewhere.

Local HTML formatting overrides all styles. HTML formatting is no longer used by Dreamweaver to format text because the `<font>` tag is deprecated (marked for deletion) in HTML 4.0, as discussed in Lesson 2. Although formatting with the `<font>` tag is still supported in manual coding through Dreamweaver as well as by browsers, taking advantage of the new standards enables you to design a more flexible and functional Website. It is best to avoid using the `<font>` tag.

3. Click the index.html tab to switch back to the index.html Document window. Apply the highlight style to the text *Universal Principles of Alignment* in the last line of the list. Click the Current button at the top of the **CSS Styles** panel.

The background color defined in the highlight style is combined with the style that controls the formatting of the list.

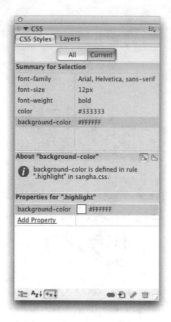

The Current view of the CSS Styles panel gives a summary of all properties and values that apply to the current selection in the top portion of the panel, in the order of which they are applied. The bottom property is the one that is closest to the current selection. In the lower portion of the panel, you will see details regarding the property that is selected in the summary. In this case, the highlight class is shown, including information about the style sheet in which the rule is located. You can select any of the properties in the summary to find out more about them. The Properties segment of the CSS Styles panel that you used to edit a style in the previous exercise remains visible.

If there is more than one style applied by the author of the Web page (the origin) to the same text with conflicting attributes, priority is given to the specifications from the innermost style (the style closest to the current selection). The most recent styles are nested inside earlier styles. Because the last formatting attributes you apply are physically the closest tags to the text, they take precedence over earlier styles and control the final look of the text.

If your document uses an external style sheet, the styles in that sheet are applied across your document. Suppose, for example, that the external style sheet has definitions for Heading 3 and Heading 4, and that you also created an internal style within your document that redefines the Heading 3 tag. The internal style takes precedence if the attributes conflict with those in the external style. For example, if the internal style defines the h3 tag to be red and the external style defines the h3 to be blue and bold, the h3 tag will actually be red and bold. Only the attributes that conflict are affected.

Text formatting applied manually to ranges of text can also take precedence over other styles. In the example just presented, suppose that you used the Property inspector to apply a different color to one of the Heading 3 lines. Dreamweaver defines color and formatting selections from the Property inspector as internal custom styles. The Style menu on the Property inspector includes both internal and external styles.

If you have attached a style sheet to a document and the browser does not display the formatting that you expect, check your style sheet and your document to see if you have other styles or local formatting that is overriding the styles you expect to see used.

Creating a Basic CSS Layout

CSS is a great way to control the layout and appearance of your Website. CSS functionality is best achieved with recent browsers (5.0 and up) that can support the widest range of features. CSS can be used in combination with, or as an alternative to, creating layouts with tables, which you'll learn about in Lesson 6. Many sites are migrating toward the use of CSS instead of tables because although tables offer a layout method that might seem to be currently more compatible with a larger number of browsers, there are a number of drawbacks to using them. Tables, particularly complicated ones, can cause your page to load slowly, require a great deal more code, and often necessitate the use of spacer gifs to force the table to hold its position. One of the primary drawbacks is the combination of content with formatting and appearance. The benefits of CSS include the ease and speed with which a CSS-based site can be updated, a consistent appearance, less code, and faster download time. With CSS, content is separated from the design and attributes that define appearance. The advantages to using CSS for layout also include increased accessibility, flexibility, and efficiency. The important things to consider when deciding which layout tools to use in a Web page are what works best for the particular layout that you are trying to achieve, and what the majority of your visitors will be able to access. Make sure that you preview your pages in multiple browsers and operating systems to test how your chosen layout method will appear.

In this exercise, you will edit the description rule that you created earlier in the lesson to obtain a basic single box for content that uses the description style. In the index.html document, the <div> containing the paragraph near the top of the document uses the description rule.

1. Click the All button on the CSS Styles panel. Select the description rule from the All Rules list and click the Edit Style button at the bottom of the CSS Styles panel.

Edit Style button

You're beginning to set up the class that will be used to define the look of a simple box for this page.

2. Select Background from the list of categories. Choose white (#FFFFFF) from the Background color picker.

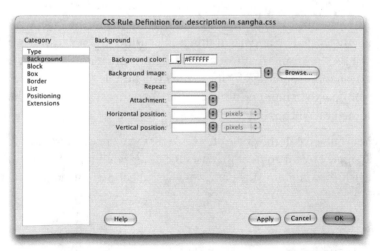

You have defined the background color of the column that will appear on top of the yellow page background.

3. Select Box from the list of categories. Enter *90* in the Width text field and verify that % is selected in the measurement menu. In the Padding section, enter *8* in the Top text field. The Same For All box should be checked, and pixels should be selected in the measurement menu (these are the default settings).

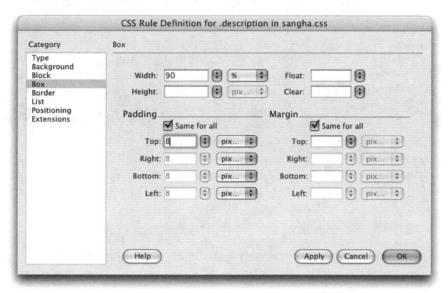

The Box category provides a number of options to control the container you are creating. In this case, you defined the width of the box you will create as 90% of the available browser width. The padding creates the specified amount of space between the edge of the box and the content it contains. The margin defines the space that will exist between the edges of the browser and the edges of the box as well as the space that would exist between the box and any additional elements that might be created outside of the box.

4. Select Border from the list of categories. Select Solid from the Top menu in the Style section. In the Width section, leave the Same For All box checked and enter *1* in the text field; then verify that the pixels option is selected in the measurement menu. Select black (#000000) from the Top color picker in the Color section and leave the Same For All box checked. Click OK to close the CSS Rule Definition dialog box.

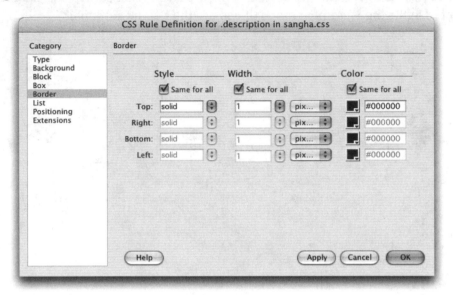

The border options allow you to define how the outline around the box appears.

Note *There are a total of eight categories available for style definition. You've used five: Type, Background, Box, Block, and Border. The other three categories are as follows:*

- **List:** *Provides options to control the formatting of ordered and unordered lists.*

- **Positioning:** *Provides options to control where elements are located. Dreamweaver considers any element with positioning options defined to be a Layer. (Layers are covered in Lesson 9.) You can integrate CSS and Layers for more complex layouts.*

- **Extensions:** *Provides additional options, some of which are not widely supported.*

At this point, the `<div>` containing the paragraph displays a white background with a black outline.

5. Roll the pointer over the border of the box. When the line turns red, indicating that you can select the `<div>`, click the border.

The `<div>` is selected, as you can see by the highlighted **`<div.description>`** in the tag selector.

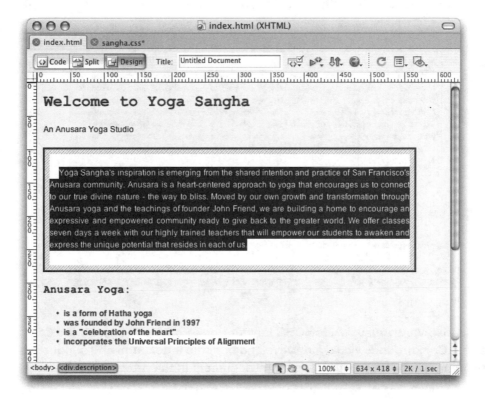

The selected `<div>` uses a number of visual aids to indicate the CSS attributes that are affected—such as the solid blue outline that designates the border property and the shaded area between the border and the text that signifies the padding property.

6. Choose View > Visual Aids > CSS Layout Backgrounds.

Dreamweaver uses color coding to identify areas of a document that have been formatted with CSS, and every div uses a different color to help you distinguish between them when creating layouts. Values of other properties, such as font and background colors, are temporarily ignored in this mode. This visual aid, which is available only in Dreamweaver, is not indicative of how the page will appear in the browser.

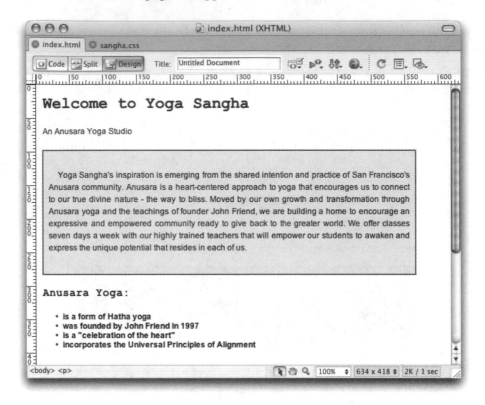

7. Choose View > Visual Aids > CSS Layout Backgrounds to turn off the CSS Layout Backgrounds visual aid. Save and both the index.html and sangha.css documents and preview the index.html document in the browser.

You now have a box surrounding content. Because this layout is created with an external style sheet, you can easily apply it to many other documents for a consistent appearance. You can use techniques such as this one to create more complex layouts without using tables.

You can close the both files.

Working With CSS On Your Own

Throughout the rest of the book you'll continue to work on creating and refining CSS styles to control appearance and layout. For additional practice, you can create your own external style sheets using the techniques learned in this lesson and link them to the pages that you've been creating in your own site through the work in the previous On Your Own sections. You can also experiment with several of the CSS documents that are provided within Dreamweaver as samples and starting pages by applying them either to pages within your own Website or to copies of the starting files in the Yoga Sangha project site. Exploring other style sheets is a good way to learn about what is possible with CSS and to discover techniques that you might be able to incorporate into your own pages.

1. Choose File > New and choose the Page Designs (CSS) category in the General portion of the New Document dialog box. Select a style sheet such as Halo Left Nav from the Page Designs list. Click the Create button.

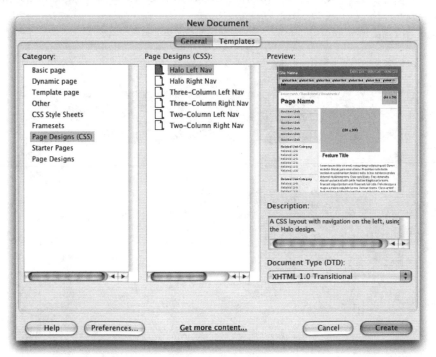

Dreamweaver will create the new document and prompt you to select the location in which the file will be saved. Some starting pages might require files such as graphics that will automatically be copied to your site. During the process of copying the necessary files to your site, you might see preliminary content appear in the HTML document—it will refresh after the files have been copied.

The Halo Left Nav style sheet will create a page that looks similar to the following example. You can preview it in the browser to see how it will look.

Note *Halo is one part of a set of components—including HTML and Flash elements, layout options, and an interface design created by Macromedia and integrated throughout the Studio programs—that are geared toward helping Web developers create positive user experiences.*

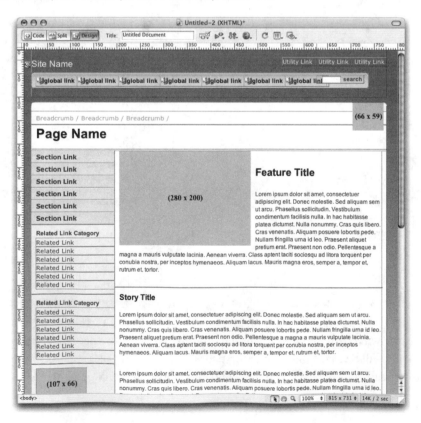

Turning on the CSS Layout Background visual aid that you used in the previous exercise will let you see the wide array of styles that work together to create the layout.

2. **Use the techniques you practiced in this lesson to create styles for your own site.**

As you create styles, remember to be aware of the differences between internal and external styles and what kinds you are creating. Think about creating styles that help to visual distinguish the hierarchy of the content.

What You Have Learned

In this lesson, you have:

- Specified a background color and font (pages 110–120)
- Created an internal style to use the same text formatting quickly and easily (pages 121–122)
- Created a class that can be applied to different kinds of text formats (pages 123–129)
- Converted internal styles to external styles so they can be used by other documents (pages 130–131)
- Linked to an external style sheet from another document to use the same text formatting (pages 131–134)
- Created external styles specifying text formatting that can be used to maintain consistency in the look of text throughout a Website (pages 134–144)
- Added multiple styles to an existing style sheet by redefining HTML tags (pages 144–148)
- Edited a style in the external style sheet to affect all documents linked to it (pages 149–159)
- Created a basic box with a `div` and CSS class (pages 159–167)

5 Working with Graphics

Graphics can play a significant part in capturing the attention of your audience and effectively communicating the intended message of your Website. In this lesson, you will incorporate graphics into the pages you are creating for the Yoga Sangha project site. In the process, you'll learn about different graphic file formats, how to control the positioning of images through CSS, and how to combine graphical elements with text.

The features in Macromedia Dreamweaver 8 give you a great deal of control over the graphics used in your site. They enable you to modify image properties quickly within Dreamweaver, as well as immediately open images within an external image editor. The Assets panel simplifies the management of graphics by allowing you to create catalogs of all the images used in your site or of specific images that you need to have available.

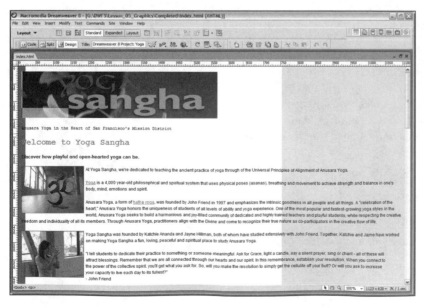

In this lesson, you'll create a page similar to this one while you learn to incorporate graphics with text on your pages.

If you want to view the final result of this lesson, open index.html in the Completed folder within the Lesson_05_Graphics folder.

What You Will Learn

In this lesson, you will:

- Identify graphics formats and explore their differences
- Insert graphics into a page
- Modify the properties of your images
- Change the positioning of graphics on a page
- Give your images names and alt attributes
- Use the Assets panel to manage graphics
- Wrap text around an image
- Make use of image placeholders
- Use basic image-editing tools to adjust graphics
- Align text with an image

Approximate Time

This lesson should take approximately two hours to complete.

Lesson Files

Media Files:

Lesson_05_Graphics/Images/green-studio.jpg
Lesson_05_Graphics/Images/studio-om.jpg
Lesson_05_Graphics/Images/teaching.jpg
Lesson_05_Graphics/Images/ys_bkg_main.gif
Lesson_05_Graphics/Images/yoga_sangha-title.jpg

Starting Files:

Lesson_05_Graphics/index.html
Lesson_05_Graphics/about/studio.html

Completed Project:

Lesson_05_Graphics/Completed/index.html

Using a Background Graphic

In this exercise, you'll add a background graphic to a page. A background graphic can be a small graphic that tiles across your page by repeating itself to the extent of the width and height of the browser window. A tiled background graphic has no effect on the appearance of scroll bars (or lack thereof) on your page. You can also use larger images as background graphics and use Cascading Style Sheets (CSS) to control their placement, as well as whether they tile horizontally, vertically, both, or not at all. Background graphics will automatically tile in old browsers that do not support CSS.

You can define both a background color and a background graphic for your pages. On slow connections or in older slower browsers, you might see the background color displayed first—a good reason to set a background color even if you plan on using a background image. After the background graphic loads, it remains onscreen, overriding the background color.

Note *In this exercise you'll work with XHTML files that have been created using the skills and techniques you learned in the previous lessons. If you want extra practice, you can re-create them using the starting pages as guides.*

1. Open index.html from the Lesson_05_Graphics folder. From the All Rules list on CSS Styles panel, select the body rule from the sangha.css style sheet and click the Edit Style button in the bottom of the panel.

Edit Style

This index.html document uses the sangha.css style sheet that you created in the previous lesson. To make the application of a background image available to other documents in the site, the style sheet must be edited. The body rule redefines the <body> tag, which contains the document's content.

When working on older sites you might come across documents that define attributes directly within the <body> tag—this method of specifying backgrounds and link colors is deprecated and should be avoided in favor of using style sheets as you are learning to do in this exercise.

Note *You can also set a background image directly in an individual page through the Page Properties dialog box—this method will create an internal style that is available only to the document to which it was applied. To do so, choose Modify › Page Properties and select the Appearance category. You can click the Browse button to locate the background image and select a repeat method if desired. Use the keyboard shortcut Cmd+J (Macintosh) or Ctrl+J (Windows) to access the Page Properties dialog box quickly. You can also control the margins of the page directly in the Appearance section as well—this can be helpful if the amount of the margin is dependent upon the background graphic. Defining a margin in the document you are working with in this exercise for example, can prevent the text from overlapping the vertical bar on the left side of the page. You can also define page margins in external style sheets by defining the margin attribute of the body tag.*

2. In the Background category, click the Browse button next to the Background image text field. Locate the ys_bkg_main.gif graphic in the Images folder of the Lesson_05_Graphics folder. Click Choose (Macintosh) or Select (Windows) to designate the image as the background for the page.

The Background category might be automatically selected because there is one attribute applied to the body tag already: the pale yellow background color, #FFFFCC.

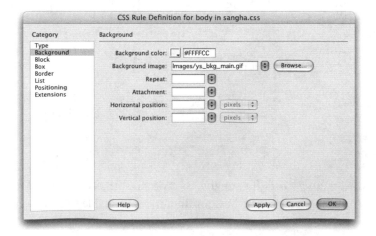

A path name, or path, describes the location of a file. The path to the ys_bkg_main.gif image is now displayed in the Background image text field; the location described by that path is relative to the sangha.css document. If you had not yet saved your file when you added the background image, the entire path name for the graphic relative to your hard disk would display in the text field. Until a file is saved, Dreamweaver has no way to make these kinds of references, so a path name based on the location of the image on the hard disk is substituted instead of a valid link. When the file is saved, the path name will update and change to reflect the location of the graphic relative to the document containing it. It is always best, however, to save your file before importing any graphics—even background images. Path names that are relative to your hard drive don't work on the remote server; if you insert graphics without first saving your page, you run the risk of having "broken" images.

Note   *If the image you select in the Select Image Source dialog box is outside of your local site, Dreamweaver displays an alert and gives you the option to copy the file into your site. The pages and elements (HTML, images, multimedia, and so on) that you use in your site will usually be located in your local root folder. You can also use elements that do not exist in your local root folder but are in a location on the Internet, whether on your own site or elsewhere, through the use of absolute paths (covered in Lesson 3)—a technique that is often used for advertising banners. Because such items do not display in the Dreamweaver Document window, you need to preview your page(s) in the browser to view them.*

You can create a background graphic in an image editor such as Macromedia Fireworks or Adobe Photoshop. Keep in mind that large graphics can significantly add to a page's size and download time—use smaller graphics whenever possible. The smaller your pages, the quicker they will load; the quicker your pages load, the more likely your visitors are to stay, browse, and return to the site.

Tip   *If you are considering several background images, you can click the Apply button to see the background image displayed on your page without closing the Page Properties dialog box.*

If you want to delete a background graphic, you can do so by opening the Page Properties dialog box and deleting the filename in the Background text field or by locating the background property for the page in the CSS panel's Properties list and changing or deleting the value.

3. Choose repeat-y from the Repeat menu and click OK to close the Page Properties dialog box.

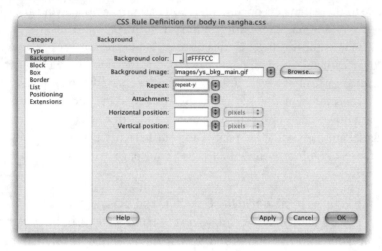

The changes you made are applied to the document, and the ys_bkg_main.gif background image now tiles vertically in the Document window. The background color you applied in the last lesson can be seen if you expand the Document window to the right, past the ending point of the background graphic.

There are a number of options available for controlling the repeat property of the background image:

- **repeat-y** will tile the selected background graphic vertically
- **repeat-x** will tile the graphic horizontally
- **repeat** will tile the graphic both vertically and horizontally
- **no-repeat** will cause the image not to tile

By default, background images tile both horizontally and vertically unless you apply the repeat properties.

The other options available are the following:

- **Attachment** allows you to specify whether the background image should be fixed or if it should scroll with the rest of the page—this property is used with background images that do not repeat.
- **Horizontal position and Vertical position** allow you to control the position of the background image. Positioning can be done either by selecting options of left, center, or right for horizontal placement and top, center, or bottom for vertical placement, or by specifying a precise location with numeric values and a measurement unit such as pixels.

Placing Graphics on the Page

Images can be placed directly in the body of the document, along with other content such as text. In this exercise you'll begin to incorporate images into your documents.

In this book, all the images you work with have already been saved for use on the Web as GIFs and JPEGs. You will not need to save or optimize any graphics.

Graphic Formats for the Web

The most common and widely supported graphic formats on the Web are GIF (Graphic Interchange Format) and JPEG (Joint Photographic Experts Group). The process of saving images for use on the Web is known as optimization, and can be done with an image editor such as Macromedia Fireworks or Adobe Photoshop. When deciding whether to save a graphic as a GIF or a JPEG, aim for the highest image quality and the lowest possible file size.

As a general rule, GIFs should be used if the artwork has large areas of solid flat colors and little or no blending of colors. GIFs works well with text, vector graphics, images with a limited number of colors, and very small image dimensions. GIF images can be saved, at maximum, using 8-bit color mode in which only 256 colors can be represented. GIF files tend to load faster, have more optimization options, and support transparency and animation. The extension used for a GIF file is .gif.

JPEGs are usually the best choice for photographic images or images with a large tonal range. The JPEG format handles blending of colors very well and can produce much higher quality photographic images at a fraction of the size of a GIF. JPEG saves the image in 24-bit mode, retaining all the colors and using a lossy form of compression in which redundant data is lost. The lower the quality of a JPEG, the more information is lost about the image through this discard of data. Because of the lossy quality of JPEGs, any edits should always be done to the source file and resaved as JPEGs to avoid degradation of the image. The extension used for a JPEG file is .jpg.

A third graphic format, PNG (Portable Network Graphic), is also used for Web graphics. The PNG format was intended as a replacement of the GIF format—it combines features of both JPEG and GIF. PNG files are lossless, can compress better than GIF files and have more options for color control, can retain all colors like a JPG or use a limited number of colors like a GIF. PNG files are not intended to replace JPEGs. PNG does not support animation and is not supported by older browsers. The extension used for a PNG file is .png.

1. Place the insertion point in front of the title **Yoga Sangha** at the top of the document and press Return (Macintosh) or Enter (Windows). Place the insertion point in the new blank line. Click the Images menu button in the Common category of the Insert bar; then select the Image option.

Image

The Select Image Source dialog box opens, which allows you to insert a graphic into the page. An alternative method is to choose Insert > Image.

Tip *For **Windows** users, the Preview images checkbox provides a useful option that enables you to see a thumbnail of the images you click as you browse. When this option is selected, images are displayed in the Select Image Source dialog box along with their dimensions, file size, and approximate download time.*

*On the **Macintosh** there is no Preview images checkbox; if you are in column view mode, you see the image preview along with dimensions, file size, and approximate download time in the right pane of the Select Image Source dialog box after you select an image.*

2. Locate the file yoga_sangha-title.jpg in the Lesson_05_Graphics/Images folder.

The Select Image Source dialog box contains a variety of options. You can specify the folder from which you want to pick an image by using the menu (unlabeled on the Macintosh; labeled Look In on Windows) and selecting from the display of folder and files beneath the menu and view tools. Macintosh users have a hierarchical view that enables users to scroll through different levels of files and folders; Windows users have a Files Of Type menu that can be used to limit the view to specific kinds of files, and a File Name text field that displays the name of the selected file (normally, minus extension).

The URL text field displays the path that will be used by the index.html document to access the selected image. Below the URL text field is the Relative To menu. Set to Document by default, the Relative To option lets you choose how Dreamweaver references images: with *document-relative* (the Document option) or *site root-relative* (the Site Root option) references. In document-relative referencing, Dreamweaver constructs the path to the image based on the relative location of your HTML document to the graphics file. When Document is selected in the Relative To menu, the filename of the document into which you are inserting the image appears to the right of the menu—in this case, you will see index.html. Site root-relative referencing constructs the path to the image based on the relative location of the selected image to the site root, also known as the top level of the local root folder. If Site Root is selected, the name of the site will appear to the right of the menu. Generally, you should use document-relative links and paths. If you have an extremely large site or plan to move pages frequently, you might want to use site root-relative referencing. Throughout the course of this book, you should use only document-relative paths for images.

You also have several additional options in the Select Image Source dialog box that are intended for use with dynamic sites. On the Macintosh, the Select File Name From section located at the bottom of the dialog box contains a Data Sources button and a Sites And Servers button; On Windows, the Select File Name From section is located at the top of the dialog box and has two radio buttons: File System and Data Sources, as well as a Sites And Servers button. The File System option is the default selection method on both Macintosh and Windows for the Yoga Sangha project site and others similar to it that do not use a server technology (such as ColdFusion, ASP, JSP, or PHP). The Data Sources and Sites And Servers options are used for dynamic sites in which a document executes on an application server. You do not need to use these options in the lessons contained in this book because you are not creating a dynamic, data-driven site.

3. Click Choose (Macintosh) or OK (Windows). Enter *Yoga Sangha* in the Alternate Text field in the Image Tag Accessibility Attributes dialog box and click OK.

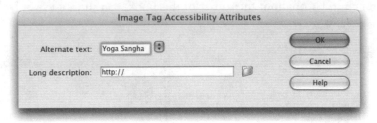

The Alternate Text option provides the opportunity to specify text that will displayed if users have graphics disabled, if their browsers are not capable of displaying graphics, if a particular image fails to load, or if another situation prevents the user from being able to see the graphic. Alternative text should be the text equivalent of the graphic—it should describe the function. For example, alternative text should be included with any graphics that are critical for site navigation. Adding alternative text is useful because if users have graphics disabled or are using a text-only browser, they can see some of the information they would otherwise miss. Additionally, people who have vision disabilities use various programs, often called *readers* or *speech synthesizers*, which relay content on Web pages audibly. In these cases, the alternative text of an image is spoken. Many browsers will display the alternate text as the user moves the pointer over the image. The more descriptive and detailed your alternative text is, the more useful it is for users of your site.

At times, you might have graphics that serve a strictly visual function and do not display words or other imagery that are important to the content of your page. Spacer images, invisible graphics that occupy a certain space, are one example of nonfunctional graphics that can make it more difficult for users with vision disabilities to use your site if they are labeled inappropriately with alternative text. For these types of images, you should click the menu button to the right of the Alternative text field and select <empty>. Avoid setting irrelevant alternative text—it does more harm than good.

In this exercise, the alternative text you specified is the same as the text that is shown in the image. Alternative text is an attribute of the <img> tag that defines images.

Tip   *Alternative text can be modified via the Property inspector when the image is selected. The menu containing the <empty> option is also available in the Property inspector.*

Creating Section 508 and WCAG-Compliant Sites

The goal of accessibility is to create sites that are accessible to the widest possible audience. Section 508 and Web Content Accessibility Guidelines (WCAG), both described as follows, address the need for accessibility on the Web.

Section 508 is an amendment to the Rehabilitation Act of 1973, which requires Federal agencies in the United States to account for the needs of people with disabilities, ensuring that all users have an equal opportunity to access the content made available through technologies such as the Internet. Section 508 defines the standards that are necessary for those who have disabilities to be provided with comparable information and services as those available to nondisabled users. Although Section 508 is not forced upon the private sector, it is important for all Websites to adhere to the practice of creating compliant code wherever possible for many reasons. Conditions ranging from poor or failing eyesight to color blindness or even total blindness affect a significant portion of the population—and your audience.

WCAG was developed by the W3C to address a wide range of accessibility issues and provide a set of clear guidelines for the development of accessible sites. Accessible sites are also important for WebTV, mobile phones, and PDAs. More information can be found at: http://www.w3.org/TR/WAI-WEBCONTENT/.

One solution is to create an alternative, text-only version of your site, but it might not be feasible or even necessary—particularly given the issues of the kinds of content and services offered, amount of space available, time and resources needed to create additional pages, and increased requirements for site maintenance. A text-only page might not even be accessible, depending on the techniques used to create it and the content it contains. Another drawback to text-only sites is that they usually contain less information than their counterparts, and/or the functionality of the site is decreased.

Incorporating accessibility features into a single version of your site is usually the best method. It provides options in one place for as many different users as possible and avoids duplication of content and maintenance efforts. There are a number of ways to use integrated solutions to address accessibility issues without creating a duplicate site and with no degrading visual impact on your page designs. Dreamweaver provides you with easy ways to create accessible Web pages through the use of elements such as CSS, alternative text, descriptions, and summaries.

Note *To turn accessibility prompts on or off, choose Dreamweaver › Preferences (Macintosh) or Edit › Preferences (Windows) and select Accessibility from the list of categories. Uncheck the boxes for any elements for which you do not want to be prompted for accessibility attributes.*

4. Delete the line of text Yoga Sangha that is formatted as Heading 1 and save the document.

The heading is no longer necessary because the image contains the name of the project site and alternative text has been included. The text, as well as the line that it is on, should be deleted.

Note *The yoga_sangha-title.jpg graphic was saved as a JPEG because of the large tonal range behind the text. To maintain the quality of the lines for the text, the image was saved as a high-quality JPEG—resulting in an increased file size. As a lower-quality JPEG, the same image would show more JPEG **artifacts**—small, blocky squares where redundant data is discarded, which are more common in areas of solid flat color like the text Yoga Sangha. In this case, JPEG was the best option to compromise between the needs of the photographic areas and the text.*

Resizing and Refreshing Graphics

When you import a graphic, the width and height of the image are shown in the Property inspector and placed into the code automatically; giving the browser the information it needs to define the layout of the page. This option can make a difference in the loading speed of your page.

1. Select the yoga_sangha-title.jpg image and use the Property inspector to change the width in the **W** text field to *220* pixels and the height in the **H** text field to *40* pixels.

You need to press Return (Macintosh) or Enter (Windows), or click in the Document window to apply the change and refresh the view.

The new width and height attributes of the <img> (image) tag cause this graphic to appear in smaller dimensions without making the actual graphic file smaller. Notice that the file size of the selected image that is displayed in the Property inspector does not change. There are many important advantages of restricting all image adjustments to being performed within an image editor, including sharpness, image quality, and file size. If you were to reduce the same image in an image editor and reoptimize it for the Web, the file would be smaller in file size and higher in image quality.

Note *File size is an especially important consideration for Web pages. The smaller the file size, the more quickly your images load. And the more quickly your pages load, the more likely your visitors will wait around long enough to see your site.*

2. Click one of the selection handles—the black squares—on the border of the selected image. Drag to resize the image and make it larger than the original size of the image.

The width and height specifications update automatically. Notice that the new dimensions are displayed in bold. This bold formatting is an indicator that the graphic has been resized. At times, you might resize a graphic accidentally, and the bold numbers will help clue you in to that change.

Tip *Hold down the Shift key while you drag the image's lower-right corner selection handles to constrain the proportions of the image.*

Notice that when you scaled the image larger, the image quality diminished. Images display in browsers at screen resolution, which is 72 dpi. This resolution is not high enough to display an image at a size that is larger than the actual size of the graphic—another reason to always adjust the image size in your image-editing software (such as Macromedia Fireworks or Adobe Photoshop) to ensure that you have the smallest file size possible.

3. In the Property inspector, click the Reset Image To Original Size button that is located just to the right of the W and H text fields.

The refresh icon indicates the Reset Image To Original Size button. It is in the center of lines connecting the W and H text fields. The refresh icon and connecting lines gives you another indication that the dimensions of the image have been altered—it appears only when the image dimensions have been modified. The image resets to the original size of the graphic. Notice that the width and height numbers revert to plain text, indicating that the image is set at the original size.

Note *When using very large images or images that are located on other servers, you can provide a visual clue to viewers by using a low source image. By defining a low source, you are choosing a lower-quality image that will appear first. The higher-quality image will appear in its place when the download is complete. When an image is selected, the Property inspector provides a Low Src text field for defining a low source image. Click the Browse For File Folder icon next to the field to choose an image. This technique is sometimes used when you know the final image will be large in file size and therefore take longer to download than a user might expect, or if the image is being obtained from a source that might experience frequent slow downs or lags. Low source images used in such situations often depict "loading" or similar messages.*

Positioning Graphics

When you place an image into a document, you have a number of options for positioning it. The following exercise demonstrates a method for creating an alignment that uses CSS.

1. In index.html, place the insertion point at the beginning of the line At Yoga Sangha, we're dedicated to teaching... Insert studio-om.jpg, which is located in the Lesson_05_Graphics/Images folder.

Use the techniques learned in the "Placing Graphics on the Page" exercise earlier in this lesson to insert the studio-om.jpg image. By default, the image appears at the beginning of the line of text.

In the following steps, you'll use CSS to align the image to the left and make the text wrap around the right of the graphic.

2. Click the New CSS Rule button in the CSS Styles panel. Select the Class Selector Type and enter .*studioPhoto* into the Name text field and click OK. In the CSS Rule Definition dialog box, select the Box category, choose left from the Float menu, and click OK.

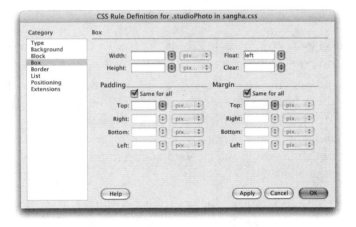

Every element in a document is considered to be a box. CSS uses the box concept to control an element's appearance, positioning, and so on. The elements—and therefore, the boxes that represent them—can either be block or inline, and each box can contain other boxes. Here, you're using the box to control the position of the inline image element to which you'll apply the studioPhoto class. Float is one of three positioning methods; the other two are absolute and fixed.

Choosing a left float causes the affected block—the element to which the studioPhoto class is applied—to be shifted to the far-left margin of the block that contains it. The body of the document is considered to be a box, and in some cases might be considered the containing block. The top of the floated element will line up with the top of the block it is in, and surrounding content will flow around the floated element.

3. Select the studio-om.jpg image in the Document window and choose studioPhoto from the Class menu in the Property inspector.

The image shifts to the left side of the page and lines up with the top of the paragraph block that contains it. The subsequent text wraps around the graphic on the right.

Working with the Align Attribute

Dreamweaver provides quick access to image alignment options in the Property inspector through a menu of vertical and horizontal alignment options. Each of the alignment options available in this menu uses the align attribute of the `<img>` tag. Use of the Align attribute as applied to an `<img>` tag is deprecated because it is inline, presentational markup. However, you might need to be familiar with the functionality if you are working on older sites. The alignment options function in relation to the current line—where the image is located—as follows:

- **Default.** No align attribute specified.
- **Baseline.** Aligns the bottom of the image to the baseline of the text line.
- **Top.** Aligns the top of the image to the highest element of the line—it can be an image.
- **Middle.** Aligns the middle of the image to the baseline of the text line.
- **Bottom.** Aligns the bottom of the image to the baseline of the text line—the equivalent to the Baseline option.
- **TextTop.** Aligns the top of the image to the tallest character of the text line; usually, but not always, the same as Top.
- **Absolute Middle.** Aligns the middle of the image to the middle of the text line.
- **Absolute Bottom.** Aligns the bottom of the image to the lowest character of the text line.
- **Left.** Causes the image to shift to the left—any subsequent text wraps around the right side of the image.
- **Right.** Causes the image to shift to the right—any subsequent text wraps around the left side of the image.

The alignment options in the menu are not the same as the Left, Center, and Right alignment buttons. The alignment options in the menu are applied to the `<img>` tag, whereas the three alignment buttons apply to the block element that contains the images, such as the `<p>` tag, and therefore everything else contained within that tag is affected by the alignment because it is part of the same block.

Adding a Border Around an Image

At times, you will need to set an image apart from the background or surrounding content to make it stand out. One way to create this effect is to place a border around the image. A border can draw attention to an image and it can be part of a stylistic look throughout a site. Sometimes, a border can also indicate a link. There are two ways to define a border—in this exercise, you'll use CSS to create the border but you'll also learn about the second method of applying the border attribute to the image tag.

1. Select the studioPhoto rule from the All Rules list in the CSS Styles Panel and click the Edit Style button in the bottom of the panel.

Rules appear in the order that you created them, with the oldest at the top of the list and the newest at the bottom.

2. In the CSS Rule Definition dialog box, select the Border category. Choose solid from the Style options, enter *1* into the top text field for the Width section, and choose #747E3F. Click OK to close the dialog box and apply the change.

Dreamweaver adds a one-pixel border around the image. The border setting uses pixel-based measurement, the default in the Rule Definition dialog box. You can set the width of the border to any number you want.

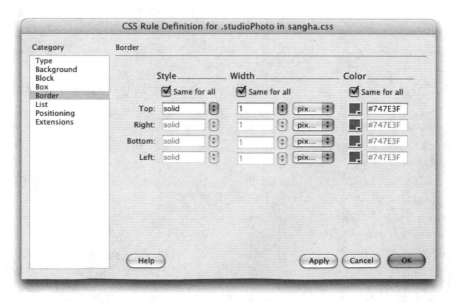

Note *You can also apply a border to an image using the border attribute of the `<img>` tag. To do so, select the image and enter a value for the desired thickness into the Border text field in the Property inspector. If you assign a link to an image, the border color will be the same as the default Link Color specified in Page Properties—unless a CSS style is applied, in which case a link will not cause any change in the border color. The border color will be the same as the default text color that was specified in the Page Properties dialog box. The following example shows an image that has a border attribute applied through the Property inspector. Avoiding the border attribute in favor of using CSS to define image borders, as you have done in this exercise, is a better coding process.*

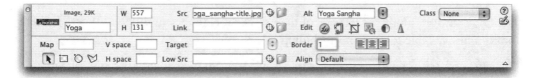

Assigning Image Names

Image names are important, although largely invisible, parts of Web pages. It is generally a good practice to assign names to images—they are used in scripting to identify the object.

Select the yoga_sangha-title.jpg image and enter *Yoga* in the image name text field in the Property inspector.

The image name text field is not labeled in the Property inspector. It is located in the upper-left corner, directly under the size of the image.

Image Name text field

The name you assign to the image is an internal name, used mainly for functions such as Behaviors (covered in Lesson 8). Although naming your images is not essential, doing so is good practice. You should keep image names short, enter them in lowercase, and avoid using spaces or special characters.

Inserting an Image from the Assets Panel

The Assets panel provides you with the ability to organize the components of your site from within Dreamweaver. You can use it to view and catalog a wide variety of media and page elements. For example, it might be difficult to manage all your images, especially if you are working on a large site. The Assets panel gives you a way to keep track of those images.

1. Select the Assets panel from the Files panel group. Click the Images button located at the top of the column of buttons on the left side of the Assets panel.

Tip *If the Assets panel or Files panel group is not visible, you can choose Window › Assets to open the Assets panel within the Files panel group.*

The other buttons along the left side of the Assets panel represent different types of assets that can be available to your site, including colors.

You can work with the Assets panel in two ways: You can view it with the Site list, which gives you a complete list of the images in your site, or view it with the Favorites list, which shows only the images that you marked as Favorites. Both views allow you to add a selected image to your page.

Images button —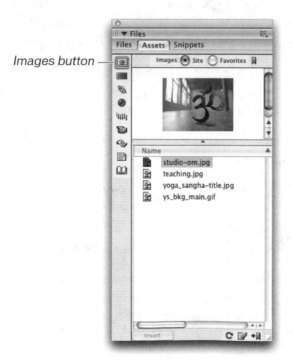

2. Click the Images: Site button (to the right of the Images button) at the top of the Assets panel if it is not already selected (as it should be by default).

> **Note** *In the Yoga Sangha project site you will see multiple copies of most images listed in the Images portion of the Assets panel because there are several copies of each image in the site as a result of the fact that the files are duplicated in each lesson folder as well as the respective completed folder. In your own sites, you will not have this situation unless you have multiple image folders that contain several of the same images. Spacer GIFs and navigation images are sometimes contained in several image folders. Usually it is not necessary to have multiple copies of an image because you can use images from any location in your site. In fact, multiple images might not be desirable—if you update an image, you might need to make changes on a number of files if you have multiple copies of the same image.*

All images within the site are shown in the Site Assets window. The images appear in this window automatically, whether or not they are used in any document. It might take a few seconds for the panel to create a catalog of the image assets available for your site.

> **Note** *If you didn't enable cache for your site when it was created, Dreamweaver will prompt you to click the refresh button in the Assets panel to enable and create the cache. Cache is enabled by default and is automatically created unless you uncheck the Enable Cache box in the Site Definition dialog box for your site.*

If you add a new asset to your site, it might not appear in the Assets panel immediately. To update the panel to match all the images in your site, you need to refresh the site catalog. To do so, click the Refresh Site List button in the lower-right corner of the Assets panel.

3. Place the insertion point at the beginning of the paragraph beginning with Yoga Sangha was founded by Katchie Ananda and Jayne Hillman. Find the teaching.jpg graphic in the Assets panel that is located in the Lesson_05_Graphics/Images folder and click the Insert button.

> **Tip** *You can also select the image in the Assets panel and drag it to the desired location.*

You can find out where a graphic file is located by selecting the file in the assets panel, Cmd + clicking for the context menu, and choosing Locate In Site.

Expanding the Assets panel horizontally will allow you to see the Full Path column, which you can use to determine where the images are located. On the Macintosh you can expand the panel by clicking and dragging the lower-right corner to the right—you might need to move the panel or panel groups to the left first so that you have room to expand the panel. On Windows you can click the vertical bar separating the panels from the rest of the interface and drag it to the left.

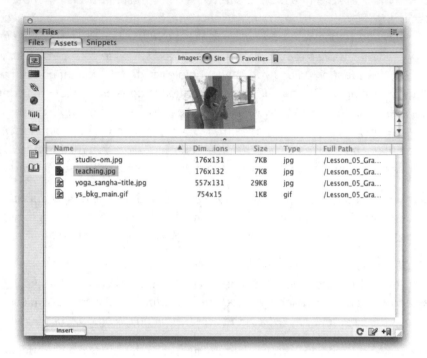

The image appears in the Document window.

As you select images in the Assets panel, you'll see a thumbnail preview at the top of the panel. You can enlarge the thumbnail by increasing the available preview area (place the cursor over the lower border of the viewing area and drag to resize) and/or enlarging the whole Assets panel. You can easily select an image from the Assets panel and click the Edit icon to open the image in your default image-editing program.

Clicking the column headers will reorder the list of images. For example, clicking the Name column header will reorder the images alphabetically in ascending (indicated by an upward-facing arrow) or descending order (indicated by a downward-facing arrow). You can use the other column headers to sort by Size, Type, and Full Path. You might need to scroll to the right to see the other columns. If you see an ellipse (…) in a column or column header, you will have to expand the panel to view the contents of that column. After the Assets panel is in focus (click an image in the list to bring it into focus), you can enter the first letter (or the first several letters in quick succession) of the file that you are looking for to select it.

Note *This photographic image was saved as a JPEG. The same image would appear posterized (rough gradations, with jagged edges to colors causing noticeable pixelation) if saved as a GIF image because all the different shades would be mapped to only a few colors. In this case, JPEG was the best option.*

4. In the Alternate Text text field in the Image Tag Accessibility Attributes dialog box, enter *A Yoga Sangha Teacher* and click OK. In the Document window, select the image you just inserted and enter *teacher* into the image-name text field in the Property inspector. Apply the studioPhoto CSS class to the image.

Giving names and alt text to your images as you insert them saves you time and make it easier to work with them in Code view later, if necessary.

At this point, your document should look similar to the preceding example.

Managing Images with the Favorites List

Placing images that you use repeatedly in the Favorites list can be a time-saver. You can add any image contained within the site to your Favorites list. Each site has its own Favorites list. This list is empty when you start using Dreamweaver. In the following exercise, you'll add an image from the Site category to your Favorites list and then organize that list.

1. In the Assets panel's Site list, select teaching.jpg and click the Add To Favorites button, located in the lower-right corner.

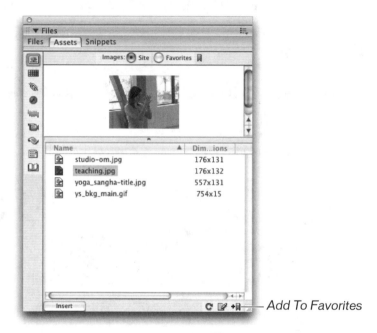

— *Add To Favorites*

A dialog box appears to let you know that the selected assets have been added to this site's Favorites list. Choose OK to acknowledge the message and close the dialog box.

Note *There are several alternative methods to add an image to the Favorites list. You can select an image in the Files panel and use the context menu in the upper-right corner of the panel to choose Add To Favorites (Macintosh Users). Yet another method is to make an image in your Document window a favorite. To do this, Ctrl-click (Macintosh) or right-click (Windows) the image and choose Add To Image Favorites from the context menu that appears. This context menu contains a wide variety of options and also works for other elements such as links and Flash objects.*

2. Use the Images options at the top of the Assets panel to select the Images: Favorites radio button.

The Assets panel now displays the list of favorites, with the image you added in the previous step.

As you begin to manage your images through the Assets panel, you probably will need to remove as well as add images. When an image is selected in the Favorites list, the Add To Favorites button becomes the Remove From Favorites button. Clicking Remove From Favorites causes the selected image to disappear from the list.

Note *In both the Site and Favorites lists in the Images category you can use the context menu to find the location of a particular image within your site. To do so, select and image and choose Locate In Site from the context menu. The Files panel becomes active, with the image selected in the site structure.*

3. Click the icon for the New Favorites Folder at the bottom of the panel. In the name text field of the folder that appears, replace the default name of untitled with Teachers and press Return (Macintosh) or Enter (Windows).

You can organize your images in folders to make them easy to locate.

Tip *You can also select the New Favorites Folder option from the context menu. This option is available only in the context menu when you are viewing the Favorites section of the Images category.*

4. Drag the teaching.jpg image into the Teachers folder.

You can double-click the small folder icon to see the contents of the folder and double-click again to collapse the folder. Images contained within a folder will appear below and slightly indented from the folder.

Note *If you need to delete a folder that you created in the Favorites list, select the folder and then click Remove From Favorites at the bottom of the Assets panel.*

Adjusting the Space Around an Image

When you wrap text around graphics, you might also need to adjust the space around the image. Initially the text in your document will be very close to the image, which can make it difficult to read. Creating a certain amount of open space will help the visual layout of your page. The space settings use a pixel-based measurement.

1. Select the studioPhoto rule from the All Rules list in the CSS Styles Panel and click the Edit Style button in the bottom of the panel.

Right now, the text is very close to the edge of this graphic. The page would look better and the text would be easier to read if space were added around the image.

2. In the CSS Rule Definition dialog box, select the Box category. In the Margin area of the dialog box, uncheck the Same For All box, enter 5 in both the right and bottom Margin text fields, and press Return (Macintosh) or Enter (Windows).

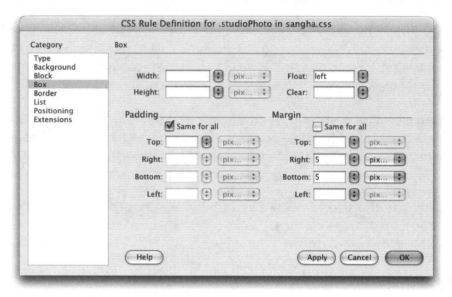

This setting creates five pixels of space on the right and bottom sides of the image. With CSS you can control the amount of space on each side of the element individually. This is useful in a situation in which the top of the image should line up with the top of the text line, and the left side of the image should line up with the left text edge.

Note *You can also add space to an image by defining the H space (horizontal space) and V space (vertical space) attributes of the <img> tag. These attributes add equal space of both sides of an image, whether horizontally or vertically—you can't add space on only one side unless you use CSS. You can define these attributes through the V space and H space text fields in the Property inspector.*

Inserting an Image Placeholder

You have the option to insert an image placeholder if you do not have the final image. A placeholder can be inserted and used to approximate how the final graphic will appear in the page in combination with text, tables, or other elements.

1. Place the insertion point at the end of the description of the Anusara Yoga Immersion announcement and press **Return (Macintosh)** or **Enter (Windows)** to create a new paragraph. In the **Common** category of the Insert bar, click the **Images** menu and select the **Image Placeholder** option.

Image placeholder

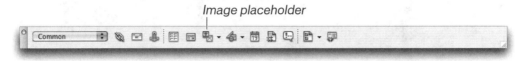

The Image Placeholder dialog box appears.

Note *The default width and height for an image placeholder is 32 × 32 pixels.*

2. In the Name text field, enter *class*. Set the width to **176** and the height to **132**. Click the color box and use the swatches to pick black; then enter *a class at Yoga Sangha* in the Alternate text field. Click **OK**.

The image placeholder appears in the Document window. It is black and displays the image name and the dimensions.

Note *If you have Fireworks installed and set as the default editor for your image files, you can select the placeholder image in the Document window and click the Create button in the Property inspector to open a Fireworks document at the size you specified for the placeholder. When you save that document, the name you used for the placeholder image is automatically assigned in the Fireworks Save As text field.*

When you preview your page in a browser, the image placeholder displays a broken image icon along with the alt text within a box with the dimensions and color you defined in the Image Placeholder dialog box. To replace this, you need to swap the image placeholder with the intended image, as described in the next exercise.

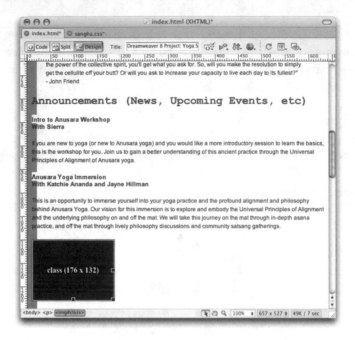

Your page should now look similar to this example.

Replacing an Image Placeholder

After you have created the final graphic or received the necessary image from your client, you need to replace the image placeholder you used to approximate the graphic.

Tip *You can also use this same technique to replace one image with another.*

1. Double-click the image placeholder in the Document window.

The Select Image Source dialog box opens.

2. Select the class.jpg from the Lesson_05_Graphics/Images folder and click Choose (Macintosh) or OK (Windows).

The image replaces the placeholder in the Document window. The name and alt text that were assigned to the image placeholder are now applied to the image.

Setting Image-Editing Preferences

As you create Web pages with Dreamweaver, you might find that you need to modify the images that you are using. For extensive editing you will need to open and adjust the image in an external image-editing program. Dreamweaver makes this process easy by providing a quick way for you to open the image in a program you specify.

1. Choose Dreamweaver Preferences (Macintosh) or Edit > Preferences (Windows) and select File Types/Editors in the Category list of the Preferences dialog box.

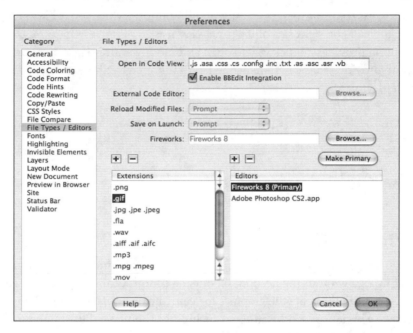

You can use this dialog box to assign different external programs as the default editors according to the file extensions.

Note *Production with Dreamweaver 8, Flash, and Fireworks can be integrated through what is known as roundtrip editing, a feature that makes it possible for file updates to be transferred between the programs. For this feature to function, Fireworks must be the default image editor.*

2. Select .gif in the Extensions list. Click the plus (+) button above the Editors list and select an image-editing program such as Fireworks. With the program selected in the application list, click the Make Primary button to set the program as the default editor for all GIF files.

Tip *To specify an editing program, be sure to use the buttons above the Editors list. The buttons above the Extensions list are for adding other extensions.*

If you do not have an image-editing program, you can skip this step.

If you do have an image-editing program, you should repeat this step for JPEG and PNG files.

3. Select the yoga_sangha-title.jpg image.

The Property inspector for images features an Edit button (which looks like a Fireworks icon) in the top half and right side of the panel as well as an option to Optimize In Fireworks. The Edit option provides a quick way to open and modify your images in an external image editor, provided that you have defined a default image editor, as detailed in the previous step.

Basic Image Editing

Several basic image-editing functions are available directly within Dreamweaver, enabling you to alter images without the need for an outside editor. Although you need an external image editor to initially create the graphics for your site or to make major changes, you can now make a variety of modifications—including cropping, adjusting the contrast, and sharpening—right in the Dreamweaver Document window using the integrated Fireworks image-editing features.

1. Select the class.jpg image.

The Image Editing options appear in the Property inspector.

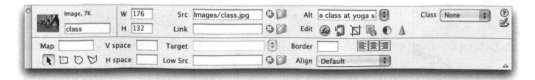

2. Click the Crop tool in the Property inspector.

An alert box informs you that the operation will change the actual image file on your disk. You can click the Don't Show Me This Message Again dialog box to avoid seeing this message again. Click OK to continue.

A selection area appears inside the image, indicated by a solid black line (Macintosh) or a dashed line (Windows). Grab handles are located in the corners and centers of each side of the selection area. The selection area might be difficult to see on dark images. By default, the selection area is slightly smaller than the image and has approximately the same proportions. The area within the selection is clear; the area outside the selection is grayed-out to show that it will be cropped. The cursor, when placed in the center of the selection area, turns into a hand (Macintosh) or a cross-hair with arrows (Windows) so that you can click and drag to move to selection area. You can click the cursor on any of the handles and drag to reduce or enlarge the size of the selection area.

3. Adjust the size of the crop area so that it is smaller than the original image and then press Return (Macintosh) or Enter (Windows) to crop the image.

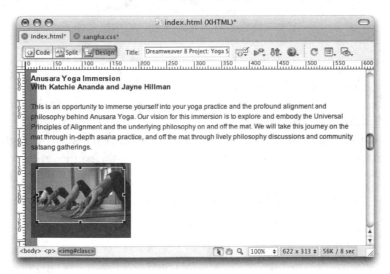

Tip *You can also double-click inside the selection area or click the crop icon in the Property inspector to apply the change. To cancel the crop, click elsewhere in the Document window outside of the image.*

The image is now cropped to the area that you selected. You might notice that the file size of the image is reduced; how much depends on the amount of the image that you cropped.

The original size of the class.jpg image was approximately 7 KB. The image size is given near the upper-left corner of the Property inspector when the image is selected.

Note *If you alter an image using Dreamweaver's Image tools, all instances of that image in your site will change. If this is not what you intend, you might want to make a duplicate of the image and perform your adjustments on the copy. If you make a crop and decide you don't like it, you can revert to the original image by using Dreamweaver's undo command. Choose Edit > Undo Crop or use the keyboard command Cmd+Z (Macintosh) or Ctrl+Z (Windows) to switch back to the original image.*

4. With the class.jpg image selected, click the Brightness And Contrast tool in the Property inspector. Change the brightness to +25 and click OK.

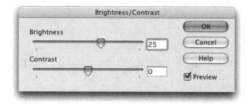

The alert informs you that the image file will be changed. Click OK to continue.

The Brightness/Contrast dialog box appears, with one slider for Brightness and one for Contrast. The sliders range from −100 to +100 with the center and default being 0. You can enter any value within the range into the text fields, or you can click and drag the sliders. Moving a slider to the left into the negative numbers decreases the brightness or lowers the contrast; moving a slider to the right into the positive numbers increases the brightness or heightens the contrast.

The Preview box is checked by default—this allows you to immediately see the effects of your adjustments in the Dreamweaver Document window.

Note *The brightness change you apply in this step is fairly drastic so that can clearly see the effect upon the image. Take care with using this option because it can severely affect the quality of an image if overused.*

5. With the class.jpg image selected, click the Sharpen tool in the Property inspector. Adjust the slider value to 2 and click OK.

The alert informs you that the image file will be changed. Click OK to continue.

The Sharpen dialog box uses one slider with a range of 0 to 10 and, like the Brightness and Contrast feature, it has a Preview option turned on by default.

You can repeat this function if necessary. Take care when using this option because it can severely affect the quality of an image if overused. Extreme sharpening can cause the image to appear pixilated.

Note *The additional image-editing options in the Property inspector include Edit, Optimize In Fireworks, and Resample. You must have Fireworks installed to take advantage of the option to optimize files. The Optimize Images dialog box allows you to make a wide variety of changes, including switching the format of images, adjusting the quality (JPEGs), and adjusting the color palette (GIFs). Keep in mind that you can lower the quality of an image and reduce its file size, but you can't increase the quality. To obtain a better image, you need to use original source files. The Launch External Editor opens in whichever editor you defined as Primary in the Preferences, which you set earlier in this lesson. The Resample tool gives you the option of increasing or decreasing the resolution of your images. It is always better to start with a higher resolution file and decrease the resolution to the desired size, rather than increasing a low-resolution file. Even when increasing the resolution, you can't add quality to an image that isn't there to begin with. Web resolution is 72 ppi (pixels per inch).*

Creating Graphic Links

You can also use images to link to documents within your site, as well as to sites other than your own. This exercise shows you how to create an external link. You can use the same techniques you used in the preceding exercise to link images to files on your site.

1. Click the class.jpg graphic to select it. Enter *schedule/immersion-details.html* in the Property inspector's Link text field.

This link is a relative path. You can use graphics to provide links just as easily as text. The immersion-details.html file does not exist in the schedule folder. You can use this method to insert links for pages that have not yet been created.

Remember, you must use an absolute path to link to a document that is located outside of your local file structure or to anything that is outside of the root folder. An absolute link begins with http:// (HyperText Transfer Protocol) to indicate that the user is connecting to a Web server. The remainder of the absolute link specifies the address of the linked site. All links to documents that exist on external Websites are absolute links.

Tip *If a URL is long or complex, you can go to that site in your browser, copy the URL, and paste it into the Link text field.*

2. Save the file and preview it in the browser.

Notice that when you roll over the graphics at the bottom of the page, you see the hand, indicating that they are linked. Depending on your browser, the link locations can appear in the browser's status bar as you roll over the links.

Creating Image Maps

In the previous exercise, you experienced how easy it is to apply a link to an image. The user can click any part of the image to go to the linked page. You also have the option of dividing the image into several linked areas called *hotspots* by using an *image map* to place individual hotspots on the image. These hotspots are not limited to rectangles; they can have other shapes. In the following exercise, you will add a rectangular hotspot and a circular hotspot.

Conceptually, image maps work quite well when applied to geographical maps; however, you can apply an image map to any image regardless of what that image represents.

1. Open studio.html from the Lesson_05_Graphics/about folder. Select the graphic green-studio.jpg.

The graphic needs to be divided into three hotspots—one for each item.

2. In the Property inspector, enter *greenstudio* in the Map text field.

Don't use spaces or special characters in the name. You can have several image maps on one page, but each map on that page must be uniquely named. If you fail to name your maps, Dreamweaver creates automatic sequential names for each (Map1, Map2, Map3, and so on). Such generic names do not provide any identifying information about the image map or the graphic that it is applied to. The name you are using in this exercise, greenstudio, suggests that the image map has to do with an environmentally conscious studio. By creating your own names in the Map text field, you can use names with distinct meanings. Short, concise, and specific names serve you best.

Tip *If you don't see the Map text field, click the expander arrow in the lower-right corner of the Property inspector.*

3. Select the Rectangular Hotspot tool below the map name text field in the Property inspector. Click and drag a square around the words floors and materials.

You might see a warning message informing you of the necessity to provide alternative text for the image.

A translucent blue-green area with handles appears around the names on that portion of the image, and the Property inspector displays the hotspot properties. Dreamweaver automatically places a null link (#) in the Property inspector's Link text field. Do not delete this character unless you immediately replace it with a link—it serves as a placeholder link to indicate that the area is clickable.

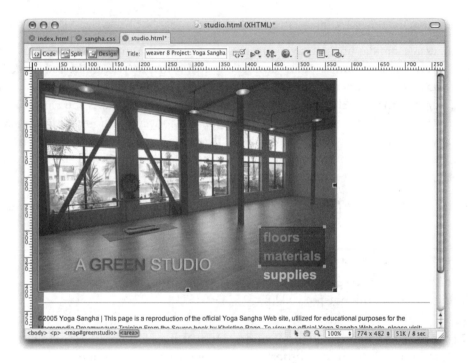

Note *The client-side image map icons are turned off by default. If you want them on, you can enable the client-side image maps option in the Invisible Elements category of the Preference dialog box. With this option, when you create one or more image maps, a map icon appears, usually at the bottom of the document. The map icon looks similar to the Named Anchor icon, and it is visible only in Dreamweaver—it does not appear in the browser.*

You can also toggle the visibility of the hotspot regions on and off by choosing View > Visual Aids > Image Maps.

4. Select the Pointer Hotspot tool below the Map text field in the Property inspector. Resize the hotspot you created in Step 3 by dragging a handle until the hotspot encompasses only the word floors.

The hotspots you create are easy to edit—you can resize, move, or delete them at any time.

To move the hotspot, position the pointer inside the hotspot and drag. After the hotspot is selected with the Pointer Hotspot tool, you can also adjust the position of hotspots using the arrow keys.

Holding the Shift key down at the same time causes the arrow keys to affect the size of the hotspot.

To delete the hotspot, select it and press Delete (Macintosh) or Backspace (Windows).

You can create circular hotspots using the Oval Hotspot tool. You can also use the Polygon Hotspot tool to click multiple points around any area with a more complicated shape for which you want to create a hotspot. When you use the Polygon tool, each click creates a point. A line connects each subsequent point to the preceding point. As you click, you'll see the translucent hotspot area begin to form. You can continue clicking until you have the shape you want. You do not need to "close" the shape by clicking back on the original point. The more points that a polygon shape uses to define the hotspots, the more code is necessary in the document to describe those areas.

Note | *If two or more hotspots overlap each other, the first one you create takes precedence over any subsequent hotspots that overlap it.*

5. With the hotspot selected, enter floors in the Alt text field in the Property inspector.

The hotspot alt text serves a similar purpose as alt text for an image; it gives an indication to where this hotspot will link.

6. Enter *green.html#floors* in the Property inspector's Hotspot Link text field, and choose _blank from the Target pop-up menu to have the link open in a new browser window.

Be sure to replace the original number sign (#) in the Link Text field with the link you entered.

In this case, the link would take the visitor to a named anchor called floors on an HTML page called green.html. The use of anchors to link to specific portions of other pages helps your site to be more functional, directing your viewers to what they are looking for immediately and reducing the amount of time they have to spend scrolling through long documents. The more functional and easy to use your site is, the more likely it is that you will have new and repeat visitors.

The hotspot must be selected to modify the link, target, or alt text.

Note *You can also create links that include named anchors to other pages using the Point To File tool, which you used in Lesson 3 to create links within the same document. To do so, you can select a hotspot, click the Point To File icon to the right of the Link text field, and point to the desired named anchor in an open HTML document.*

7. Use the Rectangular Hotspot tool to create one hotspot each for both the words materials and supplies. Repeat Steps 5 through 6 to create alternative text and links for both words. Use *materials* and *supplies*, respectively, for the alternative text; use *green.html#materials* and *green.html#supplies* for the links, respectively.

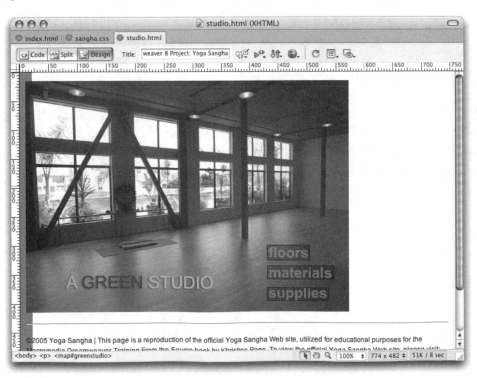

When you finish working with the image map, you can use the Pointer Hotspot tool to click outside the hotspot to another area of the image. Clicking outside the image map on to a different portion of the image resets the Property inspector to display image properties.

Tip *You can hold down the Shift key while using the Rectangular Hotspot tool to constrain the proportions to a square.*

8. **Save the file and preview it in the browser.**

Test the links in the image map you created. You can close the studio.html, index.html, and sangha.css documents.

Note *If you copy an image map and paste it into another document, Dreamweaver retains the links and hotspots.*

Using Graphics On Your Own

Including images in your site and controlling their layout with CSS, as you learned to do in this lesson, can increase the visual impact your site has upon visitors.

You'll need to select, edit, and optimize your images with an image-editing program. Consider the content of each image when deciding whether to go with GIF, JPEG, or PNG.

Use the techniques you practiced in this lesson to insert graphics into the pages in your own site.

As you incorporate the images, create CSS styles to control placement of the visuals.

Keep the accessibility issues discussed at the beginning of this lesson in mind when you are integrating images into the site.

What You Have Learned

In this lesson, you have:

- Used background image (pages 171–174)
- Placed images with accessibility attributes in the page (pages 175–180)
- Resized images and reset them to their original dimensions (pages 180–181)
- Positioned images (pages 182–183)
- Added a border around an image (pages 184–185)
- Assigned names and `alt` attributes to images (page 185)
- Used the Assets panel to manage images in the site (pages 186–189)
- Managed images with the Favorites List (pages 190–191)
- Adjusted the space around images (pages 191–192)
- Inserted an image placeholder (pages 193–195)
- Cropped an image (pages 196–197)
- Adjusted the brightness and contrast of an image (pages 198–199)
- Created an image map (pages 200–204)

6 Creating Tables

Tables allow you to present information in an organized manner; they contain rows and columns that intersect to form cells in which you can place content. Cells can then be merged to create larger cells. Tables can be used to present a wide variety of content, from tabular data that needs to be presented spreadsheet style to visual treatments with combinations of graphics and HTML text.

Tables can be used to control layout. By arranging content within table cells, you can place objects in specific locations on a page and create more complex visual arrangements. Tables were one of the HTML elements that initially gave designers and developers control over the layout of their sites. Keep in mind, however, that using CSS (Cascading Style Sheets) can be a better method of developing the layout and design of a page because it provides a wider number of layout choices and appearance options while

In this lesson, you'll create tables that contain text and graphics while learning how to augment layouts with tables and use them in conjunction with CSS.

giving designers and developers a better control over the look and feel of the entire site. Table-based layouts are generally more restrictive; you can achieve a greater degree of flexibility with CSS. Additionally, CSS is more efficient, more accessible, and meets the current standards of Web development as defined by the W3C. Because support for the latest CSS can be limited—older browsers in particular have poor support for CSS—tables can still be useful. As a result, and considering that many older sites that you might work with are likely to use tables for design purposes, it is important to understand the concepts and techniques of table-based layout.

If you want to view the final result of this lesson, open index.html from the Completed/Schedule folder within the Lesson_06_Tables folder.

What You Will Learn

In this lesson, you will:

- Learn how to create tables to control the layout of your pages
- Modify the table properties, including border, background, spacing, color, alignment, and size
- Create accessible tables
- Import tabular data from spreadsheets
- Modify a table by adjusting rows and columns
- Sort a table
- Export a table
- Determine the optimal size of your layout
- Create your page design using Layout mode
- Import a tracing image

Approximate Time

This lesson should take about two hours to complete.

Lesson Files

Media Files:

Lesson_06_Tables/Images/…(all files)

Starting Files:

Lesson_06_Tables/schedule/index.html
Lesson_06_Tables/schedule/events.html
Lesson_06_Tables/explorations/poses.html
Lesson_06_Tables/Text/schedule.txt
Lesson_06_Tables/Text/short-schedule.txt
Lesson_06_Tables/Text/events.txt

Completed Project:

Lesson_06_Tables/Completed/index.html
Lesson_06_Tables/Completed/yoga-table.html
Lesson_06_Tables/Completed/schedule/index.html
Lesson_06_Tables/Completed/schedule/events.html
Lesson_06_Tables/Completed/explorations/poses.html

Creating a Table

All content that is contained within a table is always contained within a cell, and every table has one or more cells. A cell is the area created by the intersection of a row and a column. A table must have at least one row and one column, which will create one cell.

Macromedia Dreamweaver 8 provides a variety of tools and options for creating tables. These tools are available through three viewing modes: Standard, Layout, and Extended. Each visual editing mode offers a different perspective on table design and structure while enabling you to create and edit tables.

In this exercise, you will begin to create a page in the Yoga Sangha project site using Standard mode.

Tables versus CSS

In HTML, tables were originally meant as a method to organize information—they were not intended to be a design tool. Over the years, as Web designers worked to develop more visually appealing and functional Websites, the table became a primary tool for layout. As a result, the contents and structure of Web pages have become more dependent upon one another. CSS gives designers the ability to separate the content from the structure of Web pages. This can be beneficial in terms of increasing accessibility and flexibility, decreasing download time, and decreasing the amount of time that is needed to create and maintain pages. Whether you use tables or CSS to control the layout of your Web pages will depend on a number of factors including browser support, how your pages display across different platforms and browsers, and the desired layout. CSS support is becoming more widespread, but it might not yet enable you to create the layout you want. You'll need to consider the requirements of your Website, weigh the options of using CSS and/or tables, test your pages with both, and choose a layout method(s) accordingly.

1. Open index.html from the Lesson_06_Tables/Schedule folder.

This page already contains content, has basic document formatting set, and integrates CSS to control the appearance of page elements—including text and images. You have learned the techniques used to create this page throughout the previous lessons in this book.

Tip *For additional practice, you can re-create this starting page by beginning with a new blank document and using this page as a guide.*

2. Choose the Layout category on the Insert bar and verify that the Standard mode button is selected.

The Standard mode option should be active by default—a highlighted button indicates the active mode. If Standard mode is not the active table mode, click the Standard button.

Tip *You can also check the mode or switch to another by choosing View › Table Mode—a checkmark next to a mode in the menu indicates that mode is active.*

3. Place the insertion point in the empty paragraph between the first paragraph and the horizontal rule and then click the Table button in the Layout category on the Insert bar.

> **Tip** *The Table button is also available in the Common category on the Insert bar. Alternatively, you can choose Insert > Table or use the keyboard shortcut Option+Cmd+T (Macintosh) or Ctrl+Alt+T (Windows) to open the Table dialog box.*

The Table dialog box opens.

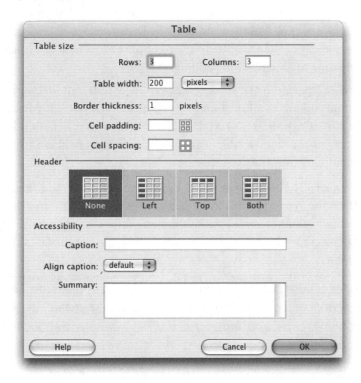

The Table dialog box is split into three sections: Table Size, Header, and Accessibility. The Table Size section contains these options:

- **Rows:** The number of table rows. The Dreamweaver default is 3 if you have not previously created a table.
- **Columns:** The number of columns. The Dreamweaver default is 3 if you have not previously created a table.

- **Table Width:** The width of the table in pixels or as a percentage of the browser window. Tables specified in pixels are good for a precise layout of text and images. Tables specified in percentages are an ideal choice when the proportions of the columns are more important than their actual widths. The Dreamweaver default is 200 pixels if you have not previously created a table.

- **Border Thickness:** The width of the table border. The Dreamweaver default is 1 if you have not previously created a table.

- **Cell Padding:** The amount of spacing between the cell content and the cell walls. If you leave this option blank, cell padding defaults to one pixel. If you don't want cell padding, be sure to type **0** in the text field. The Dreamweaver default is blank if you have not previously created a table. To the right of the text field is a small table that uses blue shading to illustrate cell padding.

- **Cell Spacing:** The amount of spacing between table cells, not including the border. If you leave this option blank, cell spacing defaults to one pixel. If you don't want cell spacing, be sure to type **0** in the text field. The Dreamweaver default is blank if you have not previously created a table. To the right of the text field is a small table that uses blue shading to illustrate cell spacing.

These properties can all be changed at a later time—the options in the Table size section are all available on the Property inspector when a table is selected in the Document window. The default values of these options might be different if you have already used the Table dialog box, in which case the values will be the same as the last values you specified for a table.

Tip *A number of table properties can also be adjusted through the Tag inspector— in a default configuration, the Tag inspector is located between the Application and Files panel groups. You can access the Tag inspector by choosing Window › Tag Inspector.*

The Header section contains four different placement options for headers: None, Left, Top, and Both. A header is essentially a row or column title that is used to label your content. Headers are most often used for data tables (those that function much like spreadsheets) as opposed to design/layout tables (those that are used to arrange and position visual elements for design purposes). The header option uses the scope attribute to make the information that is placed in header rows or columns act as identifiers for each of the cells in their respective rows or columns. For example, if you use the top header option and type **Order** in the top cell of the first column, the remaining cells in that column are prefaced verbally by the word Order when read aloud by a screen reader (a type of browser used by visitors with vision disabilities or situations that prevent them from using a standard browser) to indicate the contents of those cells. The option to make a cell (or cells) into headers is also available through the Property inspector and can be modified at a later time, although this will not set the scope attribute.

It is important to continually consider how accessible your pages will be to your visitors. The goal of creating accessible pages is to develop content that is functional for the widest possible audience, including those with disabilities. Dreamweaver makes it easy to include accessible features from the beginning through the Accessibility section, which includes the following options:

- **Caption:** When you define a caption, it is displayed to all users and can be aligned to the top, bottom, left, or right of the table. If you leave this option blank, no caption is inserted. This option is available only in the Table dialog box. If you want to add this feature at a later time, you need to do so by editing the HTML code, covered in Lesson 16.

- **Summary:** A table summary is not displayed on the page; it is read by screen readers and is used to explain the purpose and context of the table. The summary should provide a concise and descriptive, but fairly brief, synopsis of the material contained within the table. It should indicate what the content of the table is. If you leave this option blank, no summary is inserted. This option can be modified at a later time through the CSS/Accessibility portion of the Attributes tab, which is located in the Tag inspector.

4. Type *2* in the Rows text field and *4* in the Columns text field. Change the Table width to *500* pixels, set the Border thickness to *1*, and leave the Cell padding and Cell spacing text fields blank. In the Header section, select *Top*. In the Accessibility section, type *Class Schedule at Yoga Sangha* in the Caption text field and choose top from the Align caption menu. In the Summary text field, type *Information about the yoga classes available at Yoga Sangha. Each entry includes the day of the week, time, level and instructor for the class.* Click **OK** to close the dialog box.

A table with the properties you specified appears on the page and is automatically selected. A table header—the light gray bar—is attached to the top of the table. Vertical green lines indicating the left and right boundaries of the table are displayed on the sides of the bar. A green line, with the width value of the table and a menu arrow both shown in the center, spans the topmost portion of the bar. At the portion of the bar closest to the table, a series of shorter green lines, each with its own menu arrow, indicates the widths of the columns. The table header disappears whenever you click outside of the table and reappears whenever the table is active or selected. The table header can obscure nearby content above the table. If the table is the first item in your document, the table header can be attached to the bottom of the table. You cannot control where the bar appears.

Tip *You can turn the table header visual aid on or off by selecting View › Visual Aids › Table Widths. A checkmark indicates that the option is turned on; no checkmark indicates that the option is off. You can also turn all visual aids on and off through the same menu or with the use of a keyboard shortcut: Cmd+Shift+I (Macintosh) or Ctrl+Shift+I (Windows). The following exercises assume that you have visual aids, including the table header, turned on.*

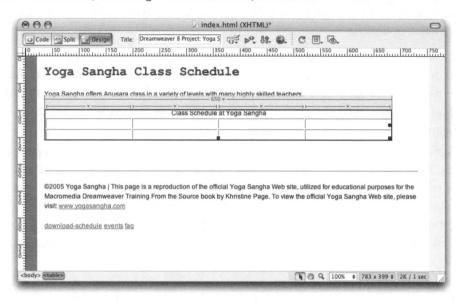

A solid black outline, with selection handles on the bottom and right sides, surrounds the table and the caption, indicating that the table is selected. The two rows and four columns are shown with a gray border, which does not surround the caption. You can see the spacing between the cells as a result of the default cell padding that is applied because the Cell spacing option was left blank.

5. Click in the first cell of the top row and left column. Type *Day* in the cell; then press Tab to move to the next cell. Type *Time* and press Tab. Type *Level* and press Tab. Type *Instructor* in the last cell.

As you type and jump to other cells, the table might automatically shift the widths of the columns to accommodate the text.

You can use the Tab key or the arrow keys to move between cells. Tab is the quickest method to jump to the next cell to the right or down to the next leftmost cell if you are at the end of a row. If you move to a cell that already has content in it, that content is selected when you press Tab.

Because the top row is the header row, the text that you type is centered and rendered in bold (a default property of table headers). You can use CSS to apply additional formatting. For this exercise, leave the headers as they are.

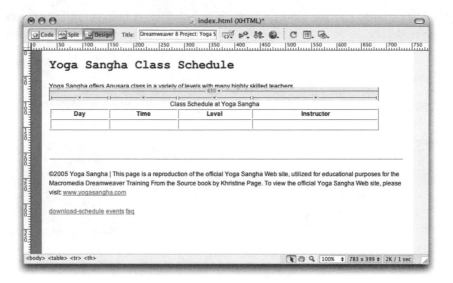

6. Place the insertion point on the blank paragraph line below the table.

Tip *If you do not have a blank paragraph line below the table, click after the table and press Return (Macintosh) or Enter (Windows).*

When you click outside the table, the columns may shift slightly, changing their widths. The insertion point is now in a new paragraph.

You can enter the data for the table by typing directly into the cells. In the next exercise, however, you will use another method to fill the table with the content.

Importing Spreadsheet Data

If you have text in a spreadsheet or even in a Microsoft Word table, you can easily insert that content into Dreamweaver documents. To do so, you need to save a document as a tab- or comma-delimited file to make it compatible with Dreamweaver. You can use tab- or comma-delimited files that have been created using a variety of programs, including Microsoft Excel and Microsoft Word. In this exercise, the tab-delimited text file has already been created for you. You'll import the data into a new table, then transfer the data from the new table into the first table you created.

1. With the insertion point on the new line that you created in the previous exercise in the index.html document, click the Tabular Data button in the Layout category on the Insert bar.

> **Tip** *You can also choose Insert › Table Objects › Import Tabular Data to open the same dialog box.*

Tabular Data button

The Import Table Data dialog box opens.

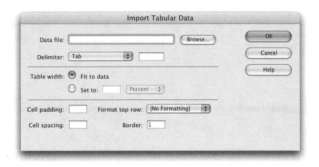

2. Click the Browse button to the right of the Data file text field and choose schedule.txt from the Lesson_06_Tables/Text folder. Leave Tab selected in the Delimiter menu. For Table width, choose Set to, type *500* in the text field, and choose Pixels from the menu. Leave both Cell padding and Cell spacing blank. You should leave Format top row set to (No Formatting), which is the default, and leave Border set to 1. Click OK when you are done.

> **Note** *If Set is selected in the Table width section when you open the Import Tabular Data dialog box, the table width text field for specifying size and /or the measurement selection might be dimmed. If this happens, try switching to the Fit To Data option and then switch back to Set.*

A table is built for you according to the options you just selected, and the data from the tab-delimited schedule.txt file that you are importing has been inserted into that new table.

> **Note** *You can also use a variety of other delimiters, including semicolons and colons, but tabs and commas are the most widely used. Choosing Other from the Delimiter menu displays a text field in which you can type the delimiter of your choice.*

When the second table is selected, the gray bar of the table header can overlap and obscure the lower portion of the first table. Click outside the tables and the table header will disappear.

Copying and Pasting Table Cells

You now have two tables: The first table contains the titles for each column, and the second table contains the data. Now you need to combine the two tables. You can copy and paste multiple table cells at the same time, which preserves the cell's formatting if there is any, or you can copy and paste only the contents of the cell.

Cells can be pasted at an insertion point or by replacing a selection in an existing table. If you want to paste multiple table cells, the contents of the Clipboard (a system feature on both Macintosh and Windows—the Clipboard is not a part of Dreamweaver) must exactly match the structure of the table or the selection in the table that the pasted cells will replace. You can copy one cell and paste it to replace a selected cell, but you can't copy two cells and paste them to replace a single cell. The number and orientation of the cells that you copy must match the number and orientation of the cells you plan to replace. You can paste multiple cells into a single cell, but the end result will be multiple cells, as you'll see in the following.

1. In the index.html document, select all the cells in the second table by clicking the upper-left cell and dragging across the cells to the lower-right cell.

The selected cells are now outlined with black borders. Selecting the cells in this manner selects the cells themselves, not the entire table.

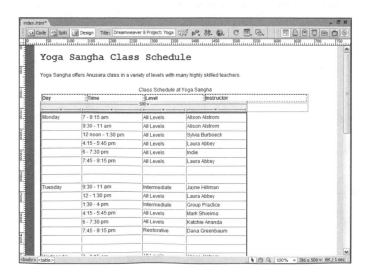

2. Choose Edit › Copy.

Tip *You can also use the keyboard shortcuts Cmd+C (Macintosh) or Ctrl+C (Windows).*

To be cut or copied, the selected cells must form a rectangle. For example, you can't select six cells in the top row and four cells in the bottom row.

3. Click once inside the first cell of the second row in the top table.

You might need to click a visible portion of the top table first or click in an area of the page that is outside both tables to show the bottom row if the table header of the second table obscures it.

This empty cell is where the copied cells will be pasted.

4. Choose Edit › Paste.

Tip *You can also press Cmd+V (Macintosh) or Ctrl+V (Windows) to paste the contents of the Clipboard—the cells you copied in Step 2.*

All the cells from the second table are inserted into the first table. Your first table will now look like the following example.

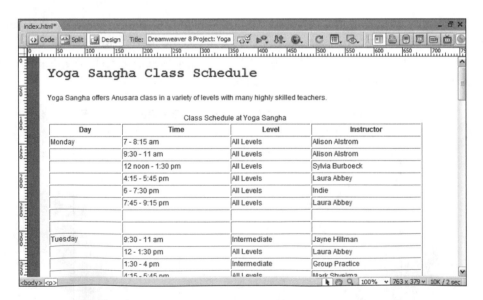

Click outside the table to deselect the cells.

Note *If you are pasting entire rows at the end of a table (as in this exercise), the rows are added to the table. If you are pasting to replace one or more cells, the contents of the selected cell(s) are replaced if the Clipboard contents match the structure of the selected cell(s). If you are pasting outside a table, the rows, columns, or cells are used to define a new table.*

If you need to remove the contents of cells, but want to leave the cells themselves intact, select one or more cells (but not an entire row or column); then choose Edit › Clear or press Delete. If you need to remove an entire row, drag across all the cells in the row to select it and press Delete.

Selecting a Table

Now that all the content from the second table is in the first table, you no longer need the second table. To delete it, you need to select the table first. Dreamweaver provides several methods for selecting a table. You will find that some methods are easier to use than others, depending on the complexity of the table structure.

1. In the index.html document, select the second table by positioning the pointer anywhere inside the table and then selecting the <table> tag in the tag selector in the lower-left corner of the Document window.

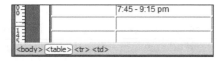

Tip *You can also select a table by clicking the upper-left corner of the table or anywhere on the right or lower edge. The pointer shows a table icon next to the pointer arrow when you are close to the edge. Wait until you see the pointer before you click. Another way to select a table is to click inside the table and choose Modify › Table › Select Table. You can also click the horizontal green table width line that spans the gray bar to select the table.*

Selection handles appear around the table when it is selected, and a black border surrounds the entire table—there are no black borders around any of the individual cells.

Note *If the insertion point is inside the table and the table itself is not selected, you can see the <tr> and <td> tags in the tag selector in addition to the <table> tag. The tag <tr> represents the table row. The tag <td> represents the table data, otherwise known as a cell. Selecting a <td> tag selects the corresponding cell and enables you to make changes to that cell in the Property inspector. You'll learn more about tags in Lesson 16.*

2. With the table selected, press Delete (Macintosh) or Backspace (Windows) to remove the second table.

The second table is gone.

Tip *When the pointer is inside a cell, the keyboard shortcut Cmd+A (Macintosh) or Ctrl+A (Windows) selects the cell. Using the keyboard shortcut a second time selects the entire table.*

Selecting and Formatting Table Cells

You can easily select a row, a column, or all the cells in the table. Earlier in this lesson, you selected contiguous cells—that is, cells that adjoin or touch one another. You can also select noncontiguous cells—those that do not touch—in a table and modify the properties of those cells. You can't copy or paste noncontiguous cells. The following steps demonstrate various selection methods.

You can change several options for each cell, either on an individual basis or for multiple selected cells. These options include background color and alignment.

1. In the index.html document, select noncontiguous cells in the top row of the remaining table by holding down Cmd (Macintosh) or Ctrl (Windows) and clicking the first cell, which contains the text Day. Continue to hold down the Cmd or Ctrl key; click the cell containing the text Level.

When you hold down the Cmd or Ctrl key as you move the pointer over a cell, an outlined square can appear next to the pointer arrow to indicate you are selecting cells.

Both noncontiguous cells should now be selected, as shown by the black borders around the individual cells.

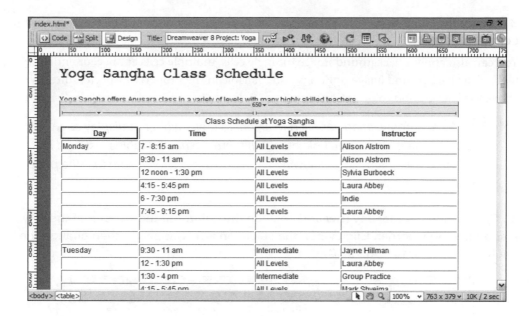

2. Type the hexadecimal code *#CCCCFF* into the Background Color text field on the Property inspector.

Background Color text field

The color of the cells change to the color you selected. You might need to click outside of the table for the change to be applied.

You can change the background color of single cells, multiple cells, or the entire table, depending on what you select. In this step, you changed multiple cells at the same time.

Notice that the Header option on the Property inspector is checked. Earlier in this lesson you set the header row to top—all cells in this row are formatted as headers. You should leave this option checked for all cells in the top row.

Note *To change the background color of the entire table, select the table and use the Background Color box on the Property inspector to choose a color for the table, or type the desired hexadecimal code into the corresponding text field.*

3. Select the noncontiguous Time and Instructor cells; change their background colors to #9999CC.

You can also apply a background image to single cells, multiple cells at once, or entire tables. The background image option is also available in the Property inspector, directly above the background color option.

Note *A background image applied to an entire table might not display as expected if the table has multiple cells or if there are nested tables inside of it. Always test your pages by previewing them in browsers to be sure that the page appears as you expect.*

4. Click inside the Monday row and position the pointer at the left end of the row, just on the table border. Click when the selection arrow appears; then change the background color to #6699CC.

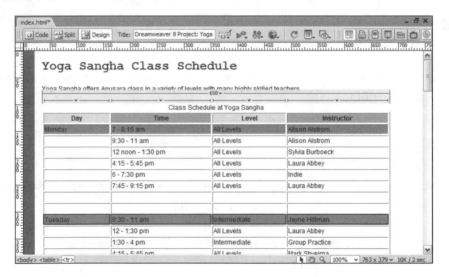

You might need to roll the pointer up and down the left border of the table to get the selection arrow to appear. As you place the cursor in position, all the cells in that row will become outlined in red. The selection arrow is a quick way to select a single row or column in a table. If you can't get the selection arrow or the red outlines to appear, try clicking the left border of the row. When you click the border, all cells in the table become selected and are displayed with black outlines.

5. Continue to change the color of other rows that contain the day names to match the example.

The rows now alternate between white and blue.

Note *You can also quickly format tables with alternating colored rows automatically. Choose Commands › Format Table to open the Format Table dialog box, which allows you to select from a variety of preset formatting options as well as customize the appearance of your table through color, style, alignments, and alternate row options. However, the Format Table command will not work on tables that have captions, such as the one you've been working with in this lesson.*

6. Place the insertion point within the table, then select the Instructor column by clicking the green column width line that spans that column on the gray table width bar.

You have selected the entire column.

Tip *You can also select the Instructor column by clicking the top cell of the column, holding down the Shift key, and clicking the bottom cell in that column.*

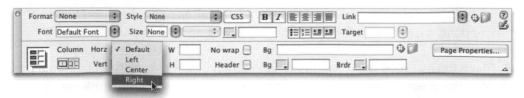

The default setting for horizontal alignment does the same thing as the left setting—it aligns the contents of the selected cells to the left. The default setting for vertical alignment does the same thing as the middle setting—it aligns the contents of the selected cells to the middle. Because the top row is a header row, the contents of those cells are automatically centered.

7. In the Property inspector, change the horizontal alignment of the entire Instructor column to Right.

The contents of all cells in the Instructor column are now aligned to the right.

The lower half of the Property inspector contains the following cell attributes:

- **Merge:** Combines two or more selected cells into one cell.
- **Split:** Divides a single cell into multiple cells.
- **Horizontal:** Sets the horizontal alignment of the cell's contents to the browser default (browser defaults are usually left for regular cells and center for header cells) or to left, right, or center.
- **Vertical:** Sets the vertical alignment of the cell's contents to the browser's default (usually middle) or to top, middle, bottom, or baseline.
- **Width And Height:** Sets the width and height of selected cells in pixels. To use percentages, follow the value with a percent sign (%).
- **No Wrap:** Prevents word wrapping; cells expand in width to accommodate all data. Normally, cells expand horizontally to accommodate the longest word and then expand vertically.
- **Header:** Formats the selected cell(s) as a table header. The contents of table header cells are bold and centered by default.
- **Background Image (the top Bg option):** Sets the background image for the cells.
- **Background Color (the bottom Bg option):** Sets the background color for the cells. Cell backgrounds appear inside the cells only—that is, the background does not flow over cell spacing or table borders. If your cell spacing and cell padding are not set to 0, gaps appear between the colored areas even if the border is set to 0. If you want to prevent these gaps, you should apply color to the entire table or set cell spacing and cell padding to 0.
- **Border:** Sets the border color for the cells.

You might need to click the expander arrow on the right side of the Property inspector if you do not see these options. You will work with some of these options in the following exercises.

Sorting a Table

You can perform a simple table sort by sorting on the contents of a single column. You can also perform a more complicated sort by sorting on the contents of two columns. You can't sort tables that contain merged cells. The following exercise demonstrates sorting.

1. Open the poses.html document in the Lesson_06_Tables/Explorations folder, select the table, and choose Commands > Sort Table.

The Sort Table dialog box opens.

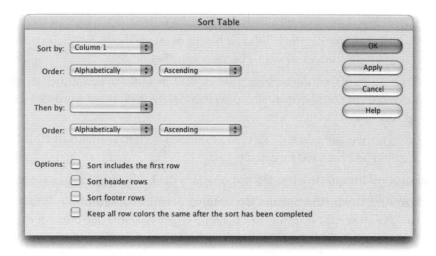

2. Set the following options.

Sort By: Select the column to sort. For this exercise, select Column 1 (default).

Order: Specify whether you want to sort the column alphabetically or numerically. For this exercise, select Alphabetically (default). This option is important when the contents of a column are numerical. An alphabetical sort applied to a list of one- and two-digit numbers results in an alphanumeric sort (such as 1, 10, 2, 20, 3, 30) rather than a straight numeric sort (such as 1, 2, 3, 10, 20, 30). Choose Ascending (A to Z or low to high) for the sort order (default).

Then By: For this exercise, leave it blank (default). Then By lets you choose to perform a secondary sort on a different column. The sort methods in the menu are the same as the methods that are available in Sort By.

Sort Includes The First Row: This option allows you to specify whether the first row is included in the sort. If the first row is a heading that shouldn't be moved, leave this checkbox unchecked (default). For this exercise, however, you should check this option.

Sort Header Rows: For this exercise, leave this option unchecked (default).

Sort Footer Rows: For this exercise, leave this option unchecked (default).

Keep All Row Colors The Same After The Sort Has Been Completed: If you changed any attributes for a row, you can retain that attribute in the row by choosing this option. Suppose that you sort a table with a color in the first row. After sorting, the data in the first row moves to the second row. If this option is selected, the color moves with the data to the second row. If this option is not selected, the color remains in the first row. For this exercise, leave this option unchecked (default).

3. Click OK.

The table is now sorted alphabetically using the data in the first column. Save your document.

Modifying a Table

After you create a table, you might find that it is too large or too small, or you might need to add columns and rows. You can adjust these table properties easily.

1. In the index.html document, select the table and change the Width value on the Property inspector from 500 to *650*. Press Return (Macintosh) or Enter (Windows) to apply the change.

You have enlarged the table.

Note   *You can also adjust the size of the table by moving the pointer over the bottom or right edges of the table border. When the pointer changes to a two-headed arrow, drag the column border to adjust the table to the desired size. You can see the new width by selecting the table and looking at the number in the Width text field in the Property inspector. Use caution when dragging a border of a table to change its size. Whenever you drag table borders in this way, Dreamweaver automatically assigns and updates widths and/or heights. Sometimes, this may not be what you want. If you want to get rid of the widths or heights, press the Clear Column Widths and Clear Row Heights buttons in the Property inspector. You can also use the Clear All Heights and Clear All Widths commands in the table width menu accessible from the gray bar at the top of the table.*

2. Click in the right cell of the last row of the table (the lower-right cell) and then press Tab.

If the pointer is in the last cell of a table, pressing Tab causes the insertion point to be placed in the leftmost cell of a new row.

Tip *You can also add new rows and columns by choosing Modify › Table and selecting one of the following options: Insert Row (inserts one row above the current row), Insert Column (inserts one column to the left of the current column), or Insert Rows or Columns (this option allows you to choose whether to insert rows or columns, specify the number of rows or columns that should be inserted, and to select where those rows or columns will appear). You can also add new columns by clicking the green line spanning a column on the gray bar and choosing Insert Column Left or Insert Column Right.*

3. In the left cell of the row you just inserted, click and drag to the right to select all the cells in the row. Click the Merge Cells button in the Property inspector.

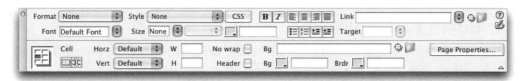

The four cells now form one long cell that spans four columns. Any attributes of the first cell, such as color and alignment, are applied to the merged cell.

Note *You can split cells in the same manner by clicking the Split Cell button in the Property inspector or by choosing Modify › Table › Split Cell. This method returns the number of cells to the original number if you merged them, or it can split a cell into any number of rows or columns.*

You can merge any number of cells in one column or any number of cells in one row. You can also merge cells in multiple rows and columns, but the cells to be merged must form a rectangle. You can't merge cells to create an L shape.

Tip *To merge cells, you can also choose Modify › Table › Merge Cells. The keyboard shortcuts for merging rows are Option+Cmd+M (Macintosh) or Ctrl+Alt+M (Windows). Pressing just the M key also merges the selected cells.*

4. In the cell you have just merged, type © 2006, Yoga Sangha.

Merging cells gives you a great deal of additional options for layout.

Note *If you need to delete a row, click the row and then choose Modify > Table > Delete Row. You can also Ctrl-click (Macintosh) or right-click (Windows) on the table and choose Table > Delete Row from the context menu.*

5. With the insertion point in the last row of the table, choose Modify > Table > Insert Rows or Columns. In the Insert Rows or Columns dialog box that appears, choose Rows from the Insert options, type *1* in the Number of rows text field, and choose Above the Selection in the Where options. Click OK.

The Insert Rows or Columns dialog box allows you to specify whether to insert before or after the current row. When you use this dialog box, you have control over where the new rows or columns are placed, and you can insert any number of rows or columns.

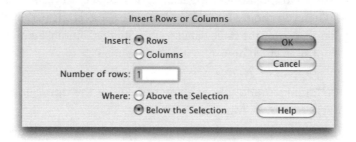

Note *If you choose Modify > Table > Insert Row, the new row is inserted above the current row by default. You can also Ctrl-click (Macintosh) or right-click (Windows) the row above and choose Table > Insert Rows Or Columns from the context menu.*

This new row you have inserted acts as a spacer between the copyright and the information about the class schedule above it. Giving each section or block of information on your page a little space helps the viewer to differentiate between the text on the page—it is difficult to read information when there is a lot of text that all runs together.

Exporting a Table

If you need to extract information from a table to place in a database, a spreadsheet, or a word-processing or page-layout application, you can't just copy and paste the text. All you get is text with no row and column formatting. But you can export the table and save the file as a tab-delimited file that most word-processing and spreadsheet applications can read.

1. In the poses.html document, select the table.

You will export the selected table from Dreamweaver into a new file in the following steps.

2. Choose File > Export > Table.

The Export Table dialog box opens.

3. From the Delimiter menu, choose Tab (default).

Most word processing and spreadsheet applications can read both comma- and tab-delimited tables. When you choose File > Export > Table, Tab is selected by default. Your choices of delimiter values for the table data are Tab, Space, Comma, Semicolon, and Colon. If you are not sure which option to use, choose Tab.

4. From the Line Breaks menu, choose line breaks for the operating system you are using (default): Windows, Macintosh, or Unix.

Line breaks are the characters inserted at the end of each line. You worked with them in Lesson 2 when you imported text. When choosing which type of line breaks to use, select the operating system for which you are exporting the file. You might need to choose an operating system other than your own if the file will be used on a different platform.

5. Click Export. In the dialog box that opens, name the exported file *yoga_poses.txt* and save it in the Lesson_06_Tables/Text folder.

The entire table is exported to a new file with the name you chose. The file you created is a plain text file. If you have Excel or Word, you can import the information into those programs using the delimited ASCII format. Check the documentation included with those programs for details on how to import such files.

Using Images in Tables

Tables are often used to construct the layout of a page with multiple images or to reassemble an image that has been sliced. An image can be sliced into several smaller images for it to be optimized for the Web (the process of optimizing includes decreasing the file size of the image while maintaining the highest possible image quality). The resulting pieces need to be aligned with each other using a table. Many graphic editing programs, such as Adobe Photoshop and Macromedia Fireworks, allow you to designate slices that are exported automatically along with the creation of the necessary table in a corresponding HTML document.

In this exercise, you'll create a table that can be used on pages in the Yoga Sangha project site. This same layout can be done with the use of CSS—which you'll work on creating throughout the remainder of the book.

1. Create a new HTML page, save it as *yoga-table.html* in the Lesson_06_Tables folder, and title it *Yoga Sangha*.

This page will contain a number of tables.

2. Create a new table with the following settings: 5 rows, 4 columns, 754 pixels wide, 0 Border Thickness, 0 Cell Padding, and 0 Cell Spacing. Set the Header to None, leave the Caption text field blank, and type *Yoga Sangha Content* in the Summary text field.

Tip *Each time you use the Table dialog box, Dreamweaver will automatically populate all options with the same values as you used for your last table.*

The table you create should look like the following example.

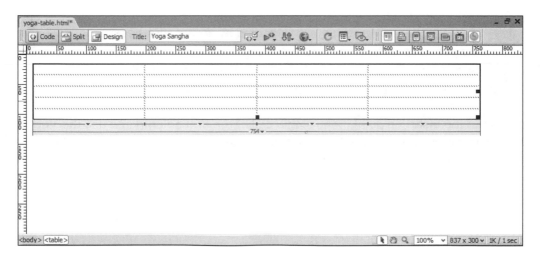

Note *Be sure to type the number 0 into the Border, Cell Padding, and Cell Spacing text fields. Leaving these fields blank will result in an actual value of 1 for both the Cell Padding and Cell Spacing fields.*

3. Select all five cells in the first column and merge them. In the second column, select and merge the two cells in the second and third rows from the top. In the fourth row, select and merge the two cells in the second and third columns. In the fifth row, select and merge the two cells in the second and third columns. In the fourth column, select and merge the two cells in the fourth and fifth rows.

Your table should now look like the following example.

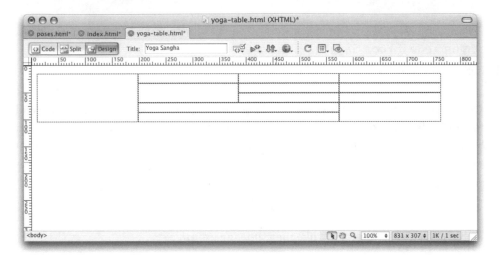

Tip *The structure of your table is represented by dotted lines because you defined the border as 0. With the cursor positioned over the green line that spans the with of the table in the gray Table Width bar, you can press Cmd (Macintosh) or Ctrl (Windows) to see the table structure displayed in a solid red line.*

4. Place the insertion point in the single cell of the first column and use the Vert menu on the Property inspector to change the vertical alignment of the cell to Top. Insert into the cell the green-bar.gif from the Lesson_06_Tables/Images folder. In the Image Tag Accessibility Options dialog box, choose **<empty>** from the Alternative text menu and leave the Long description field as-is.

The green bar you just inserted will now stay at the top of this column, regardless of how tall the table eventually becomes.

This image serves as a visual design element, so alternative text is unnecessary. As mentioned in Lesson 3, avoid specifying alternative text for images that serve only layout or design purposes. Such images should use the <empty> option—do not leave the Alternative text field blank.

When you insert images into cells in Dreamweaver, the empty cells have a tendency to collapse and look as if they are no longer there. They are actually still there, but they have just been squished together. You can see this happen if you click outside of the table or into another cell. You should not try to resize the cells at this point. When cells become squished together, you have several options for moving through the tables. Avoid dragging the borders of your table and its columns and rows in these cases—instead, navigate through tables using the arrow keys as well as the Expanded Tables mode, which you will learn to do in the following steps.

5. Click the Expanded button in the Layout category on the Insert bar.

Tip *You can also use the keyboard shortcut F6 to turn this mode on and off, or switch modes by choosing View › Table Mode and selecting the desired viewing mode from the submenu.*

An introductory dialog box, Getting Started In Expanded Tables Mode, appears. You can click OK to close the dialog box when you are done reading it.

A bar that reads "Expanded Tables Mode [exit]" appears across the top of the Document window, just under the toolbar, to indicate that the Expanded Tables mode is active. You can return to Standard mode by either clicking the [exit] link on the bar or the Standard button in the Layout category on the Insert bar.

The Expanded Tables mode appears to enlarge your tables slightly and simultaneously gives the illusion of increasing the border, cell spacing, and cell padding. These appearance changes happen only in this mode—no actual changes are made to the size of your table or the properties of border, cell spacing, and cell padding. This mode does not represent the way tables appear in browsers. Given the distortion that occurs when viewing your page in this mode, you should refrain from making any size changes to your tables in this mode. If possible, resize tables in Standard mode.

6. Place the insertion point in the second column of the first row and use the Horz menu on the Property inspector to change the horizontal setting of the cell to Center. Insert above-nav.jpg from the Images folder. In the Image Tag Accessibility Attributes dialog box, select <empty> from the Alternative text menu and leave the Long description field as-is.

This image, now located in the center cell of the top row, is a minor graphic for visual effect for the Yoga Sangha site. Using the alternative text to communicate the same message that is contained in the image is an important step. If it doesn't convey any information, choose the <empty> option.

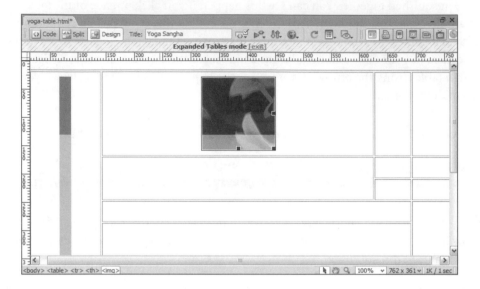

7. Click to place the insertion point in the cell that is located in the first row of the third column. Insert yoga-s-header.jpg from the Images folder into the cell. Use *Yoga Sangha* as the Alternative text.

Because the Expanded Tables mode is active, you can easily click inside the cell.

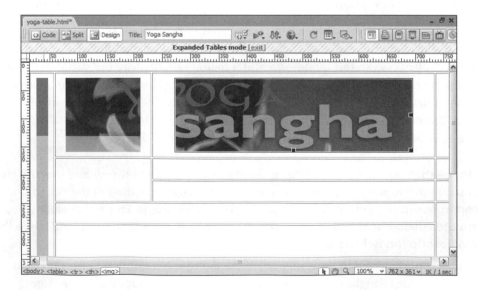

Note *If you were using Standard mode, you could still navigate through a collapsed table by using the arrow keys. To do so, you would select the title image Yoga Sangha and press the right arrow key once to move off the image. The insertion point would then be in the cell that contains the nav_titlebar.gif image, directly to the right of that image. At the right edge of the image, you would see a blinking cursor the same height as the image. You would press the right arrow key once more to move into the next (third) column and then use the down arrow key once to move the insertion point into the third row. When columns collapse completely, it can be difficult to see the blinking cursor between the dotted lines that indicate the boundaries of the cells. Refrain from dragging the borders of the table and resizing it to see columns that have collapsed. Resizing your table changes its dimensions by adding height tags and width tags. The dimensions defined by those tags could create problems, such as causing the images to not line up flush with each other. If height or width tags are created, you can select the table and click the clear row heights and clear column widths buttons on the Property inspector. You might need to redefine the width of the table after clearing column widths. After the pointer is in the correct cell, typing a small amount of text causes the cell to expand, which might help you see the columns more clearly. If you use this method, it is very important to be sure that you delete the text or replace it with the appropriate text or image(s). Extra characters can cause problems in some tables, particularly if you've calculated the table size solely for specific images.*

8. **Click to place the insertion point in the cell that is located in the first row of the fourth column. Insert om.jpg from the Images folder into the cell. Use** *OM* **as the Alternative text.**

The image now appears in the cell.

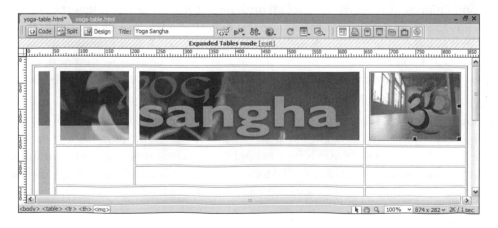

9. Click the Standard button in the Layout category on the Insert bar to switch back to Standard mode.

In Standard mode, the columns now align flush with the images. In the following exercises, using Standard mode allows you to see how the tables and images work together to create a seamless layout. You need to make sure that extra spaces don't get worked into the tables you create, which is difficult to watch for in Expanded mode because that viewing mode causes additional spacing.

As you insert images, if your tables contain images that line up flush with one another as they do in this table, they might obscure the dotted lines separating the individual cells.

> **Note** *As you work with tables, keep in mind that the dotted lines, which Dreamweaver uses to indicate the cell and table borders, each take up one pixel of space. Those extra pixels of space created by the dotted lines do not exist when the document is seen in a browser. However, those pixels of space might cause tables viewed within Dreamweaver to look slightly larger than they really are. For example, you might have two tables of the same width in a document. The first table might have five columns, and the second table might have only one column. The first table would appear in Dreamweaver to be four pixels wider than the first, even though both tables would be the same width if viewed in a browser. You can always turn off table borders by choosing View > Visual Aids > Table Borders. On the other hand, table borders are generally very useful, and it can be very difficult to work with tables when you have them turned off.*

10. Place the insertion point in the cell located in the second row of the third column, and insert flower.jpg with ‹*empty*› alternative text. Place the insertion point in the cell located in the third column and third row, and insert tag-bkg.jpg with ‹*empty*› alternative text. Place the insertion point in the cell located in the second column that spans the second and third rows of the table. Insert the image cell-nav.jpg from the Images folder into the cell. Place the insertion point in the cell that is located in the fourth column, second row and insert teaching.jpg with *Teachers at Yoga Sangha* for the alternative text. In the cell below that one, insert class.jpg with *Classes at Yoga Sangha* for alternative text. Click outside the table.

When you click outside the table, Dreamweaver causes the table to refresh, and the cells now fit exactly around the edges of the images. At times you might need to make use of a spacer image—often a small, one-pixel by one-pixel GIF that can be either transparent or the same color as the background—which is used to hold the dimensions of rows and columns in tables that are necessary to create the final look of a page. Tables often need images to force them to hold the dimensions you want. Without an image to hold that space, your columns may shift around. You can use spacer GIFs (usually 1×1 pixel transparent files) stretched to fill the dimensions you want to ensure your columns size correctly.

Tip *When working with small images in tables, using the arrow keys can make it easier to navigate through the tables as you're creating and modifying them.*

Your table now looks similar to the following example.

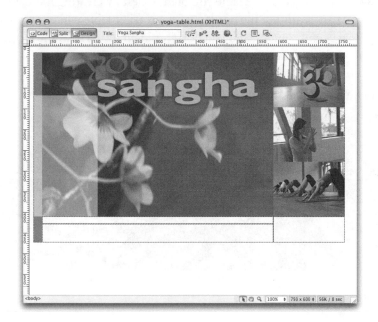

Tip *If your table doesn't look like this, it may be that Dreamweaver is adding spaces to your cells. Open the Preferences dialog box, select the Code Format category, and verify that No Break After TD is checked.*

Nesting Tables

A nested table is one that is placed within the cell of another table. Nested tables are used for a variety of purposes. In the earlier days of the Web, nesting tables was usually considered a bad practice because of the problems it caused (sometimes crashing a viewer's browser, for example). These days, however, browsers are capable of a great deal more. Nested tables are commonly used to create pages that otherwise have to use one incredibly complicated table or not be able to use the intended design at all. Nesting tables allows you to create more complex layouts and keep each of your tables as simple as possible. The more complex a single table is, the harder it is to create and the more likely it will be to break or have other viewing problems in browsers.

1. In the yoga-table.html document, click outside the table you created in the previous exercise and press Return (Macintosh) or Enter (Windows). Create a new table with the following properties: 2 rows, 1 column, 176 pixels wide, 0 Border, 0 Cell padding, and 0 Cell spacing. Set the Header option to None, leave the Caption text field blank, and type *Schedule of Classes* in the Summary text field. Click OK.

It is often easier to put together the table you plan to nest by creating it outside the larger table because you can clearly see the borders of the smaller table while you are inserting the necessary images and content, and you don't accidentally click in the larger table as you're trying to work with the smaller one.

2. Place the insertion point in the second row and type *Schedule*.

Your small table should now look like the following example.

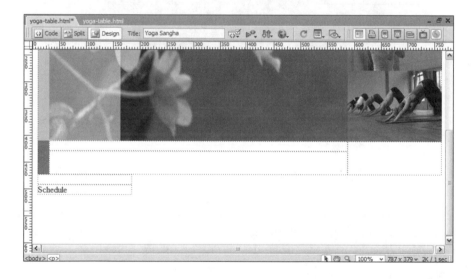

3. Press Tab to add a row below the last one. Click the Split Cell into Rows or Columns button on the Property inspector, choose Rows from the Split Cell Into section, and type *7* into the Number Of Rows text field.

Split Cell into Rows or Columns button

You have prepared the table and are now ready to insert the content into the cell you just split.

4. Using the short-schedule.txt document from the Text folder, copy and paste the text using one row for each day.

Tip *There are a variety of ways to approach tasks such as this within Dreamweaver, and the method you choose will depend on circumstances such as how the data is formatted. For example, another way to import the text is to save the .txt file as a delimited file and import it as a table. You can then copy and paste the cells to replace those in the current table, or modify the imported table to match the one you are creating in this exercise.*

Each row represents one day.

Your table should now look like the following example.

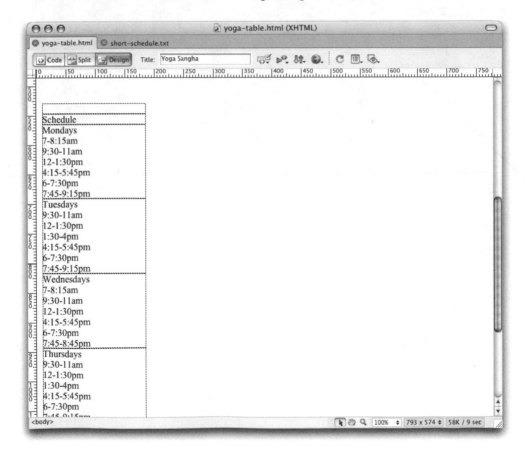

5. Select the table you've been working with containing the class schedule table and choose Edit > Cut. Place the insertion point into the cell located in the fourth column and fourth row of the table that you created in the previous exercise and choose Edit > Paste.

Your document should now look like the following example.

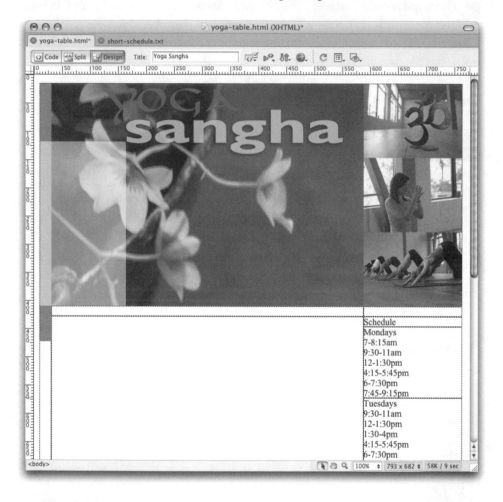

The smaller table is now nested into the first table. In this exercise, you have nested a table to simplify the layout of the large table.

Try to avoid nesting tables more than five or six levels deep. Keep in mind that older browsers—especially older versions of Netscape—might have difficulty displaying too many levels of nested tables (sometimes due to the increased memory required to display those nested tables). To determine whether the nested tables you create will work correctly for your visitors, you need to test your pages in a variety of browsers on different platforms.

Don't get in the habit of creating extraneous nested tables. Nesting is a good technique that can be used to achieve cohesive, advanced layouts, but it should be done in a carefully considered and purposeful manner. If you find yourself nesting many levels of tables, you should probably rethink your layout. A simpler layout means that less code is created, which makes it more likely that the page will download quickly and there will be less potential for problems. If you end up with an improper display in a browser, multiple levels of nested tables can also make it more difficult to find the cause of those errors in the code.

Designing for Computer Screens

In the print world, a designer creates pages to be viewed in final form at a fixed size. The paper stock, printing quality, and size are all controlled. A Web designer, on the other hand, has to account for a greater number of possibilities. You have to consider not only the variety of browsers users might have but also the size and resolution of their monitors. The number of screen types on which users can view Web pages has increased and will continue to do so. Users view Web pages on computers, TVs, cell phones, PDAs (such as the Palm), and more.

If you have only text on a page, the text reflows within the page based on the size of the browser window. As a Web designer, you then have no control over the look of the page. The user can maximize the window, making long and hard-to-read lines. If you want to control the flow of the text on the page, you can place your text within a table or use CSS to limit line length for text in a cell.

When you design a page with a fixed width, you might want to design to the lowest common denominator of monitor sizes that your audience will be using. If you think most of your users have 13-inch monitors, you should use that size. Remember that the browser takes up some room to the left and right of the screen, even if the user maximizes the window. There is no set rule for the amount of room a browser uses, so you should allow for the browser. For 13-inch monitors, for example, make the maximum page width 600 pixels (not accounting for space taken up by the browser and operating system). To determine the maximum page width, refer to the following chart.

Resolution (in Pixels)	Device
160×160	Palm-type device
240×320	Pocket PC
544×372	Web TV
640×240	Windows CE
640×480	13-inch monitor
800×600	15- to 17-inch monitor
1024×768	17- to 19-inch monitor
1200×1024	21-inch monitor

Note *The visitors' need to be able to print Web pages is important to consider. It is particularly important to make your pages printable or provide printer-friendly versions for pages with a great deal of text or pages that viewers will be likely to need to print. The dimension for a printable page is 535 pixels. Although tables provide quick and dirty layouts, printing is one of the many reasons to consider using Cascading Style Sheets (CSS). It offers more flexibility in design; and gives you the ability to create specify CSS files used only for printing, allowing you to ensure that your layout is printer-friendly.*

Using Window Size to Check Layout

You can check your layout directly within Dreamweaver to determine what your page will look like on different-sized screens using the Window Size menu.

At the bottom of the Document window, click the black arrows located to the right of the current window size dimensions. Choose 760×420 (800×600 Maximized).

Windows Users: You must first click the Restore/Maximize button on the Document window—not the Restore/Maximize button for the entire application. The Document window will reduce to a floating window in the document space. You can only adjust the window size in this view. You can switch back to the tabbed interface after this exercise by clicking the Document window Restore/Maximize button again.

The Document window resets to 760 × 420. This size accounts for the space taken up by the browser and operating system on a screen at the 800 × 600 resolution.

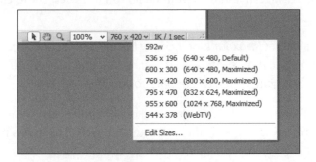

Tip *You can also add your own size presets to the list by choosing Edit Sizes at the bottom of the menu.*

As you change the size of the Dreamweaver Document window, you'll notice that the dimensions in the window size change to reflect the new size.

Creating a Table in Layout View

Dreamweaver 8 also provides Layout mode for creating tables. Layout mode works much like a page-layout program in which you can draw boxes on the page and then fill the boxes with text or graphics. You can resize the boxes and place the boxes anywhere on the page.

Some Dreamweaver features such as layers (covered in Lesson 9) do not function in Layout mode—you must use Standard mode when you need to use those features.

Note *In Layout mode, the exact numeric values of the widths and heights of the table and cells you create, as well as the placement of those cells, will be somewhat different from the examples shown here. Use the examples as guides for the general layout of your page.*

1. Open events.html from the Lesson_06_Tables/Schedule folder.

You will use the Layout mode to create a table in this document in the following steps.

2. Click the Layout button in the Layout category on the Insert bar.

You have switched to Layout mode, in which you can easily place elements on the page. You may see the info box titled Getting Started In Layout Mode which briefly describes the main tools: the layout cell and the layout table. You can click OK to close this dialog box.

Note *There is a checkbox for Don't Show Me This Message Again. If you leave this box unchecked, the next time you restart Dreamweaver, you will see this dialog box again if you switch to Layout mode.*

A bar, with the text Layout Mode [exit] centered on it, appears just below the Document window toolbar, appearing to be within the document itself. This bar is not visible in the browser because it is used only in Dreamweaver to indicate that you are working in Layout mode. As with Expanded mode, you can switch back to Standard mode by either clicking the Standard button in the Layout category on the Insert bar or by clicking the [exit] link that appears on the bar across the top of the document while in Layout mode.

Tip *You can also choose View > Table Mode > Layout Mode or use the keyboard shortcut Cmd+F6 (Macintosh) or Ctrl+F6 (Windows) to switch to Layout mode.*

3. Make sure that the Insert bar is displaying the Layout category and click the Draw Layout Cell button.

After you select the Draw Layout Cell tool, the pointer changes to a plus sign (+) when you move it into the Document window. The tag selector is replaced with a description of the tool you have selected.

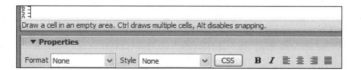

A layout cell lets you draw a cell anywhere on the page. In Layout mode, you don't need to worry about the number or arrangement of rows and columns when creating your table—Dreamweaver automatically creates and manages the rows and columns when you designate the location of the cells on your page.

Note *You can't use the Layout Table tool to draw a table within the cell of another table in Layout mode. You must use Standard mode to nest tables.*

4. Place the pointer in the center of the page; then click and drag to draw the cell.

A layout table is drawn automatically to contain the cell. The layout table is drawn nearly as wide as the Document window, although you can resize the table to any dimensions.

The cell is outlined in blue to distinguish it from the table, which appears outlined in green. A solid blue line indicates that the insertion point is within the cell, whereas a dotted blue line indicates that the insertion point is not in the cell. All parts of the table other than the cell are shown in gray. The thin white lines indicate the rows and columns that Dreamweaver creates to construct the table when you draw layout cells. When you move the pointer over the border of the cell, it turns red to indicate which cell you are over.

By default, layout tables appear with a tab at the top, which makes it easier to identify the table. The tab causes the table to drop down slightly from the top of the page; this extra space does not exist in the browser. The table also appears with a bar at the bottom containing column widths and menus and the table width and menu. The bar, which serves the same purpose as the table header bar in Standard mode, might not be initially visible until you roll the pointer over the bottom boundary of the cell that you just created.

Note *To hide the tab and bar, choose View › Visual Aids › Table Widths. The rest of this lesson assumes that the default visual aids are active and that you can see the tab and bar on the layout table.*

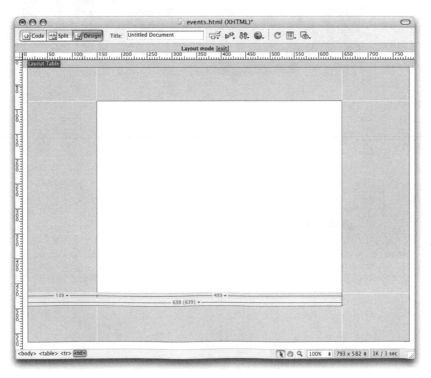

5. Insert the yoga_sangha-title.jpg graphic from the Lesson_06_Tables/Images folder into the layout cell you just drew. Use *Yoga Sangha* for the alternative text.

Tip *From the Site portion of the Image Assets panel, you can just select and drag the graphic from the Assets panel into the cell on the page.*

You have inserted an image. The cell expands to fit the graphic if it was smaller than the size of the graphic. The new size is displayed in parentheses next to the original size of the column on the table widths bar.

Note *The table widths bar might disappear when you insert the image. To view it again, roll the pointer over the bottom edge of the cell.*

Modifying Table Layout

As you design your pages in Layout mode, you will want to move, resize, or add new cells while adding content. A layout cell cannot overlap other cells and cannot be moved outside the layout table.

1. In the events.html document, select the cell by moving the pointer over the border and clicking the border when it turns red.

The cell border turns blue and handles appear. Drag the handles to resize the cell.

Tip *You can also Cmd-click (Macintosh) or Ctrl-click (Windows) within a cell to display the resize handles.*

2. If the cell is larger than the image, use the handles to drag the cell border to resize the cell, fitting it closely around the graphic. The cell should be the same size as the graphic.

Tip *Use the selection handle on the lower-left corner of the cell to adjust the size if the table widths bar is obscuring the other selection handles on the bottom of the cell. Alternatively, you can use the keyboard shortcut Cmd +Shift+I (Macintosh) or Ctrl+Shift+I (Windows) to hide all visual aids—turn the visual aids back on by repeating the command when you are done resizing the cell.*

On the Table tab, the size listed in the parentheses replaces the old size display. If the cell you initially created was smaller than the size of the graphic, the cell will have enlarged automatically to fit around the image exactly, and you don't need to resize it. If the cell you created was larger than the graphic, you must resize the cell to make sure that the borders of the layout cell line up flush with the edges of the image.

3. Click on the border of the cell (not on the resize handles) and drag the cell, moving it to the top and center of the page.

If you moved the cell to the right or left to center it, notice that the column numbers in the surrounding layout table change to display the new size.

4. Use the arrow keys to move the cell to the left.

The arrow keys move the cell one pixel at a time. Hold down the Shift key to move the cell 10 pixels at a time. Leave some space in the column between this cell and the side of the table.

5. Choose the Draw Layout Cell tool again, and draw three more cells in a single column down the middle of the page below the top cell, with a little space between them.

Your page should look similar to the example shown here. Don't be concerned about the sizes of the columns listed on the table width bar; they vary according to the exact placement of your layout cells.

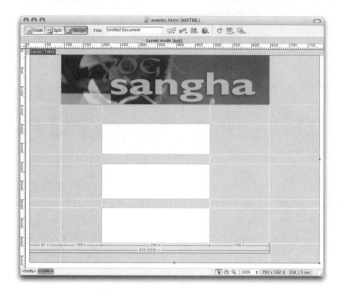

When you draw a cell on the page, white guides appear to help you place other cells that you want to align with the first cell. Use the horizontal guides to align the tops of the cells.

Tip *To draw multiple cells without clicking Draw Layout Cell more than once, hold down Cmd (Macintosh) or Ctrl (Windows) as you draw the first cell. You can continue to draw new cells until you release the modifier key.*

6. Of the three cells you just created, expand the topmost cell so it's as wide as the cell that contains the yoga_sangha-title.jpg graphic. Open events.txt from the Lesson_06_Tables/Text folder. Copy the first header line and the paragraph below it, paste the text into the first cell below the yoga_sangha-title.jpg graphic.

The cell expands if necessary to fit the content.

7. Insert the om.jpg image from the Lesson_06_Tables/Images folder into the empty cell beneath the one you pasted the text into. Adjust the cell so it is the same size as the image and move it to the center of the page. Copy the remaining text from the events.txt file and paste it into the last cell.

Your page should now look similar to the example shown here.

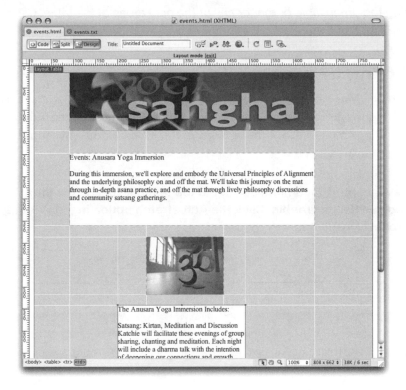

Applying Cell Formatting

As with Standard mode, you can change several table attributes, including cell color and alignment.

In the events.html document, select the cell above the om.jpg by clicking the cell border. Type the color code **#FFCC99** into the Background Color text field in the Property inspector. Set the background of the cell for the second text cell to the same color.

The color of the cell changes to the color you selected. Be sure to select the cell so you can see the selection handles, as opposed to placing the insertion point inside the cell.

Note *To change the background color of the entire table, select the table by clicking the green table border or any of the gray areas of the table. Click the Bg color box and choose a color for the table.*

Specifying Layout Width

In Layout mode, you can control the width of tables in two ways: You can set a fixed width, which is the default, or you can use Autostretch, which causes the cells to change width depending on the width of the browser. In this exercise, you will control the width by applying Autostretch.

1. In the events.html document, select the top text cell just below the yoga_sangha-title.jpg graphic. Click the Autostretch option in the Width area on the Property inspector.

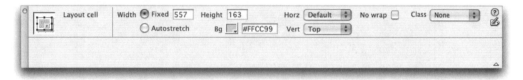

The Choose Spacer Image dialog box appears if a spacer image is not associated with your site.

In the dialog box that appears, choose Use an existing spacer image file, click OK, and locate spacer.gif in the Lesson_06_Tables/Images folder. The spacer file location will be saved with your preferences. To change or remove the spacer image, choose Dreamweaver > Preferences (Macintosh) or Edit > Preferences (Windows) and select the Layout Mode category and adjust the spacer image settings for the Yoga Sangha site.

Note *The Choose Spacer Image dialog box includes an option to create a spacer image file. If you are working on a site for which there is no existing spacer image, you should choose this option and click OK to navigate to the directory in which you want Dreamweaver to save the spacer image. The Images folder is the best place.*

The Autostretch column is displayed in the table widths bar as a zigzag line—you might have to scroll down to the bottom of the document to see it. Dreamweaver inserts spacer images to control the layout of the fixed-width columns when you select Autostretch. A spacer image controls the spacing in the layout, but is not visible in the browser window.

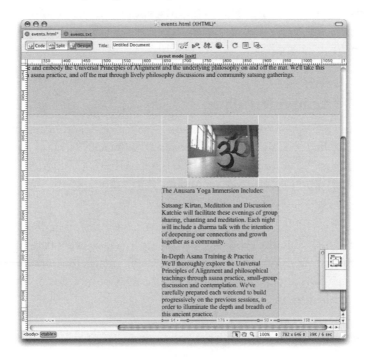

Tip *You can also click a column's menu on the table width bar and choose Make Column Autostretch to apply the Autostretch option.*

2. Save and view the page in the browser; then change the width of the browser.

Notice that the column stretches as you change the width. When you select a column to Autostretch, you cause all cells in that column to Autostretch. Use the white guides on the page to determine whether another cell is within the column you selected.

If you choose not to use spacer images, columns change size or even disappear if they do not hold content. You can insert and remove spacer images yourself or let Dreamweaver add them automatically when it creates an Autostretch column. To insert and remove these images yourself, choose one of the following options from the column-header menu:

- **Add Spacer Image:** The spacer image is inserted into the column. You do not see the spacer image, but the column might shift slightly.
- **Remove Spacer Image:** The spacer image is removed, and the column might shift.
- **Remove All Spacer Images:** Your whole layout might shift slightly or dramatically, depending on your content. If you do not have content in some columns, they might disappear.

The column menus are contextual and change depending on which column you select. All three preceding options are not available in all columns.

You can close the events.html document.

Using a Tracing Image

At times, you might be given pages that someone else has designed in a graphics program (such as Macromedia FreeHand, Adobe Photoshop, or QuarkXPress) or you may have a screen shot of a page. If you can convert the design to a JPEG, GIF, or PNG graphic, you can import that image into Dreamweaver and use it as a guide, or tracing image, to re-create the HTML page.

The tracing image is visible only inside Dreamweaver. It is not embedded in the HTML code and is not displayed in the browser. The tracing image appears behind everything on your page in Dreamweaver. While you're using a tracing image, the background color or background image of your page is hidden, but that background color or image displays when you look at the page in a browser.

1. Open the layout.html document from the Lesson_06_Tables folder and switch to Standard mode.

In this exercise, you'll insert a tracing image into this document.

2. Choose View › Tracing Image › Load.

The Select Image Source dialog box opens.

3. Choose the file design_trace.jpg, located in Lesson_06_Tables/Images; then click Choose (Macintosh), or OK (Windows).

The Page Properties dialog box opens.

4. Select the Tracing Image category. To see your image on the page, click Apply. Drag the Image Transparency slider to the left to lighten the image to 50 percent. Click Apply to see the change.

You want to be able to see the image but not be distracted by it.

5. Click the Appearance category in the Page Properties dialog box and set the Left, Right, Top, and Bottom margins to 0. Click OK to close the Page Properties dialog box.

Dreamweaver simulates the margin between the edge of the browser window and the items in the page. If you change this margin in the Page Properties dialog box, Dreamweaver uses the margin options you specify to place the tracing image. The default margin (used if the margin text field is left blank) can vary depending on the browser, but it is approximately seven pixels.

Note *You can change the position of a tracing image by choosing View › Tracing Image › Adjust Position and specifying the x and y coordinate values. If you move the tracing image into the space reserved for the margin, as defined in the Page Properties dialog box, the coordinate values appear to be negative numbers. Choosing View › Tracing Image › Reset Position returns the tracing image to the top-left corner of the Document window with margin space (0 + margin, 0 + margin). Choosing View › Tracing Image › Align With Selection aligns the tracing image with the selected element. The top-left corner of the tracing image is aligned with the top-left corner of the selected element.*

6. Type *Download the latest schedule of classes at Yoga Sangha* at the top of the page.

Notice that the text is displayed with the tracing image behind it. A tracing image can be your guide while you lay out a page. The use of a tracing image emphasizes how it is helpful to have a clear and thought-out plan for the way your page will appear ahead of time.

You can save and close all open documents.

What You Have Learned

In this lesson, you have:

- Created a table in Standard mode (pages 209–215)
- Imported tabular data from an external document as a Dreamweaver table (pages 215–219)
- Modified the table properties including border, background, spacing, color, alignment, and size (pages 220–225)
- Sorted the information in a table (pages 226–227)
- Modified a table by adding and merging rows and columns (pages 227–229)
- Exported a Dreamweaver table to an ASCII text file that other applications can read (pages 229–230)
- Created a table in which you inserted a variety of images (pages 230–237)
- Nested tables by placing one table inside another table (pages 237–241)
- Learned how the variety of screen sizes and screen resolutions can affect how you determine your page layout (pages 241–243)
- Used tables to lay out your pages in Layout mode (pages 243–252)
- Imported a tracing image to use as a guide for layout (pages 252–254)

7 Using Multimedia

Multimedia elements, including Macromedia Flash and QuickTime movies, can help expand the content offered through your site. With the use of these elements, you can include animation and video media to get your message across to your site's audience.

In this lesson, you will create Web pages that incorporate Flash and QuickTime movies.

If you want to view the final result of this lesson, open index.html in the Completed folder within the Lesson_07_Multimedia folder.

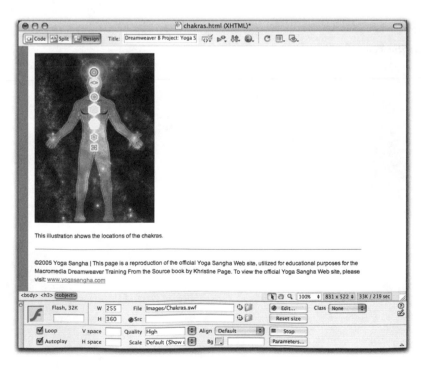

In this lesson, you'll create a page similar to this one while you learn to incorporate multimedia elements on your pages.

What You Will Learn

In this lesson, you will:

- Work with Flash text to quickly create text in a variety of fonts and sizes
- Insert buttons and animations from Flash
- Develop a slideshow using the Image Viewer
- Incorporate a QuickTime movie in a page

Approximate Time

This lesson should take approximately one half hour to complete.

Lesson Files

Media Files:

Lesson_07_Multimedia/Images/Chakras.swf
Lesson_07_Multimedia/Images/Videos/

Starting Files:

Lesson_07_Multimedia/index.html

Completed Project:

Lesson_07_Multimedia/Completed/

Creating Flash Text

When you add a heading to your page, you can use text and differentiate it from body text in some way—such as formatting it as a heading tag—or you can create a graphic and insert it into the page. Text has the advantage of loading on the web page quickly, but the appearance is limited, even with Cascading Style Sheets (CSS). Using graphics as headings solves the problem of lack of available fonts, but you might not have access to a graphics program or you might not have enough time to create the graphic you need.

Flash text provides the best of both these options. You can use any font you choose and create the text directly within Dreamweaver. The text you create is saved as a small Flash file—these files use the extension .SWF.

Tip *Although creating and working with Flash text is quick and easy, you should always consider whether your audience is likely to have the correct plug-ins before adding it to your site.*

1. Open the index.html document in the Lesson_07_Multimedia folder. Position the insertion point on a new blank paragraph line below the text *Welcome to Yoga Sangha* **near the top of the document. Click the Media menu on the Common category of the Insert bar and select the Flash Text option from the menu.**

Make sure that you don't click the Flash or Flash Button options. This exercise deals with creating Flash text. The Flash option enables you to insert Flash movies into your page, whereas the Flash Button option lets you create buttons—both of which are different from Flash text.

The Insert Flash Text dialog box appears.

2. Set the following options.

- From the Font menu, choose Comic Sans MS. If Comic Sans MS is not available, choose another font.

- In the Size text field, type *22.*

- Use the Color box to choose the *#FFCC00* orange color.

- In the Text window, type *Welcome to Yoga Sangha.*

- For Rollover color, type *#FFFFCC.*

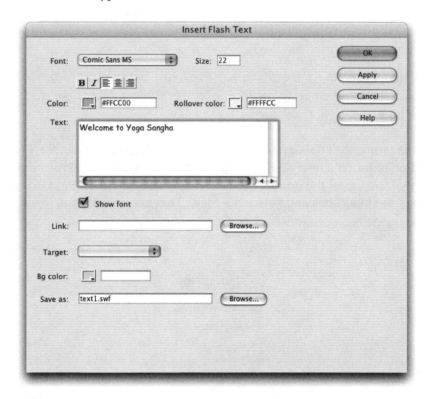

3. In the Save as text field, type *welcome.swf* and then click **OK.**

The Insert Flash Text dialog box closes, the Flash text appears in the Document window, and the Flash Accessibility Attributes dialog box appears.

Note | *Initially, a default filename is automatically included in the Save as text field. This default name is generated with a numeric identifier: text1.swf, text2.swf, and so on. It's recommended that you replace the generic name with one that is descriptive of the Flash text file you are creating. The default location to save the Flash text is in the same folder as the HTML file into which you are inserting the Flash text, although you can save it into another folder (such as an images folder or a media folder) if you prefer.*

4. Type *Welcome to Yoga Sangha* into the Title text field, and click OK.

The other options include Access key and Tab index—you'll learn more about both in Lesson 11.

The Flash text appears in your document. The Property inspector reflects the attributes of the welcome.swf Flash text file.

5. In the Document window, select the Flash text and resize it by dragging one of the handles.

It doesn't matter what size you make the Flash text. Because the text is vector-based Flash text and not normal body text or a bitmap graphic, you can resize it directly in the Document window. You can increase or decrease the image size without concern about loss of image quality.

Although you can resize graphics within Dreamweaver, it is not recommended because you won't be able to adjust the resolution. You can, however, resize the Flash text image that you create because it is a vector graphic. Vector graphics retain the integrity of the image when scaled; bitmap graphics (such as GIF files and JPEG files) do not.

Tip | *Hold down the Shift key to constrain the proportions while you resize the Flash text.*

6. You can now delete the original Welcome to Yoga Sangha text located above the Flash text. Save the file and preview it in the browser.

The text appears as it did in Dreamweaver.

Note | *You can also set a link and rollover color on Flash text. The Play button on the Property inspector will enable you to see such effects directly within Dreamweaver. You'll work rollovers and other interactive elements in Lesson 8.*

Modifying Flash Text

Changing Flash text objects within Dreamweaver is easy. You might need to change these text objects if you have to rephrase the text, use a different font, or otherwise adjust the content.

1. In the Document window, double-click the Flash text.

If you can't select the text, first click Stop in the Property inspector.

The Insert Flash Text dialog box opens.

2. Change the options to your liking and then click Apply to see the results of your changes. When you finish, click OK to close the Insert Flash Text dialog box.

The edited Flash text is refreshed on the page, and the SWF file is updated.

Adding Flash Buttons

You can achieve special effects by using Flash objects such as text, buttons and movies. Because Flash graphics are vector-based, their file sizes can be very small, which helps them load more quickly than the equivalent graphic files in the user's browser. Similar to Flash text, you do not need to have Flash to create Flash buttons—you can develop them directly in Dreamweaver.

Flash buttons have several states, depending on the position of the pointer and whether the mouse button has been clicked. The first state is the appearance of the button when the pointer is not on it. The second state occurs when the pointer is on the button, but the mouse button has not been clicked. The third state occurs when the pointer is on the button, and the mouse button has been clicked. You can create and maintain Flash buttons in Dreamweaver from a set of pre-made button styles.

1. In the index.html Document window, position the insertion point at the beginning of the line Email:info@yogasangha.com near the bottom of the document.

You'll insert a Flash button on this page.

2. From the Common category of the Insert bar, click the Media menu and then select the Flash Button icon.

The Insert Flash Button dialog box opens.

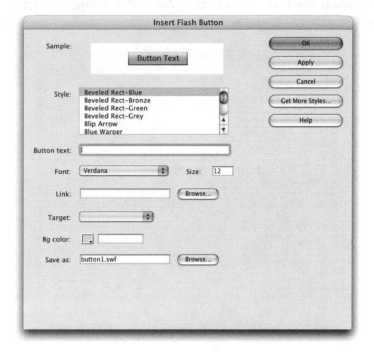

3. In the Style list, scroll down and select Glass-Silver. In the Button text text field type *Email*. Leave the Font and Size options at their defaults: Verdana and 12 respectively.

A sample area at the top of the dialog box shows a preview of the button style. You can move the mouse over this sample image to see how it will function.

You can edit these settings later, if necessary. The next exercise shows you how.

Note *In this exercise, you leave the optional Link text field blank.*

4. Click the Bg color text field and enter #FFFFCC.

The background color hexadecimal code #FFFFCC represents the background color that will be used for the button. To make the button appear seamlessly on your page, you would instead select the same color as was used for the background of the page.

5. In the Save as text field, type *email-button.swf*; then click **OK** at the upper right of the dialog box. In the Flash Accessibility Attributes dialog box, type *Email* into the Title field.

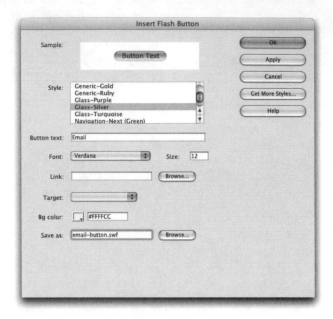

You should always name your Flash button files and provide clear accessibility information. If you don't, Dreamweaver automatically assigns generic names.

Tip *The preview does not change dynamically as you alter the settings; it only shows the button style. If you want to view the button as you make changes, you need to click the Apply button so that you can see the changes in the Document window.*

The Insert Flash Button dialog box closes, and a button with the specifications you set appears in the document. Because you just inserted the button, it is selected.

6. With the button still selected, click the Play button in the Property inspector.

Clicking Play allows you to see the Flash button effects in the Document window. The button appears as it will in a browser, and the selection handles disappear. The Play button becomes a Stop button.

7. In the Document window, move the pointer over the Main button; then click the button.

The button changes to its rollover state when the pointer is moved over it. The button changes to its clicked state—a different visual appearance—when clicked.

8. Click Stop in the Property inspector. Save the file and preview it in the browser.

The button changes states just as it did in Dreamweaver, depending on the pointer position and mouse click.

Modifying Flash Buttons

You can easily change many of the button attributes at any time.

1. In the Document window, double-click the Flash button you created.

The Insert Flash Button dialog box opens.

2. Make changes in the Flash button settings. Set the options however you want.

Change the font to Arial, for example.

3. Click Apply to see the changes. Click OK when you finish.

You can add your own template buttons to those in the Style list by using Flash to create SWT Generator Template files outside Dreamweaver. To add these files to Dreamweaver, you need to open the Dreamweaver program folder and place them in the Configuration > Flash Objects > Flash Buttons folder.

Adding Flash Animations

Using Flash, you can create vector-based graphics, animations, and movies. Unlike bitmap graphics such as GIF files and JPEG files, vector graphics use mathematical formulas to create the images and objects that you see.

You can add Flash animations to your documents as easily as you can add any bitmap image, provided that the animation already exists. You can't create these kinds of animations directly within Dreamweaver—you must use Flash. For this exercise, an animation that was created in Flash is provided for you.

1. Open the chakras.html document from the Lesson_07_Multimedia folder. Add an extra paragraph above the text and place the insertion point on the new line.

Be sure to use a paragraph return, not a line break. You need a new text block.

2. From the Common category of the Insert bar, click the Media menu and select the Flash icon. In the Select File dialog box, select Images/Chakras.swf and then click the Choose button (Macintosh) or Select button (Windows).

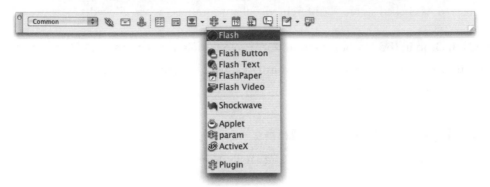

Similar to images, you can also insert a Flash animation from the Assets panel.

3. In the Object Tag Accessibility Attributes dialog box, type *chakras* into the Title menu.

The Flash animation is placed on the page.

4. In the Property inspector, make sure that the boxes for Loop and Autoplay are checked. Click Play to view the animation in Dreamweaver.

To view animation files in Dreamweaver, click Play. Click Stop when you are done testing.

> **Tip** *You can resize animations by dragging their selection handles. Hold down the Shift key to constrain the proportions.*

5. Click Stop on the Property inspector. Save the file and preview it in the browser.

Autoplay causes the Flash animation to begin playing as soon as the page is loaded into the browser. The animation plays repeatedly because you chose Loop in the Property inspector.

> **Tip** *Always be sure to select a SWF file when you insert a Flash animation. Do not insert FLA or .SWT files because they do not show up in a browser.*

Using the Image Viewer

Flash Elements enable you to quickly add interactivity to your pages. The Image Viewer Flash Element creates a slide show interface that you can use to present a series of images. This interactive presentation format, which can be configured easily within Dreamweaver, gives you a variety of options including the ability to set captions and links for each image in the slide show.

Note *The Image Viewer is the only Flash Element that Dreamweaver 8 initially contains. Additional Flash Elements may be created in the future by Macromedia or third-party developers and made available through the Developers Exchange on the Macromedia Web site.*

1. Open yogastudio.html from the Lesson_07_Multimedia/about folder. Choose the Flash Elements category on the Insert bar, and click the Image Viewer button.

The Save Flash Element dialog box opens.

2. Type *yogastudio* into the Save as text field and save the file into the Lesson_07_Multimedia/about folder.

The Image Viewer Flash Element file is saved, and Dreamweaver automatically adds the required SWF extension. If the new file yogastudio.swf does not immediately appear in the Files panel, click the Refresh button at the top of the panel to update the list of files.

The Image Viewer appears in the Document window as a large gray placeholder with the Flash icon in the center.

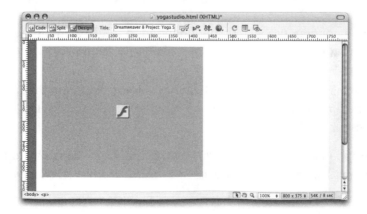

3. Click the Play button on the Property inspector.

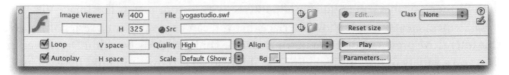

The Image Viewer now appears in the Document window with default settings. A control bar is located at the top of the Image Viewer, which contains a blank area to the left for a title; a text field that displays the number of the current image and allows the user to type in a number and jump to a different image; and three buttons: Back, Play/Stop, and Forward. Below the control bar is the image area.

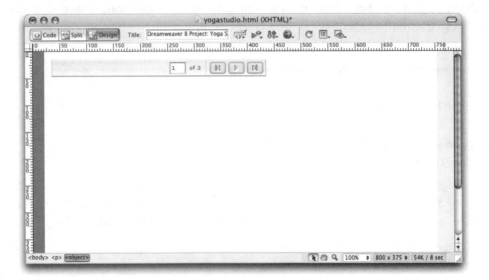

4. In the Tag inspector, whose title bar changed to read **Flash Element** when you selected the Image Viewer, click the Color picker for **frameColor**, and choose the **#666666** gray.

You will do the majority of the configuration for the Image Viewer in the Tag inspector, which opens automatically when the Image Viewer is inserted and displays the initial default settings for this Flash Element.

Tip *If the Tag inspector is collapsed, click the Expand/Collapse button to the left of the name to expand it. If you do not see the Tag inspector, choose Window > Tag Inspector.*

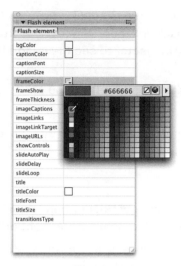

The frameColor option determines the color of the border that outlines the Image Viewer. The control bar uses several different shades of gray, and the #666666 gray color matches the darker shades. After you select a color, the Flash Element might automatically switch back to the placeholder image in the Document window. In the following steps, you'll continue to configure the Image Viewer before making it visible in the Document window again.

5. In the Tag inspector, click the (No) value for the frameShow option to make menu buttons available. Choose (Yes) from the menu that appears.

The frameShow option turns the border option on for the Image Viewer.

6. In the Tag inspector, click the value field for frameThickness and change it to *1*; then press Return (Macintosh) or Enter (Windows) to apply the change. Click the Play button on the Property inspector to see the Image Viewer again in the Document window.

The border is now set to a width of one pixel and you can see the gray outline around the Image Viewer.

The background color of the Image Viewer, defined by the bgColor option in the Tag inspector, is set to white by default. You should leave the background color set to white for this exercise.

7. Click the value field for the imageURLs option in the Tag inspector; then click the Edit Array Values button that appears at the right of the text field.

The imageURLs option defines the images that the Image Viewer will contain. You need to use this option to specify the location of the images.

Note *A series of values in Flash Elements is called an array. The Image Viewer uses arrays for the image, caption and URL options.*

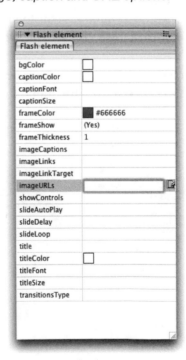

The Edit 'imageURLs' Array dialog box opens.

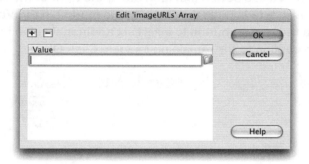

8. With the cursor placed in the line for the first item, click the folder icon that appears to the right of it. Use the Select File dialog box to browse to the Lesson_07_Multimedia/about/Images folder and select studio_photo.jpg.

The values, which are the paths to the images, will be contained in single quotes—these quotes must be included for the Image Viewer to work properly.

Note   *If the Edit 'imageURLs' Array dialog box shows any images in the Value list when you first open it (perhaps in the form 'img1.jpg'), delete them all before adding the studio_photo images by selecting each one and clicking the minus (-) button.*

9. Click the plus (+) button to another value field and select the studio_photo2.jpg image. Continue to add additional value fields and set their sources to studio_photo3.jpg, studio_photo4.jpg, studio_photo5.jpg, studio_photo6.jpg, and studio_photo7.jpg. Click OK to close the Edit 'imageURLs' Array dialog box.

Tip   *You can also press the Tab key to create add another item to the list when the insertion point is in the last value.*

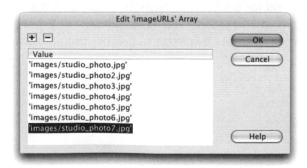

You now have seven images defined in the Image Viewer.

10. Click the value field for the imageCaptions option in the Tag inspector; then click the Edit Array Values button that appears at the right of the text field. Type *'Yoga Sangha'* (be sure to include the single quote marks) in the Value text field. Press Tab or use the plus (+) button to insert six additional value fields while adding the same caption to the remaining images. Click OK.

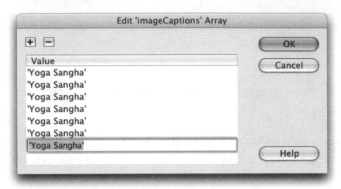

Similar to the image values, the captions must be contained in single quotes for the Image Viewer to work properly.

When creating captions you need to add captions text in the same order that the images were added. If your image and captions are not listed in the same order, your captions, if different from one another, might not match up correctly with their corresponding images.

Note *You can control the font color as well as the font face and size of the captions using the captionColor, captionFont, and captionSize options on the Tag inspector, respectively. For this exercise, you should leave the caption-formatting options at their default settings.*

11. Click the value field for the title option in the Tag inspector; then type *Yoga Studio* into the text field and press Return (Macintosh) or Enter (Windows). Click the Play button on the Property inspector to see the Image Viewer again in the Document window.

The title is placed in the space on the left of the control bar.

Note *You can control the font color as well as the font face and size of the title using the titleColor, titleFont, and titleSize options on the Tag inspector, respectively. For this exercise, you should leave the title formatting options at their default settings.*

By default, the transitions between images are set to Random. You can modify the transition effect and choose a single transition by clicking the transitionsType value text field and choosing an option from the menu. Leaving the transition value set to Random for this exercise will allow you to see the different transition effects when you preview the page in a browser or use the control bar buttons to view the images in Dreamweaver.

Your document should now look similar to the following example.

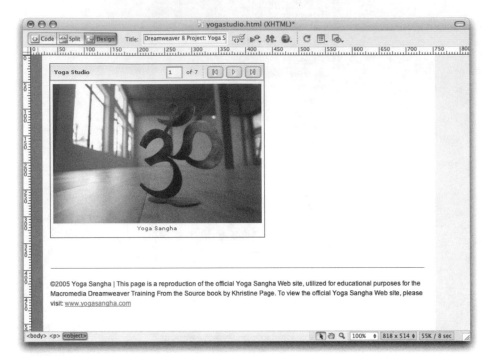

Note *You can add, change, or remove links associated with the images by clicking the imageLinks value text field and then clicking the Edit Array Values button. The Edit 'imageLinks' Array dialog box is similar to the ones you used to set the images and captions. Each URL must be contained by single quotes. Just as when you added captions, you need to take care to add links in the same order of the images so that the links correspond with the appropriate images. Targets define where the links will be opened and can be set through the imageLinkTarget option, the default is _blank, which causes the links to open in a new window.*

12. **Click off of the Image Viewer in the Document window to deselect it. Save the document, preview it in the browser, and test the Image Viewer.**

You can close the yogastudio.html document when you are done viewing it in the browser.

Note *You can change the size of the Image Viewer through the Property inspector.*

Embedding Quicktime Movies

QuickTime is a popular, widely used format for video on the web that is available for both Macintosh and Windows. QuickTime movies can be straightforward videos, or they can include interactive elements including Flash, as well as interactive QTVR (QuickTime Virtual Reality) movies with 360-degree panoramas. You can insert QuickTime movies as easily as you can insert Flash movies.

1. Open pose-demo.html from the Lesson_07_Multimedia/explorations folder and place the insertion point on the blank line below the first header in the document. Select the Common category on the insert bar, click the Media menu, and choose the Plugin option.

Dreamweaver treats QuickTime movies as plug-ins.

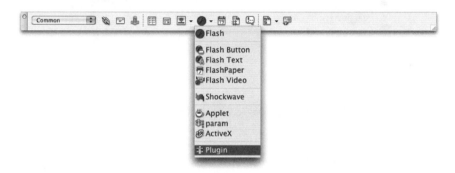

The Select File dialog box opens, enabling you to choose the plug-in.

2. Locate the file Lesson_07_Multimedia/explorations/Videos/Yoga1.mov and click Choose (Macintosh) or OK (Windows) to select it.

The plug-in is embedded into the page using the <embed> tag, at a default size of 32 × 32 pixels and appears in the Document window as a gray square with a plug-in icon in the center.

3. With the plug-in selected, use the Property inspector to change the width to *320* and the height to *256*.

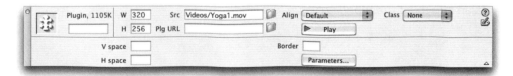

The standard dimensions of small QuickTime web movies that are made for the web are 320 pixels wide by 240 pixels tall. The QuickTime controller is 16 pixels tall, so you need to add 16 pixels to the height of the movie. Sometimes when you insert movies, they might appear cropped or the controller might seem to be missing. In these cases, try enlarging the amount of space allotted to the movie by increasing the width and height. When inserting your own movies, be sure to obtain the correct dimensions of the movie and add an additional 16 pixels for the controller.

4. **With the plug-in selected, click the Parameters button on the Property inspector.**

The Parameters dialog box opens.

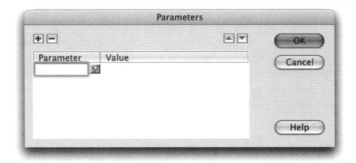

5. **Click in the Parameter column and type** *controller* **into the text field. Macintosh users should press Tab once; Windows users should press Tab twice. Type** *true* **and then click OK.**

Parameters define the properties of the movies. Specifying a controller parameter with the value as true will include the QuickTime controller beneath the movie. You can set the value to either true or false. In the case of the controller, true will turn the controller on, whereas false will turn it off. If you do not specify the controller parameter with a value of true, your visitors may not see a controller.

> **Note** *Another parameter that you can set is autoplay, which will define whether your movies start after the page is loaded or are dependent upon the visitor pressing Play. To define this parameter, you would need to add an item to the Parameters list, type* autoplay *in the parameter text field and type either* true *or* false *into the corresponding value text field.*

6. Click in the Document window outside the plug-in to deselect it. Save and preview the document.

It's always a good idea to let your visitors know how to use the materials that you include on your Web site.

You can click the Play button on the Property inspector to view the movie in the Dreamweaver Document window, or you can preview the page in the browser. You must have the QuickTime player installed on your machine to view QuickTime movies. You can obtain the free QuickTime player at Apple's website: http://www.apple.com/quicktime.

You can save and close the pose-demo.html file.

What You Have Learned

In this lesson, you have:

- Created Flash text (pages 257–259)
- Modified Flash text (page 260)
- Added and modified Flash buttons (pages 260–263)
- Added Flash animations (pages 263–264)
- Used the Image Viewer to create a slideshow (pages 265–272)
- Incorporated a QuickTime movie on your page (pages 273–275)

8 Adding User Interactivity

Interactivity and user feedback are important components of Websites that can bring about a variety of benefits when integrated effectively. These benefits include helping your visitors better understand the content and purpose of your site, assisting users to more easily and directly navigate your pages, and providing visitors with a more enjoyable and productive user experience.

There are many ways to bring interactivity to a Website. Dynamic and database-driven pages, Macromedia Flash, and Quick Time Virtual Reality (QTVR—movies that support 360-degree panoramas and interactive components) are a few examples of the many tools that can be used to create interactive pages. One of the most common and effective tools for creating interactive Websites is JavaScript, which is used primarily for client-side scripting; that is, the scripts are included on the Web pages and processed by the browser. Other scripts, including those used by Java Server Pages (JSP) are server-side scripts—they are processed by the server and delivered to the user.

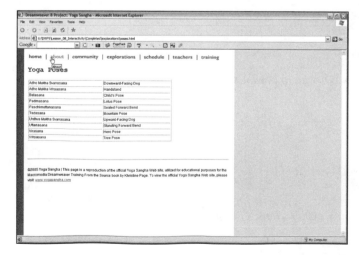

In this project, you will create rollovers with images that are already on the page and learn how to make more than one image on the page change at the same time.

Macromedia Dreamweaver simplifies the process of using standard JavaScript functions by providing *behaviors* — prewritten JavaScript code routines that you can easily incorporate into your Website. A behavior combines a user event (such as moving the pointer over a graphic button in the browser) with an action or series of actions that take place as result of that event. You can use behaviors to add interactivity to your pages, enabling your users to receive feedback based on their actions, and to change or otherwise control the information they see. In this lesson, you will use Dreamweaver behaviors to create rollovers, new browser windows, and menus. Dreamweaver includes a number of predefined behaviors; you can extend Dreamweaver by obtaining additional behaviors or, if you are proficient with JavaScript, you can create your own behaviors.

To see examples of the finished pages: open Completed/explorations/poses.html and Lesson_08_Interactivity/Completed/explorations/meditations.html.

What You Will Learn

In this lesson, you will:

- Create rollovers
- Add user interactivity to your pages by using behaviors
- Add multiple behaviors to one user action
- Add behaviors to image maps
- Create a status bar message
- Redirect users based on the version of their browser
- Open a new browser window
- Create a pop-up menu

Approximate Time

This lesson should take about two hours to complete.

Lesson Files

Starting Files:
Lesson_08_Interactivity/explorations...(all files)

Completed Project:
Lesson_08_Interactivity/Completed/explorations...(all files)

Inserting a Rollover Image

One of the most common uses of JavaScript on Web pages is to create a *rollover*—an image that changes when the user moves the pointer over it. Rollovers combine the use of two images within the same space. When a visitor first arrives at a page that uses rollovers, those image combinations are displayed in their original states. As the pointer moves over the rollover image, a new image is swapped into its place. The new image is sometimes referred to as the *on* or *over* state of an image. As the user rolls the pointer off of the image, it can either swap back to the original image or remain changed. A rollover is a basic application of interactivity—it gives the user a response to the act of moving the pointer over the image. This response is often a visual effect to the existing image, such as lighting up a button, highlighting a tab, or changing the apparent depth to make a navigational element appear active. The rollover response can also incorporate additional information into the new image such as a description or explanation of content.

Website interactivity primarily concerns the user experience; it is what occurs between the visitor and the Website. Interaction requires an action and a response—it is a two-way communication process. Incorporating interactivity into your pages—designating the response that your site gives to visitor's actions—can bring more complexity and depth to the experience of visiting your site. Websites that encourage action or participation are likely to be more successful, functional, and memorable—to have a greater impact upon the visitor—than those in which the user is stuck in a passive situation.

You can create rollovers in Dreamweaver without ever looking at the HTML or JavaScript code. A rollover is a simple behavior that is included in the Common category of the Insert bar. When you use this method, Dreamweaver creates the behavior behind the scenes.

1. Open poses.html from the Lesson_08_Interactivity/explorations folder. Click in the first empty cell of the table at the top of the Document window. From the Common category of the Insert bar, select the Rollover Image button from the Images menu.

The Insert Rollover Image dialog box opens.

Dreamweaver steps you through the process of creating rollovers in this dialog box. If you haven't already placed the images that you want to create rollovers from on the page, you might prefer this method because it enables you to insert an image and define it as a rollover at the same time. In the next exercise, you will create rollovers for images that have already been placed on the page.

Tip *Alternatively, you can choose Insert > Interactive Images > Rollover Image to insert a rollover image using the same dialog box.*

2. In the Image name text field, type *home* for the image name.

This field is used to name the image. If you don't name your rollover images, Dreamweaver will assign generic names automatically in a numeric order: Image1, Image2, and so on. When creating your Web pages, it is helpful if you make a standard practice of giving all rollovers specific and meaningful names that clearly indicate what they are for. When naming your images, don't use spaces or any special characters, and do not begin the name with a number; any of these actions can cause problems with scripting and your rollovers might not function properly as a result.

3. Click the Browse button next to the Original image text field and select home.gif in the Lesson_08_Interactivity/explorations/images folder.

This image appears on the page before the user rolls over it.

4. Click the Browse button next to the Rollover image text field and select home-on.gif from the Lesson_08_Interactivity/explorations/images folder for the rollover image.

When this page is viewed in a browser, the visitor initially sees the home.gif image. The home-on.gif image replaces the home.gif image when the user rolls over home.gif in the browser window.

Note *When making rollover graphics, create both the original image and the image that will swap at the same dimensions. If both images are not the same size, the second rollover image may be resized to the size of the first image. Resizing distorts the second image because that image has only the space held by the first image available to it.*

5. Type *Home* in the Alternate text text field. Click the Browse button next to the When clicked, Go to URL text field and find the file index.html in the Lesson_08_Interactivity folder. Leave the Preload rollover image box checked and then click OK.

The Preload rollover image option is checked by default and it is highly recommended. This setting causes the secondary image to load when the document loads into the visitor's browser. If this setting is not checked, the image does not load until the visitor rolls over the primary image and the browser requests that rollover image from the server. Loading the image along with the rest of the page makes the rollovers happen more quickly, eliminating any lag caused by the download occurring at the time the user rolls over the image.

The rollover now links to the file you chose. The file you chose in the When clicked, Go to URL text field now appears in the Link text field on the Property inspector when the image is selected.

When the rollover image is selected, the resulting behavior appears in the Behaviors panel, which you'll use in the next exercise.

6. Save your file and test it in the browser.

You can close this file.

> **Note** | *When creating your graphics, make the file sizes as small as possible. Remember that with rollovers, you are downloading not one but two images for the same button. The file size of a rollover like the one you inserted in this exercise is increased because there are two images to download. The amount of increase depends upon the size of the images.*

Adding Behaviors

This exercise demonstrates the process of creating rollovers from graphics that have already been placed on the page. The result is the same as the last exercise—an image swaps to show a different image when the user rolls over it. In this exercise, however, you are using a different method to insert rollovers: You will insert the behavior for the rollover using the Behaviors panel. When you are creating your own Web pages, you should use this method if you have already placed your original images on a page. If the original images are not yet on the page, you can use the method from the previous exercise to set both the original image and the rollover image in one step.

1. Name the six section navigation images in the table at the top of the page using the image name text field in the Property inspector. The image names should be as follows: about.gif should be named *about*, community.gif should be named *community*, explorations.gif should be named *explorations*, schedule.gif should be named *schedule*, teachers.gif should be named *teachers*, and training.gif should be named *training*. For each of the navigation images, link them to their respective pages using the technique described in Chapter 5 in the section "Creating Graphic Links."

Naming the images to match their content or their function is a good method. This naming practice helps to clearly indicate which images are associated with the chosen names.

2. Select the about link using the tag selector, being careful not to select just the image. Open the Tag inspector panel and click the Behaviors tab.

The Behaviors panel opens.

Tip *You can also choose Window > Behaviors to open the Behaviors panel.*

3. Click the plus sign (+) button on the Behaviors panel and choose Swap Image from the Actions menu.

The Swap Image dialog box opens. The Swap Image behavior is what creates the rollover effect you used in the previous exercise: It swaps a new image in to replace the original image that the visitor rolled over. The behavior is a combination of an action and an event.

An *action* is what happens as a result of user interaction. When you select an action, Dreamweaver adds that action to the list in the Behaviors panel. The Actions menu displays or disables actions depending on which element you selected in the Document window. The action is this case is the swapping of one image for another.

Dreamweaver also adds an appropriate event (or events) for that action automatically. The *event* is what causes the action to occur. An event could be the user rolling over an image or clicking a button, for example. In this case, the event is onMouseOver, which is the Dreamweaver default for rollovers. You will learn to select specific events later in this lesson.

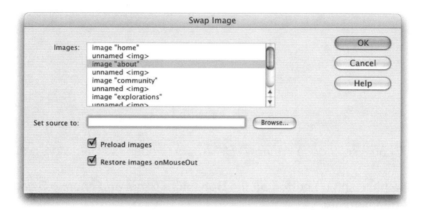

4. In the Images list, make sure that the about image is selected.

The image is listed as "about," which is the name that you defined (in Step 2 of this exercise) for the image that you selected and added an action to through the Behaviors panel (in Step 4 of this exercise). By selecting the about image in the image list in the Swap Image dialog box, you designate that when a user rolls over that image, it is replaced with a rollover image. You will choose the rollover image in the next step.

> **Note** If you were to choose a different image from this list, the selected image would be replaced with the rollover image when the user rolls over the about image because the about image is the one to which the behavior is applied—you will do that in the next exercise.

Keep in mind that if you don't name your images, they all appear with the name, "unnamed <img>" in this dialog box. You can see a number of instances of "unnamed

<img>" in this dialog box because you named only seven images. This is why it is so important to name your images properly; it is very hard to work with behaviors if the images are not clearly and logically named. In a list full of unnamed images, it can be difficult to distinguish which images you are working with.

5. Click the Browse button next to the Set source to text field and find the about-on.gif image in the Lesson_08_Interactivity/explorations/images folder. Click Choose (Macintosh) or OK (Windows) to select the image for use as the rollover image.

Set the source to define what the rollover image will be. Setting the source is the same as choosing the rollover in the previous exercise. Generally, the original appearance of an image is known as the "off" state, and the instance of the rollover when the user moves the pointer over the image and the image changes is known as the "on" state. Images used for the "on" states often look as if a button has been pressed or a word has been highlighted to indicate to the visitor that the object is an active or linked element.

All the rollover graphics you will use for this exercise are in the images folder, and the names of the rollover-image files have the suffix -on. Developing a logical and ordered naming system for your images, such as about.gif for the original image and about-on.gif or about-over.gif for the rollover image, will help you keep graphics organized and will make it easier to find the appropriate image.

After choosing the image, you are returned to the Swap Image dialog box. An asterisk appears at the right end of the image name in the Images list to indicate that an alternative image has been assigned to it for the rollover.

6. Make sure that the Preload images and Restore images onMouseOut checkboxes are checked; then click OK.

As with the rollovers you inserted in the previous exercise, the Preload images option is checked by default. This option causes the images to be loaded at the time the page is called up by the browser instead of waiting to load until the browser needs to display the image.

The Restore images onMouseOut option is also checked by default and is recommended. This option makes your swapped images revert to the original images when the user rolls off them.

Note *Restore images onMouseOut is done by Swap Image Restore, which is available as a separate action in the Behaviors panel.*

Both portions of the behavior are now listed in the Behaviors panel: The onMouseOver event causes the Swap Image action and the onMouseOut event causes the Swap Image Restore action. The combination of these actions and events creates the rollover effect—the image swaps when the visitor moves the pointer over the image and it swaps back when the visitor moves the pointer off the image.

7. **Repeat Steps 3 through 7 for the remaining navigation section titles using the -on versions for the rollover images that you define in the Set source to text field.**

If you ever need to delete a behavior, you can select the object in the Document window that contains the behavior, select the action in the Behaviors panel that you want to delete, and then click the minus sign (–) button at the top of the Behaviors panel. You can also delete a behavior by selecting it and then pressing Delete (Macintosh) or Backspace (Windows).

Note *In Dreamweaver 8 it is no longer necessary to have a link applied to an image for rollovers to function. Instead, rollovers can be applied directly to the images themselves. However, there are two good reasons not to do this: first, it doesn't work in older browsers, and second, you'll have rollovers that don't actually do anything when the visitor clicks them. Web surfers have learned that rollovers mean clickable, and if your image just has a rollover without also being a link, your site will be confusing.*

8. Save your file and test the rollovers in your browser.

Notice the images change when you roll over them.

Swapping Multiple Images with One Event

You can create more complex interactions with visitors by applying multiple actions to a single event. For example, you can have several images swap from their original images to their rollover images at the same time as a result of the same event. This technique might be used to cause two images to swap out, each from their original image to the rollover image, when the user rolls over one button.

In this exercise, you will apply a behavior to the meditation graphic, which causes the spacer image that exists below it to swap to another image as the user rolls over the initial graphic. For the additional rollover to occur using the same event, you will edit the existing Swap Image action and define the additional image swap in this exercise.

1. Open the meditations.html document from the Lesson_08_Interactivity/ explorations folder. Select the meditation image and then double-click the existing Swap Image action in the Behaviors panel.

Make sure that you double-click the Swap Image action, not the Swap Image Restore action.

The Swap Image dialog box opens.

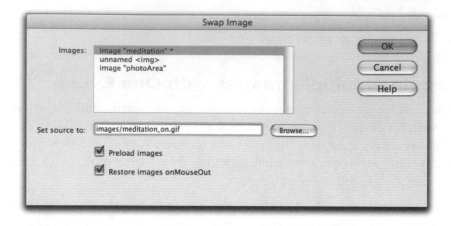

2. In the Swap Image dialog box, select the image named photoArea. Click the Browse button on the right of the Set Source To text field and choose the med_hands.jpg image from the Lesson_08_Interactivity/explorations/images folder.

The photoArea image area, which contains the blank image underneath the meditation graphic, has already been named for you. In this step, you are selecting that blank image in the Swap Image dialog box so you can replace it with the image of the meditating woman.

Look at the Images list in the Swap Image dialog box. Images with an asterisk at the end of the name have been assigned a rollover image. The meditation image, for example, has an asterisk next to it because that rollover has already been defined. Now the photoArea image also has an asterisk next to it because you have assigned a rollover for that image in this step. Checking this list is a quick way to verify which images will swap from their original images to rollover images.

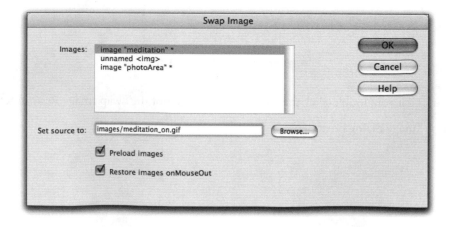

3. Click OK to close the Swap Image dialog box. Save your file again and test it in the browser.

Swapping multiple images can be useful for giving the user additional information, but keep in mind that too many extra image swaps on one action can slow a browser down.

When you move your pointer over the meditation image, the word will change to a lighter color, and the corresponding image below will also change. When you move the pointer away, both images will return to the original images.

Adding Behaviors to Image Maps

Moving the pointer over any portion of a standard rollover image calls up the JavaScript script and causes the image swap to happen. There might be times, however, when you want the rollover to occur only when the user rolls over a certain part of the image. In such cases, you can use image maps to define those hotspot areas.

1. In meditations.html, select the med_img_map.jpg image and give it the name nav. Next, use the Rectangular Hotspot tool on the Property inspector to draw an image map closely around the word meditations.

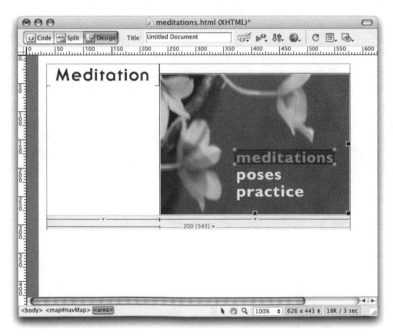

The image map makes only the word meditations on the med_img_map.gif image clickable.

2. Click the plus sign (+) button on the Behaviors panel and choose Swap Image from the Actions menu.

You might get a dialog box informing you that a description should be provided in the alt text field on the Property inspector. In this exercise, the description has already been assigned, so you can ignore this message.

You are applying a swap image behavior to an image map. The behavior does not apply to any area of the image surrounding the image map.

Note *Because you just created the image map on the med_img_map.jpg image, the hotspot is automatically selected. If you are not applying the behavior directly after creating the image map, you should choose the pointer tool on the Property inspector and click the image map to select it to make the hotspot active—you don't want to apply the rollover to the entire image.*

3. In the Images list, select the photoArea image. Click the Browse button next to the Set source to text field and find med_hands.jpg in the images folder. Click Choose (Macintosh) or OK (Windows) to pick the image and return to the Swap Image dialog box.

You have now selected the image that will appear on the left when you roll over the hotspot in a browser.

Note *If you designate the image with the hotspot as the one to be replaced, the entire image will be replaced even though the clickable area is only on a certain portion of the original image.*

4. Make sure that the Preload images and Restore images onMouseOut checkboxes are checked; then click OK.

The dialog box closes, and you return to the Document window. Whenever the image map on the med_img_map.jpg image is selected, you can see the Swap Image listed in the Behaviors panel. If you have the image selected but do not have the image map selected, you will not see the swap image listed in the Behaviors panel.

5. **Save the file and test your work in the browser.**

Using image maps in combination with behaviors can give you a significant amount of additional control over your images, actions, and events.

Editing Actions and Events

You can edit the actions and events that combine to make behaviors in several ways: You can change the event to which an action corresponds, you can attach several actions to a single event, and you can change the order in which those actions occur. For example, in the previous exercise, Swap Image was the action, and OnMouseOver was the event that corresponded to the rollover behavior. In this exercise, you will add an action for a pop-up message and select a corresponding event.

1. **In the meditations.html document, draw a rectangular image map hotspot around the word "poses" on the med_img_map.jpg image. With the hotspot selected, click the plus sign (+) button in the Behaviors panel and choose Popup Message from the Actions menu.**

The Popup Message dialog box opens, displaying a text field in which you can type your message.

2. Type *Explore a variety of different yoga poses* and click **OK**.

The Popup Message action and the corresponding event, onClick, appear in the Behaviors panel.

3. Click the onClick event in the Behaviors panel. From the menu that appears on the right of the current event, select the *onMouseOut* event.

Note *You can choose what browser type to display events for by making a choice from the Show Events For portion of the Add Behavior menu. You can choose to show events for a specific browser version, such as IE 6.0, or for all browsers of a specified version number, such as 4.0 and later browsers. After you select a browser type, you can select an event in the Behaviors panel to make the Events menu available. The Events menu then lists only those events that are available for the browser type that you chose.*

The events that are available in this menu might differ depending on the action and the browser type you choose. The Events menu appears only when you select an event in the Behaviors panel.

The up and down arrow buttons on the Behaviors panel can be used to adjust the order in which events appear in the Behaviors panel list. The up arrow moves the selected item up in the list; the down arrow moves it down in the list. Use these buttons to change the order in which actions are executed by the browser.

4. Save and preview the page in the browser.

Use care when adding the Popup Message behavior to your pages. Similar to pop-up windows, which you will learn to create later in this lesson, pop-up messages can quickly annoy your visitors when overused.

Leave this file open to use in the next exercise.

Creating a Status Bar Message

A status bar message can give users extra information about where links will lead them. This message, which appears in the status bar at the bottom of the browser window, replaces the default display of the URL or path to the linked page.

Note   *The status bar message you create will be visible only when the page is viewed in Internet Explorer or Netscape.*

1. In the meditations.html document, draw a rectangular image map hotspot around the word "practice" on the med_img_map.jpg image. With the hotspot selected, click the plus sign (+) button in the Behaviors panel and choose Set Text > Set Text Of Status Bar from the Add Behavior menu of actions.

The Set Text Of Status Bar dialog box opens, displaying a text field in which you can type your message.

2. Type *Developing a personal yoga practice* and click OK.

If you use status bar messages, a concise description of the linked material helps users navigate your pages.

The Set Text Of Status Bar action now appears in the Behaviors panel.

3. Save the file and test it in the browser.

When you move your pointer over the word "practice," you see the message you created displayed in the status bar at the bottom of the browser window. You can leave the meditation.html file open; you will use it again later in this lesson.

Checking the Browser

Not all browsers support JavaScript events and other features—some, particularly pre–4.0 browsers, have very limited support. With the Check Browser action, you can detect which browsers are being used by the visitors to your Website and redirect users to another page if you want to provide features that won't display correctly in older browsers. For example, if your page contains layers (covered in Lesson 9), you could create a page without the layers and redirect users with 4.0 or later browsers to the page that uses layers. Users with older browsers or with JavaScript turned off would remain on the page that doesn't use layers.

In this exercise you will add a Check Browser behavior to one page and redirect the users with 4.0 or later browsers to another page.

If you do use this feature, it can be good to keep the page that contains the Check Browser behavior very small so that it loads and redirects the visitor quickly. If it is too large, it might take a considerable amount of time to load, causing visitors to have to wait not only for that page to load but also for the one to which they are redirected to load.

1. Open sequences.html from the explorations folder. Select the <body> tag by clicking <body> in the tag selector (in the lower-left corner of the Document window).

The action will be attached to the <body> tag to redirect a user when the page loads. You should see <body> displayed in the title bar of the Behaviors panel, indicating that the <body> tag is selected.

| **Note** | When the *<body>* tag is selected, all content in the document appears selected. |

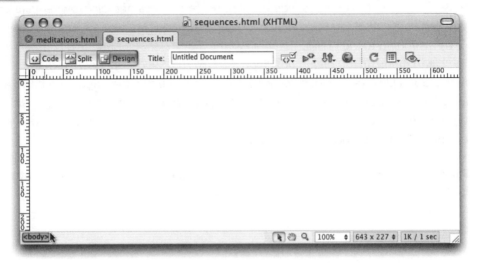

2. Click the plus sign (+) button in the Behaviors panel and choose Check Browser from the Add Behavior menu of actions.

The Check Browser dialog box opens.

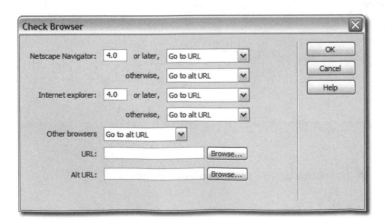

3. For both Netscape 4.0 and Internet Explorer 4.0 or later, choose Go to URL from the appropriate menu. For both Netscape and Internet Explorer; otherwise, choose Stay on this page. For Other browsers, choose Stay on this page.

When you use the Check Browser behavior, if you tried to use this behavior to redirect users with older browsers to another page, it would not work for anyone who uses a browser that does not support JavaScript or who simply turned off JavaScript.

Note *To redirect all users to a different page, regardless of their browser version, you can use a meta tag refresh by choosing Insert › HTML › Head Tags › Refresh or by switching to the HTML category of the Insert bar and choosing Refresh from the Head menu. In the dialog box, type the URL that you want users redirected to in the Go to URL text field. If you want users to remain on the page for a certain length of time before the browser loads the page that you are redirecting them to, type the time in seconds into the Delay text field. The Refresh this document option reloads this page in the browser.*

4. Click the Browse button next to the URL text field and locate the poses.html file in the Lesson_08_Interactivity/explorations folder.

The poses.html file is the page to which users of the latest browsers will be redirected.

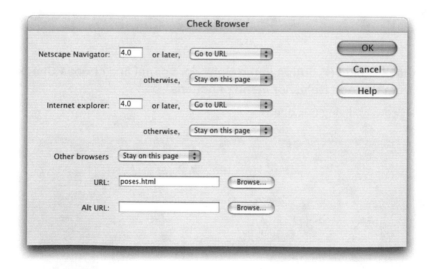

5. Click OK to insert the JavaScript into your page.

The onLoad event appears with the corresponding Check Browser action in the Behaviors panel.

6. Save the file and test the page in your browser.

If you do not have a 4.0 or later version of Internet Explorer or Netscape, you remain on the static page. This includes such commonly used browsers such as Firefox, Safari, and Opera.

If you have a 4.0 or later version of Internet Explorer or Netscape, you might briefly see the sequences.html page before the browser redirects you to the other page, poses.html.

You can close the sequences.html file.

Opening a New Browser Window

This exercise will demonstrate how to open a new browser window when the page loads, which can be used for displaying an advertisement, definition terms, or a wide variety of other information. You could open a browser window by using the _blank target along with a standard link, but you wouldn't have any control over the attributes of that new window. On the other hand, the Open Browser window lets you control the size along with a number of attributes of the new browser window, such as scroll bars and menu bars.

Note *Although the Open Browser Window option is easy to add, think it through before using it on a Web page. Make sure that the extra window is necessary. Users are often irritated with new windows that continually pop up as they browse the Web. Moderation is important—whether you are creating new browser windows or using other behaviors, be sure to consider the amount of feedback or interactive options you are offering the visitor, and strike a balance between too little (which doesn't provide enough information) and too much (which can often be overbearing). Understanding your visitors' prior experiences with Websites and other media helps you tailor the experience they will have while viewing and interacting with your site.*

1. In the poses.html file, select the word Uttanasana in the eighth row of the first column. Click the plus sign (+) button in the Behaviors panel to add a new behavior and then select Open Browser Window in the list.

The Open Browser Window dialog box opens.

2. Click the Browse button and locate the fwd-fold.jpg file in the explorations/images folder.

This file is the image that will load in the new window.

3. Type *405* for the window width and *605* for the window height; then click OK.

The width and height are chosen based on the size of the content in the new window. If you are simply displaying a banner ad, you should set the size of the new window to the width and height of that ad image. If the content is larger, you should adjust the size of the window accordingly. You can also set a number of window attributes as needed. The additional attributes for new windows are as follows:

- **Navigation toolbar:** The row of browser buttons that includes Back, Forward, Home, and Reload. Leave this box unchecked for this exercise.

- **Location toolbar:** The row of browser options that includes the location field. Leave this box unchecked for this exercise.

- **Status bar:** The area at the bottom of the browser window in which messages (such as the load time remaining and the URLs associated with links) appear. Leave this box unchecked for this exercise.

- **Menu bar:** The area of the browser window (Windows only) in which menus such as File, Edit, View, Go, and Help appear. You should set this option if you want users to be able to navigate from the new window. If you do not set this option, users can only close or minimize the window from the new window. Leave this box unchecked for this exercise.

- **Scrollbars as needed:** Specifies that scroll bars should appear if the content extends beyond the visible area. Scroll bars may not appear if you do not set this option. If the Resize Handles option is also turned off, users may have no way of seeing content that extends beyond the original size of the window. If this is the case, you need to make sure that the window is sized appropriately for the content of the page. If the window is too small or too large and has no scroll bars, it will be very frustrating for users. Some browsers will disregard this setting (along with the one for resize handles) and provide them whenever they're necessary. Leave this box unchecked for this exercise.

- **Resize handles:** Specifies that users should be able to resize the window, either by dragging the lower-right corner of the window or by clicking the Maximize button (Windows) or size box (Macintosh) in the upper-right corner. If you do not set this option, the resize controls are usually unavailable, and the user cannot resize the window. Leave this box unchecked for this exercise.

- **Window name:** The name of the new window. You should name the new window if you want to target it with links or control it with JavaScript. Leave this text field blank for this exercise.

The Open Browser Window action is now displayed in the Behaviors panel. The current event will vary depending on what browsers you're showing events for. Here, we end up with onFocus.

4. Change the onFocus event to onClick.

The onClick event will enable users to access the new window by clicking inside the table cell. You might wish to provide some indication that the table cell is clickable, such as setting the word to a different color, adding an underline, or other variation.

5. Save your file and test your page in the browser.

A new window opens with the selected image when you click inside the table cell containing "Uttanasana."

Creating a Pop-Up Menu

You can integrate JavaScript pop-up menus with your navigation to give your visitors a list of choices and quick access to various sections of the site. Dreamweaver's Pop-Up Menu script works in both Netscape (versions 4 and up) and Internet Explorer (versions 4 and up), along with other popular current browsers.

1. In the poses.html document, click the explorations image in the table at the top of the page.

When it is selected, you should see two actions listed in the Behaviors panel from when you created a rollover for this link earlier in this lesson.

2. Delete the text "index.html" from the Link field on the Property Inspector and press Return (Macintosh) or Enter (Windows). Click OK in the alert box that warns you that the JavaScript events will be removed.

There is no longer a link attached to the explorations image, and the behaviors you added previously have been removed.

3. Click the explorations image to select it, then click the plus sign (+) button in the Behaviors panel and choose Show Pop-Up Menu from the Actions menu. Click Continue on the Show Pop-up Menu dialog box.

The Show Pop-Up Menu dialog box first appears with a tip to let you know that the Fireworks program can allow you to build more advanced pop-up menus. Click the Continue button to go ahead with creating the pop-up menu in Dreamweaver.

The Show Pop-Up Menu dialog box appears with the Contents tab active. You will use this portion of the dialog box to define the choices to present to your visitor.

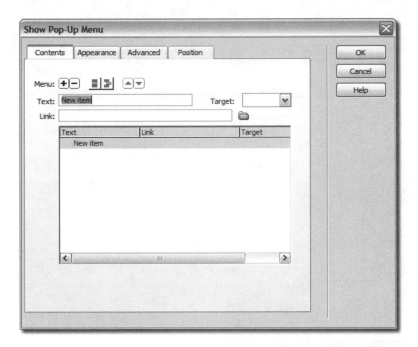

4. In the Text text field, replace the default text New Item by typing *Meditations*. Click the folder icon next to the Link text field, browse for meditations.html in the explorations folder, and select it. Click Choose (Macintosh) or OK (Windows) to close the dialog box.

The Meditations item is added to the list of menu items.

5. Click the Menu plus sign (+) button to add a new item. Replace the default text New Item by typing *Sequences*. Click the folder icon next to the Link text field, browse for sequences.html, and select it. Add a third item to the list, name it *Philosophy*, and link it to philosophy.html. Add a fourth item to the list, name it *Media*, and link it to media.html.

The names of menu items and the corresponding pages to which they link can be edited by selecting an item in the list and using the Text and Link text fields to make changes.

Tip *Shorter and more concise menu options help to keep your design clean and easy to use.*

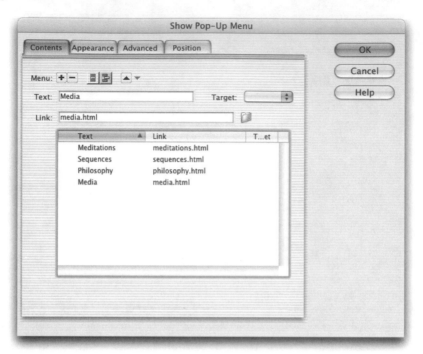

Tip *To delete an item, select it in the list of menu items and click the Menu minus sign (–) button.*

6. Select Sequences in the list of menu items. Click the Move item up arrow button to move the Sequences item to the top of the list. Select Philosophy in the list and click the Move item down arrow button to move it to the bottom of the list.

The order of menu items can be rearranged easily with the menu arrow buttons.

Note *You can create subcategories of menu items by selecting the item you want to make a subcategory and clicking the indent item button. Use the Outdent Item button to move an item to a higher category level.*

7. Click the Appearance tab on the Show Pop-Up Menu dialog box. Select Vertical menu from the orientation menu. Select the Verdana font set from the Font menu and enter *10* in the Size text field. There should be no bold or italic styling, and the alignment should be left.

You might need to click back onto the Font menu for the preview area to refresh and show your menu at the size you chose. The preview will also refresh when you specify the colors in the next step.

Here, you are matching the text options for the Pop-Up menu to the styles used in the "Lights of the Coast" project site.

Note *If you have fewer than four choices in your menu list, Dreamweaver repeats the last entry until there are four choices in the preview shown in this dialog box— this is for display purposes only and won't happen in your document.*

8. **Use the color boxes to set the following: Up state Text #666600 (grayish green), Up state Cell #FFFFFF (white), Over state Text #FF9900 (orange), and Over state Cell #FFFFFF (white).**

These options enable you to set the look of the pop-up menu to match the style of the navigational images as closely as possible. You can see how the menu will look in the preview area of the Show Pop Up Menu dialog box. The second menu option appears with the Over State colors applied to it; the other menu options appear with the Up State colors. The preview is approximate; it might not appear in a browser exactly as you see it here.

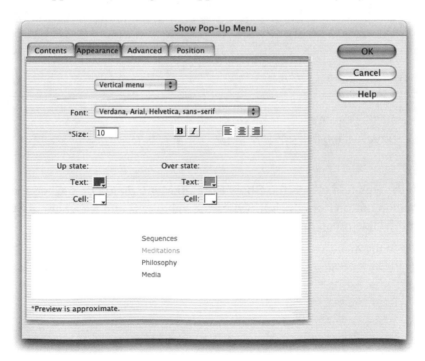

9. Click the Advanced tab on the Show Pop-Up Menu dialog box. Verify that the default settings are as follows: Cell width and Cell height menu choices should be set to Automatic, the Cell padding to 3, the Cell spacing to 0, the Text indent to 0, and the Menu delay to 1000. Make any changes necessary to match the settings listed here. In the Pop-Up borders section, leave the Show borders box unchecked.

The Menu delay controls how long it takes for the menu to disappear after the visitor rolls off of it.

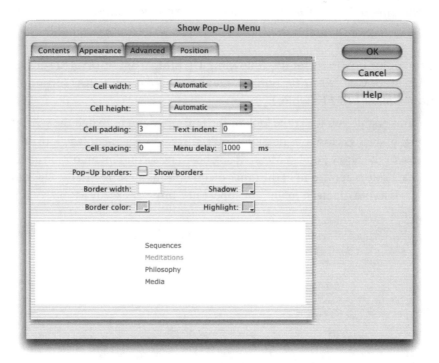

10. Click the Position tab on the Show Pop-Up Menu dialog box. Click the second Menu position button from the left. Type an X value of *5* and a Y value of *26*. Make sure that the Hide menu on MouseOut event box is checked. Click OK.

In addition to the X and Y axis, you can use the four general placement buttons on this portion of the Show Pop-Up Menu dialog box to position your menu on the page.

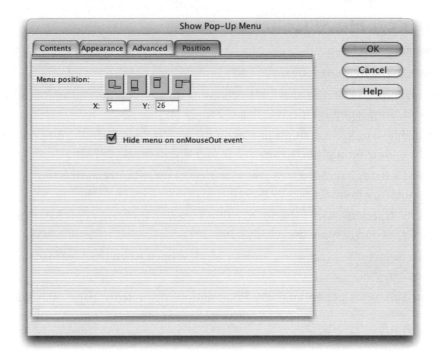

11. Save the file and preview it in your browser.

The Show Pop-Up Menu behavior is now listed in the Behaviors panel. It is split into two portions: Show Pop-Up Menu and Hide Pop-Up Menu.

Note *An external JavaScript file with the .js extension is created. Usually named mm_menu.js, this file is necessary for the pop-up menu to function. The external file can be rather large, so you need to judge whether the addition of scripts like this one are of a size that your visitors can download quickly and easily.*

Test your menus as much as is possible. When you roll over the explorations navigation image, you see the pop-up menu that you created in this exercise appear below the "explorations" graphic. The settings that you applied for appearance and position make the menu look integrated with the rest of the navigation.

Note *With the Show Pop-Up Menu behavior, there might be some discrepancies between how the menus appear in various browsers on the Macintosh versus Windows. You may need to adjust the positioning of the menu.*

What You Have Learned

In this lesson, you have:

- Created basic rollovers (pages 279–282)
- Learned how to edit the behaviors by choosing different events and adding actions while creating a pop-up message (pages 282–287)
- Learned how to make multiple images on the page change when the user rolls over one by adding multiple behaviors to one user action (pages 287–293)
- Created a status bar message to give your viewers more information about a link when they roll over it (pages 293–294)
- Used the Check Browser behavior to redirect users to different pages based on the browser version they are using (pages 294–297)
- Used a behavior to make a new browser window open when the page loads (pages 297–300)
- Created a JavaScript pop-up menu with multiple menu items (pages 300–305)

9 Creating Layers

A **layer** is a rectangular container for HTML content that you can position at an exact location in the browser window. Layers can contain a wide variety of elements: text, images, tables, and even other layers. Anything you can place in an HTML document you can also place in a layer. Layers are especially useful for placing elements atop each other or making them overlap. Layers are supported by 4.0 or later browsers only. They can control layout and appearance when used in combination with Cascading Style Sheets (CSS), and they provide interactivity when used in combination with behaviors.

In this lesson, you will learn several ways to create layers in Dreamweaver. You will draw a layer on the page to the size you want and place a layer on the page using a predetermined width and height. You will learn to modify layer attributes including size,

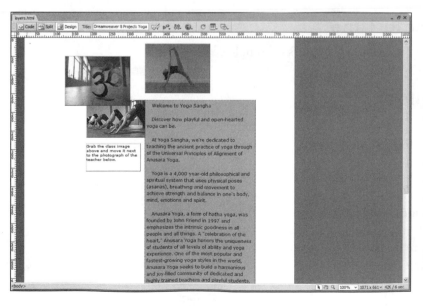

In this project, you will create layers, place text and images in them, move them to exact locations on the page, and change their properties. You'll also learn about layer-based animations that make use of multiple layers in a timeline with keyframes to control visibility and create movement.

placement, and visibility. You will also convert your layers to tables to make it possible for users with older browsers to view your pages.

To see an example of the finished page, open layers.html from the Lesson_09_Layers/ Completed folder.

What You Will Learn

In this lesson, you will:

- Create layers
- Name layers
- Modify layer sizes and locations
- Use layers to control content on your page
- Change the stacking order of layers
- Nest and unnest layers
- Change layer visibility
- Set rulers and grids
- Use a JavaScript fix for a Netscape bug
- Make pages designed with layers compatible with earlier browsers
- Learn about timelines

Approximate Time

This lesson should take about two hours to complete.

Lesson Files

Media Files:

Lesson_09_Layers/Images/…(all files)

Starting Files:

Lesson_09_Layers/layers.html

Completed Project:

Lesson_09_Layers/Completed/layers.html
Lesson_09_Layers/Completed/layers_table.html
Lesson_09_Layers/Completed/transparent.gif

Creating Layers

A layer is simply a container, known as the <div> tag, that makes use of specific CSS properties (absolute positioning and z-index) that allow it to overlap other elements.

There are several different ways to create a layer. The method you choose might depend on how you plan to use the layer and where you want to place it. In this exercise, you will create several layers and insert content into them.

1. Open layers.html from the Lesson_09_Layers folder. Switch to the Layout category on the Insert bar and verify that the Standard button is selected.

Tip *You should be using Design view for this lesson.*

Standard view is the default, and the Standard button on the Insert bar will be highlighted to indicate that it is active. You must be in the Standard view to create a layer.

Draw Layer button

2. Click the Draw Layer button in the Layout category of the Insert bar. Move the pointer into the Document window; then click and drag to create a new layer on the right side of the page.

The pointer changes to a crosshair (+) when you move the pointer into the Document window. After you drag and release the pointer to create the layer, a rectangle appears, displaying the new layer.

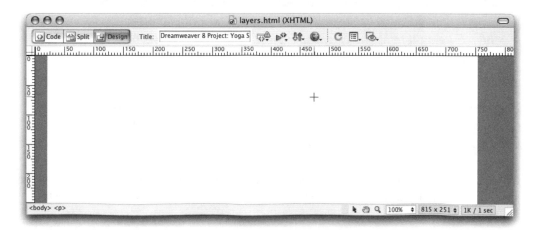

3. Choose Dreamweaver > Preferences (Macintosh) or Edit > Preferences (Windows). Select the Invisible Elements category and check the Anchor Points For Layers box. Click OK.

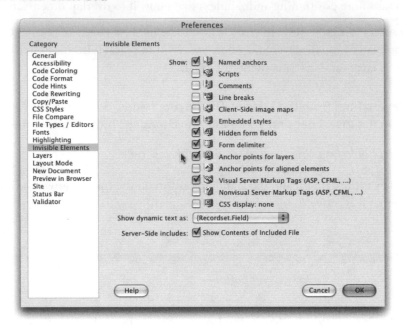

You should now see a layer marker at the top left of the Document window. The outline of the layer appears blue when it is selected.

Note *You can use the layer marker to select the layer, but if your layer is positioned at the top left of the Document window, the marker could appear to shift the position of the layer. This shift happens only in the Document window; when the page is viewed in the browser, all elements will be in their correct positions. Turn the markers off temporarily by using View > Visual Aids > Invisible Elements. A checkmark next to the command in the menu indicates that the option is on.*

By default, the layer code is inserted at the top of the page, just after the <body> tag. Dreamweaver uses the <div> tag to create layers that use absolute positioning to determine the placement of the layer in relation to the top and left sides of the browser window. The <div> tag is a block-level element, which is a container that structures portions of your page—it begins on a new line or a new block. Other block-level elements include <p>(paragraph) and <ul> (unordered list). Block-level elements can contain other block-level elements as well as inline elements. Inline elements usually contain only text and other inline elements, and are used within block elements—they do not create new blocks or lines. Some examples of inline elements include <span> (span),
 (line break) and <a> (anchors, otherwise known as links).

Note *Dreamweaver recognizes several additional tags that can be used to create layers (<span>, <layer>, and <ilayer>), but it does not provide the option to use these tags to create layers. The <span> tag, which is an inline element, uses relative positioning to determine the placement of the layer depending upon the position of other elements around it. The <layer>and <ilayer> tags were supported only in Netscape Navigator 4. Netscape no longer supports these tags, and Internet Explorer has never supported them. The Design view does not render or display these types of layers, although it does insert a layer marker for the layer.*

4. **Position the pointer over the border of the layer. Click to select the layer when the pointer turns into a hand (Macintosh) or a four-headed arrow (Windows).**

When the pointer rolls over the lines that indicate the border of the layer, the lines turn red to indicate that you can select the layer.

The layer is now shown with a square tab at the top left. This tab is the layer selection handle. The blue squares on the borders of the layer are sizing handles.

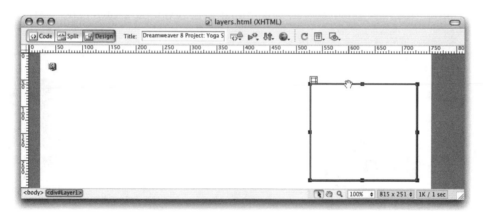

5. **Place the insertion point inside the layer. Insert a table into the layer with the following attributes: 1 row, 1 column, 300 pixels wide, border of 0, cell padding of 5, cell spacing of 0, no header, no caption, and no summary. Open about.txt from the Lesson_09_Layers/Text folder, copy all the text, and paste it into the table you created inside the layer.**

Tip *The Layout category of the Insert panel contains an insert Table button.*

The layer expands if necessary to accommodate the size of the table and the text that the table now contains. Layers expand to show you all their content unless you change the overflow setting in the Property inspector.

6. **Place the insertion point in the document outside the layer. Click the Draw Layer button and draw a small second layer on the left side of the page. Insert the studio-om.jpg image from the Lesson_09_Layers/Images folder, into the layer. Use OM for the alternative text for the image.**

The layer expands if necessary to the dimensions of the image. The layer does not change size if it is larger than the image.

Tip *To draw multiple layers continuously without clicking Draw Layer more than once, hold down Cmd (Macintosh) or Ctrl (Windows) as you draw the first layer. You can continue to draw new layers until you release the modifier key.*

If the insertion point is within a layer when you insert the layer, the new layer is nested inside the other layer.

Tip *Be aware that nested layers can cause problems in older browsers.*

At this point, your document should look similar to the example shown here.

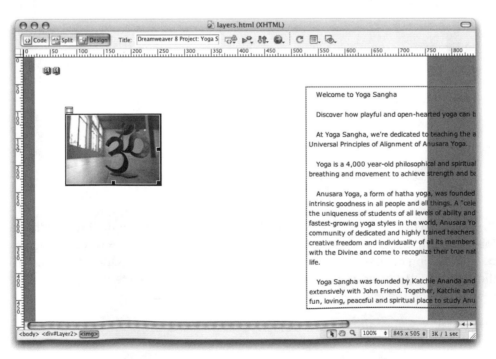

Note *Layers that are not selected and not activated are displayed with a faint, thin gray line marking their borders. You can turn this on or off by choosing View > Visual Aids > Layer Borders. A checkmark next to the command in the menu indicates that the option is on.*

7. Place the insertion point in the document outside the first and second layers and then choose Insert > Layout Objects > Layer. Insert the teaching.jpg image from the Lesson_09_Layers/Images folder into the layer and type *teaching* for the alternative text for the image.

The layer appears in the upper-left corner of the Document window with the default width and height specified by the layer preferences. This third layer might overlap the second layer you created earlier.

Note *Dreamweaver's default is 200 pixels for the width and 115 pixels for the height, but you can change these options in the Layers category of the Preferences dialog box. To open the Preferences dialog box, choose Dreamweaver > Preferences (Macintosh) or Edit > Preferences (Windows) and choose the Layers category. You can also use the Layers preferences to set default visibility, background, nesting, and compatibility options, all of which will be covered later in this lesson.*

Depending on the location of the insertion point, markers might not be visible for the layer you just placed, although the layer code has been inserted. The layer markers might be hidden behind the new layers. When adding layers by drawing them onto the pages, the layer code will be placed at the top of the page, with no paragraphs or other code between them. Using other methods to insert layers might place them between or inside of other tags, such as the <p> (paragraph) tag. You can remove these tags in the code, which you'll learn to work with in Lesson 16. At this point, the third layer might partially obscure the layer markers and portions of the other layers.

8. Click in the Document window outside of the existing layers to deselect the layer you inserted in the previous step. Drag the Draw Layer icon from the Insert bar into the Document window and drop it outside the existing layers. Click inside the new layer to place the insertion point inside of it and insert the class.jpg image from the Lesson_09_Layers/Images folder into the layer; type *class* for the alternative text for the image.

Don't drop the Draw Layer icon into another layer; dropping it would cause the layers to be nested.

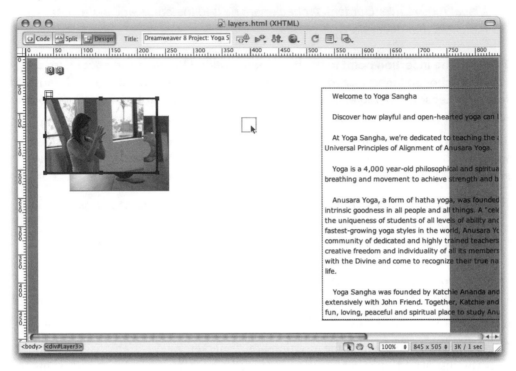

A fourth layer with the default width and height is created in the Document window, over top and offset slightly to the right of the last layer you created, similar to the following example. After you insert the layer, the insertion point will automatically be in that layer.

9. Save the layers.html document.

Leave this file open for the next exercise.

With each method of creating a layer that has been used in this exercise, the `<div>` tag was placed in the body of the document, whereas the CSS properties that define those layers were placed in an internal style sheet in the head of the document. CSS was covered in Lesson 4. Another way to create layers would be to specify the CSS properties that define the placement and positioning of the layers in an external style sheet—either by exporting the internal styles or by initially creating the styles in the external style sheet.

Naming Layers

Dreamweaver assigns generic names automatically in a numeric order: Layer1, Layer2, and so on. These names are not very descriptive, especially when you create complex pages with multiple layers. It's best to get in the habit of giving your layers short descriptive names.

1. Choose Window > Layers to open the Layers panel.

Tip *You can also bring up the Layers panel by opening the CSS panel group and clicking the Layers panel tab.*

The Layers panel, located in the CSS panel group, gives you a list of the layers on the page. You can use this panel to select a layer, name a layer, change the layer's visibility, change the layer stacking order, or select multiple layers on the page. When you create a layer, the new layer is placed at the top of the list on the Layer panel before other layers, if there are any—layers are listed in descending order. If the layer is hidden or placed off the page, using the Layers panel and layer markers might be the only methods for selecting the layer.

Note *If the insertion point is inside a layer, that layer's name appears in bold on the Layers panel, and the selection handle appears in the Document window to indicate that the layer is active but not selected.*

The four layers you just created are named Layer1, Layer2, Layer3, and Layer4.

2. Double-click the Layer1 layer in the Layers panel, type *textlayer* for the layer name, and press Return (Macintosh) or Enter (Windows). Double-click the Layer2 layer in the panel, type *om*, and press Return (Macintosh) or Enter (Windows). Don't change the name for the Layer3 layer. Double-click the Layer4 layer in the panel, type *class*, and press Return (Macintosh) or Enter (Windows).

Do not use spaces or special characters (including the underscore character) for layer names. A layer name must be unique—don't assign the same name to more than one layer or to a layer and another element such as a graphic. It is a good idea to use a consistent naming scheme for all layer names.

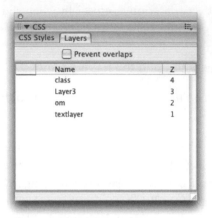

Tip *You can also type the name in the Layer ID text field on the Property inspector if the layer is selected.*

As you assign names to the layers, they become selected in the Document window. A selected layer temporarily appears to be in front of any other layers that might actually overlap it while it is selected. You can click in the Document window, outside of all the layers, to deselect a selected layer.

3. Save the layers.html document.

Leave this file open for the next exercise.

Modifying Layers

After you create a layer, you might want to add a background to it, move it around, or resize it. One of the advantages of using layers is that you can place them in precise locations on the page. You can use the Property inspector and type in values for placement, and you can align layers to other layers. You need to select a layer first before you can make any modifications to it. There are several methods for selecting a layer—the method you use depends on the complexity of your layout.

1. In the layers.html Document window, position the pointer over the border of the textlayer layer and click the border line when the pointer turns into a hand (Macintosh) or a crosshair with arrows (Windows), and the border turns red.

Note *If no layers are selected, Shift-clicking inside a layer selects it, whereas simply clicking inside a layer places the insertion point in the layer and activates it, but does not actually select the layer itself. You can select multiple layers by Shift+clicking other layers. Additional ways to select a single layer are to click the yellow layer marker that represents the layer's marker in the Document window, the layer's tag in the tag selector, or the name of the layer in the Layers panel.*

The layer becomes selected, and square black sizing handles appear around the layer. The name of the selected layer in the Layers panel is highlighted.

The Property inspector changes to reflect options for the selected layer. To see all properties, click the expander arrow in the lower-right corner of the Property inspector.

Tip *To delete a layer, select it and press Delete (Macintosh) or Backspace (Windows).*

2. **Resize the textlayer layer by typing *320px* for the width in the W text field on the Property inspector and pressing Return (Macintosh) or Enter (Windows).**

In the Property inspector, the W and H text fields display the specified width and height of the layer. Resizing a layer changes these values. The default unit of measurement is px (pixels).

Note *You can also specify the following units: pc (picas), pt (points), in (inches), mm (millimeters), cm (centimeters), or % (percentage of the parent's value). The abbreviations must immediately follow the value, with no space between (for example, 3mm). Pixels or percentage are the recommended units.*

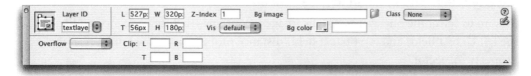

You can also resize the layer by dragging any of the sizing handles.

Note *To resize the layer one pixel at a time using the keyboard, select the layer and press Option+right-arrow key (or any arrow) for Macintosh or Ctrl+right-arrow key (or any arrow) for Windows. To resize the layer by the current grid increment, press Shift+Option+right-arrow key (or the arrow for the direction that you want the layer to expand in) for Macintosh or Shift+Ctrl+right-arrow key (or the arrow for the direction that you want the layer to expand in) for Windows. See the Grid and Ruler Settings exercise later in this lesson to learn how to set the grid increment.*

As you learned while inserting the text and images earlier in this lesson, layers expand to fit their content. When the content of the layer exceeds the specified size, the original values for width and height will be overridden. The Overflow setting on the Property inspector controls how layers behave when this occurs. There are four Overflow options: Visible, Hidden, Scroll, and Auto.

- **Visible**, the default option, increases the size of the layer, expanding the layer down and to the right as much as is needed for all the layer's contents to be visible.
- **Hidden** maintains the size of the layer and clips any content that doesn't fit without providing scroll bars.
- **Scroll** adds scroll bars to the layer, whether or not the contents exceed the layer's size.
- **Auto** makes scroll bars appear only when the contents of the layer exceed its boundaries.

You might need to click the expander arrow on the Property inspector to make these options visible.

Note *You can also set the clipping area to specify the part of the layer that is visible. The clipping area can be smaller, larger, or the same size as the layer. Use the Property inspector to define the visible area by typing values in all four Clip text fields: L (left), T (top), R (right), and B (bottom). Any content outside of the clipping area is hidden. This setting is available with all four Overflow options.*

3. **With the textlayer layer still selected, type *375px* in the L text field and *50px* in the T text field on the Property inspector. Select the om layer and type *125px* in the L text field and *100px* in the T text field.**

Be sure to select the om layer—not the image it contains—before trying to modifying the left (L text field) and top (T text field) distance properties for the om layer in the Property inspector.

Note *The layer position can be off the page if the values in L and T are set to negative numbers. You might do this if you want to animate the layer and want it initially placed off the page. You will learn to animate layers later in this lesson.*

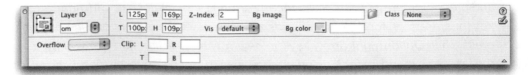

Be sure to use the L and T text fields on the top half of the Property inspector. Do not use the Clip text fields for this step. The L text field on the top half of the Property inspector defines the space between the layer and the left side of the browser window. The T text field on the top half of the Property inspector defines the space between the layer and the top side of the browser window.

Note *You can also drag the selection handle or border of the selected layer to move it to a different location on the page. To move a layer from the keyboard one pixel at a time, select the layer and use the arrow keys. Hold the Shift key and press an arrow key to move the layer by the current grid increment.*

4. Select the class layer in the Layers panel and drag the layer selection handle in the Document window down on the page so the layer appears farther down the page, below the om layer. Select the Layer3 layer and drag it farther down the page, below the class layer.

Dragging the layer selection handle will help you to be sure you are dragging the actual layer, not just the contents of the layer.

Note *When dragging Layer3, pausing the layer over top of the bottom edge of the Document window causes the document to scroll upward, giving you the space you need for the layer at the bottom of the window.*

When layers are hiding other layers that appear below them, you need to use the Layers panel or the layer markers to select a hidden layer that you want to modify. You can also adjust the order in which layers are overlaid (their stacking order), as demonstrated in the next exercise.

Your document now looks similar to the example shown here.

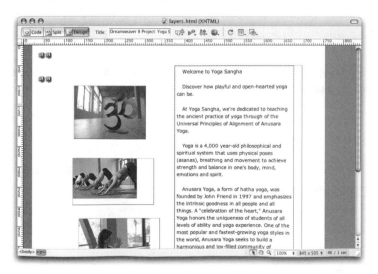

5. Select the textlayer layer. In the Property inspector, click the Bg color box, and select pale tan or type *#CCCC99* into the text field.

Tip *Be sure to select the layer, not the table that contains the text.*

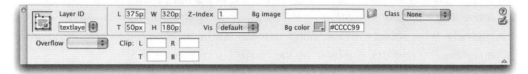

The background of the layer changes to pale tan.

There are two options for the backgrounds of layers:

- **Bg image:** Specifies a background image for the layer. Type the path for the image in the text field or click the folder icon to select a source image. The background of a layer might not display in all browsers.

- **Bg color:** Specifies a background color for the layer. Leave the text field blank or choose the default no color (the empty color swatch with a red line through it) at the top of the color menu to specify transparency.

When using either option, test your pages in all browsers—the results might not be what you expect, depending on the content of the layer. In this case, you have text in the layer. When viewed in the browser, the size of the text can vary greatly depending upon the visitor's browser and system, particularly if the text size is relative. The text might exceed the defined length of the layer, in which case the background might be either too big or too small. To avoid this, you can assign the pale tan color to the background of the table instead. Another way to solve the problem is to use CSS to define an absolute size for the text and then set the size of the layer accordingly.

6. Select the om layer; then press and hold down the Shift key while selecting the textlayer layer by clicking the border of that layer.

Tip *You can also hold down the Shift key and click the layer name in the Layers panel to select multiple layers.*

Because multiple layers are selected, the most recently selected layer appears with solid handles—the other layer has outlined handles.

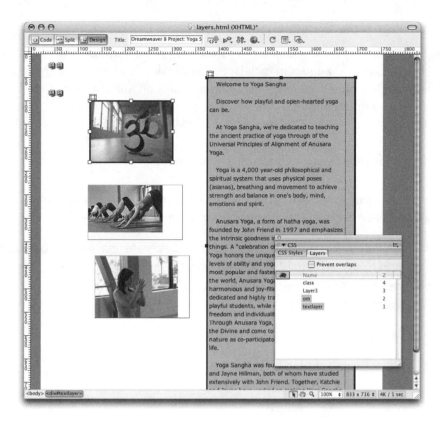

Note *To resize multiple layers at once, select two or more layers in the document and choose Modify > Align > Make Same Width or Make Same Height. The first selected layers change to the width or height of the last selected layer. You can also enter width and height values in the Property inspector to apply the values to all selected layers.*

7. Choose Modify > Arrange > Align Top.

When you choose an alignment option, all the selected layers are aligned to the position of the last layer selected. The alignment options in this menu also include Left, Right, and Bottom.

The tops of the textlayer and om layers are now aligned to each other.

8. Save the document.

Leave this file open for the next exercise.

Changing the Stacking Order of Layers

You can use either the Property inspector or the Layers panel to change the stacking order of layers by adjusting the z-index of each layer. The *z-index* determines the order in which layers are drawn in a browser. A layer with a higher z-index number appears to be laid atop layers with lower z-index numbers. Values can be positive or negative. This is particularly useful when you have overlapping layers and you need to specify which layer(s) will be atop others. It is also possible for more than one layer to have the same z-index number, in which case the layer that appears in the code first appears on top.

1. In the layers.html document, select the class layer and drag it upward until it partially overlaps the om layer. Preview your page in the browser.

Tip *When working with images in layers, you can create images with transparent backgrounds—saved in the GIF image format, which supports transparency. Using images with transparent background in layers over other images can give a more layered visual effect.*

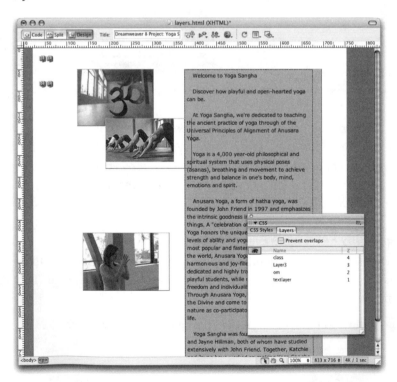

In the following steps of this exercise, you will adjust the stacking order of the layers to make the om layer appear above the class layer.

2. Select the class layer in the Layers panel and drag it downward in the list, below the om layer. Stop dragging and release the layer when a thin black line appears between the class and textlayer layers in the Layers panel.

You will see the changes applied in the Layers panel—the class layer now appears between the om and textlayer layers. The z-index numbers on the Layers panel also change automatically. It can be easier to change the stacking order when you move layers in the Layers panel than it would be to change the z-index values yourself via the Property inspector because Dreamweaver automatically changes the z-index values.

The class layer's z-index text field located on the Property inspector has changed from 4 to 2.

Your document now looks similar to the example shown previously.

Save this file and leave it open for the next exercise.

Nesting and Unnesting Layers

Nesting is a way to group layers together. A nested layer moves with its parent layer and inherits the parent's visibility. There might be times when you want to nest or unnest a layer, and this exercise demonstrates that process. Be cautious; the results might be unreliable because nested layers might not display correctly in all browsers. If you do choose to nest layers, test your pages with your target browsers to be sure the result is what you expect. (Testing is covered in Lesson 15.)

Note *The top (T) and left (L) values in the Property inspector for a nested layer are relative to the parent layer, not the top-left corner of the page. T and L specify the location of the layer from the top-left corner of the page or parent layer.*

1. In the layers.html document, use the Layers panel to select the Layer3 layer and drag the layer name (not the layer itself) over the textlayer layer while pressing Cmd (Macintosh) or Ctrl (Windows). Release Layer3 when it is over top of the textlayer.

In Windows, a solid outline will appear around the textlayer name as you drag Layer3 over it. There is no visual indication on the Macintosh.

Tip *Don't release when the area between the layers is highlighted by the display of the thin black line—doing so changes the stacking order of the layers instead of nesting the layers.*

In the Layers panel, the Layer3 layer now appears indented below its parent layer: textlayer. Next to the textlayer layer is a downward-pointing triangle (Macintosh) or a minus sign

(–) button (Windows) that allows you to see the nested layer. You can collapse this view by clicking the triangle (Macintosh) or minus sign (Windows) to display only the parent layer with a triangle pointing to the right (Macintosh) or a plus sign (+) button (Windows). You can click the plus sign or triangle again to show the list of nested layers. The position of the Layer3 layer in the Document window shifts to be in the lower right of the textlayer layer because the left value of the Layer3 layer is now relative to its parent layer: textlayer.

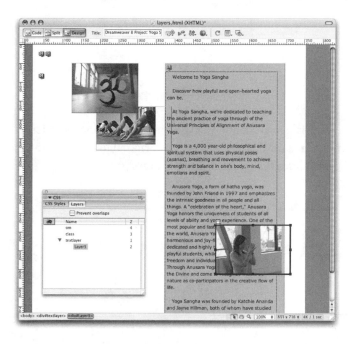

In the Document window, the layer icon representing the nested Layer3 layer appears at the top of the textlayer layer, just above the table. The space created by this icon is seen in Dreamweaver only if you have visual aids enabled. The icon is not seen in (nor does it take up space in) the browser window.

If you preview the layers.html file in several different browsers, you might notice differences that occur in the display of layers. The display might vary depending on the system visitors' operating systems and browsers, so always make a practice of checking your work in multiple browsers.

Note *You can also create a layer within an existing layer by selecting Draw Layer on the Insert bar and drawing the layer within an existing layer. For this to work, the Nest When Created Within A Layer box must be selected in Preferences. To change the Layer Preferences, choose Dreamweaver > Preferences (Macintosh) or Edit > Preferences (Windows) and select the Layers category.*

2. On the Layers panel, select the nested Layer3 layer and drag it above the textlayer layer so a thin black line shows just above the textlayer layer.

The nesting of a layer is removed, and the layer no longer appears indented in the Layers panel. The Layer3 layer is now moved back to its original location in the Document window and appears above the textlayer in the Layers panel.

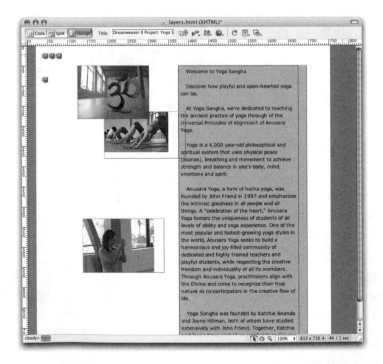

3. Save the layers.html document.

Leave this file open for the next exercise.

Changing Layer Visibility

You can change layer visibility to show or hide a layer, which can be useful when using layers to add user interactivity. You might need to change the visibility of a layer if you are creating dynamic content that displays in response to user interaction.

1. Select the Layer3 layer in the layers.html document. Click once in the Visibility column on the left side of the Layers panel to change the visibility of that layer.

A closed eye icon will appear in the column on the Layer3 row to indicate that the visibility has been changed to hidden, and the layer temporarily disappears.

Tip *To change the visibility of all layers at once, click the eye icon at the top of the column.*

There are three visibility options on the Layers panel: Inherit, Visible, and Hidden.

- **Inherit** uses the visibility property of the layer's parent. For this option, there is no icon displayed in the visibility column.

- **Visible** displays the layer contents, regardless of the parent's value. For this option, there is an open eye icon displayed in the visibility column.

- **Hidden** displays the layer content as transparent, regardless of the parent's value. If you set a layer to hidden, the layer markers and the Layers panel might be the only ways for you to select that layer. For this option, there is a closed eye icon displayed in the visibility column.

On the Property inspector, there is a fourth visibility option: Default does not specify a visibility property, but most browsers interpret it as inheriting the parent's value.

Tip *Choose Dreamweaver > Preferences (Macintosh) or Edit > Preferences (Windows) and select the Layers category to set the default visibility for new layers.*

2. Save the layers.html document and preview it in the browser.

When the Layer3 layer is selected in Dreamweaver, you can see it in the Document window. When it is not selected, the layer disappears, making the Document window look just as it does in the browser.

If the content in a hidden layer extends past the content of a visible layer, the browser window will continue to scroll past the end of the visible layer because of the hidden class content.

3. Select the Layer3 layer in the Layers panel and choose Edit › Clear (Macintosh) or press Backspace (Windows).

Pressing Delete might not work with the Layers panel on the Macintosh. You can choose Edit > Clear or remove the layer from the Document window instead.

Leave this file open for the next exercise.

Setting Grid and Ruler Options

When you work with layers, you might want to use grids and rulers as visual guides for the placement of layers on your page.

1. Select the class layer and use the Property inspector to change the size of the layer to *158 W* and *100 H*.

Having the layer size match the size of its contents will help you when adjusting the placement of the layer in this exercise.

2. In the layers.html document, choose View › Grid › Show Grid.

The grids display in the Document window. A checkmark next to the command indicates that the option is on.

3. Choose View › Grid › Snap To Grid.

This option turns snapping on or off. A checkmark next to the command indicates that the option is on. When this option is on, the layers snap to the grid lines when you move them close.

4. Select the om layer; then press the Shift key and select the class layer. Use the class layer selection handle to move them to the right so that the right edge of the class layer snaps to the seventh vertical grid line from the left and one grid box is showing between the top edge of the Document window and the top edge of the om layer.

The class layer appears to be on top of the om layer while you move them because you selected the class layer last—you can see that they are both selected in the Layers panel because both layer names are highlighted. After you click off of the layers in a blank area of the Document window, the om layer appears above the class layer again.

The class layer will have snapped to the grid line. If you click in the Document window to deselect both layers, select only the class layer; the L value should now be 200px. You might be able to see the faint gray border of the class layer just to the left of the grid line in the Document window when it is deselected. The layer is actually aligned exactly with the grid line, even though the border appears to be one pixel to the left of the grid line; the one-pixel gray layer border that you see is a Dreamweaver visual aid that does not display in the browser.

> **Note** *You can change the grid setting by choosing View › Grid › Grid Settings. The Edit Grid dialog box appears, in which you can change the color, set the spacing value and units (pixels, inches, or centimeters), and switch the grid display to lines or dots. The grid can be useful when you need to align layers.*

5. Choose View › Rulers › Show to turn the rulers on if they are not already visible.

The rulers display at the top and left sides of the Document window. A checkmark next to the command indicates that the option is on. The units for rulers can be changed by choosing View > Rulers > Pixels, Inches, or Centimeters. A checkmark next to a unit of measure indicates which one is set.

6. Select the textlayer layer and move it just to the right of the class layer, aligning the tops of both layers and aligning the left side of the textlayer along the grid line along the right edge of the class layer. Change the width of the textlayer layer to *300px*.

7. Preview the page in the browser. If necessary, adjust the L value of the textlayer layer on the Property inspector or move the layer by using the left and right arrow keys so there is no white space between the class layer and the background color of the textlayer layer.

> **Note** *If the tan background of the textlayer does not continue to the bottom of the text inside the table and you see white space near the bottom of the table when viewed in the browser, you can either set the background of the table to the same tan color or you can increase the height of the layer.*

You can also temporarily turn off the layer borders visual aid by choosing View > Visual Aids > Layer Borders. The rest of this lesson assumes that you have the layer borders visual aid turned on.

Note *The zero point is the point where the horizontal and vertical rulers intersect. The default location for the zero point is the upper left corner of the page, where the top and left sides of the page meet. You can set the zero point to a different location by clicking in the square between the vertical and horizontal rulers, dragging the zero point downward and to the right and then releasing. When the zero point is moved to a point inside the document, you see negative values appear upward and to the left of the zero point. Choose View > Rulers > Reset Origin to reset the zero point.*

Your document should now look similar to the example shown here.

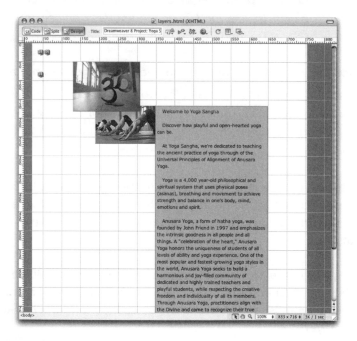

8. Turn off the Grid, Snap To Grid, and Ruler options.

Note *Choose View > Grid > Show Grid to remove the checkmark and hide the grid. Use the same method to remove the checkmarks for the Snap To Grid (View > Grid > Snap To Grid) and Ruler options (View > Rulers > Show).*

The rest of the book assumes that you have the grid turned off. You can either turn off the rulers or leave them on. Save this file and leave it open for the next exercise.

Using the Drag Layer Behavior

Layers can be combined with behaviors, which were covered in Lesson 8, to enable your visitors to interact with your page. The Drag Layer behavior makes it possible for the visitor to grab a layer in the browser window and move it to a different spot on the page. This is a great way to create interactive games or teaching tools with elements that can be moved by the user.

1. Place the insertion point in the text that is in the textlayer layer. Click the `<table>` tag in the tag selector at the bottom of the Document window. Press the right arrow key once to move the insertion point after the table and insert the teaching.jpg image—type *teaching* as the alternative text for the image.

The teaching.jpg image that you used previously in Layer3 is now in the textlayer, just below the table containing the text.

2. Create a new layer just below the class layer. Name it *grab* and type the following inside the layer: *"Grab the class image above and move it next to the photograph of the teacher below."*

Your document should now look similar to the example shown here.

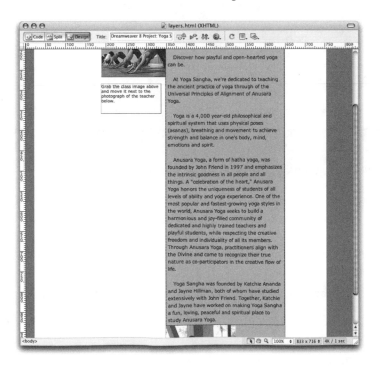

It is a good practice to let your visitors know when an item can be moved. Now that you've included text to let the visitor know the class image is draggable, you can apply the behavior.

3. Click the \<body> tag in the tag selector at the bottom of the Document window to select it.

The Drag Layer behavior cannot be applied directly to a layer, so you will apply it to the document's \<body> tag.

Tip *You can also apply the Drag Layer Behavior to other tags, such as link <a>, which can be either inside or outside of a layer.*

4. In the Behaviors panel, click the plus sign (+) button and select the Drag Layer action from the Actions drop-down menu.

Tip *The Behaviors panel is located in the Tag inspector panel group. (Behaviors were covered in Lesson 8.)*

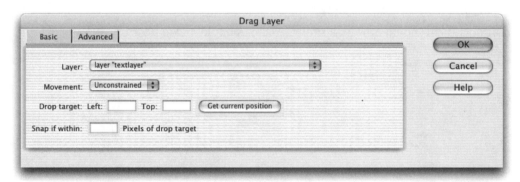

The Drag Layer dialog box appears with the Basic tab active.

Note *The Drag Layer action is not available if you have a layer selected. If it is dimmed, you should make sure that the <body> tag is selected.*

5. Select layer "class" from the Layer menu and choose Constrained from the Movement menu.

Four text fields appear to the right of the Movement pop-up menu: Up, Down, Left, and Right.

6. Type *10* in the Up text field, *600* in the Down text field, *10* in the Left text field, and *10* in the Right Text field. Leave the text fields for Drop Target and Snap If Within blank.

The coordinates allow the visitor to place the class layer only within the area of the teaching image. The amount of allowable movement is relative to the original position of the class layer. You are restricting the visitor to moving the class layer only 10 pixels upward of where it is now, only 600 pixels downward, and so forth.

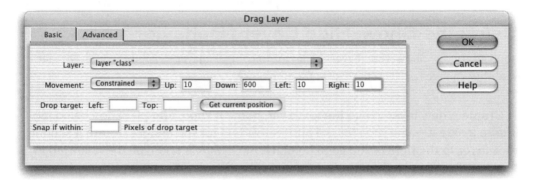

Tip *If you choose Unconstrained from the Movement menu, the visitor can move the class layer anywhere on the page.*

You can use the Constrain option to control the direction and amount of pixels in which the visitor can drag a layer. You can restrict the visitor to moving the layer only in a horizontal direction by setting the Up and Down text fields to 0 so that the layer could not be moved up or down. Likewise, you can restrict movement to a vertical direction by setting the Left and Right text fields to 0.

Note *If you have a target area where you want the visitor to place the layer, you can specify that location by typing into the Drop Target text fields the left and top values that the layer should have in its target position. You can make it easier for a visitor to place the layer in the target location by causing the layer to snap to the target location if the layer is moved within the range of pixels that you specify; use the Snap If Within text field to set the snap-to range.*

7. Click OK. Save the file and preview it in the browser.

Test the movement of your class layer by trying to move it. Notice that you can move it only within the region specified by the numeric values you entered in Step 6. This behavior might not work in all browsers.

Note *The Advanced tab in the Drag Layer dialog box allows you to specify an area of the image as a handle that the visitor can use to grab and move the layer. It also gives you control over what happens to the z-index of the layers when the layer is moved. You also have the option to call additional JavaScripts while the layer is moving, when the layer is dropped, or when the layer snaps to the target. The Drag Layer behavior gives you the ability to create a more interactive experience for the visitor.*

Using the Show-Hide Layers Behavior

You can use the Show-Hide Layers behavior to control a layer's visibility and have that visibility change based on the visitors' actions.

1. Create a new layer above the textlayer, name it *yoga*, and place the jayne.jpg image inside it—use *yoga* for the alternative text for the image. Create a second new layer to the right of the yoga layer. Name it *details* and type the following in the new layer: *Learn about a variety of yoga poses in our classes.*

Your document should look like the following example.

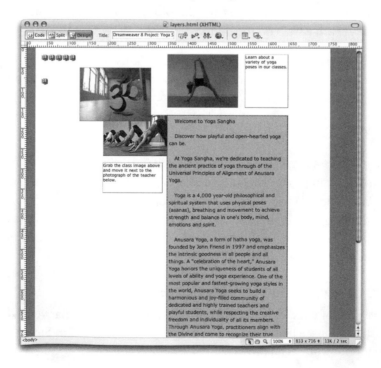

2. Set the visibility of the details layer to hidden by selecting the layer and choosing hidden from the Vis menu on the Property inspector. Click outside the layer in the Document window to deselect it.

Note *You can also set the visibility of the layer by clicking in the Visibility column to show the closed eye icon that indicates the layer is designated as hidden. Clicking on the visibility icon in the column for any given layer will change the visibility for that layer.*

The details layer now disappears.

3. Select the jayne.jpg image, type # into the Link text field on the Property inspector, and press Return (Macintosh) or Enter (Windows). With the image still selected, click the plus sign (+) button in the Behaviors panel (located in the Tag Inspector panel group) to add a behavior. Choose Show-Hide Layers from the behaviors menu.

The Show-Hide Layers dialog box appears with a list of the layers on the page.

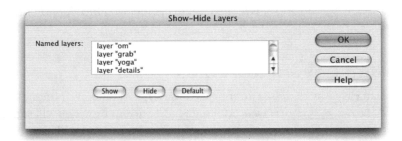

4. Select the details layer from the Named Layers list and click the Show button. Click OK to close the Show-Hide Layers dialog box.

When you click the Show button, (show) is displayed next to the details layer in the list on the Show-Hide Layers dialog box.

5. In the Behaviors panel, click the Event menu and choose <A> onMouseOver from the Event menu.

This behavior is now triggered when the visitor rolls over it. Selecting events for behaviors was covered in Lesson 8.

6. Save the layers.html file and test it in the browser.

Leave this file open for the next exercise.

Tip   *If you want the layer to hide again when the visitor scrolls off the image, repeat steps 3-5 choosing "Hide" instead of "Show" in step 4, and choosing "<A> onMouseOut" instead of "<A> onMouseOver" in step 5.*

Converting Layers to Tables

Layers can be an easy way to design your page; however, your audience might be limited because not all browsers support layers. Although most current browsers will support layers, earlier browsers display layer contents without any positioning and without any control about the placement. If you decide to design your page using layers, you might want to convert the layers to a table to provide an alternate page for those viewers with browsers that do not support layers. Test your pages in different browsers and see what your audience is using to help determine if you want to provide an alternative page. After you have converted the layers to a table, you can switch to Layout view to complete any design changes. You can then use the Check Browser behavior to redirect users based on their browser version.

The following exercise shows you how to convert layers, but the recommended method of creating tables is using Standard view to create tables or Layout view to draw tables and table cells (you worked with both methods in Lesson 6).

A few restrictions apply when you're converting layers to tables: You can't have nested layers, and the layers can't overlap. If these conditions exist, Dreamweaver displays an alert and does not create the table. You also cannot convert a single layer or group of layers to a table while leaving other layers as layers—the entire page and all the layers that it contains will be converted to a table.

1. In the layers.html document, choose File › Save As and type *layers_tables.html* in the Save As (Macintosh) or File name (Windows) text field. Save the file in the Lesson_09_Layers folder.

The layers in this document will be converted and replaced with a single table.

| Tip | *The conversion to a table removes the layer names.* |

2. Click in the Document window. On the Layers panel, check the Prevent Overlaps box. Adjust the placement of the layers at the top of the page so that the layers are not next to another and do not overlap.

Overlapping layers cannot be converted to a table. If you select this option before you begin drawing layers, Dreamweaver prevents the layers from overlapping. After the Prevent Overlaps box is checked, you might want to test it by trying to move the class layer over the om layer. By using the Prevent Overlaps option, you can move layers as close as possible to other layers.

If you already have layers that overlap, checking the Prevent Overlaps checkbox does not move those layers. You have to move them to stop them from overlapping.

3. Select the <body> tag in the tag selector, select the Drag Layer behavior in the Behaviors panel, and click the Remove Event button. Select the jayne.jpg image in the Document window, select the Show-Hide Layers behavior in the Behaviors panel, and click the Remove Event button.

When you use behaviors that apply to or are intended to affect layers, those behaviors are no longer be necessary after you convert the layers to a table. Such behaviors should be removed to keep your document clean, keep it free of errors and unnecessary code, and reduce the file size.

4. Choose Modify > Convert > Layers to Table.

The Convert Layers to Table dialog box opens with a number of options:

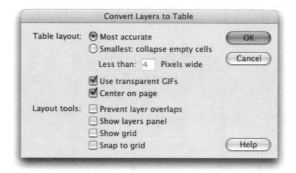

- Most accurate creates a table cell for every layer plus any additional cells that are necessary to preserve the space between layers.

- Smallest: collapse empty cells specifies that the layers' edges should be aligned if they are positioned within the specified number of pixels. If this option is selected, the resulting table might have fewer empty rows and columns.

- Use transparent GIFs fills the last row of the table with transparent GIFs, which ensures that the table displays the same way in all browsers. When this option is selected, you cannot edit the resulting table by dragging its columns. When this option is deselected, the resulting table does not contain transparent GIFs, and its appearance might vary slightly in different browsers.

- Center on page centers the resulting table on the page. If this option is deselected, the table is left-aligned.

- Layout tools allows you to set any desired layout or grid options.

5. Keep the default settings of Most accurate, Use transparent GIFs, and Center on page; then click OK.

If you have any layers that overlap, you get a warning dialog box, informing you that Dreamweaver cannot convert the layers to a table. If this happens, go back to your document and make sure that none of the layers overlap.

Any hidden layers are deleted. After you convert your layers to a table, you can make any necessary adjustments to the table.

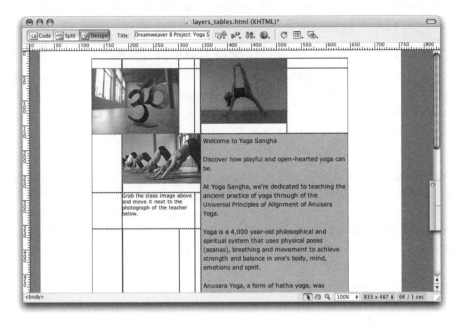

6. Select the `<style>` group in the **CSS Styles Panel and click the trash icon at the bottom of the panel. In the Document window, select the instruction text located in the table cell below the class image and delete it.**

The process of converting layers to tables replaces the `<div>` tags in the body of the document with a corresponding `<table>` tag; however, the internal CSS properties that were defined in the head of the document still remain. You can use the CSS Styles panel to delete the internal style sheet entirely or remove only those styles that defined the layers. If you look in the CSS Styles panel you will see two groups of styles: sangha.css and `<style>` . The external style sheet that is used throughout the project site is sangha.css, whereas the `<style>` group is the internal style sheet that was created while you worked with layers in this lesson. The textlayer layer for example, is defined in the `<style>`group as `#textlayer` . Any styles that use the names of the layers that you previously created are no longer necessary and can be deleted. Although in this case the entire internal style sheet can be deleted, you might want to be cautious when deleting an internal style sheet and check to be sure that there are no additional styles that were included that specify properties that defined things other than the layers themselves, such as font styling.

When performing operations such as converting layers to tables, certain functionality might be lost. In this case, the user can no longer drag the class image to a different location on the page—so any references to or instructions regarding such features should be removed.

Using the Netscape Resize Layer Fix

Netscape 4.x versions have a problem with layers that occurs when the user resizes the browser window: The layer changes its shape when the browser window is resized, which can cause problems with the page. You can fix this problem by inserting the Netscape Resize Layer Fix JavaScript code into your document whenever you use layers. The JavaScript code fixes the Netscape 4.x problem and does not affect other browsers.

Dreamweaver will automatically add the Netscape Resize Fix when you create a layer in a document. When you delete all layers from a document you should run this command and remove the code if the script is still in your document. Because you converted from layers to a table in the previous exercise, you'll remove the script now because it is no longer needed.

1. In the layers_tables.html document, choose Commands › Add/Remove Netscape Resize Fix.

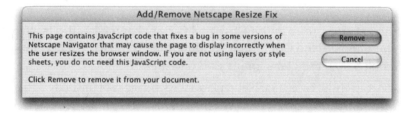

In the Add/Remove Netscape Resize Fix dialog box that opens, you can either add or remove the JavaScript code, depending on whether or not the script is in the document. The code causes the page to reload if the user resizes the browser window. Dreamweaver adds this code to your page automatically. If it is not in a page that uses layers, you can add it easily with this dialog box.

The Netscape Resize Fix Javascript is located in the head of the document, before the <body> tag and can be seen in either Split or Code view. You'll work with the code more in Lesson 16.

2. Click Remove.

The Netscape Resize Fix JavaScript code is removed from the page.

3. Save the layers_tables.html document.

You can close this file.

Animating with Timelines

HTML pages are generally motionless unless you add an animated GIF or a Macromedia Flash movie. You can roll over a button that might appear to move slightly as it swaps out with another image, but it remains static on the page. With Dynamic HTML (DHTML), you have the option to add more extensive animations to your Web page directly within Dreamweaver. These animations are controlled with JavaScript within the HTML page, without the need of a plug-in. The limitation on DHTML animations is that users must use a 4.0 or later browser to view the pages; however, these animations are far more restricted than Flash with which you can do far more—Flash files are also generally more compatible and less buggy. It is recommended to use Flash movies instead of timelines whenever possible. The timelines feature was removed from Dreamweaver MX 2004 for these reasons. It has been added back into Dreamweaver 8 to provide Web developers with the ability to easily edit and maintain legacy pages that were created with previous versions of Dreamweaver. The general features and components of timeline animations are outlined here, for background information on working with older pages. If you are creating an animation, however, the best method is to use Flash.

Understanding How Timelines Work

All objects that are included in a timeline animation are contained in layers. The layers are arranged in a timeline, which generates a path of movement and controls timing. A timeline consists of a series of frames, much like frames in a movie. Each frame displays on the Web page at a specific point in time, depending on how many frames per second you specify and how long the animation is. You can control the placement and properties of each layer in a frame. A frame can also trigger a behavior during the animation.

To move an object (such as text or a graphic), the object must be contained in a layer. Objects such as images can be added to the timeline without placing them in a layer, but you will not be able to animate their positions.

Timelines Panel

Open the Timelines panel by choosing Window > Timelines.

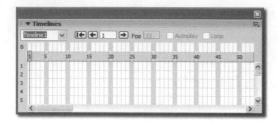

The Timelines panel represents the properties of layers and images over time.

Each row on the Timelines panel is called an *animation channel* and represents elements on the page. Because you can only animate layers, each row on the timeline can only contain layers. You can use the Timelines panel to control a layer's position, dimension, visibility, and stacking order.

Each column on the Timelines panel is called a *frame* and represents a unit of time. Frame numbers indicate the number of frames each animation occupies.

Adding an Object to a Timeline

To add an object to the timeline, select the layer in which the object is contained and choose Modify > Timeline > Add Object to Timeline. When you use this method, the layer is added to the Timelines panel in the first animation channel (the first row).

> **Tip** *You can also use the layer selection handle to grab the layer and drag it from the Document window into the Timelines panel. When you drag a layer into the Timelines panel, the layer will appear in whichever animation channel (row) that you drop it into.*

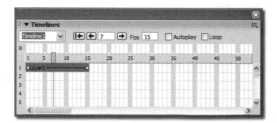

You can also add more timelines to a page by choosing Modify > Timeline > Add Timeline. The timeline drop-down menu allows you to select a timeline if you have created more than one.

The Animation Bar

When you add an object to a timeline, a horizontal blue *animation bar* appears in the new channel on the timeline and displays the name of the layer in the bar.

Animation bars show the duration of each object. A single row can include multiple bars representing different objects. Different bars cannot control the same object in the same frame. The animation bar can be relocated to any frame and any channel. The initial placement of the animation bar in the channel is based on the position of the playhead. The playhead shows which frame of the timeline is currently displayed on the page. If the playhead is in Frame 1, the animation bar begins in Frame 1; if the playhead is in Frame 8, the animation bar begins in Frame 8. As you move the animation bar, the playhead will also move. You can move animation bars on the Timelines panel by dragging the solid area of the bars.

By default, animation bars are initially 15 frames long when you add layers to the Timelines panel. The frame numbers show the duration of the animation. You can control the speed and length of the animation by setting the total number of frames and the number of frames per second (fps). Set the total number of frames by dragging the last keyframe to the right, as you did in this exercise. Set the number of frames per second in the Fps text field. The default setting of 15 frames per second is a good average rate to use—faster rates might not improve performance. Browsers always play every frame of the animation, even if they cannot attain the specified frame rate on the user's system.

To change the start time of an animation, select the animation bar (click in the middle of the bar and not on a keyframe) and drag left or right. Press Shift to select more than one bar at a time.

Using Keyframes

All animations are controlled by keyframes. *Keyframes* are the pivotal instances that define what happens in the animation. After you place a layer on the timeline, you use keyframes to control the movement of that layer on the page. A keyframe marks a point in the animation when a change is made to specified properties (such as position or size) for the layer. Dreamweaver interpolates values—that is, it creates the values needed for all frames between keyframes to come up with the path of the layer. The path line that is automatically generated between the keyframes is based on the values and locations of the layers at the keyframes. By default, there will always be a beginning keyframe and an ending keyframe, which are indicated by open circles at the beginning and end of the animation bar. An animation with only these two keyframes will move in a straight line. To create an animation that doesn't move in a straight line and has movement that is more fluid and follows a more complex path, you need to add keyframes at other frames in the timeline.

To add a keyframe, in the Timelines panel, hold down Cmd (Macintosh) or Ctrl (Windows) until the pointer changes to a circle; then click on the animation bar at the desired point or type the number of the frame into the frame text field to select it and choose Modify > Timeline > Add Keyframe. To remove a keyframe, select the keyframe and choose Modify > Timeline > Remove Keyframe.

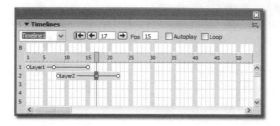

The frame text field will tell you which frame number the selected keyframe is on. You can move keyframes on the timeline by dragging them left or right to new frames. If you want to shorten and speed up the animation or expand and lengthen it, drag the last keyframe to the left or right (respectively) to change the size of the animation bar—all the keyframes will automatically move proportionally to stay in the same position relative to the other keyframes. To prevent the other keyframes from moving, press Ctrl (Windows) or Cmd (Macintosh) while dragging the keyframe at the end of the animation bar. The modifier keys restrain the movement to only the last keyframe.

> **Note** *When animating a layer containing an image, users with a Macintosh and Internet Explorer 5.0 might notice a trail of pieces of the image as it moves across the screen. Internet Explorer 5.0 on a Macintosh cannot calculate the layer dimensions as it moves across the page if the layer is the same size as the image. To fix this, you will need to change the size of the layer (or the layer you are animating) to make it larger than the image. When the layer is on the timeline, you have to change the size of the layer at each keyframe. Use the Property inspector to exactly match the sizes of the layer at each keyframe. If you have a timeline with more than two keyframes, it might be easier to remove the layer from the timeline and start again.*

Controlling Timelines with Behaviors

Adding a behavior to the timeline is similar to adding a behavior to any other object, except that you attach the behavior to a single frame in the timeline and not to the entire animation bar. The behavior is added to the Behaviors channel, and a dash in the Behaviors channel indicates which frame the behavior was applied to.

Events don't have to start at the beginning of the timeline. You can use the timeline to delay action on the page until a certain time after the page loads by moving the animation bar to the right to create the desired number of empty frames.

To add a behavior, click the desired frame in the Behaviors channel above the playhead. Open the Behaviors panel and add the desired behavior.

- **Autoplay.** Uses JavaScript to make the timeline play when the page loads. A behavior is attached to the page's <body> tag; the behavior automatically executes the Play Timeline action when the page loads in a browser—using the onLoad event, which will cause the animation to begin once the document has finished loading in the browser. At times you might want the user to control the playback of the timeline. You can add a Start Timeline button to play the animation when the user rolls over a button or clicks an image. Select the first frame in the Timelines panel. Select the image or button you want to use. In the Behaviors panel, click the plus sign (+) button to add a behavior and choose the Timeline > Play Timeline behavior.

- **Loop.** If you select Loop on the Timelines panel, a behavior is added in the last frame that returns the playback head to Frame 1 and plays the timeline again. The behavior is added to the Behaviors channel and appears as a dash above the last frame. You can edit the parameters for this behavior to define the number of loops by selecting the dash in the Behaviors channel and double-clicking the corresponding action in the Behaviors panel. A dialog box will allow you to set how many times the animation will loop and in what frame it will begin to loop.

- **Show / Hide.** You can make multiple layers appear and disappear at once by selecting other layers in the Named Layers list and clicking the Show or Hide buttons. Default will restore the layer's default visibility. Layers do not have to be in the Timelines panel for you to show or hide them with this behavior.

Positioning an Object

The arrow keys will move the layer one pixel at a time. Holding down the Shift key and pressing an arrow key will move the layer by the current grid increment.

You can also type a negative number in the L (Left) text field at the top of the Property inspector to move the layer off the screen. The top-left corner of the browser is the zero point (covered early in this lesson, when you worked with rulers), where Dreamweaver's horizontal and vertical rulers intersect when they are visible. Anything to the right or down from that point is a positive value; anything to the left or up from that point is a negative value. To make the layer begin outside of the visible window of the browser you have set the starting point of the layer to a negative horizontal value.

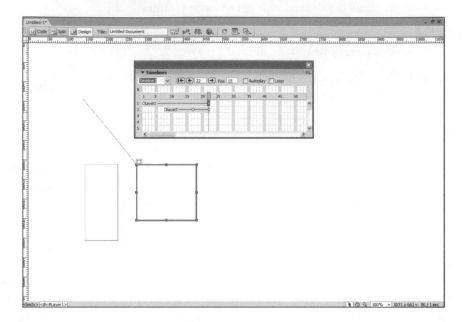

To shift the location of an entire animation path, select the animation bar on the timeline and then drag the layer on the page. Dreamweaver adjusts the position of all keyframes. Making any change when an entire bar is selected changes all the keyframes in the bar.

Note | *The z-index determines the order in which layers will overlap each other, designating their level not horizontally or vertically, but in the third dimension. If you wait until you place a layer in the timeline, adjusting the z-index will change the stacking order only for the keyframe that is selected in the Timelines panel. This is useful if you want the stacking order of your layers to change over the course of the animation.*

Recording the Path of a Layer

Another method of specifying the movement of the animation is by recording the path. To do this, Dreamweaver follows your pointer as you drag the layer on the page. Dreamweaver tracks your movement and creates the keyframes on the timeline for you. Dreamweaver also matches the time you take when dragging the layer. The slower you drag, the more keyframes are added, and the longer the animation bar becomes. You can then alter the time or the keyframes on the timeline. Recording the path of a layer will automatically add that layer to the timeline.

To record a path, select the first frame in the Timelines panel by clicking the 1 in the row of frame numbers. Select the desired layer in the Document window and choose Modify > Timeline > Record Path of Layer.

As you drag the layer, a gray dotted line will show the resulting path. You can drag the layer in any direction, cross back over the path you are creating, and vary the speed with which you drag the layer to affect the way the path is recorded. When you stop dragging and release, the dotted line is converted to the animation line. Dreamweaver adds the layer to the timeline with the necessary keyframes to control the layer's movement.

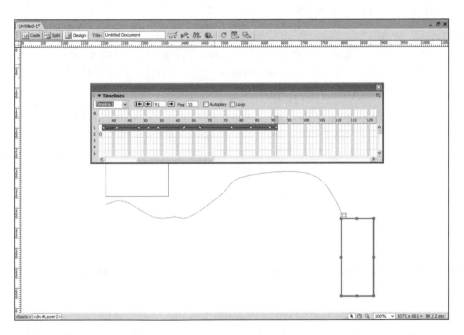

Depending upon the amount of time that you take to drag the animation bar while recording the path of the layer, this animation might be very long. The longer the path you create, the longer the animation will be. Keep in mind that long, complicated animations and pages with many different animation channels will take much longer to load and increase the possibility of crashing the visitor's browser.

As you shorten the animation bar, all the keyframes in the animation shift, so their relative positions remain constant. The keyframes will stay in the same positions relative to other keyframes and the beginning and end of the animation bar.

Changing Image Properties

Timelines allow you to change the source properties of an image by selecting the point at which you want the change to occur. You would need to add a keyframe to the title animation bar at the desired frame.

Using a spacer image as the initial image is one way to make the image appear. You can also achieve this effect by changing the visibility of a layer.

Changing the Visibility and Size

Timelines allow you to do more than simply move layers. You can also use timelines to change the visibility of a layer over time. For example, you might want a layer to be displayed only after another layer animates across the screen. The initial state of the second layer would be hidden and would then become visible at a certain frame.

In addition to changing the visibility of a layer, you can also change the size of a layer. The process is the same as the techniques you used to change the visibility during the animation: To change the size of a layer, you would select the keyframe at which you want the change to occur on the animation bar for the layer you want to affect and then change the W and H text fields on the Property inspector or use the resize handles in the Document window. Keep in mind, browsers have varying capabilities and not all will display properly—test your pages to be sure.

Previewing the Animation in Dreamweaver

To preview the animation, click Rewind on the Timelines panel and then hold down Play to preview the animation on the page. The layer will jump back to its original position in the Document window, and the playhead will move to the first frame in the Timelines panel. If you click the Play button once, you will see the layer move one frame per click, and the play head will advance one frame to the right. When you click and hold the Play button, you will see the animation play continuously. The animation will repeat for as long as you continue to hold down the Play button. As the animation plays, the playhead shows which frame of the timeline is currently displayed on the page. You can also use the Back button to move one frame to the left or back. Hold down the Back button to play the timeline backward.

What You Have Learned

In this lesson, you have:

- Created layers by drawing them in the Document window and by inserting default presized layers (pages 309–314)

- Named layers to keep track of them in the Layers panel (pages 315–316)

- Selected single and multiple layers, modified their sizes and locations, and aligned them relative to each other (pages 315–316)

- Used layers to control the placement and display of content on your page (pages 316–321)

- Changed the stacking order of layers to specify the order in which they display from top to bottom (pages 322–324)

- Nested and unnested layers to understand how layers can work in groups or become nested accidentally (pages 324–327)

- Set rulers and grids to help when moving layers on the page (pages 328–330)

- Combined layers with behaviors to let users interact with your pages (pages 331–334)

- Changed layer visibility to hide and show entire layers (pages 334–336)

- Made pages designed with layers compatible with earlier browsers by converting the layers to a table (pages 336–340)

- Learned to insert or remove a JavaScript to remedy a Netscape bug that causes viewing problems with layers (pages 340–341)

- Learned about the Timelines feature (pages 341–348)

10 Creating Frames

A standard HTML page consists of one region that encompasses the entire browser window. Frames split the browser window into two or more panes; each pane contains independent HTML content. Each of these independent regions is a subset of the larger browser window that contains them. Frames are commonly used to define navigation and content areas for a page. Typically, the navigation area remains constant, and the content area changes each time a navigation link is clicked. This use of frames can be extremely helpful to a user for navigation through a site. Using frames can also make a site easier to modify because there is only one navigation page to update. On the other hand, frames can degrade a Website if they are poorly implemented: They might be confusing and disorienting to users if they do not provide a clear site structure, they

In this lesson, you'll create and change the properties of a frameset and frames, resize frames, and use links to control their contents.

might make it difficult for users to bookmark or find their way back to a previous page, or they might make the content difficult to view if they are not properly sized and formatted.

When a user views a Web page that was created with two frames, the browser is actually using three separate files to display the page: the frameset file and the two files containing the content that appears inside each of the two frames. A *frameset* is an HTML file that is invisible to the user and defines the structure of a Web page with frames. A frameset stores information about the size and location of each frame, along with the names of the files that supply the content for each of the frames. Each frame is a separate HTML file. Frames have borders that can be turned off so the frames are not readily apparent to the user or they can be turned on to clearly split the window into different panes. Other options include scroll bars and the possibility of allowing the user to resize the frames by dragging the borders.

In this lesson, you'll work with frames to create a Web page with a navigation area and a content area. You'll develop a set of pages that all appear in the content frame when the user selects a link from the navigation frame and you'll learn how to target links to different frames. You'll also learn how to include content for browsers that do not support frames.

To see an example of the finished page for this chapter, open community.html from the Lesson_10_Frames/Completed folder.

What You Will Learn

In this lesson, you will:

- Create a frameset
- Save a frameset
- Create frames and nested frames
- Resize frames
- Change frameset and frame properties
- Create documents within frames
- Target frame content
- Create NoFrames content

Approximate Time

This lesson should take about one hour to complete.

Lesson Files

Media Files:

Lesson_10_Frames/Images/...(all files)

Starting Files:

Lesson_10_Frames/Text/...(all files)
Lesson_10_Frames/Community/sidebar.html
Lesson_10_Frames/Community/ys_nav.html
Lesson_10_Frames/sangha.css

Completed Project:

Lesson_10_Frames/Completed/Community/AboutGreen.html
Lesson_10_Frames/Completed/Community/BeginningGreen.html
Lesson_10_Frames/Completed/Community/community.html
Lesson_10_Frames/Completed/Community/community_intro.html
Lesson_10_Frames/Completed/Community/sidebar.html
Lesson_10_Frames/Completed/Community/top.html
Lesson_10_Frames/Completed/Community/ys_nav.html

Creating a Frameset

A frameset defines the overall look of a page that uses frames—the number of frame areas on the page, the size of each frame, and the border attributes. A frameset itself does not contain any content; it specifies what HTML document will be used in each frame. The frameset document is the file that you link to when calling up a frames-based Web page. In this lesson, you create a Web page consisting of three frames. The left frame holds navigation elements that remain constant, the right frame displays pages with content relative to the links clicked in the navigation frame, and the top frame contains the title of the site.

There are two ways to create a frameset in Macromedia Dreamweaver: You can manually insert the frames or you can choose from several predefined framesets. If you choose a predefined frameset, the frameset and frames are automatically set up for you. The predefined frameset method is one of the quickest ways to create a layout using frames because most of the work is done for you. You just need to name the individual pages.

In this exercise, you will use a predefined frameset to create a Web page that uses frames.

1. **Choose File › New and select Framesets from the Category list in the General portion of the New Document dialog box.**

> **Tip** *You can also access the Framesets portion of the New Document dialog box by clicking Framesets in the Create From Samples list in the Start page.*

The New Document dialog box contains a variety of presets that you can use when creating a new frameset. As you browse the Framesets list, samples showing the basic frame structure are displayed in the preview area at the right, along with a description.

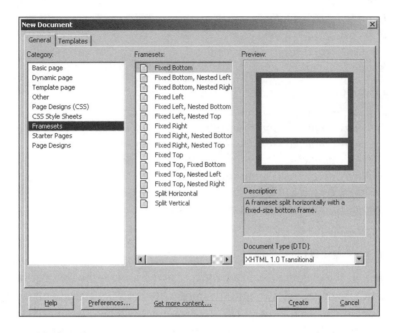

> **Note** *You can also create a frameset from a standard HTML document by selecting the Layout menu on the Insert bar and choosing a frameset preset from the Frames menu.*

The Frames menu in the layout category of the insert bar

2. **Select Fixed Right, Nested Top from the Framesets list and click Create.**

A frameset can be made of either rows or columns, but not both. Framesets can be nested to create a layout like the one you chose with multiple rows and multiple columns.

3. In the Frame Tag Accessibility Attributes dialog box, use the Frame menu to select the frames and the Title text field to set the corresponding titles as follows:

Set the title of rightFrame to Right Navigation

Set the title of topFrame to Title and Navigation

Set the title of mainframe to Main Content

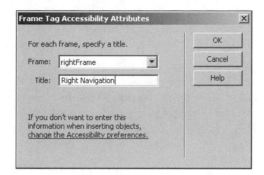

Note *If the Frame Tag Accessibility Attributes dialog box does not appear, you can turn on the Frames accessibility feature by choosing Dreamweaver > Preferences (Macintosh) or Edit > Preferences (Windows) and selecting Accessibility from the Category list. Under the Show attributes when inserting option ensure that Frames is checked.*

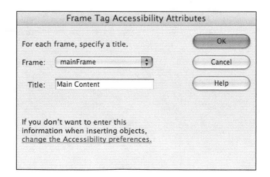

The Frame Tag Accessibility Attributes dialog box enables you to select an appropriate title for each frame. The title provides context for the content of each frame, so users can determine which frame has the information they seek. A frame title is defined through the `title` attribute, which is easily accessed when you first create the frames via the Frame Tag Accessibility Attributes dialog box. However, you can also apply or edit frame titles at a later time by selecting a frame and using the CSS/Accessibility portion of the Attributes section of the Tag panel to modify the `title` attribute.

The title attribute is not interchangeable with the name attribute. The title labels the frame for users; the name labels it for scripting and window targeting. Only the title is presented to users. You'll work with frame names later in this lesson.

Accessibility and Frames

The drawbacks of using frames include the lack of full accessibility and nonfunctionality of onscreen readers and mobile devices such as PDAs and cell phones. Other issues include impaired browser back button functionality, printing problems, maintenance issues, and poor usability.

Frames are used to organize a page visually into different panes. For nonvisual users, the relationships between the content in frames must be conveyed in a nonvisual way; therefore, using the accessibility features that Dreamweaver prompts you with while creating frames is an important step in creating more accessible documents.

After you apply the accessibility attributes, you will see the frameset in the Document window. A dotted border appears around the page edges in the frameset, and lines show the frame structure.

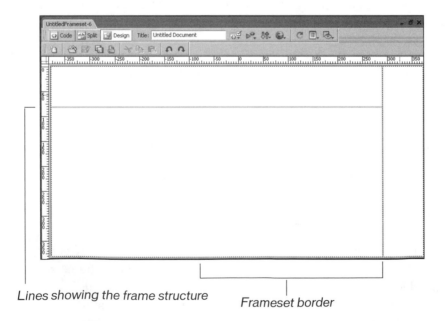

Lines showing the frame structure   Frameset border

The page is divided into three frames with the use of two framesets. Framesets can contain only horizontal frames or only vertical frames—they cannot contain both vertical and horizontal frames at the same time. To achieve the combination of vertical and horizontal frames, framesets must be *nested* within each other. A nested frameset is one that is contained inside a frame that was defined by a previous frameset. The initial frameset of your document contains two vertical frames—one on the left and one on the right. The left frame contains a nested frameset that is divided into two horizontal frames: a short frame on the top and a longer frame on the bottom. Several of Dreamweaver's predefined framesets use nested framesets. You can use combinations of these predefined framesets to come up with any frame layout you want. Thin gray lines mark the divisions between frames.

Note *To insert frames manually, open a new HTML document and choose View > Visual Aids > Frame Borders to turn on the dotted frame border around the page edges of the Document window. Click the border and drag it into the Document window. The document becomes split horizontally (if you drag from the top or bottom of the border) or vertically (if you drag from the left or right sides of the border). If you drag the border from the corner, the document becomes divided into four frames. You can also choose Modify > Frameset > Split Frame Left, Right, Up, or Down. If you selected the wrong frames configuration or need to reduce the number of frames in your frameset, you can remove the extra frames by dragging the border of the unwanted frame to the edge of the page or atop another frame. The extra frame disappears.*

Leave this file open to use in the next exercise.

Saving a Frameset

When you have the number of frames you want, you need to save the frameset. The frameset file is the file that you reference when linking to this Web page. The frameset, as well as the files for each frame, needs to be saved before you can preview the page in a browser. If you attempt to preview the page in the browser prior to saving, Dreamweaver displays a message stating that the frameset and frame files all need to be saved to preview. You can save each file individually or you can save all open files at once. In this exercise, you save only the frameset.

1. In the Document window, verify that the frameset is selected by checking the tag selector, in which the `<frameset>` should be highlighted.

When you create a frameset, it is automatically selected. Clicking anywhere in the Document window deselects the frameset because you would be clicking inside a frame. Clicking inside a frame is similar to clicking inside a table cell; placing the insertion point inside a cell will make that cell active, but will not give you access to the same properties that you would be able to edit if the entire table itself were selected. Likewise, to modify a frameset, you must select the frameset itself.

The Document window with the frameset selected

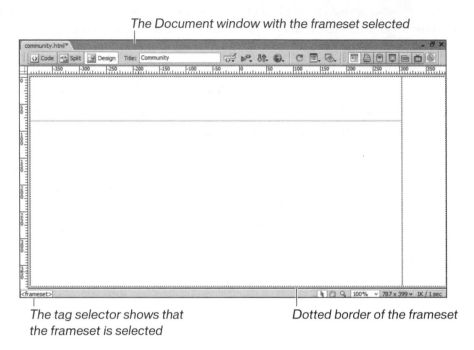

The tag selector shows that the frameset is selected

Dotted border of the frameset

If the frameset is not selected, you can select it by clicking the border around the edges of the Document window. You can also select the frameset by choosing Window > Frames and then clicking the outermost border enclosing the frames in the Frames panel. The Frames panel shows you a simplified version of the structure of frames in the document.

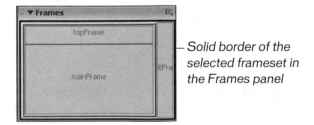

— Solid border of the selected frameset in the Frames panel

When the frameset is selected, the Document window is outlined by a dotted line and the tag selector at the bottom of the window displays <frameset>. The document's title bar shows "UntitledFrameset-1" and the Property inspector shows the frameset properties. The number (-1, -2, and so on) of your untitled document might vary depending on how many new documents you created since you opened Dreamweaver.

> **Note** *If the frameset is not selected, an individual frame is selected instead and the frames border around the Document window is a solid black line. If a nested frameset is selected, the border of the frame that contains it is surrounded with a dotted line.*

In the Frames panel, a selected frameset is displayed with a thick border around the perimeter of the panel and the frames are displayed with a grayed-out border.

2. **Choose File › Save Frameset As and save the file as** *community.html* **in the Lesson_10_Frames/Community folder.**

The document's title bar shows the filename.

3. **With the frameset still selected, type** *Yoga Sangha: Community* **for the page title. Save the frameset.**

If you don't have the frameset selected when you title the page, you might be titling one of the pages that correspond with an individual frame—not the actual frameset file. Refer to the Frames panel to check what is selected; it helps to ensure that you are working within the frame or frameset that you intend to edit.

Leave the community.html file open to use in the next exercise.

Resizing Frames in a Frameset

You can use the Property inspector to specify the size of your frames or you can simply drag the borders in the Document window to perform the same task. In addition to specifying a size in the Property inspector, you can also determine how browsers allocate space to frames when there is not enough room to display all frames at full size.

1. In the Document window, verify that the nested frameset is selected by positioning the pointer over the horizontal border between the top and bottom frames. When the pointer changes to a double arrow, click the border once to select the frameset.

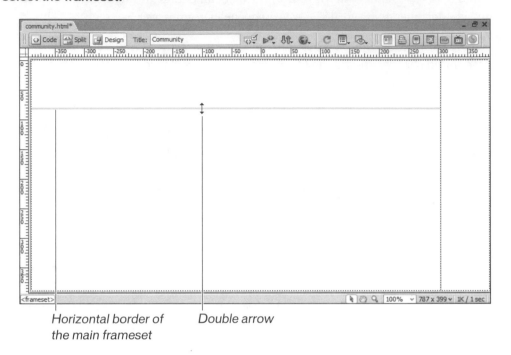

Horizontal border of   Double arrow
the main frameset

The nested frameset is selected, and the Property inspector shows the frameset properties. The Property inspector changes depending on whether you selected a frameset or a frame. To change the size of the frames, you need to make sure that you selected the frameset.

The Property inspector showing frameset properties for the nested frameset   *Top row selected*

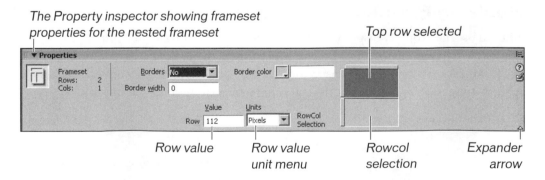

Row value   Row value   Rowcol   Expander
                   unit menu   selection   arrow

Tip *Click the expander arrow in the Property inspector to view all Frameset properties if they are not already visible.*

2. Drag the border between the top and bottom frames until the top frame is 112 pixels high.

Use the Row Value in the Property inspector to check the height or type **112** in the Row Value text field when the top row is selected in the RowCol Selection area to get the exact height. Make sure that Pixels is selected from the Units menu. The top row in the RowCol Selection should be dark to indicate that it is active.

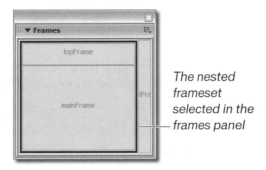

The nested frameset selected in the frames panel

3. With the frameset still selected, click the bottom row in the RowCol Selection area in the Property inspector to select the bottom row within the nested frameset. Next to the Row Value text field, verify that Relative is selected from the Units menu.

When you use the RowCol Selection in the Property inspector to select a row or column, you are selecting that row or column within the frameset, which enables you to modify the properties of the frameset as they apply to that specific row or column. You are not selecting an individual frame.

Setting the value unit of the bottom row to Relative allows the bottom row to expand or contract depending on how large the user's browser is and how much space is left after the top row is allocated the 112 pixels that you assigned to it. By default, Dreamweaver automatically places a 1 in the Row Value text field of rows that are defined as Relative.

Note *If you view the HTML code for the frameset size, you see* frameset rows="112,*"*. The 1 in the Row Value text field, in conjunction with the Relative unit chosen from the menu, is the same as the asterisk (*) in the code; it represents a size that is relative or proportional to the other rows in the frameset.*

4. In the Frames panel, click the entire frameset to select it. In the visual representation of the frame in the Property inspector, click the left column in the RowCol Selection area to select the left nested frames column.

In your document, the outer frameset is made up of columns, whereas the nested frameset is composed of rows.

The left column in the Property inspector darkens to indicate it has been selected.

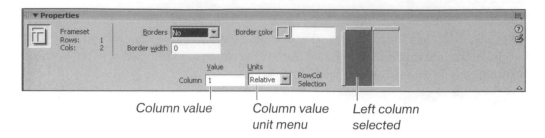

Column value

Column value
unit menu

Left column
selected

5. In the Column Value text field of the Property inspector, type *484* and press Return (Macintosh) or Enter (Windows). Verify that Pixels is selected from the Units menu.

The left column's width is adjusted to 484 pixels.

When you are deciding how to resize the column, keep these units of measurement in mind:

- **Pixels:** This option sets the absolute size of the selected column or row to the number of pixels that you enter. It is the best option for any frame that needs to have a set size. If other columns or rows are defined by a different unit, those other columns or rows are allocated space only after rows or columns specified in pixels are their full size.

- **Percent:** This option specifies a percentage that the current column or row should take up in its frameset. Columns or rows specified with units set to Percent are allocated space after columns or rows with units set to Pixels and before columns or rows with units set to Relative.

- **Relative:** This option specifies that the current column or row is allocated space using the current proportions relative to the other columns and rows. Columns or rows with units set to Relative are allocated space after columns or rows with units set to Pixels and Percent, but they take up all remaining space. If you set the bottom or the right frame to Relative, the frame size changes to fill the remaining width or height of the browser window.

6. In the Property inspector, click the right column in the RowCol Selection area to select the right column of the frameset. Next to the Column Value text field, verify that Relative is selected from the Units menu.

This procedure enables the right column to expand or contract, depending on how large the user's browser is and how much space remains after the left column is allocated the 484 pixels assigned to it.

7. **Save the frameset by choosing File > Save Frameset.**

If this command is not available, first select the outer frameset by clicking the border between the top and bottom frames.

> **Tip** *If you have the frameset selected, Cmd+S (Macintosh) or Ctrl+S (Windows) saves the frameset only.*

Leave the community.html file open to use in the next exercise.

Specifying Frame Properties

When you create a frameset, get in the habit of naming each frame. The name you assign to a frame is not the filename or title of the document that corresponds with the frame, nor is it the title of the frame itself. A frame name serves to identify the framed area of the document for your reference and is generally used for scripting purposes. Naming your frames is important when you create links to display pages within a framed area. It is also important to name your frames for accessibility, especially when the frame title is not supported by technology used to view the page. In the previous exercise, you worked with the predefined framesets. Each frame was already given a default name. In this exercise, you will change the frame names to indicate the functions that they serve.

1. **Select the top-left frame by clicking the top-left frame in the Frames panel.**

> **Tip** *If the Frames panel is not open, choose Window > Frames.*

Selecting the top-left frame in the Frames panel is not the same as placing the insertion point inside the top-left frame by clicking in the Document window. Selecting the frame makes the properties for that frame available to you in the Property inspector. Clicking in the frame in the Document window makes the standard text properties appear for that frame's document. If the insertion point is in the top-left frame, it is the active frame; however, you can't make changes to the frame properties. To affect the properties of the frame itself, it needs to be selected.

> **Tip** *You can also use Shift+Option-click (Macintosh) or Alt-click (Windows) in the top frame in the Document window to select the frame.*

Top frame selected in the frames panel —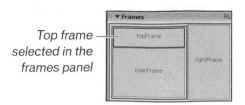

The Frames panel shows a thin black border around the top left frame with the name topFrame shown in the center. The Property inspector displays frame properties for topFrame.

2. In the Frame name text field in the Property inspector, type *titleNav* to replace the default name topFrame. Press Return (Macintosh) or Enter (Windows) to apply the name change.

The frame name text field in the Property inspector

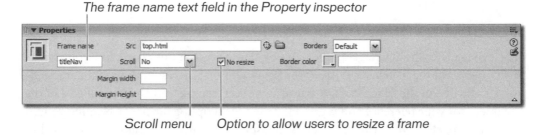

Scroll menu   Option to allow users to resize a frame

The Frames panel displays the word titleNav in the top frame. You can always refer to the Frames panel for the name of a particular frame. Frame names are often used to target links to load in specific frames. You learned about targeting links in Lesson 3.

> **Note** *When naming frames, don't use spaces, hyphens, periods, or special characters in the frame name; and don't begin the name with an underscore. Using any of these characters can cause problems with code or scripting. Also, most coding languages are case sensitive, so make sure you maintain consistency with your frame names.*

3. Verify that No is selected in the Scroll menu and that the No Resize box is checked in the Property inspector.

The scroll option, which defines when scroll bars appear, applies to both vertical and horizontal scroll bars. The Auto setting displays scroll bars whenever there is not enough room in the frame to display the content of the page. The Default option is the browser default setting, which is usually Auto. Be careful how you set this option: if it is set to No and the frame is not large enough to display all the contents, the user cannot scroll to see the rest of the content; if it is set to Yes and the contents fit within the frame, scroll bars that are dimmed still take up space on the page, even though it isn't possible to scroll.

No Resize locks the size of the frame when viewed in the browser. If this option is unchecked, users can drag the frame borders in their browser window. Regardless of whether this option is checked or unchecked, it does not affect your ability to resize frames within Dreamweaver.

Don't forget that visitors to your Website have a wide range of monitor sizes and resolutions. With frames, it is particularly important when designing sites on large, high-resolution screens to account for smaller screens. Frames-based pages might encounter problems on screens that are larger or smaller than those that they were designed for. Small screens, for instance, might cause your pages to suffer problems such as too much scrolling, which can make it extremely difficult for users. By testing your pages in a variety of environments, you can be sure to accommodate the widest possible range of sizes and resolutions. Be aware that such size issues can also lead to printing problems. You might want to provide alternatives, such as printer-friendly pages, if you use frames in your site.

Note *Printer-friendly pages are 530 pixels wide (printable width) and use a bare minimum of graphics. Navigation should also be minimal, such as text links at the bottom of the page. A background color of white and the use of black text is best for readability against the white background of paper. Serif fonts are good choices for pages intended primarily for printing; likewise, keep your text at a size that can be read easily, such as 12 points.*

4. **Select the lower-left frame and name it** *content.* **Scroll should be set to Auto, and the No resize box should be checked.**

In the Property inspector, notice that the Borders menu has Default selected. The predefined framesets that you used to create the page layout are automatically set to have no frame borders. When the Default setting is selected for the Borders option of an individual frame, that frame uses the setting of the parent frameset. If another setting (Yes or No) is selected, the frame overrides the setting of the parent frameset.

The Frames panel displays the name **content** in the lower-left frame.

The Frames panel displays the names you set for the frames —

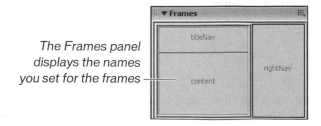

5. Select the right frame and name it *moreContent*. Scroll should be set to No, and the No Resize box should be checked.

In the Property inspector, notice that the text fields for Margin Width and Margin Height are blank. This is the default for the predefined framesets you used to lay out your page. Margin Width sets the left and right margins of the frame in pixels. Margin Height sets the top and bottom margins of the frame in pixels. Leaving them blank uses the browser default, which might vary in size depending on the browser version and type.

The Frames panel displays the name **moreContent** in the right frame.

6. Choose File > Save Frameset.

When you change Frame properties, you are actually modifying the frameset community.html. Frame and frameset properties are both defined within the frameset.

Leave the community.html file open to use in the next exercise.

Creating and Editing Frames Content

Remember that the content of a frame resides in a separate HTML page—not in the frameset. You can create the individual frame pages separately or within the constraints of a frame. Using the frameset to help you design the pages to be contained in each frame is always a good idea. That way, you don't create a page that's too wide or too narrow for the frame. Your users will find the pages difficult to view if they have to scroll in multiple directions to see all the content.

In this exercise, you will add content to each page in the frameset.

1. Place the insertion point in the title frame (the top frame) in the Document window.

The document title bar (Macintosh) or the Dreamweaver program title bar (Windows) changes to show that this is an untitled document.

2. Choose File > Save Frame. Save the file as top.html in the Lesson_10_Frames/ Community folder and title it *Yoga Sangha: Title*. Attach the sangha.css style sheet in the Lesson_10_Frames folder.

The document title bar (Macintosh) or the Dreamweaver program title bar (Windows) changes to reflect the title and filename for the document in this frame. Visitors are not likely to see the title of this page because the browser uses the title of the frameset in the browser window. However, it is still good practice to always title your documents so that if the page is opened in a window by itself for any reason, it has a title.

3. Insert the image ys_header.jpg from the Lesson_10_Frames/Images folder into the title frame and give it an Alt text of *Yoga Sangha*. Save the frame.

As you edit your pages, remember to save often. When you use the Save keyboard shortcut Cmd+S (Macintosh) or Ctrl+S (Windows), you save only the file that corresponds with the currently selected frame or the frameset if it is selected. The Save command does not save each document; you must save them individually or use the File > Save All option. If you want to save the file displayed in another frame, just click inside that frame in the Document window and then click Save. You can refer to the Frames panel to check which frame is selected when you are saving. The names of all frames displayed in the Frames panel are dimmed except for the name of the frame in which the insertion point is located.

4. Place the insertion point in the content frame (the lower-left frame). Save the file as *community_intro.html* in the Lesson_10_Frames/Community folder and title it *Yoga Sangha Community: Introduction to Green Yoga*. Attach the sangha.css style sheet located in the Lesson_10_Frames folder.

The document title bar (Macintosh) or the Dreamweaver program title bar (Windows) changes to reflect the title and filename for the document in this frame.

5. Open Lesson_10_Frames/Community/ys_nav.html, copy the toolbar, and paste it into the content page.

The main navigation toolbar will be contained within the content pages, so it will be included in all pages in this frame.

6. Press Return (Macintosh) or Enter (Windows) to add a new paragraph below the toolbar. Open Lesson_10_Frames/Text/green_page1.txt, copy the text and paste it into the page. Change the text *Green Yoga at Yoga Sangha* to a paragraph and apply the tagline-style style in the Property inspector. Save the page.

This is the content page that corresponds with the Community link that you will create in the navigation frame later in this lesson.

Your content frame should now look like the example shown here.

Note *You can use an interactive element called a navigation bar in frame-based pages to create a way for visitors to get visual feedback while exploring pages. Although you can create a navigation bar yourself, Dreamweaver provides a tool that you can use to create one. A navigation bar is a set of images that are linked to a variety of pages. Navigation bars use JavaScript (covered in Lesson 8), allowing you to add up to four states based on user interaction for each image. The first state of an image occurs when the page loads; the second state of an image is displayed when the user rolls over the image. When the user clicks the image, the third state is shown. The fourth state of an image is used when the visitor rolls over an image after that image is clicked. The navigation bar is effective for giving visitors responses to their actions so that they understand what pages they are looking at based on the state displayed by the navigation images.*

Creating Other Content Documents

You now need to create additional documents that will also appear in the content frame.

1. Create a new HTML document from the Basic Page category of the New Document dialog box. Save the file as *AboutGreen.html* **in the Lesson_10_Frames/ Community folder and title it** *Yoga Sangha: Community: About Green.* **Attach the sangha.css style sheet located in the Lesson_10_Frames folder.**

The document title bar changes to reflect the title and filename for the document.

2. Open Lesson_10_Frames/ys_nav.html, copy the toolbar, and paste it into the AboutGreen.html page.

The main navigation toolbar is contained within each content page.

3. Press Return (Macintosh) or Enter (Windows) to add a new paragraph below the toolbar. Open Lesson_10_Frames/Text/green_page2.txt, copy the text, and paste it into the page. Change the text *About Green Yoga* **to a paragraph and apply the tagline-style style in the Property inspector.**

This is the content page that will correspond with an About Green link; you will create a link to this page from the rightNav frame later in this lesson.

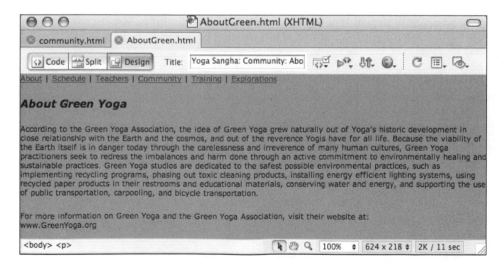

4. Repeat steps 1 to 3 to create BeginningGreen.html in the Lesson_10_Frames/ Community folder. Title it *Yoga Sangha: Community: Beginning Green Yoga* including the text in the green_page3.txt file.

This is the content page that will correspond with a Begin link you will create in the rightNav frame later in this lesson.

You can close AboutGreen.html and BeginningGreen.html. Leave the community.html file open to use in the next exercise.

Opening an Existing Page in a Frame

The content for the moreContent frame has already been created for you. You will want to assign this page to the frame. Also, you already started several content pages, so now you need to make sure that they fit in the content frame. You can open those files directly in the frame to check or edit them.

1. In the community.html Document window, click inside the moreContent frame.

This is the frame in which you want the sidebar page to appear.

2. Choose File > Open in Frame. Choose sidebar.html from the dialog box. Save the frameset.

The page is loaded into the content frame and is available for editing. Notice that the secondary navigation items do not yet have links associated with them.

3. Within the content frame, open AboutGreen.html. Verify that the page fits correctly into the frame.

> **Tip** *Take care when saving your frames and exercise caution when using the Save All Frames command in the File menu. This command saves all open pages contained in your frames and the frameset. The files that initially appear within each frame are defined in the frameset. If you choose File > Save All Frames while you are editing other pages within the frames (by using File > Open In Frame), you redefine the frameset.*

4. Open BeginningGreen.html in the content frame.

Your page should now look like the following example. Verify that it fits in the frame.

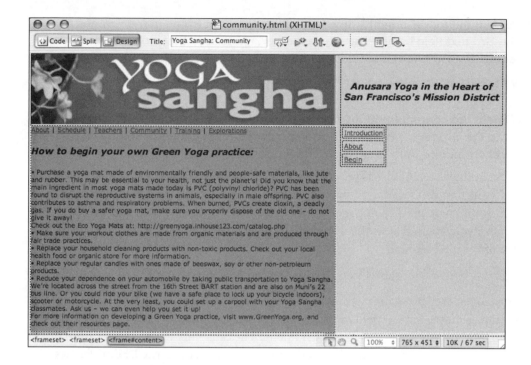

Checking Frame Content

As you create and edit pages within frames, it can be easy to accidentally place the wrong content in a frame. You can use the Property inspector to ensure that the correct pages are loaded into each of the frames for the initial view of your Web page.

1. Select the title Nav frame by clicking the top frame in the Frames panel. In the Src text field in the Property inspector, make sure that top.html is selected. If it isn't, click the folder icon to find and select it.

The Property inspector shows Frame properties for the title frame.

Source for the file that appears in the selected frame

2. Select the moreContent frame by clicking the right frame in the Frames panel. In the Src text field in the Property inspector, make sure that sidebar.html is selected. If it isn't, click the folder icon to find and select it.

The Property inspector shows Frame properties for the moreContent frame.

3. Select the content frame by clicking the lower-left frame in the Frames panel. Next to the Src text field in the Property inspector, click the folder icon to find and select community_intro.html. Save the frameset.

The BeginningGreen.html was selected because it was the last document that you worked with in this frame. If you open a page within a frame to edit it, saving the frameset causes that file to become the default page for that frame when the frameset document loads. The community_intro.html file is the document you want to appear at first in the content frame of the final frameset.

The Property inspector shows frame properties for the content frame.

You can open Web pages from a variety of sources in a frame by typing the URL of the desired page in the Src text field in the Property inspector. The page you call up does not have to reside on the same server as the frameset. The capability to open pages from other servers can be a drawback where the ethical use of content is concerned. Some frames-based pages are used to open content developed by others, without their permission. Be sure to respect the copyright of content that is not your own and avoid giving visitors the impression that materials are from your Website if they aren't.

Note | *If you are concerned about your pages being called up in someone else's frame, you can use JavaScript to cause the browser to open your page in its own window if it is called from a frame. You might be able to determine whether this is a problem by reviewing your site logs; check with your system administrator or Web host for more information.*

Controlling Frame Content with Links

After you have created the content document pages, you need to link the navigation elements to those pages that should display in the content area of your Web page. To get the content to appear in its proper location, you need to target the link to the desired frame.

1. Place the insertion point in the text link Introduction in the moreContent frame (the right frame). In the Property inspector, replace the null link (#) by clicking the Browse for File icon next to the Link text box. Select the community_intro.html page in the same directory. Press Return (Macintosh) or Enter (Windows) to apply the link. Select content from the Target menu while the link is still selected.

By default, links are targeted to the frame or window in which they are located; however, these links should open their corresponding documents in the content frame, not the moreContent frame.

Link text field

Target menu

Each time you create a new frame, the name of that frame is automatically added to the Target menu. Clear, concise, and descriptive names serve you best. Although Dreamweaver's default frame names give you an idea of the frame location, those generic names can still be difficult and confusing to sort out when you try to make a document open in a certain frame.

Note *If you are working on a document that will be loaded in a frame and you are not working on it inside the frameset, as you are in this lesson, you don't have the option in the Target menu to select the names of any frames. Dreamweaver displays only the names of frames that are available in the current document in the target menu. In these cases, you need to type the exact name of the frame in which you want the page to open into the target text field.*

2. Repeat step 1 to link the text About to AboutGreen.html and the text Begin to BeginningGreen.html. Each of these links should be targeted to the content frame.

There are other options available in the Target menu:

- **_blank** loads the linked document in a new, unnamed browser window.
- **_parent** loads the linked document in the parent frameset of the frame that contains the link. If the frame containing the link is not nested, the linked document loads into the full browser window.
- **_self** loads the linked document in the same frame or window as the link. This target is implied, so you usually don't have to specify it.
- **_top** loads the linked document in the full browser window, thereby removing all frames.

3. Save the file and preview it in the browser.

When previewing your frames pages in the browser, you might get a dialog box informing you that all the frames need to be saved. Click OK to save all frames and the frameset.

When you click the About link, the AboutGreen.html document displays in the content frame.

> **Tip** *If your pages don't appear in the frames you expect them to, check to see that you have selected the correct frame from the Target drop-down menu in the Property inspector for each link.*

The links should open all the pages in the content frame—if not, you need to correct the target using the Target menu for any links that do not open in that frame.

Creating NoFrames Content

In Dreamweaver, you can create content that is ignored by frames-capable browsers, and is displayed in older and text-based browsers or in other browsers that do not support frames. This information, called NoFrames content, is also used by search engine spiders, screen readers, and portable Internet devices that do not support frames. The NoFrames content you create is placed in the frameset file. When a browser that doesn't support frames loads the frameset file, the browser displays only the NoFrames content.

1. In the community.html document, select the frameset.

The community.html document is the page the browser loads initially, so the NoFrames content is specified here.

2. Choose Modify > Frameset > Edit NoFrames Content.

> **Tip** *If the Frameset option in the Modify menu is dimmed, you might have a frame selected.*

The Document window changes to display the NoFrames page, and the words "NoFrames Content" appear at the top. This is still the community.html document; you are just seeing a different view of the page's content.

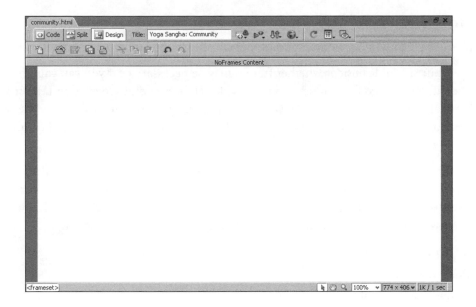

3. Open the green_page1.txt document; then select and copy all the text. Create the NoFrames content in the Document window by pasting in the text you copied from the green_page1.txt text file.

Alternative content can contain elements from a standard html page. It will be enclosed between the <noframes> and </noframes> tags. Only browsers that do not support frames see this content. The content should be relatively simple—browsers that do not support frames are likely to not support JavaScript, image maps, and other types of complex elements. Some Websites use NoFrames content to provide simple alternative pages or to direct users to a text-based version of the Website, whereas other sites use NoFrames content to display a message to users that the site is available only to frames-capable browsers.

4. Make sure there is a checkmark next to Modify > Frameset > Edit NoFrames Content.

The Document window changes to hide the NoFrames content and returns to the normal view of the frameset document.

Note *When you finish editing the NoFrames content, you might be inclined to close the window because you can't see the original document. If you do, you close the frameset and all the frame pages. You then have to open them up again if you want to continue editing them.*

5. Choose File > Save All and close all your documents.

Using Frames On Your Own

Frames can be a useful Web development tool when they are properly implemented.

Review your site and consider whether frames may be necessary or if you can gain the functionality you need from other elements, such as Library items (covered in Lesson 12) or Templates (covered in Lesson 13). For additional practice, you might want to develop two versions of a portion of your site—one with frames and one without—and compare them.

When developing pages with frames, remember to use the accessibility options that Dreamweaver will prompt you to include, and always develop no-frames content for browsers or devices that are not capable of displaying frames-based Web pages. If you develop two versions, compare the usability of each, considering the following:

- Ease of navigation
- Maintenance
- Browser functionality

What You Have Learned

In this lesson, you have:

- Created a frameset to define the layout of frames within your document (pages 353–357)

- Saved a frameset and learned how to save other frames individually, as well as how to save them all at once (pages 357–359)

- Created frames and nested frames to modify the layout of your page using predefined framesets (pages 357–361)

- Resized frames by changing the dimensions in the Property inspector (pages 359–363)

- Changed frameset and frame properties using the Frames panel and the Property inspector (pages 363–366)

- Created documents within frames by inserting elements directly into the frames and by opening existing documents in the frames (pages 369–371)

- Targeted frame content into other frames to control where the pages appear (pages 371–374)

- Created NoFrames content for browsers that are unable to display frames (pages 374–376)

11 Creating Forms

You might sometimes need to collect information from the visitors to your Website. The types of information that might need to be gathered can include feedback about the site, user registration, responses to polls, and buying products (e-commerce). From gathering different types of information to creating an opportunity for visitors to interact with your site, forms provide the necessary user interface that enables you to obtain data. Forms allow you to ask visitors for specific information or to give them an opportunity to send feedback, questions, or requests to you. Visitor registrations and product orders often require the functionality of forms. Forms are often used in conjunction with databases and can enable visitors to perform searches and post information to be included in a database. A form contains fields in which users enter information. These fields can be text fields, radio buttons, checkboxes, menus, or lists, to name a few.

Form data is usually sent to a database on a server, to an e-mail address, or to an application that will process it. The processing of forms can be done through dynamic pages (which use languages such as PHP, JSP, ColdFusion, and more to access

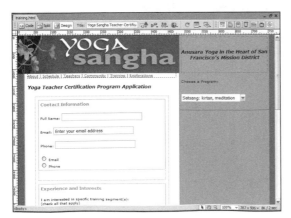

In this project, you will build a form with various text fields, checkboxes, radio buttons, submit and reset buttons, and a menu.

dynamic content sources such as databases) or Common Gateway Interface (CGI) scripts. CGI is a standard protocol that acts as the communication link between the data from the form and the server. In this lesson, you will be creating the form that a visitor will see. Because you will not be working with dynamic pages or CGI scripts, you do not need access to a server to complete this lesson.

To see an example of the finished page for this lesson, open training.html from the Lesson_11_Forms/Completed/Training folder.

What You Will Learn

In this lesson, you will:

- Create a form on a Web page
- Divide form content into groups
- Create accessible forms
- Add single-line text fields
- Add a multiline text field
- Add checkboxes
- Add radio buttons
- Add list/menu items
- Add hidden fields
- Add buttons
- Format a form using Cascading Style Sheets (CSS)
- Create a jump menu
- Test a form

Approximate Time

This lesson should take about one hour to complete.

Lesson Files

Starting Files:

Lesson_11_Forms/training/training.html

Completed Project:

Lesson_11_Forms/Completed/training/training.html

Building Your Form

Before you add elements such as individual fields and buttons to a page, the form that contains those elements must be created. Forms act as the containers for fields, buttons, menus, and other objects that visitors can use to enter or select information; forms also specify what happens with the data when it is submitted. In this exercise, you will create the form area.

1. Open the training.html document from the Lesson_11_Forms/Training folder. Position the insertion point in the blank paragraph below the text *Yoga Teacher Training Certification Program Application*. **Click the Form button in the Forms category of the Insert bar.**

> **Tip** *You can also insert a form by choosing Insert › Form › Form.*

Forms category   Form

The area occupied by the form is identified visually by red dotted lines in the Document window; that area is defined by the <form> and </form> tags in the code. These red lines are invisible elements that are displayed only in Dreamweaver; when you view the page within a browser, there is nothing to mark the form area. These red lines are not draggable—the size of the form area depends on what you place inside the form, and it expands horizontally to the full extent available and vertically as much as necessary to accommodate the contents. The form you placed on the page extends to occupy the entire width of the container, whether that is a div, a table cell, or the page itself.

Red dotted lines indicate the area occupied by the form

Note *If invisible elements are not turned on, a message box appears, letting you know that you won't be able to see the form. Click OK to close the message box and then choose View > Visual Aids > Invisible Elements so you can see the red dotted boundary of the form. If invisible elements are turned on, you do not see the warning message. The Form delimiter box must also be checked in the Invisible Elements category of the Dreamweaver preferences—it is checked by default.*

You can place multiple forms on one page; however, it is not possible to nest a form inside of another form in HTML. Because of this restriction, Dreamweaver prevents forms from becoming accidentally nested by disabling the insertion of one form into another form. The option to insert a form will not be dimmed, but no form is inserted if you attempt to place one form inside of another. If form tags have been inserted manually within a form, Dreamweaver highlights the tags that are incorrect to bring the error to your attention.

2. Select the form by clicking the red dotted line.

Tip *You can also use the tag selector to select the form if the insertion point is inside the form.*

The Property inspector changes to display form properties.

Note *If the Property inspector is not visible, choose Window > Properties.*

3. Replace the default name form1 in the Form name text field on the Property inspector by typing *training*.

Dreamweaver generates generic names for forms. The names automatically increment numerically each time you create a form: form1, form2, and so on. All form names must be unique and use no special characters. Form names are important identifiers, particularly if you have more than one form on a page or if you are using a database for information that is collected or requested via the form. Form names are also used to control forms through the use of scripting languages such as JavaScript.

4. Place the insertion point into the form and choose Insert › Table. Set the table to 3 rows and 1 column. The table width should be 90 percent. Set the border to 0, cell padding to 0, and cell spacing to 10. Choose None for the Header and then click OK.

The table improves the layout of the form. Using tables makes it easy to align text or images with the form fields to label them.

You can place a table inside a form or you can place a form in a table, but the table in question must completely contain or be contained by the form.

Grouping Form Content

Before you start to put your form together, you should take the time to develop a thorough outline of the contents. After you have an outline of the information that you will be requesting from visitors, you can divide that information into logical groups based on similarity of content. The form that you are creating in this lesson can be split up into three sections: Contact Information, Experience and Interests, and Send Your Answers. After you determine the sections into which your form will be divided, you are ready to use *fieldsets* to create those sections within the form itself. Fieldsets are form elements that are used to create individual sections of content within a form. Grouping the contents of your form into smaller, self-contained sections makes it easier for visitors to understand and complete the form. It offers a way for them to immediately grasp the overall structure of the form.

1. Place the insertion point in the first row of the table you created in the previous exercise. In the Forms category of the Insert bar, click the Fieldset button.

Fieldset

The Fieldset dialog box opens.

2. In the Legend text field, type *Contact Information* and click **OK**.

A fieldset expands to occupy the full amount of space that is available to it. The top cell of the table you created in the previous exercise serves to establish the boundaries of the fieldset and control the layout. Similar to forms, fieldsets can be placed within a table, or you can place a table in a fieldset, but the table must completely contain or be contained by the fieldset.

3. Place the insertion point in the second row and click the Fieldset button on the Insert bar. In the Legend text field, type *Experience And Interests* and click **OK**.

The legend that you specify for a fieldset serves as a caption for the section; a way to identify the contents. When creating legends for fieldsets in your own forms, be as clear as possible. These legends should accurately reflect what their fieldsets contain.

4. Place the insertion point in the third row and click the Fieldset button on the Insert bar. In the Legend text field, type *Send Your Answers* and click **OK**.

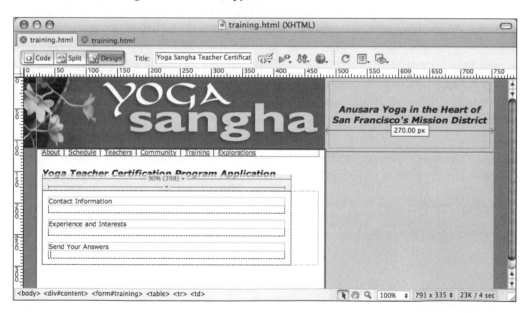

A fieldset surrounds its contents with a pale gray line.

5. Save the file and preview it in the browser.

Leave this file open for the next exercise.

Adding Single-Line Text Fields

Text fields are for gathering information that the user can type in. Single-line text fields are used for short concise answers such a word or phrase. Typical single-line text fields collect names, portions of addresses, and e-mail information from users. Single-line text fields are also used for basic searches, in which the visitor types words describing the desired information into the field.

You must place all form fields and buttons within the red dotted lines; otherwise, they are not a part of the form. If you try to insert form fields outside the red lines, Dreamweaver displays an alert box with Yes or No options, asking whether you want to add a form tag. If you choose No, the field or buttons will not function as a part of any form.

1. In the training.html document, place the insertion point in the text Contact Information. Use the tag selector to select the **<legend>** tag, press the right arrow key once, and press Return (Macintosh) or Enter (Windows).

Form objects must be inserted in the fieldset, but not inside the legend. If you were to place the insertion point at the end of the legend and press Return, a second set of legend tags would be created. There should not be a second set of legend tags.

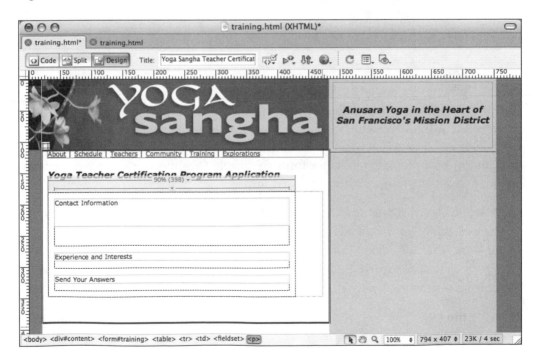

2. In the Forms category on the Insert bar, click the Text Field button.

Tip | *You can also choose Insert > Form > Text Field.*

Text Field

The Input Tag Accessibility Attributes dialog box opens.

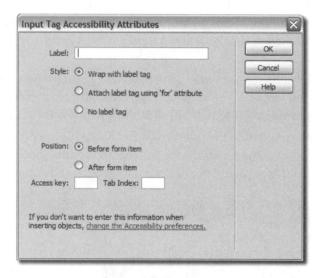

Creating accessible forms from the beginning helps to reach a wider audience. It is important to include accessible attributes to enable users who might need to use assistive technology such as screen readers. If your forms do not include these attributes, it can be difficult for some people to fill out the form. By default, Dreamweaver will prompt you to include accessibility features when you insert forms.

Note | *If Dreamweaver does not provide the Accessibility Attributes dialog box automatically, you might need to turn the accessibility features on for form objects. To do so, choose Dreamweaver > Preferences (Macintosh) or Edit > Preferences (Windows). Select the Accessibility category and check the Form objects box; then click OK.*

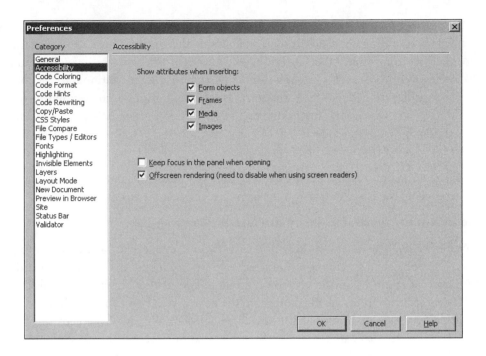

3. Type *Full Name:* in the Label text field.

Labels provide clear information that specifies the purpose for all your form objects (text fields, checkboxes, and so on) so your visitors know what information they are supposed to enter into those fields. Without being identified with labels, forms can be very confusing. Labels are included in both the Document window as a visual description of the text field and as an attribute within the HTML code that identifies the corresponding text field. Use concise and descriptive labels whenever possible.

4. In the Style section, select Wrap with label tag. In the Position section, select Before form item. Leave the Access key and Tab Index text fields blank.

The *Wrap With Label Tag* option surrounds form objects with a label tag. With this option selected, the form object should always remain next to the text label in the Document window. If the form object is moved, this option prevents it from being separated from the label tag—not using this option can cause a great deal of confusion for viewers using screen readers because the label will no longer be associated with a form object that has been moved. A text field created using this method appears in the code as `<label>Full Name: <input type="text" name="textfield" /></label>`.

The *Attach Label Tag Using For Attribute* option creates a stand-alone label that is identified with the corresponding text field through an id. Using this option allows you to separate the form object from the text that labels it in the Document window, which you might need to do for layout purposes. This method is more flexible because it continues to function properly regardless of whether the form object is separated from the corresponding text. If you are not sure which Style method to use, select this one. A text field created using this method appears in the code as `<label for="textfield"> Full Name: </label> <input type="text" name="textfield" id="textfield" />`.

The *No Label Tag* option bypasses the *Label* option. If you use this option, you can add labels later using the Label button in the Forms category on the Insert bar.

There are two additional accessibility attributes that are available:

- **Access Key:** The Access Key text field allows you to create a keyboard shortcut for the form object by specifying a character that visitors can use in combination with the Option (Macintosh) or Alt (Windows) modifier keys. Although visitors can use the Tab key to jump from one form object to the next, access keys can provide a much quicker way to jump immediately to any form object on the page. When creating access keys, take particular care to not use characters that might conflict with standard keyboard shortcuts. If you use access keys, it is a good idea to let your visitors know—provide instructions at the top of the form or in a pop-up window (which you will learn to create in Lesson 11) and indicate the keyboard shortcut next to its corresponding text field. Keyboard shortcut indicators should be as clear and unobtrusive as possible. On the Macintosh keyboard, shortcuts are listed next to menu items with a visual icon representing the modifier key. In Windows, however, the appropriate character is underlined to indicate the shortcut. Whichever method you decide to use, be consistent and clear—and let your visitors know by mentioning it in the instructions or help information.

- **Tab Index:** Many Web users use the Tab key when filling out forms; the Tab key provides a way to move through a form quickly by switching the focus from one form object or link to another. The order in which the Tab key changes the focus depends upon the order in which the object and links occur in the code. Although the default order in which the focus changes is usually what you expect, it is possible that the visual layout of a form might be presented so that the perceived order is different from the actual order of those objects in the code. In such cases, using the Tab Index field to specify the focus order by assigning numbers to form objects can help visitors to move through the form. Alternatively, you might want to apply the Tab Index only to fields that are required. When specifying a Tab Index, you need to start with 1, followed by 2, and so on. Do not skip any numbers.

If you do not use the accessibility feature when inserting form objects, you will not be prompted to specify a label. Although you can enter a label for the form object in the Document window, that text will not be contained in <label> and </label> tags unless you add those tags to the code manually or use the Label button in the Forms category on the Insert bar.

5. Click OK to insert the text field.

The single-line text field is placed in the form along with the text label; both are automatically selected.

6. Click in the Document window just to the right of the text field to deselect it and the label. Click the text field to select only the text field; then replace textfield in the TextField name text field on the Property inspector by typing *fullName*.

Note *Names are required for all fields. Dreamweaver assigns generic names automatically in a numeric order: textfield, textfield2, and so on. When the form is submitted, the name of the text field identifies the information that was entered into the field. In this case, fullName signifies that the information entered into this field is the visitor's full name.*

Do not use any spaces or special characters in the name and remember that names are case-sensitive when used with scripts such as CGI scripts or JavaScripts.

It is important to remember to name all your fields with short descriptive names. Suppose that you have two text fields on a page with labels next to them, prompting the user to enter a home phone number into one field and a work phone number into the other. If those fields are named textfield and textfield2, their names will not give you any indication about which number is the home number and which is the work number. On the other hand, by giving the fields more descriptive names, such as worknumber and homenumber, you can avoid confusion over the identity of the information. Visitors will not see or be affected by field names—naming the fields is for the benefit of you and your Web team.

7. With the text field form object still selected, click in the Char Width text field on the Property inspector and enter *40*. Press Return (Macintosh) or Enter (Windows).

Char Width, or character width, is the number of visible characters that will display in the text field. The width of the text field increases the available space so that it can show approximately 40 characters. The initial width of the text field is approximately 24 characters. The actual dimensions of the text field vary from browsers to browser, based on the text size used for that text field, which might be defined through Cascading Style Sheets (CSS) or left to browser defaults. The height of the text field is also dependent upon the text size.

Tip *You can apply a CSS style to a text field by selecting the desired style from the Class menu on the Property inspector when the text field is selected.*

8. **With the text field form object still selected, click in the Max Chars text field on the Property inspector and type** *50.* **Press Return (Macintosh) or Enter (Windows).**

Max Chars, or maximum characters, limits the total number of characters a user can enter. Initially, this text field is blank, and the number of characters a user can enter is unlimited.

If the Max Chars value is larger than Char Width, users can continue to type, and the text will scroll to the left within the field as the user types beyond the visible area. The scrollable area ends at the Max Chars value.

Note *If your form sends information to a database, you need to make sure that the value for maximum characters matches the maximum set for the corresponding field in the database.*

9. **Place the insertion point on the Full Name text label in the Document window. Select the <label> tag in the tag selector, press the right arrow key once and then press Return (Macintosh) or Enter (Windows). Click the Text Field button on the Insert bar and type** *Email:* **in the Label text field on the Input Tag Accessibility Attributes dialog box. Verify that Wrap with label tag is selected in the Style section and that Before form item is selected in the Position section, leave the other fields blank, and click OK. Select the text field and use the Property inspector to set the name of the field to** *email,* **Char Width to** *40* **and Max Chars to** *70.* **Press Return (Macintosh) or Enter (Windows), or click in the Document window to apply the change.**

This field accepts the user's e-mail address.

It is important to create a new paragraph that exists outside the <label> tags that wrap around the previous form object; otherwise, the new form object can become nested within the previous object's label tags, or the tags might overlap or cause other difficulties. You can avoid this by selecting the<label> tags in the tag selector and using the arrow keys to move just outside those tags, as you have done in this step. It might help to use Split view while you are inserting these objects.

Tip *Be careful when setting Max Chars for fields that accept information such as e-mail addresses and URLs. Users can't enter a complete URL or any other information if that information is longer than the Max Chars value because they can't type past the limit you set.*

10. **With the email field still selected, type** *Enter Your Email Address* **in the Init Val text field on the Property inspector.**

Init Val, or initial value, enables you to set text that will appear in the text field when the visitor loads the page. Init Val can help give the user an example of the kind of information that is being requested of them. Visitors can replace the initial value text with text of their own. Initial values are useful for prompting users to enter information or displaying example text. Although the user can change the text, use this option with caution. Users who want to get through the form quickly might accidentally skip a field that already has text in it, perhaps thinking they have already filled it out. Initial values might be a disadvantage if a visitor skips over the field because it looks as if it has already been filled out.

11. **Place the insertion point on the Email text label in the Document window. Select the <label> tag in the tag selector, press the right arrow key once and then press Return (Macintosh) or Enter (Windows). Click the Text Field button on the Insert bar and type** *Phone:* **in the label text field on the Input Tag Accessibility Attributes dialog box. Verify that Wrap with label tag is selected in the Style section and that Before form item is selected in the Position section, leave the other fields blank and click OK. Select the text field and use the Property inspector to set the name of the field to** *Phone*, **Char Width to** *40*, **and Max Chars to** *50*. **Press Return (Macintosh) or Enter (Windows), or click in the Document window to apply the change. Save the file and preview it in the browser.**

Leave this file open for the next exercise.

Note *A regular text field displays the information in the browser as you type it in. A password text field looks the same as any other text field, but the text displayed onscreen is hidden by bullets or asterisks as you type. The password option only hides the text in the field from someone looking over your shoulder as you type— it does not encrypt or secure your data. To encrypt data, you must have secure server software running on the Web server—talk to your Web administrator for detailed information on securing data using SSL (Secure Sockets Layer). To create a password field, insert a standard single-line text field and select Password for the Type option on the Property inspector. This option causes asterisks or bullets to appear when a user enters data in this field. Password text fields can be only single-line text fields. The Max Chars value for passwords should be set at the limit for passwords on your server.*

Adding Radio Buttons

Radio buttons are used when you want the user to choose only one out of a set of options. Selecting one option automatically deselects all other options. Typical uses for radio buttons are selecting credit card types, and questions that take a yes or no answer. In this exercise, you will insert a group of radio buttons into the table.

1. Place the insertion point on the Phone text label in the Document window. Select the <label> tag in the tag selector, press the right arrow key once and then press Return (Macintosh) or Enter (Windows).

In the next step, you will place the radio buttons in this new paragraph.

2. In the Forms category of the Insert bar, click the Radio Group button.

Tip *You can also choose Insert > Form > Radio Group.*

The Radio Group dialog box appears.

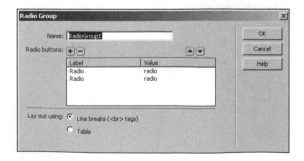

3. In the Radio Group dialog box, type *contact* in the Name text field.

When using radio buttons, you must use the same name for each radio button in the same group. Radio buttons are meant to allow only one selection.

| Note | *If you insert radio buttons one by one (either by using the Radio Button button on the Insert bar or by using the Insert › Form › Radio Button menu option), you can make those buttons all part of the same group by giving them the same name. Using the same name for multiple radio buttons indicates that those buttons are part of the same group. If the names are not the same, the radio buttons will be treated as different groups and negate the purpose of using radio buttons. You can also insert a single radio button, but keep in mind that after your visitor clicks the button, the only way for that visitor to deselect the button will be to reset the form, which will also clear any information the visitor has typed or selected in other form objects.* |

Also keep in mind that the names of form objects are case-sensitive when used with CGI and JavaScripts, so *contact* is not the same as *Contact*.

4. Click the first instance of Radio in the Radio Buttons list area and replace that text with *Email*. Use the same name in the corresponding Value text field. Click the second instance of Radio and replace it with *Phone*. Use the same name in the corresponding Value text field.

By default, every Radio Group has at least two radio buttons. You can add more as needed. Clicking an instance in the Label or Value lists highlights the text and allows you to change it.

You can add or delete entries by using the plus (+) and minus (–) buttons. You can also adjust the order of entries by selecting them and using the arrow buttons to move them up or down in the list.

When a form is submitted, the values are sent to the script that processes the form on the server. It is important to be sure you give each radio button a different value so you know which option the user chose.

5. Leave the Line breaks option selected in the Lay out using area and click OK to close the Radio Group dialog box. Delete the last line break that occurs just beneath the last radio button.

The line breaks option places the radio buttons in your document with each entry on a separate line. The table option inserts a table with each entry in a separate row.

6. Preview the page in the browser and test the radio buttons by clicking each one.

When you click one to select it, the other one should deselect. You must preview the file in the browser to see the effect; form objects do not appear selected or checked in the Dreamweaver Document window.

Save the training.html document and leave it open for the next exercise.

Adding Checkboxes

Checkboxes allow users to choose one or more options in a group of related items. Checkboxes are typically used when you want the user to choose as many of the listed options as desired. If you want your user to choose only one selection, you should use a radio button as demonstrated in the exercise that follows this one. In this exercise, you will insert a group of checkboxes.

1. Place the insertion point inside the Experience And Interests legend, select the **<legend>** tag in the tag selector, press the right arrow key once, and press **Return** (Macintosh) or **Enter** (Windows). Type *I am interested in specific training segment(s):*. Add a line break after the text by pressing **Shift+Return** (Macintosh) or **Shift+Enter** (Windows); then enter *(check all that apply)*, followed by another line break.

Recall from Lesson 2 that a line break moves the insertion point to the next line without inserting a blank line, as a regular paragraph return would do.

2. In the Forms category on the Insert bar, click the Checkbox button.

Tip *You can also choose Insert > Form > Check Box.*

Checkbox

The Input Tag Accessibility Attributes dialog box opens.

3. In the Label text field, type *Anusara Yoga Immersion*. Select **Wrap with label tag** in the Style section and select **After form item** in the Position section. Leave the other fields blank and click **OK**.

A checkbox is inserted into the form, along with the corresponding label text.

4. Select only the checkbox. In the CheckBox Name text field on the Property inspector, replace *checkbox* with *segment*. In the Checked Value text field, enter *immersion*.

Tip *If both the label and checkbox are selected, the Property inspector does not display the CheckBox properties.*

If a visitor checks the Anusara Yoga Immersion checkbox, the immersion value indicates that the corresponding checkbox has been selected, and the sources value identifies the group of checkboxes. You can designate a number of checkboxes as a group by giving them all the same names—be sure, however, to give them individual, clear, and accurate values.

5. Place a line break after the space that exists after the Anusara Yoga Immersion label. Repeat Steps 2 through 5 to add checkboxes using *In-Depth Asana Training & Practice*, *Yoga Philosophy Series*, and *Satsang: Kirtan, Meditation and Discussion* for the labels. Each checkbox and its corresponding label should be on its own line. In the CheckBox Name text field on the Property inspector, replace *checkbox* each time with *segment*. Enter *asana, philosophy*, and *satsang* in each Checked Value text field, respectively.

Placing the insertion point after the space that exists after the labels is important because the insertion point will be placed outside of the label tag that surrounds the checkbox and text. You can verify this by looking at the tag selector. If you see <p><label> at the right end of the tag hierarchy, the insertion point is still between the label tags, and you need to move it. If you see only the <p> tag, you are ready to insert the line break in preparation for the next checkbox.

The last tag in the hierarchy of code for the position of the insertion point is displayed at the right end of the tag selector. The tag selector hierarchy always begins with <body>; however, you might not see the <body> tag at the left (beginning) of the tag selector if the hierarchy of tags is too long to be fully displayed. Tags in the tag selector will begin to disappear on the left to make room for the more recent tags. Expanding the Document window will give the tag selector more room if you want to see the other tags.

As you continue to insert form objects, the table expands downward to accommodate its content. As this happens, the red dotted line of the form might appear to overlap the table and not be pushed down along with the bottom of the table. If this happens, click outside the table in the Document window to cause Dreamweaver to refresh the view.

6. Preview the page in the browser and test the checkboxes by clicking each one.

Your document should now look similar to the example shown here.

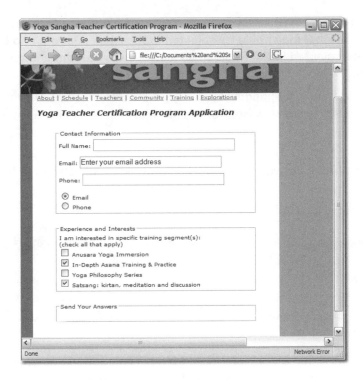

Save the training.html document and leave it open for the next exercise.

Adding List and Menu Items

You can create a scrolling list or menu from which visitors can make selections. A *scrolling list* gives you the option to allow users to make multiple contiguous or noncontiguous selections. A menu restricts users to one selection. In both types, items chosen by the user are highlighted.

1. Still inside the Experience and Interests fieldset, after the label tag that surrounds the Satsang checkbox, press Return (Macintosh) or Enter (Windows). Click the List/Menu button in the Forms category of the Insert bar.

| Tip | *You can also choose Insert > Form > List/Menu.* |

List/Menu

The Input Tag Accessibility Attributes dialog box opens.

2. Type *What type(s) of yoga have you studied and/or practiced?* in the Label text field. Wrap with label tag should be selected in the Style section, and Before form item should be selected in the Position section. Leave the remaining fields blank and click **OK**.

A small menu and the corresponding label are inserted into the form. Dreamweaver inserts a drop-down menu by default (on the Macintosh this takes the form of a pop-up menu).

3. Insert a line break between the label text and the menu. Select only the menu to display the properties in the Property inspector.

The Property inspector displays List/Menu properties.

4. On the Property inspector, select *List* for the Type option and change Height to *4*. Check the Allow multiple checkbox for the Selections option.

You changed the format to a scrolling list. You must change the height to a value that is greater than 1 for the form object to change from a menu to a list.

The list format has an additional option that is not available for menus: You can choose to allow or not allow multiple selections by checking or unchecking the Allow Multiple checkbox for the Selections option. This option is unchecked by default. If you check the Selections box, users can make multiple noncontiguous selections by using Cmd-click (Macintosh) or Ctrl-click (Windows). Users might make contiguous selections by using Shift-click on both Macintosh and Windows. If you decide to allow multiple selections, it is a good idea to inform your visitors that they can make multiple selections (and to tell them how to do so). Many users might not know these commands. It is always best to provide your visitors with all the information and tools they need to interact with your site.

You can also set a height for the scrolling list by entering the number of lines you want to be visible in the Height text field. Be sure to enter a line height value of more than 1; otherwise, the scrolling list displays as a menu.

5. In the List/Menu name text field on the Property inspector, replace *select* with *yogaTypes*; then click the List Values button.

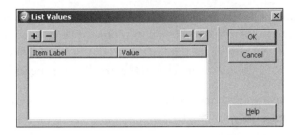

The List Values dialog box opens. This dialog box is the same for both List and Menu entries.

6. In the Item Label field, type *Anusara* and then press Tab. In the Value field, type *anusara*.

The longest item in the list values box determines the width of the list/menu. You can't resize a list or menu by dragging it or specifying dimensions.

7. Press Tab or click the plus sign (+) in the upper-left area of the dialog box to add another option to the menu.

Use the minus sign (−) to delete items from the List Values box.

8. Repeat Steps 6 and 7, adding *Ashtanga, Bikram, Dynamic Hatha, Hatha, Integral, Iyengar, Kripalu, Vinyasa, Other Western-style*, and *Other Eastern-style* to the list. Change the Value field to match the name of each region using *ashtanga, bikram, dynHatha, hatha, integral, iyengar, kripalu, vinyasa, otherWest*, and *otherEast*, respectively.

Use the arrows above the Value field if you want to reorder the list.

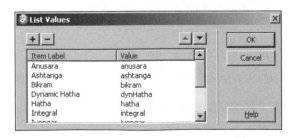

9. Click OK to close the dialog box.

The list shows the items you just added.

An additional option on the Property inspector for list/menu items is the Initially selected box. You can choose to have any one of the items in the list be selected when the page loads. This option might not be desirable for scrolling lists, but it is helpful to have a sample choice or instruction such as "Choose one" appear on the first line for menu items.

> **Note** *If you choose an item to select initially, there is no way to deselect it. To deselect it, you have to open the List Values dialog box, delete the item that was selected, and add it to the list again.*

10. Insert a line break after the list and type *(select the most appropriate options——make multiple selections with Cmd-click on the Macintosh and Ctrl-click on Windows).*

It is good to always give instructions for selecting items in case a visitor doesn't know how to make multiple selections. It can save your users a lot of frustration, making it more likely that they will finish filling out your form!

Adding Multiline Text Fields

You can use *multiline text fields* to collect larger amounts of information from a user by providing a text area with multiple lines in which the visitor can type. Typical multiline text fields collect comments and feedback from visitors. In this exercise, you will place a multiline text field in the table inside the form.

1. Place the insertion point anywhere inside the text below the list control. Use the tag selector to select the <label> tag, press the right arrow key once, and press Return (Macintosh) or Enter (Windows).

The insertion point is now where it should be: inside the fieldset but outside of the list control.

2. In the Forms category on the Insert bar, click the Textarea button.

> **Tip** *You can also insert a multiline text field by choosing Insert › Form › Textarea.*

Textarea

The Input Tag Accessibility Attributes dialog box opens. In Dreamweaver, a multiline text field is known as a *textarea*.

3. In the Label text field, type *Have you had any teaching experience in general?* *Please describe.* **Wrap with label tag should be selected in the Style section and Before form item should be selected in the Position section. Leave the remaining fields blank and click OK.**

The multiline text field and its corresponding label text appear in the Document window.

4. Place a line break between the label text and the multiline text field. Select the multiline text field.

> **Tip** *To place a line break directly between the label and the text field, select the text field and press the left arrow key once; then insert the line break.*

The Property inspector shows Text Field properties because the multiline text field is selected.

> **Note** *You can convert a single-line text field to a multiline text area by selecting the text field and choosing Multi line in the Type option on the Property inspector.*

5. In the Name text field on the Property inspector, replace *textarea* **with** *teachingExp.* **In the Char Width text field, enter** *40.*

When you use multiline text fields, you see an additional option on the Property inspector. The Wrap menu is available only for multiline text fields. It is dimmed for both single-line and password text fields. Wrap specifies how text that is typed into a multiline field is displayed if there is more text than will fit in the visible area. Leave the Wrap option set to Default for this exercise.

The Wrap options are Default, Off, Virtual, and Physical:

- **Default** uses the browser default. This option is selected automatically when you select Multi line for the Type option.

- **Off** stops text from wrapping to the next line. Text continues on one line until the Return or Enter key is pressed. The text scrolls to the left as the visitor types beyond the limit of the visible area.

- **Virtual** wraps text to the next line, but wrap is not applied to the data when the form is submitted.
- **Physical** wraps text to the next line, and wrap is applied to the data when the form is submitted.

6. Type *4* in the Num Lines text field on the Property inspector.

This option dictates how many lines appear in the scrollable area. It does not limit the number of lines users can enter. The text will scroll upward as the user types beyond the number that is set to display.

7. Place the insertion point on the multiline text field and select the `<label>` tag in the tag selector. Press the right arrow key once and press Return (Macintosh) or Enter (Windows). Repeat Steps 2 through 6 to create a second text area. Use *What do you want to gain from this program? If you have specific goals or areas of interest that you would like to explore, please explain. Please be specific.* for the label; the other accessibility attributes should be the same as those in Step 3. Name the field *gain* and apply the same attributes that you set for the previous multiline text area in Steps 5 and 6.

Your document should now look similar to the example shown here.

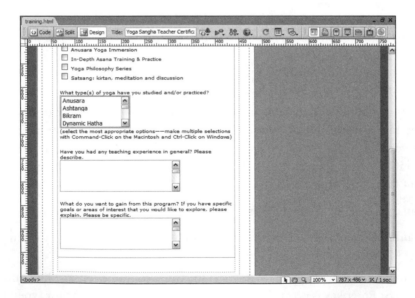

8. Preview the page in the browser and test the list by selecting multiple options.

Save the training.html document and leave it open for the next exercise.

Adding Buttons

Forms often have two buttons: one to send the form data (Submit), and one to clear the form (Reset). The Submit button tells the browser to send the data. The Reset button clears all the information from the fields on the page.

Note *A form created for a basic search function usually has only one Submit button, which is often labeled Search or Go.*

1. Place the insertion point in the text Send Your Answers in the third fieldset. Use the tag selector to select the <legend> tag, press the right arrow key once, and press Return (Macintosh) or Enter (Windows). Click the Button button in the Forms category on the Insert bar.

Tip *You can also choose Insert › Form › Button.*

The Input Tag Accessibility Attributes dialog box opens.

2. Leave the Label text field blank and select No label tag in the Style area. Leave the Position options as they are and leave the remaining fields blank. Click OK.

A Submit button is placed in the form, and the Property inspector displays Button properties. The accessibility attributes are unnecessary because the label is on the button itself. Because a Submit button is the default, you do not need to change any of the options for this button.

3. Position the insertion point to the right of the Submit button. Click the Button button on the Insert bar and repeat Step 2 to set the accessibility attributes to the same value that was used for the Submit button.

A second Submit button is placed in the form. The only difference is the name—this button is called Submit2 because no two buttons can have the same name. The only form objects that can have the same name are radio buttons that are in the same group and checkboxes that are in the same group. The button you are working with in this exercise is different because it cannot be grouped with other buttons and it will have its own action assigned to it in the next step.

4. With the second Submit button selected, choose Reset Form from the Action options on the Property inspector.

The text in the Label text field automatically changes to Reset. The action of this button causes all text fields, checkboxes, and radio buttons to clear and revert to their original state (when the page was first loaded in the browser).

The third Action option is None. Unlike Submit and Reset, the None button option has no action attached to it. It can be used in conjunction with a script to perform another task. A JavaScript routine, for example, can be used to perform calculations such as totals or interest and return the end value to the user.

5. In the Label text field, replace *Reset* by entering *Clear Form*. In the Button Name text field, change the default name to *reset*.

It is a good idea to name your buttons clearly, with consideration for your users' expectations. Submit and Reset are standard form-button labels that people understand because of their widespread use. Take care with the placement of the Reset button and make the label obvious so that visitors do not accidentally click it when they are trying to submit the form.

Tip *You can use images in place of the standard buttons by using the image field button on the Property inspector to insert an image as a form element and then inserting the appropriate value, such as `value="Submit"`, into the code. You might want to use images to customize the appearance of buttons. It is important to make sure that any images you use in this manner are obviously meant to be buttons.*

Creating Hidden Fields

Sometimes, you might need to include information with your form that shouldn't be displayed to the visitor or left to the visitor to fill in. In these kinds of circumstances, you can use *hidden fields*, which do not display in the browser. Hidden fields are often used with server-side scripting when specific information is required for processing the form: for gathering the name, order number, or other relevant information about a product that is being purchased; to provide an e-mail address and a subject header if the form will be sent to e-mail; for including the URL of a page to which you want to redirect visitors after they have filled out your form; for passing information from one form to another; or for requiring certain fields to be completed by the visitor. In such cases, server-side scripting is required to process the hidden fields. JavaScript can also be combined with hidden fields (in what is known as *client-side scripting*) for situations in which server-side scripting is not needed or available. In client-side scripting, the visitor's browser (the client) processes the scripts. You learned about JavaScript in Lesson 8.

If no scripting is used in connection with the hidden field when the form is submitted for processing, the hidden fields embedded in the form are included just like values from other form objects.

1. Place the insertion point along the very bottom of the second row of the table.

The insertion point is now in the cell above the one that contains the Send Your Answers fieldset. You can place hidden fields at any point in the document.

Now that the insertion point is in the line at the bottom of the second cell, it is no longer inside of the fieldset labeled Experience and Interests. This is okay in this case because the hidden field that you will insert in the following steps will not be visible to the Visitor; the placement is not important.

2. On the Forms category on the Insert bar, click the Hidden Field button.

Hidden Field

A hidden field is inserted into the document. The hidden field icon is a visual aid for invisible elements similar to named anchor icons—it is not displayed in the browser.

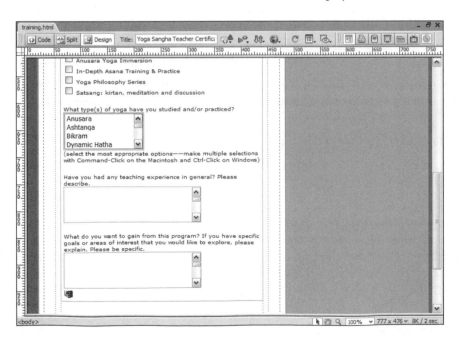

3. With the hidden field selected, replace the default name of hiddenfield by typing *webRequest* into the HiddenField text field. Type *true* into the Value text field on the Property inspector.

In this case, you are including the title of this form as a predefined value for the hidden field. Information that always remains the same can be passed to dynamic pages and CGI scripts through these kinds of hidden fields. Hidden fields using values that are set in this manner are not encrypted or secure—they can easily be seen in the document source code through the browser. Do not place any information that is sensitive (such as passwords) into these kinds of hidden fields. Secure hidden fields can be created when dynamically generating the value of the field through the use of dynamic pages or CGI scripts.

The name and value of hidden fields are usually dependent on the script that is being used to process them. For example, some scripts that send the data to an e-mail address might use "recipient" as the name of the hidden field and the e-mail address to which the data should be sent as the value. This name and value pair does not function unless you have the script that processes the recipient field on your server.

Note | *File fields are another field type that you can use in forms. A file field makes it possible for you to let visitors send files to you via your form. This capability can be useful when you need to receive documents relating to the data collected in the form. For example, a file field might be made available on a job application for which you want the visitor to submit a resume. File fields rely on the server to process the data received by the form and upload or otherwise direct the file to an appropriate location.*

Formatting Forms

You can use CSS styles (covered in Lesson 4) to make forms more consistent with the look and feel of your site.

1. Place the insertion point in the legend Contact Information in the first fieldset. In the tag selector, select the **<fieldset>** tag. Click the New CSS Rule button on the CSS Styles panel. For the Selector Type, choose Tag. Use the menu to the right of the Tag text field to select fieldset if it is not already displayed in the text field. In the Define In section, choose This Document Only and then click OK. The CSS Rule definition for fieldset dialog box opens.

You can create a style for the fieldset to control the look of the outlines surrounding individual sections of the form.

2. Select Box from the category list. In the Padding section, type *5* into the Top text field and leave the Same For All box checked.

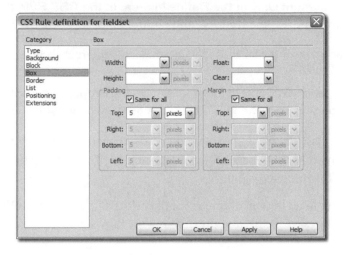

The padding gives the form objects some space so that they are not right up against the fieldset outline.

3. Select Border from the category list. In the Style section, select solid from the Top menu and leave the Same for all box checked. In the Width section, type *1* into the Top text field, make sure that Pixels is selected, and leave the Same for all box checked. In the Color section, type *#CCCC99* into the Top text field and leave the Same for all box checked. Click OK.

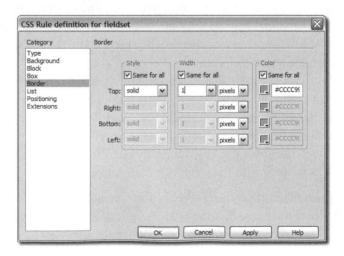

Each fieldset is now surrounded by a border.

4. Click the New CSS Rule button on the CSS Styles panel. For the Selector Type, choose Tag. Use the menu to the right of the Tag text field to select H5 and choose This Document Only in the Define In area. In the CSS Rule definition dialog box, select the Type category, and set the color to #999999. Click OK.

This style will be used for the legends that designate the different sections of the form.

5. Select the legend text Contact Information. On the Property inspector, change the format to Heading 5. Style the legends for the other two fieldsets in the same way.

Tip *You can also just place the insertion point within the text and choose H5 from the Format menu on the Property inspector instead of selecting it because headings are applied to entire text blocks.*

Your form now matches the feel of the rest of the colors and style used in the Yoga Sangha project site. You can save the file and preview it in the browser.

Processing Forms

Whether your form is intended to submit information to or retrieve information from a database, perform a search function, or otherwise process data, you need to define what will happen with that data and how it will be handled to make your form functional. This definition is done through Action and Method options in the Property inspector while the form is selected. To select the form, place the insertion point somewhere within the form and click the <form#training> tag in the tag selector.

You can use Dreamweaver to develop dynamic Web pages and applications that can be used to process forms and make use of databases. Creating and working with a dynamic, database-enabled Website requires a connection to a server. The type of server and its configuration determine which scripting language (such as PHP, ASP, JSP and ColdFusion) can be used. Because creating a site that makes use of dynamic pages and databases is beyond the scope of this book and because you might not have access to a server with the dynamic pages or CGI scripts needed to process forms while you complete this lesson, the following information is presented as reference material only. Talk to your Internet Service Provider (ISP) or Web administrator to get the information you need to set the Action and Method options to work with the scripts used on your server.

- **Action** tells the browser what to do with the form data. It specifies the path or URL to the location and the name of a server-side application (usually a CGI script or a dynamic page) that processes the information when the user clicks the Submit button. CGI scripts are located on the Web server that processes the data sent by a form.

- **Method** defines how the form data is handled: GET, POST, or Default. Data sent by a form is a continuous string of text from the information typed by the user. GET appends form contents to the URL specified in the Action text field; that information is therefore visible in the browser's address bar. GET is not a secure method of transferring data, so it should not be used for sensitive information such as credit card information or Social Security numbers. The GET method can send only a limited amount of information because restrictions are often imposed on the lengths of URLs by browsers and servers. This limitation can vary, so the GET method is also not a good choice for forms in which the visitor might have entered a lot of information—long forms lose any information exceeding the size or length restriction. The POST method, on the other hand, is capable of sending far more information and is more reliable and secure. It is the most common method used in scripts to send form data. POST uses an HTTP request to send the form value in the body of a message. Default uses the browser's default method, which is usually GET.

Testing Your Forms

It is possible to send a form to an e-mail address if you don't have a CGI script running on your server through the use of a mailto (an e-mail link, covered in Lesson 3) for the form action, which should be used only to test your forms. This method has a number of flaws, including errors that occur as a result of the browser not being configured to send mail or not being able to connect with an e-mail program, and the absolute lack of security. You should always use dynamic pages or CGI scripts for processing forms.

Note *Although the mailto action gives you a way to initially test your form, it is not a substitute for testing your form with the corresponding server scripts. You should always be sure to thoroughly test pages in a live environment to be sure that your scripts are working as expected before making them available to visitors.*

1. In the training.html document, select the form by clicking `<form#training>` on the tag selector. In the Action field of the form on the Property inspector, type *mailto:* followed by your e-mail address, with no spaces after the colon.

You should remember to include the colon and no spaces. This is the same way you inserted manual e-mail links in Lesson 3.

2. Choose POST from the Method menu and type *text/plain* into the Enctype text field on the Property inspector.

You have set the encode type to plain text; otherwise, the text sent will be encoded into an almost unreadable form.

The enctype defines how the data in the form is encoded. The text/plain value formats the information with each form element on a separate line. Using this value makes it easier to read the results in an e-mail. If you don't define an enctype value, browsers use a default value that formats the data. Because the default is the one that should be used in most circumstances, you will usually not need to specify an enctype. This example is an exception because you are sending the data in an e-mail to test the form.

Note *To add a subject line to your form, change the Action to this:*
mailto:YourEmailAddress?Subject=Title for Subject goes here. The ?Subject= defines the text that follows as the subject. You can uses spaces in the subject, but do not use any other special characters such as quote marks, apostrophes, periods, or slashes (other than the ?Subject= that separates the e-mail and the subject) because they will interfere with the HTML code. This might not work with every browser and should not be used in any way other than the testing of your form.

Remember that the mailto action does not work reliably in all browsers. Use it only for testing. If your browser is not configured to send e-mail, you can't test the form in this manner.

3. Save the file and test it in the browser.

Depending on the preview browser, you might receive warning messages about sending e-mail. If you choose to do so, the form results should be sent to the e-mail address you specified.

4. Use the tag selector to select the `<form#training>` tag. Delete the text in the Action text field and change the Method to GET. Save the file and test it in the browser.

This is another way to test your forms. Instead of the results being sent via e-mail, the browser will remain on the page with the form, and the results of the form are appended to the URL in the Address field on your browser window.

You can close this file.

Creating Jump Menus

A *jump menu* is a menu that contains links to other pages in your site or to other Websites. Similar to regular links, the jump menu can link to any type of file, including graphics or PDF files. The jump menu provides an easy-to-use interface for linking to pages in your site, if you don't make the list too long.

A jump menu, which is embedded in a form, looks like a menu list in the browser. It does not need an action or method, as described in the previous section because the jump menu doesn't cause data to be sent, received, or processed.

1. Open the training.html file from the Lesson_11_Forms/Training folder. In the upper right corner of the page, place the insertion point anywhere in the text Anusara Yoga in the Heart of San Francisco's Mission District. On the tag selector, click the `<table.tagline>` tag. Press the right arrow and press Return (Macintosh) or Enter (Windows) to open a new line. Type the text *Choose a Program*. Insert a line break. Click the Jump Menu icon from the Forms category in the Insert bar.

 **Tip** *Alternatively, you can choose Insert › Form › Jump Menu.*

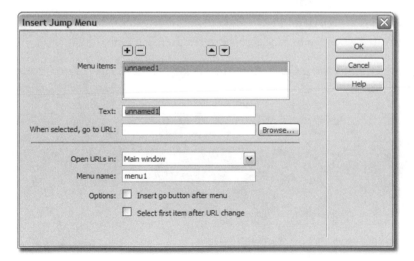

The Jump Menu dialog box opens. By default, there is one item listed in the menu: unnamed1. Dreamweaver assigns generic names automatically in numerical order: unnamed1, unnamed2, and so on.

2. In the Text text field of the Jump Menu dialog box, type *Pick One*. Type # in the When selected, go to URL text field.

The first item in the Menu items list will appear in the first line of the menu. Because the user sees this item initially in the menu list, the first line should be a short description of the list or a short instruction to let the user know that this is a jump menu.

3. In the Options area, choose Select first item after URL change.

This selection forces the menu list to display the first menu item in the list when the user returns to this page; otherwise, the list displays the most recent option chosen.

> **Note** *The Open URLs in menu can be used to target links to specific frames, as you did in Lesson 10. For this exercise, you should leave the default Main Window selected.*

4. Click the plus sign (+) button to add a new menu item. Type *Anusara Yoga Immersion* in the Text field, press Tab, and type *immersion.html* in the When selected, go to URL text field. Repeat this step, typing *In-Depth Asana Training, asana.html; Yoga Philosophy Series, philosophy.html*; and *Satsang: kirtan, meditation, satsang.html*. Click OK after you finish.

When these items are selected in the browser window, they link to their appropriate pages. A link is activated when the user selects the corresponding item.

> **Tip** *If you want to add a Go button to your list, select the Insert go button after menu checkbox.*

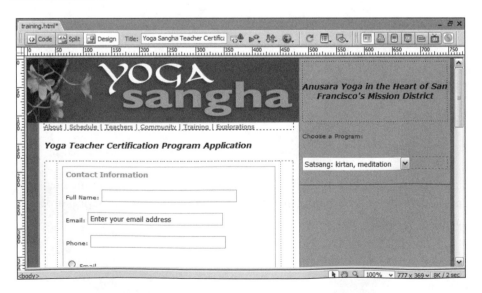

Dreamweaver automatically inserts the required form when you insert the jump menu, as you can see by the dotted red lines. Because the insertion point was at the end of the line of text, the jump menu is created just below the text. If you want the prompt text "Choose a program" to appear on the same line as the jump menu, you need to move that text into the form. Using tables gives you more control over the layout of your forms.

Tip *Use the up and down arrow icons to adjust the order of the items in the menu.*

When you click OK, the inserted menu might appear to be very short. You'll preview the page in the browser to see how it will really look to a visitor.

5. **Save the file and preview it in the browser.**

After you create the jump menu, you can make changes by using the Property inspector. The Property inspector gives you limited editing capability, allowing you to change the text the user sees and change the order in which the text appears in the list.

Tip *For more extensive editing control, JavaScript can be incorporated with jump menus.*

Creating Forms On Your Own

Forms are a great way to gather information about the audience of your Website.

Review the content of your site and decide what kinds of information you might need to gather from your visitors. Begin by outlining the kinds of information you need. After you have a clear idea of what data you will gather through the use of the form, you can create a more functional and efficient form. Use the techniques learned in this lesson to create the necessary text fields, menus, and buttons.

Test your forms early and often. Consider their usability and functionality.

What You Have Learned

In this lesson, you have:

- Created a form on a Web page to place form fields into, enabling visitors to send information to you (pages 379–381)
- Divided the form contents into groups and used fieldsets to contain their form objects (pages 381–382)
- Added single-line text fields using options including width and maximum number of characters (pages 383–390)

- Used accessible attributes to create a form that can be used by a wide audience (pages 384–390)
- Added radio buttons to limit users to a single choice (pages 390–393)
- Added checkboxes to allow users to select multiple choices (pages 393–395)
- Added list boxes and menus with multiple items and specified an item to be selected initially (pages 395–398)
- Added a multiline text field and set options for the number of lines, maximum characters, and wrap method (pages 398–400)
- Added buttons for Submit and Reset for users to send or clear the form (pages 401–403)
- Inserted a hidden field to include information in the form that is not visible to visitors (pages 403–404)
- Formatted the form using CSS (pages 404–407)
- Tested a form with a mailto action to be sure it is functioning correctly (pages 407–408)
- Created a jump menu that allows users to navigate through the site (pages 409–411)

12 Using Library Items

There are many items and groups of items that you may need to use repeatedly throughout your Website. These items may include, but are not limited to, navigation, copyright information, headers, and footers. Dreamweaver gives you the option to store these often-used portions of content as *library items* — a single portion of content is called a library item, which can be inserted into multiple pages with each instance being linked to, and controlled by, the original item. Creating library items allows you to quickly and easily insert the same content into many documents. If you need to change information, such as copyright dates that might appear on a large number of pages throughout your site, library items allow you to edit the content and update all documents that contain it with a single command. Without a library item, you have to open each page and modify the information individually or use Find & Replace (covered in Lesson 17). On a small site, doing this might not be difficult; however, on a very large site, it can be time-consuming and can greatly increase the probability of errors.

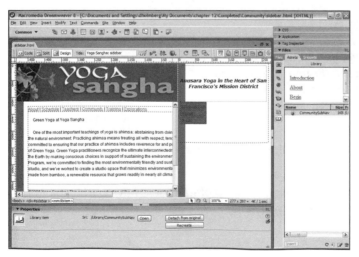

In this project, you will add a library item to a page. After you modify the library item, you will use the update feature to quickly and efficiently make the same changes to all pages containing that item on the site.

Library items provide a way for you to maintain consistency and automate the process of updating your site. Library items enable you to repeat certain elements on pages that can still have different layouts. Effective use of library items can be a timesaver, not only in the development stage of your Website but also in ongoing maintenance tasks.

To see examples of the finished pages for this chapter, open Community/community.html from the Lesson_12_Libraries/Completed folder.

What You Will Learn

In this lesson, you will:

- Learn when and why to use library items
- Create and insert a library item
- Re-create a library item
- Edit an existing library item
- Update all references to a library item
- Detach a library item

Approximate Time

This lesson should take about one hour to complete.

Lesson Files

Starting Files:

Lesson_08_Interactivity/index.html
Lesson_12_Libraries/Community/community.html
Lesson_12_Libraries/Community/community_intro.html
Lesson_12_Libraries/Community/BeginningGreen.html
Lesson_12_Libraries/Community/AboutGreen.html
Lesson_12_Libraries/Community/sidebar.html

Completed Project:

Lesson_12_Libraries/Completed/Community/Community.html

> **Note** *Library items contained within the Completed folders have had "_solution" appended to their names to differentiate them from the library items that you create in this lesson.*

Creating a Library Item

A library item is a portion of content that can be reused on multiple pages. It is separated from the pages in your site and kept in a file located in the Library. The library item consists only of the code for specific content; it is not an HTML page in and of itself. You can create a library item by selecting one or more elements in a document and adding them to the Library. When you do this, Dreamweaver converts the selection into non-editable content that is linked to the corresponding library item. The following exercise demonstrates this process.

1. Open the index.html file in Lesson_08_Interactivity. Scroll to the bottom of the page and find the copyright text. Select this entire paragraph.

Library items can only include content that appears between the <body> and </body> tags. They can include any document elements such as text, tables, forms, images, Java applets, plug-ins, or ActiveX elements.

To create a library item out of multiple elements, those elements must form a contiguous selection in the document. If you need noncontiguous items to function as a library item does, you need to create multiple library items.

The copyright text, email address, and modification date are standard information that might be used at the bottom of all pages within a Website. Libraries can be useful for this type of information.

Note *A library item containing relative paths (such as links to pages or images) can be placed in any level of your site's directory structure. Dreamweaver automatically calculates the correct paths to any elements that the library item might contain. Document-relative and site root-relative paths were covered in Lessons 3 and 5.*

2. Click the Assets tab in the Files panel group and click the Library button on the lower left of the Assets panel to open the Library.

Library button —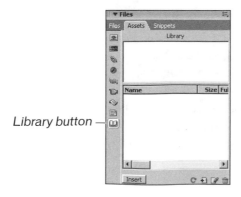

The Library category of the Assets panel opens, in which you will manage all your library items.

3. **Drag the selected copyright text into the Assets panel.**

> **Tip** *You can also choose Modify > Library > Add Object to Library to create a new library item.*

A new library icon appears in the Library category of the Assets panel alongside a text field highlighting the generic name Untitled.

> **Note** *When you create a library item, Dreamweaver creates a folder named Library at the top level of your local root folder and stores every library item that you create in that location. The Library folder must remain in its original location at the root level of your site for the library feature to function. This Library folder and the library files it contains are only stored locally; they do not need to be uploaded to a server unless you want to share them with other members of your Web team. Dreamweaver saves each library item with the .lbi file extension.*

4. **Type** *copyright* **as the name for the new library item and then press Return (Macintosh) or Enter (Windows).**

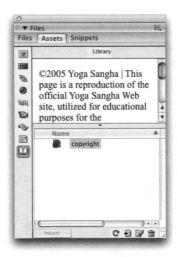

The library item is now known as copyright in the Library panel. Giving your library items descriptive names will help you to manage them throughout your site. The names are for your reference only and will not be displayed to the user in a browser window.

A preview of the library item appears at the top of the panel. You might need to click the library item icon to refresh the preview to see the elements.

Close the index.html file.

Placing a Library Item on a Page

Placing a library item in a document inserts the contents of the library item file and creates a reference to that library item. When you insert a library item, the actual HTML is inserted, meaning that the content always appears—even if the library item is not available in the Library folder. Dreamweaver inserts comments in the code around the item to show the name of the library file and the reference to the original item. The comments and reference are not visible in the browser window. The reference to the external library item file is what makes it possible to update the content on an entire site all at once simply by changing the library item.

1. Open the community_intro.html file in the Lesson_12_Libraries/Community folder. Place the insertion point in the empty paragraph just below the paragraph beginning "One of the most important teachings..."

In the following steps, you will place the library item you created in the previous exercise into this document.

Tip   *If the Library panel is not visible, choose Window › Assets and click the Library button in the Assets panel. The Assets panel is located in the Files panel group.*

2. Select the copyright library item in the Library category of the Assets panel and click the Insert button in the lower-left corner of the panel to insert the item into the document.

Tip Alternatively, you can drag the copyright file icon from the Library panel to the location where you want it to appear in the document window.

The text is added to the document. The copyright library item is shown with a yellow background. Although library items are highlighted with yellow by default, the color can be changed or turned off completely in the Preferences dialog box. This item cannot be modified directly on the page. You will modify library items in the next exercise.

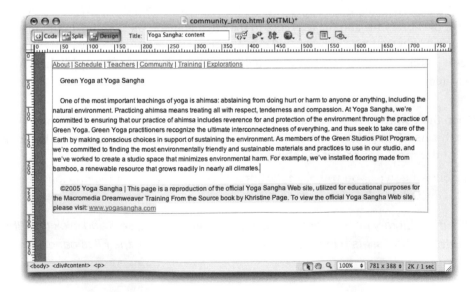

You can use the Property inspector to see the name of the source file and to perform maintenance functions for the library item that is selected in the document window. The Property inspector has several options:

- **Src:** Displays the filename and location of the source file for the library item. You can open the library item for editing by clicking the Open button. You must save the file to keep the changes you make.

- **Detach from original:** Breaks the link between the selected library item and its source file. The content of the library item becomes editable, but it can no longer be updated by the library update functions.

- **Recreate:** Overwrites the original library item with the current selection. Use this option to create library items again if the library file isn't present, the item's name has been changed, or the item has been edited.

3. Repeat Steps 1 and 2 to insert the copyright library item at the bottom of the Community/BeginningGreen.html file.

The benefit of library items becomes apparent when you reuse the library item in multiple pages.

4. Open the Community/AboutGreen.html file and place the insertion point in the empty paragraph below the paragraph that begins "For more information..."

You will place a detached copy of the library item with copyright information on this page so it is editable in the document.

5. Hold down Option (Macintosh) or Ctrl (Windows) and drag the copyright file icon from the Library panel to the bottom of the document.

The library content is copied into the document but is not linked to the library, so there is no yellow highlighting. The elements can be modified directly on the page because they are not connected to a library item. Because these elements are detached, they are not updated if any changes are made to the original library item.

6. Save and close all files.

Re-creating a Library Item

If a library item is accidentally deleted from the Library category of the Assets panel and you still have a page showing the library item, you can re-create it.

1. Open the sidebar.html document and select the navigational library item at the bottom of the page by clicking it once.

This is a library item that is not available in your Library folder. It is a simple table with three rows of navigation links for the frame-based Community pages. When you clicked the table, the entire library item became selected and grayed-out to show that it can't be edited within the document. You can also tell that it is a library item by looking at the tag selector, which displays <mm:libitem>. Although this element was marked as a library item in the Document window, it does not appear in the Library category of the Assets panel because the original item is not contained in your site.

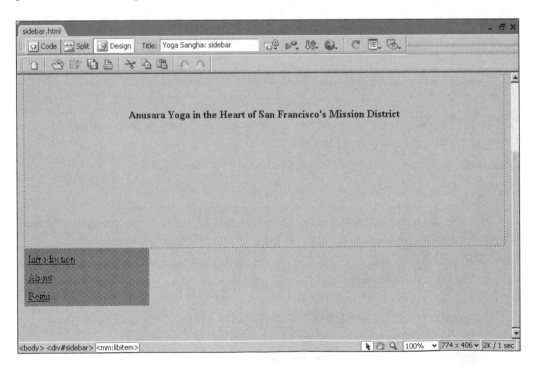

2. Click Recreate on the Property inspector.

The library item file is re-created with the item name used on this page; it now shows up titled as CommunitySubNav in the Library category of the Assets panel.

Tip *You can also right-click (Macintosh and Windows) or Control-click (Macintosh single button mice) to open a context menu that contains the Recreate option and other choices related to the selected library item.*

3. Close the sidebar.html document.

Modifying a Library Item

When you edit a library item, you need to edit the item's source file in the Library folder. A source file can be either the original library item or one that was re-created using the techniques from the previous exercise. Editing a library item changes the library item only. When you finish editing, Dreamweaver prompts you to update all the pages in the site that use the item, letting you choose whether or not to make these changes throughout the entire site. Dreamweaver accomplishes the update by searching for comments that reference the library file you just edited and then replacing the old HTML code with your new HTML code. If you remove the library comments from the code, the contents are no longer associated with the library item and can no longer be changed by updating the library item.

Note *Any modifications to the library item must be made to the source file that is located in the Library folder. If you want to edit the content directly in a document, you must first break the link to the library item. To do this, either hold down Ctrl (Windows) or Option (Macintosh) when inserting the item, or select the item on the page and click the Detach from original button on the Property inspector.*

1. Double-click the copyright file icon on the Library category of the Assets panel.

Tip *If the Library category of the Assets panel is not open, choose Window › Assets and click the Library button on the Assets panel.*

Dreamweaver opens the copyright library item for editing. When library items are inserted on a page, they take on the properties of that document; text and link colors change according to the default colors set for the document, unless you have specified inline Cascading Style Sheets (CSS) styles or other formatting directly in the library item).

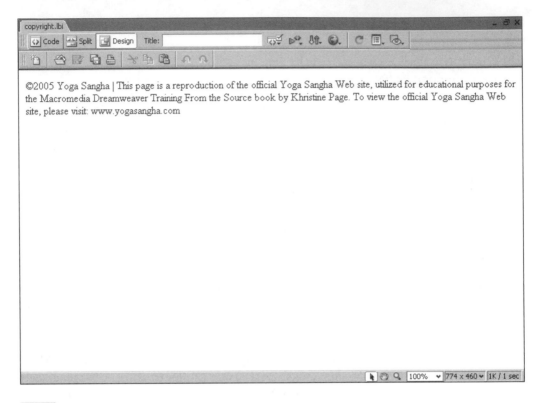

Tip *Alternatively, you can select copyright on the Library panel and then click Edit on the panel. You can also select the library item on a page and click Open in the Property inspector.*

2. In the Document window of the copyright library item, copyright.lbi, insert a horizontal rule above the copyright text. Change the height of the horizontal rule from undefined to a value of *1* in the Property inspector. Save the document.

Tip *You can insert a horizontal rule as you learned in Lesson 2: Either by clicking the Horizontal Rule button in the HTML category of the Insert bar or by choosing Insert > HTML > Horizontal Rule.*

The Update Library Items dialog box opens with a list of all the files in your site that use the copyright library item.

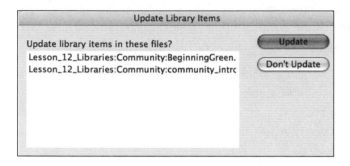

3. Click Update to update all the documents in your site that use the copyright library item.

The Update Pages dialog box shows which pages have been updated with your changes.

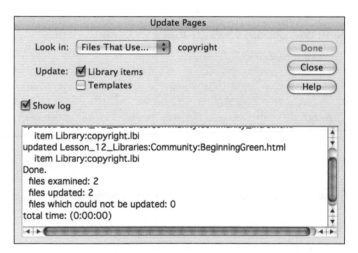

Tip   *If you have a large site, you might prefer to wait to update your site with all your changes at once. In that case, click the Don't Update button when you save the library item.*

4. Click Close to close the Update Pages dialog box.

The horizontal rule should be in its new location in both community_intro.html and BeginningGreen.html.

Updating Library References

If you choose not to update your pages at the time you edit a library item, but decide to do so later, Dreamweaver lets you do all the updating with a single command. For instance, you may want to wait to update pages at a later time if your Web team members have pages checked out that contain library items.

Note | *If you are using Check In and Check Out, a site-maintenance feature covered in Lesson 14, and you want to make updates to pages using a library item, Dreamweaver asks you if you want to check out the pages containing that library item. You must say yes to allow Dreamweaver to check out the file if you want it to be updated.*

1. In the copyright.lbi file, change the copyright date to *2006* and save the document. Click Don't Update in the Update Library Items dialog box.

Neither community_intro.html nor BeginningGreen.html shows the new copyright date yet.

2. From the menu bar, choose Modify > Library > Update Pages.

The Update Pages dialog box opens.

3. In the Look In menu, verify that Entire Site is chosen.

The menu to the right displays the current site, Yoga Sangha. You're choosing to update all files that use library items. Using these options, all library item references throughout the site will be updated—for all library items, not just copyright.lbi. You can choose to update references to a single library item by choosing Files That Use from the Look in menu and selecting the desired library item from the menu to the right.

4. In the Update check boxes, verify that the Library Items box is checked and the Templates box is unchecked. Check the Show Log box and click Start.

The Update Pages dialog box shows which files were updated.

5. Click Close to close the dialog box.

The new copyright date appears in both BeginningGreen.html and community_intro.html. You can close the copyright library item document.

Note | *Similar functionality can be achieved through the use of Server Side Includes (SSI). To include SSI on your pages however, your server must be configured to support SSI.*

Note | *Snippets are another Dreamweaver feature—they allow you to insert often-used portions of code, although they are not updateable because they are not linked to an original item. Snippets are covered in more detail in Lesson 14.*

What You Have Learned

In this lesson, you have:

- Learned how to use library items for elements that need to be repeated on many pages within a site (pages 415–419)
- Created a library item using the Library category of the Assets panel, inserted it on a page with a link to the library item, and inserted it on another page without a link to the library item (pages 415–419)
- Used the Property inspector to re-create a library item that was missing from the Library panel (pages 420–421)
- Edited an existing library item from the Library panel and applied the changes to all pages in the site that used that item (pages 421–423)
- Updated all references to a library item (pages 423–425)

13 Using Templates

A template is a document you can use as the base for creating other documents. Each document based on a template uses the same layout and structure as the template. Creating a template involves designating the areas that need to be editable in documents that are based on the template; all other portions of a template are locked and controlled by the parent template. Templates are similar to Library items in that they provide a quick way to update structure and content across many pages.

Whether you have a large Website with many sections or a number of pages that all use a common design, you can create a template to speed up the production process. By using a template, you can change or update the look of your site, changing multiple pages within a few minutes. Templates are useful when you have a team working

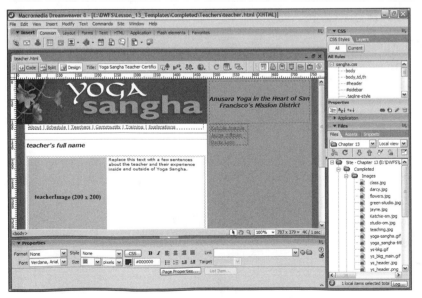

In this lesson, you will create a template from an existing page, build other pages using that template, and modify the pages by editing the template.

together to build an area of the site. The Web designer can create a template, inserting placeholders for the parts of the page that can be edited. The overall design of the page remains locked. Team members can build and edit pages based on a template using either Macromedia Dreamweaver or Macromedia Contribute, a program geared toward nontechnical users such as content editors who might have little or no experience creating Websites.

The advantages of templates are best seen in two situations: when you have a section or set of pages that need to use an identical design and layout, or when a designer creates the look of the pages but content editors add the content to the pages. If you simply want pages with the same headers and footers but different layouts in-between, use Libraries (covered in Lesson 12). But if you want to use the same design on several pages, use templates. Libraries allow you to have certain elements or groups of elements repeated throughout your site, giving you more control over the layouts of the individual pages, whereas templates enable you to make use of the same layout and design. For example, say you have an online catalog of your products and you want all the pages to look the same except for the product picture, description, and price. If you create a template, you can have your team build the pages, either with Dreamweaver or Contribute, and each page will look the same.

To see examples of the finished pages for this chapter, open Katchie.html, Hillman.html and Lyon.html from the Lesson_13_Templates/Completed folder.

What You Will Learn

In this lesson, you will:

- Create a template
- Add editable regions to the template
- Remove editable regions from the template
- Create optional regions
- Insert repeating regions
- Change the template highlight colors
- Build multiple pages based on the template
- Update a site by changing the template
- Define editable tag attributes
- Create a nested template

Approximate Time

This lesson should take about two hours to complete.

Lesson Files

Media Files:

Lesson_13_Templates/Images/...(all files)

Starting Files:

Lesson_13_Templates/Teachers/teacher.html

Text Files:

Lesson_13_Templates/Text/katchie.txt
Lesson_13_Templates/Text/hillman.txt
Lesson_13_Templates/Text/lyon.txt

Completed Project:

Lesson_13_Templates/Completed/Teachers...(all files)

> **Note** *The template used to create the files in the Completed folder is teacher_completed.dwt. This file is located in the Completed/Template_Files folder, so the files will not conflict or be confused with the template files you will be creating in this lesson. In an actual site, the correct location for these files would be the Templates folder that is created by Dreamweaver as you work through this lesson. If you need to use the templates for the completed files, you should move them into the Templates folder.*

Creating Templates

A template defines the layout and design of the subsequent pages you will create from it. In this lesson, the template you create provides the navigation, the site identity, and the look and feel of the teacher profiles section in the Yoga Sangha project site.

When creating a template, your first step usually includes the development of the page design—which has already been done for you in this project. The teacher.html document has the structure, layout, and navigation—it contains everything except for the contents that will be defined in pages based on the template you create from this page.

In this lesson, you'll create a series of Web pages from a common template, each profiling a different teacher. You'll begin the process in this exercise by using an existing page to create the template and then create other pages from that template in subsequent exercises.

1. Open teacher.html from the Lesson_13_Templates/Teachers folder.

In this document, the materials that would be placed in the content areas and that are intended to change from page to page are represented by descriptive placeholder text.

2. Choose File › Save As Template.

The Save As Template dialog box opens. You can select the site in which you want to save the template. For this project, you should save it within the Yoga Sangha site.

Dreamweaver automatically names the template teacher—the name of your file. For this exercise, use this automatic name. It accurately describes the purpose of the template.

Note *If you want to change the name of the template, type the new name in the Save As text field. The template name is for reference by you and your team only—it will not be known to the visitors of your site. Try to use names for your templates that are as descriptive as possible.*

This page has now been saved as a template, and you can use it to build other pages later in this lesson.

3. Click Save to close the dialog box. Click Yes when Dreamweaver displays an alert box that asks Update Links?

Updating the links will allow Dreamweaver to keep the paths to links and images correct.

Your template has been added to your site and saved in the Templates folder with an extension of .dwt. Dreamweaver automatically adds the Templates folder if one doesn't already exist. You might need to click the Refresh button on the Files panel to see the Templates folder. Leave this file open to use in the next exercise.

The file you are working with is now teacher.dwt, and the top of the Document window displays <<Template>> (teacher.dwt).

4. Click the Assets tab in the Files panel group and click the Templates button.

Note *Because you have a template open, teacher.dwt, the Assets panel may open the Templates category automatically.*

The Assets panel is now open to the Templates category. The template you just created appears in the list, and any future templates you create in this site will also appear here. When a template is selected in the list, a portion of that document will appear in the preview area at the top of the panel.

Templates button —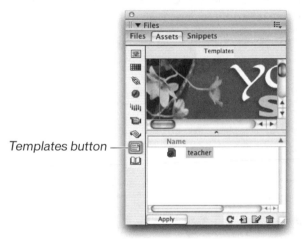

Note *Instead of saving a page as a template from one that was already created, as you just did, you can also create a new blank template by clicking the New Template icon at the bottom of the Templates Assets panel. A new untitled template is added to the list of templates in the panel. While that template is still selected, enter a name for the template. Alternatively, you can create a template from scratch by choosing Template Page from the Category list in the General portion of the New Document dialog box. The Templates tab of the New Document dialog box is for creating pages based on already existing templates—it does not allow you to create new templates.*

Adding Editable Areas to a Template

The second step of creating a template is to define the areas of the page that should be editable in documents that are based on the template. (*Editable areas* are the portions of the document that can be modified in pages that are based on the template.)

As a rule, all areas of a template are initially locked. If you want to change information on pages that use the template, you need to create the editable areas or regions. In many Websites, these regions are often content areas. Everything in the template that is not explicitly defined as editable is locked in pages that are based on the template. You can make changes to both the editable and locked areas while editing the original template, but on a page built from a template, you can make changes only in the editable regions.

1. In teacher.dwt, click the Split view button on the Document toolbar to show both Code and Design views simultaneously. Select the text *teacher's full name* at the top of the area for teacher bios; look at the code to ensure that neither the opening `<h2 class="tagline-style">` nor closing `</h2>` tag is included in the selection.

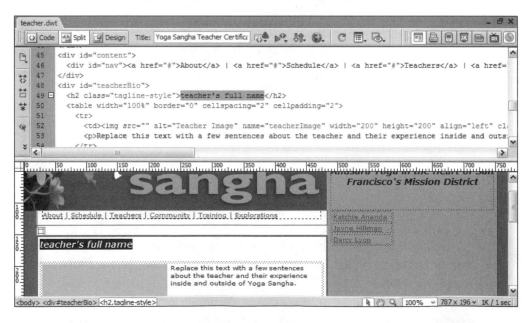

This section of the page needs to be editable so you can change the content in subsequent pages. In this instance you are selecting only the content within the <h2> block tag; therefore, any page created with this template will only allow changing of the text—it will not allow the addition of any block tags within this editable region.

Note *If the file «Template» (teacher.dwt) is not already open, you can open it from the Templates category of the Assets panel. The template you just created in the previous exercise—teacher.dwt—appears in the list as **teacher**. In the Assets panel, double-click the name of the template to open it. Alternatively, you can select the name in the Assets panel list and click Edit at the bottom of the panel.*

2. From the Templates menu in the Common category of the Insert bar, choose the Editable Region icon.

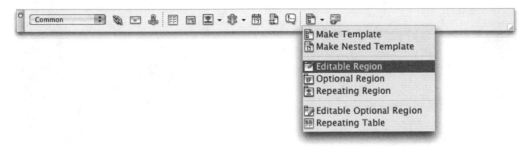

The New Editable Region dialog box opens. The Name text field will initially contain a generic name that is generated by Dreamweaver—the number at the end of the name is automatically incremented and might vary from the one shown in the following example.

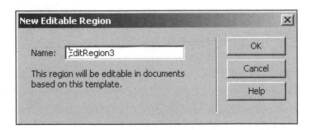

3. Type *teacherName* in the Name text field and click OK. Click the Design button on the Document toolbar to switch back to Design view.

Don't use any special characters (quotation marks, brackets, and so on) for region names. Make each name unique—you can't use the same region name more than once in the same template.

In the Document window the editable area appears outlined in blue with a tab at the top displaying the name of the region. The extra space that appears between the top border of the table and the placeholder image is due to the editable region tab. No extra space is actually inserted.

If you don't see the region names and outlines, choose View > Visual Aids > Invisible Elements.

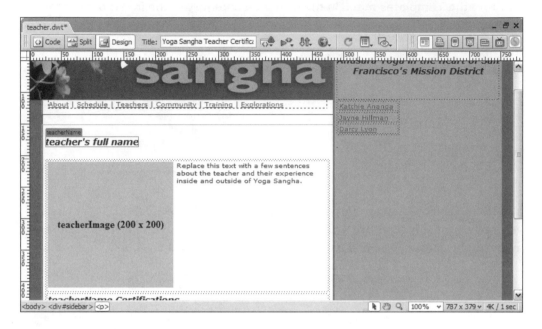

A new editable region is created inside the header. You'll see the same blue outline with a tab at the top displaying the name of the editable region, and the word description is placed inside the editable area. Later, when you apply this template to a document, you will select the text inside this area and replace it with text.

4. Choose File › Save to save the template. Click OK to the warning message.

If you have any editable regions that are within a block tag you will receive a warning each time you save the template.

5. Use the tag selector to select the table cell that contains the teacherImage image placeholder and bio text. Click the Editable Region button in the Templates menu on the Insert bar, name the region *teacherBio*, and click **OK**.

> **Tip** To select the table cell using the tag selector, click the teacherImage in the Document window and then select the *<td>* that immediately precedes it in the tag selector.

The names of all editable regions that you create are listed at the bottom of the Modify > Templates menu. A checkmark appears next to an editable region in this list if it is selected, if the insertion point is in that region, or if an item in that region is selected.

6. Select the table cell that contains the copyright text. Click the Editable Region button in the Templates menu on the Insert bar, name the region *copyright*, and click **OK**.

Anything that has to change in documents based on the template, including links, needs to be in an editable region.

7. Save your file. Click **OK** at the warning message about the editable region inside a <h2> tag.

The region names appear on tabs above all the outlined areas to help you identify which areas you designated as editable.

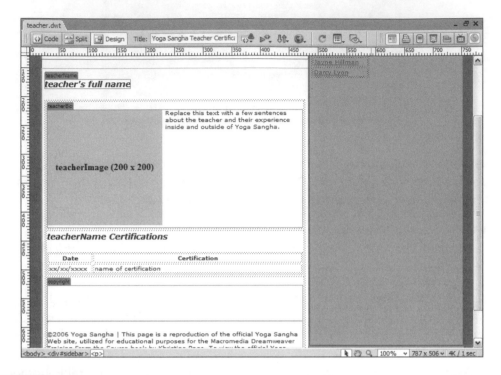

Note *Many of the tools and features available for creating and editing your original templates will be available only in the Design view, in which you have been working. Some template controls are not available if you are in Code view, which you will work with in Lesson 16. If you are working in Code view and find yourself unable to perform certain template operations, switch to Design view.*

Leave this file open to use in the next exercise.

Removing Editable Regions

You have designated certain areas of the template as "editable." You can also lock them again. Elements in locked areas can't be changed on a page that was created from the template. Any elements located in locked areas must be edited on the original template file.

1. In the teacher.dwt document, click the tab for the region copyright in the Document window to select it.

The Tag Selector at the bottom of the Document window displays the template markup `<mmtemplate:editable>`. Dreamweaver highlights the tag on the tag selector to indicate that it is selected.

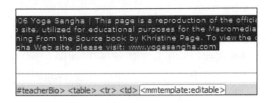

Note *If the template file that you want to edit is not open, you can double-click the name of the desired template in the Templates category of the Assets panel to open it. You can use the Assets panel to move, rename, and delete template files. Use caution when deleting template files because they cannot be re-created as easily as library items can.*

2. **Choose Modify > Templates > Remove Template Markup.**

The outline designating the copyright cell as editable disappears, and that portion of the template is now locked and can no longer be changed in files that are based on this template.

Note *If you remove an editable region from a template that has already had subsequent pages built from it, any of those pages that you modified previously in the editable region are changed when you update the pages after saving the template (you will learn how to update pages later in this lesson). Any modifications to the region are deleted on those pages because the area of the previously editable region changes to reflect the area as it appears in the template. You have the option of selecting a region in which the content that is located in the area being removed will be placed.*

Creating Optional Content

The optional content feature allows you to define whether the content is hidden or displayed in the pages based on the template. It enables you to set conditional or specific values for displaying content. You control these values through template parameters and conditional expressions.

You can create an optional content region to use certain elements in some template-based pages but not others. The capability to allow specific elements to be included on an individual basis gives your template a great deal of flexibility. Some pages, for example, might need illustrations and descriptions. You can create a table that controls the layout for such illustrations and descriptions and then define it as an optional content region. Documents based on the template will then provide you with the option to insert those regions or leave them out.

1. In the teacher.dwt document, use the Tag selector to select the <td> for the table cell that contains *teacherName Certifications* and the nested table.

The selection looks grayed-out to indicate that it has been selected. This section will be optional on pages that use the teacher template.

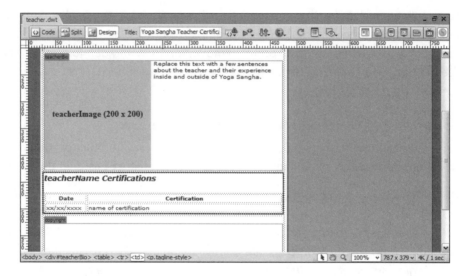

2. Click the Optional Region button in the Templates menu on the Insert bar.

The New Optional Region dialog box opens with the Basic tab active.

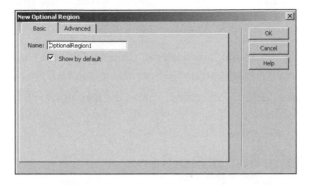

3. In the Basic tab of the New Optional Region dialog box, uncheck the Show By Default box. Click OK to close the dialog box.

When creating your own Website, if the content you define as optional will be used on the majority of your pages, you should leave this box checked. In this lesson, however, only one of the pages will use this content, so it is easier when creating subsequent pages if this content is hidden by default.

In this example, you are using the default name for the optional region.

Note *If you already created an optional content region elsewhere on the page, the Advanced tab of the Optional Content dialog box lets you link that existing optional content region with the new one that you are creating. The Advanced tab also lets you create Template Expressions.*

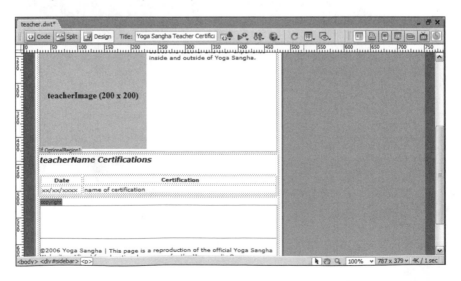

An optional region is not editable. You must define the area of the optional region that should be editable. This allows you to define only a portion of the area as editable, which you will do next.

4. Select the text *teacherName Certifications*. Choose Editable Region from the Templates menu on the Insert bar, name the region *teacherNameCert*, and click OK.

When creating optional regions, all content within those regions will be locked until you define one or more editable regions.

Inserting Repeating Regions

A *repeating region* is an area on the page that needs to be duplicated one or more times. Repeating regions can be particularly useful when you need to have multiple entries, possibly a varying number, placed on pages built from your templates. For example, if a template is created for food recipes and each page based on the template covers a different recipe, the list of ingredients varies on each page. If the list items are defined as repeating regions, you can then add as many of those regions as necessary to each individual page. Repeating regions allow you to have specific control over the appearance of multiple entries. In this exercise, the table listing customer quotes will use repeating regions.

1. In the teacher.dwt document, use the tag selector to select <tr> for the table row that contains the placeholder text for teacher certifications.

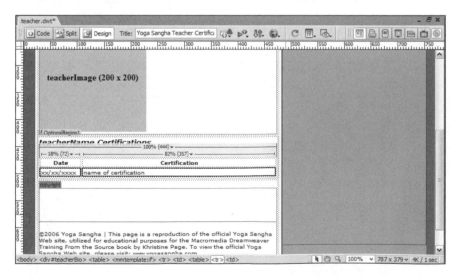

Outlines appear around the row to indicate that it is selected.

2. Choose Repeating Region from the Templates menu on the Insert bar.

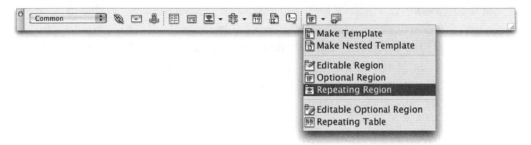

The New Repeating Region dialog box opens.

3. Name the region *certs* and then click OK.

The row you selected becomes outlined in a light blue color, and a tab at the top of the outline displays the name "certs." The highlight color for repeating regions is the same as the highlight color for optional regions and is lighter than the color for editable regions.

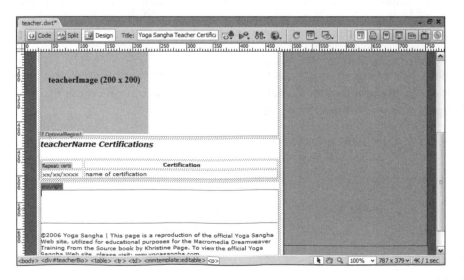

Note | *When developing your own Websites, you might want to change the color of the highlighted regions if they don't show up against the colors used in your page. Choose Dreamweaver > Preferences (Macintosh) or Edit > Preferences (Windows) and select the Highlighting category. Click the Editable regions color box and select a highlight color or enter the hexadecimal value directly into the text field. Do the same as needed for the other highlight colors. The editable region color appears in the template itself and in documents based on the template; the locked region color appears only in documents based on the template. The default colors are blue (#66CCCC) for editable regions and pale yellow (#FFFFCC) for locked regions. You can click the Show boxes to enable or disable the display of these colors in the Document window. These highlight colors show in the Document window only if the option to view invisible elements is enabled. If invisible elements such as the highlighting on template regions do not appear in the Document window, choose View > Visual Aids > Invisible Elements and check that the Show boxes are checked for the template visual aid elements in the Highlighting category in the preferences. If template-based pages are being built by a number of people on your team, remember that other team members can use the default color settings.*

4. Select the <td> on the tag selector for the table cell that contains the place-holder certification date: xx/xx/xxxx. Choose Editable Region from the Templates menu on the Insert bar and type *certDate* for the region name.

Multiple table cells can't be designated as a single editable region. If you need multiple cells to be editable, you must either make the entire table editable or break it up into several editable regions. If you try to select multiple cells within a table and make them editable, the whole table becomes an editable region.

5. Select the <td> on the tag selector for the table cell that contains the place-holder name of certification. Click the Editable Region button on the Insert bar and type *certName* for the region name.

Tip | *In addition to clicking the corresponding <td> tag on the tag selector, you can also select a cell easily by placing the pointer in the cell and use the keyboard shortcut Cmd+click (Macintosh) or Ctrl+click (Windows).*

To make changes within a repeating region in any subsequent documents that are based on your teacher template, the repeating region must contain as many editable regions as necessary. Repeating regions are locked by default; you must define which areas inside of the repeating region need to be made editable.

Note *If it is difficult to see the outline or tab indicating an editable region; you can confirm that the cell you made editable is indeed an editable region by clicking inside the cell and looking at the tag selector. The highlighted `<td>` tag corresponds to the cell you clicked in. Following that `<td>` tag is the template markup `<mmtemplate:editable>`.*

Your document should look like the example shown here.

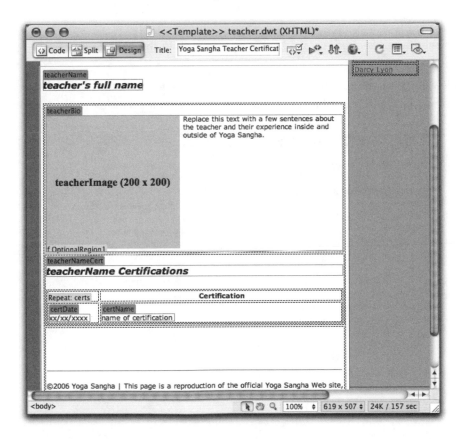

You should save and close the teacher.dwt file.

Building Pages Based on a Template

The next step in creating a site that makes use of templates is to create the actual pages that are based on your original template.

In this exercise, you will create new pages that use the teacher template you created in the previous exercises of this lesson. These pages will inherit the contents of that original template. The only portions of the page you can change in these new pages are those parts you defined as editable in the template.

The graphics you need for building the pages are located in the Lesson_13_Templates/Images folder.

1. Choose File › New and select the Templates tab in the New Document dialog box.

The New Document dialog box opens. In the Templates portion of the box, a list of the sites you defined and a list of all the templates you created for the chosen site appear.

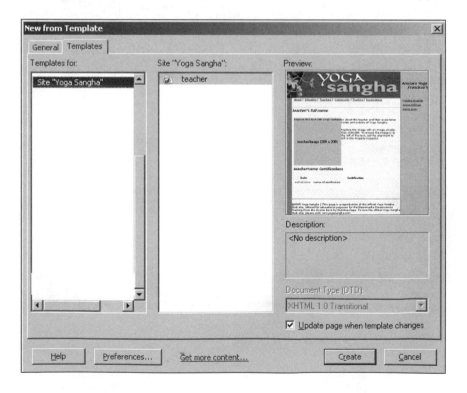

2. Choose teacher from the list of templates for the Yoga Sangha site, leave the Update page when template changes box checked, and then click Create.

A new page is created from the template. Although this document displays the inherited content, it still needs to be saved.

3. Save the file as *Katchie.html* in the Lesson_13_Templates/Teachers folder. Change the title of the page to *Yoga Sangha: Teachers: Katchie Ananda*.

In the new page, you see the highlight color of the locked regions (the default color is pale yellow) outlining the page. You also see the template name on a tab of the same color at the upper-right corner of the Document window.

Note *Dreamweaver automatically creates an editable region named doctitle around the title of the document so that you can change the name of all pages created from the template.*

The pointer changes to a circle with a line through it when you roll over it or try to click any of the locked regions, which indicates that those areas are not editable.

4. Replace the teacher's full name placeholder text with *Katchie Ananda*.

The placeholder header text is now replaced with real content in this template-based document.

5. Open the katchie.txt file from Lesson_13_Templates/Text. Select and copy all the text and paste it over the placeholder text for the teacher bio.

The text and image appears within an outlined border. The border color is the color of the editable regions. A tab at the upper-left corner of the region displays the name of the region.

Note *Formatting text sometimes causes the table to expand. If you change to a style that uses smaller sized text, you won't be able to get the table to shrink back to the proper size by clicking outside the table, as you would do in a regular document. Because this document is based on a template, you have to close and reopen the file for tables to adjust to the proper size in regard to their contents. You won't be able to change the size of the text in this document, unless you create a new style because the internal style sheet that defines the text is not editable.*

6. Select the image placeholder and use the Property inspector to change the Src to the Katchie_sm.jpg image in the Lesson_13_Templates/Images folder.

Your page should now look like the following figure.

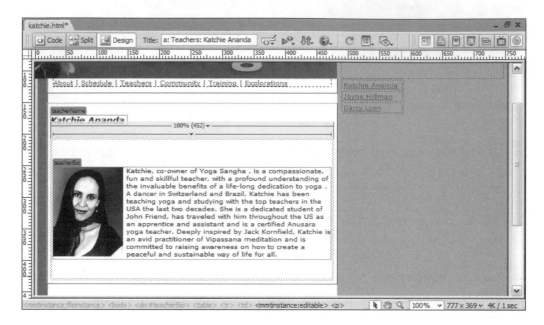

You can save the Katchie.html file.

7. Repeat steps 1 through 6 to create two more template-based files, saving them as *Hillman.html* and *Lyon.html* in Lesson_13_Templates/Teachers. Replace the placeholder text with the text from the hillman.txt and lyon.txt files in the Text folder, and replace the placeholder image with the jayne.jpg and darcy.jpg images from the Images folder on the respective pages.

> **Tip** *Clicking the More option in the Create New Column on the Start Page is a quick way to open the New Document dialog box.*

The title for the Jayne Hillman document should be Yoga Sangha Teacher: Jayne Hillman.

The title for the Darcy Lyon document should be Yoga Sangha Teacher: Darcy Lyon.

You have now created three pages from the teacher template. You can close the Hillman.html and Lyon.html files. Leave the Katchie.html file open for the next exercise.

Controlling Optional Content

When you created the teacher template at the beginning of this lesson, you defined the table for a list of certifications as an optional region that is hidden by default on pages based on that template. When you create and edit new pages using a template, you can show or hide any optional content areas that were created in the original template. In this exercise, you will prepare to develop the optional content for the Katchie Ananda profile by displaying the region.

1. In the Katchie.html document, choose Modify › Template Properties.

Tip *The Template Properties option is located near the top of the Modify menu, next to the Page Properties option.*

The Template Properties dialog box opens.

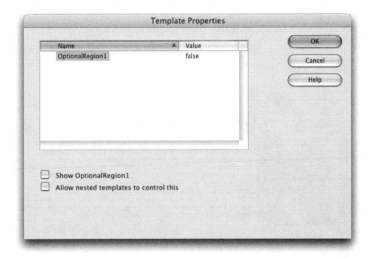

2. Select OptionalRegion1 from the list of names and check the Show OptionalRegion1 checkbox.

The value listed for OptionalRegion1 in the list of values changes from false (hidden) to true (shown).

3. Click OK to close the Template Properties dialog box.

You return to your document, and the table you created in the optional region on the teacher template is now displayed in the Katchie.html document. Keep this file open for the next exercise.

Adding Repeating Entries

The table for teacherName Certifications that is now displayed in the Katchie.html document contains the repeating region you created earlier in the teacher template. In this exercise, you will use the repeating region to insert entries for two certifications.

1. In the certDate editable region in the Katchie.html document located on the now visible optional region, type *05/15/2000*; **and type** *Sample Yoga Certification* **in the cert editable region.**

The editable regions you placed in each cell allow you to enter content into the repeating regions.

> **Note** *You can use the Tab key to jump from one region to another in this row, just as you would in a table to move from cell to cell. You can't, however, use the Tab key to create a new row. To insert a new row, you must follow the next step.*

2. On the Repeat: certs tab, click the plus sign (+) button.

A duplicate of the repeating region is added below the row in which you typed the information for the Sample Yoga Certification.

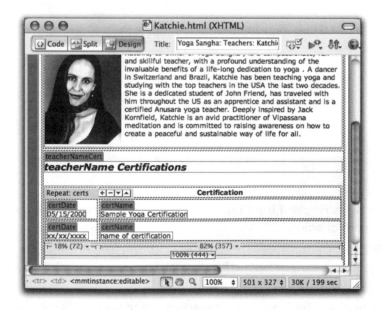

The four buttons on the repeating region tab allow you to add, delete, and change the order of the entries in this region.

3. In the certDate editable region in the newly added row type *01/20/1998*; and type *Sample Yoga 200 Hour Certification* in the cert editable region.

You now have two entries of certification information in this table.

4. Place the insertion point in the cell for the Sample Yoga 200 Hour Certification. Use the up arrow button on the repeating region tab to move this entry up to the top of the list.

The arrow buttons allow you to move the entries up or down in the region.

5. Select the teacherName Certifications text above the certifications and change the text to *Katchie's Certifications*. Save the file.

Save and close the Katchie.html file.

Modifying a Template

The use of a template makes it very easy to build multiple pages using the design of your original template. The person creating the page can just add the content that changes from page to page, but can't make changes to any of the locked areas.

The real time savings come when you need to make changes to all the pages that were built using the template. Without a template, you'd have to edit each page. With the use of a template, you simply edit the original template file to update all the pages built with the template.

1. In the Templates category of the Assets panel, double-click the teacher template.

The original template you created earlier in this lesson opens.

2. Place the insertion point within the sidebar navigation text Katchie Ananda and use the Property inspector to change the link to *Katchie.html*. Change the link for Jayne Hillman to *Hillman.html* and the link for Darcy Lyon to *Lyon.html*. Save the template.

Click OK to accept the warning message about the editable region within a block tag. Then, because you made changes to the template, the Update Template Files dialog box opens, displaying a list of all the files that were built from this template.

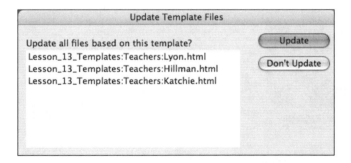

Tip *When creating your own Websites, you can choose Don't Update if you want. You can later update the pages by choosing Modify › Templates › Update Pages.*

3. Click Update to modify all the pages with the changes you just made. Close the Update Pages dialog box after examining its update log.

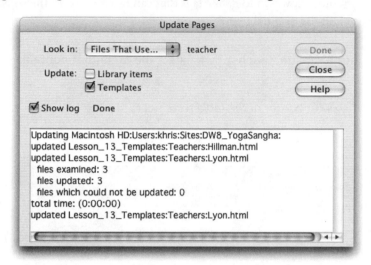

The Katchie.html, Hillman.html, and Lyon.html documents that you created earlier from the template are all updated with the new links. The ability to update all pages associated with a template can be very useful. If you have a navigation section of the template with links (like the Yoga Sangha pages you're working with), you can set those in the template. If the links change, you simply change the template, and all pages designed with the template are updated.

Note *You can detach a page from a template by choosing Modify > Templates > Detach from Template. A detached page is completely editable, but it no longer updates if the template changes. You can also uncheck the Update page when template changes checkbox on the New Document dialog box to create a copy of the page, completely independent from the template. This procedure creates a page that functions much like stationery and does not have any template markup. Pages created in this manner don't update if the template changes.*

4. Open the Katchie.html file and preview it in the browser.

The sidebar links on this page should now point to their corresponding pages, as will those on the other two pages created from this template.

Note *If you want to create content that is controlled by Cascading Style Sheets (CSS), covered in Lesson 4, you can use an external style sheet to make it possible to update the style sheet without having to update the template.*

Creating Editable Tag Attributes

Editable tag attributes allow you to define tags that can be changed in the subsequent documents based on the original template.

1. In the teacher template, teacher.dwt, select the table that contains the teacher image and bio.

| Tip | *Click the outer border of the table to select it.* |

The Document window outlines the table to show that it is selected.

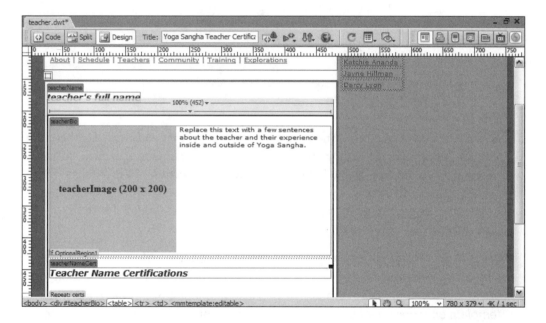

2. Choose Modify > Templates > Make Attribute Editable.

The Editable Tag Attributes dialog box opens.

3. In the Editable Tag Attributes dialog box, click the Add button and type *BGCOLOR* as the Attribute. Click OK and note the attribute is added to the Attribute menu.

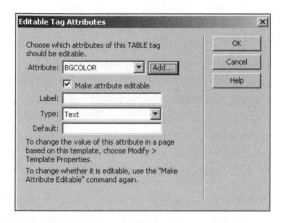

The BGCOLOR attribute does not appear in this menu only because a background color was not defined for the table. For an attribute to appear, you must set that attribute initially. The other attributes listed are WIDTH, BORDER, CELLPADDING, and CELLSPACING— all properties of the table that were defined.

Note *Attribute names must be typed in uppercase. Adding an attribute yourself requires you to be familiar with HTML tags and their attributes. You can use the Reference panel to learn more about tags and their attributes. For example, if you select TD in the Tag menu on the Reference panel, you can learn about that tag's attributes by clicking the Description menu and selecting one of the tag attributes, such as bgcolor. You'll learn more about HTML and the Reference panel in Lesson 16.*

4. Click the Make attribute editable checkbox. Set the Label text to bgcolor; choose Color for the Type, #FFFFFF for Default, and click OK. Save the teacher template, click Update, close the Update Pages dialog box, and close the template file teacher.dwt.

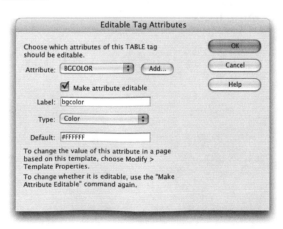

When you click the Make attribute editable checkbox, the value of the attribute is inserted into the table tag as it is defined in the template.

The Editable Tag Attributes dialog box closes. The background color of the table is now an editable tag attribute. The teacher.dwt template might not display as expected if you preview it in the browser after making the bgcolor attribute editable. For Dreamweaver to create the necessary template markup that allows it to control all documents based on the template, the code displayed in the Bgcolor text field is @@(bgcolor)@@. This kind of markup is necessary for the template to function, and it doesn't cause viewing irregularities in the final documents that are based on the template.

Note *To relock a tag that has previously been defined as editable, you must select the tag and choose Modify › Templates › Make Attribute Editable. Select the attribute you want to lock from the Attribute drop-down menu and uncheck the Make attribute editable checkbox.*

Modifying an Editable Tag Attribute

The ability to create editable tag attributes makes the possibilities for creating templates much greater. You can potentially make a wide variety of tag attributes editable, which gives you a great deal of control over the individual documents created from your original template. Attributes such as background color, alignment, and size can increase the usefulness and flexibility of your template-based documents.

1. **Open the Katchie.html document and choose Modify › Template Properties.**

The Template Properties dialog box opens, and the bgcolor tag attribute that you made editable in the previous exercise now appears in the Name list. You can see in the Value column that the default setting for this attribute is #FFFFFF.

2. Select the bgcolor attribute.

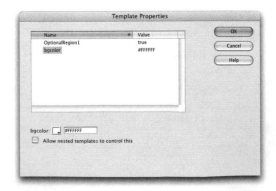

Options for editing the tag appear below the list. In this case, you are provided with a text field in which you can change the color.

3. Replace #FFFFFF in the bgcolor text field with *#FFFFCC* and then click OK to close the dialog box.

The color of the optional table is now changed to light yellow.

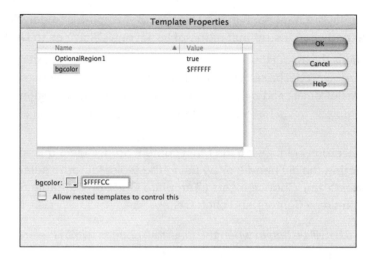

You can save and close the Katchie.html file.

Note   *Knowing HTML helps you to make the most of editable tag attributes. If you don't know HTML, using the Reference panel helps you understand the different tags and the functions of their attributes. Defining the attribute before you choose to make it editable also helps. If you do know HTML, you can make use of a very powerful template feature.*

Creating Nested Templates

A nested template is one that inherits a master layout from a base template. You can create a base template with the main content that should appear on all pages and then use a nested template to create specific content or a layout style for a certain section in your site. If you have an additional section—in which you want to use a different layout while keeping the main site components such as main navigation, footer, and header—you can create another nested template that is also based on your main template. Nested templates are most useful for creating a series of page styles with variations in their layout and design that derive their common content from a main template.

Normally, the process of creating nested templates begins with planning. You will need to first plan the look and feel of the site and create a parent template, then create nested templates for each of the site sections, and finally the sites pages from the nested templates. Typically with nested templates, the parent template is never used to create pages directly—it is used to define a container for the site design with nested templates acting to perform the site page work.

1. Open the ys-layout.html page in the Lesson_13_Templates folder. Save this file as a template and keep the default name of ys-layout. Click Yes to Update Links.

This page contains the overall look and feel of the Yoga Sangha site. All site pages (except the frame-based pages) can be created from this overall site design. Notice it has two main content areas: mainContent and rightContent. You will create editable regions in these areas so that child templates can define a custom look and feel for each section of the Website.

2. Place the insertion point inside the main content area. Select the entire area by either selecting the div handle or by using the tag selector to select the `<div#mainContent>` tag. Choose Insert > Template Objects > Editable Region. Name the region *mainContent* and click OK.

Note | *The `div` will be active when the insertion point is within the area, but it will not be selected. The small solid squares at the corners and midpoints indicated that the div is selected.*

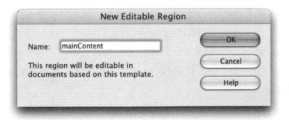

This area is intended to contain the main content for all child pages—that is, pages that are created from this template.

The editable region tab and visual aids will not appear around divs—however, you can verify that the region has been made editable by looking at the tag inspector, which should read `<mmtemplate.editable><div#mainContent>`.

3. Repeat step 2 to create an editable region out of the `rightContent` area. Name the new editable region *rightContent*. Save and close the file.

Now that you have created the original Yoga Sangha template, you are ready to create the nested template in the remaining steps.

4. Choose File › New. From the Templates tab, locate the `ys-layout` template and click Create.

A new page using the `ys-layout` template is created. You'll use the `ys-layout` template as your base template in the next step.

5. Choose File › Save As Template, name the nested template you are creating *ys-teacher*, and click Save.

By saving the document you created from the original template as a template itself, you create a nested template. Now that you have created the nested template, you can edit it. Dreamweaver automatically adds the extension .dwt so you don't have to specify it yourself.

Each page in the Teachers section of the site can be created using the `ys-teacher` template. You can create child templates for each section of the site from the parent `ys-layout` template.

You must create editable regions in the parent template to make modifications to the child template; you must make editable regions in the child template to edit areas in subsequent pages made from the nested template.

What You Have Learned

In this lesson, you have:

- Created a template from an existing page by saving the page as a template (pages 429–431)

- Added editable areas to the template to allow changes to be made on pages built from that template (pages 432–436)

- Removed editable areas from the template to prevent changes from being made on pages built from that template (pages 436–437)

- Created optional content areas that can be shown or hidden in subsequent pages (pages 437–440)

- Inserted repeating regions that allow pages based on the template to have as many or as few entries as needed (pages 440–443)

- Changed the template highlight colors for both editable and locked regions (page 442)

- Built multiple pages based on the template to create pages with the same layout (pages 450–451)

- Made changes to the template and updated multiple pages within the site to reflect those changes (pages 450–451)

- Created and used editable tag attributes for more control over specific elements (pages 452–455)

- Nested a template to create a variation on the main layout that is still controlled by the original template (pages 455–457)

14 Managing Your Site

Developing a Website generally begins with the planning phase, during which you conceive of the idea for a site, develop the site file and navigational structures, gather content, and design the look and feel of the site. These steps of preparation usually occur before you start working in Macromedia Dreamweaver—for the project site you are working with throughout this book, Yoga Sangha, these steps were already done for you, as described in Lesson 1. The planning phase is followed by the production phase, during which you use Dreamweaver to build and test the actual pages of a site, as you learned to do over the course of Lessons 2 through 13.

The work that is put into a Website does not end when you complete the production phase. After production, the Website needs to be made available to the audience—this is done through a procedure known as launching, in which the site is announced and

In this lesson, you'll work with the Files panel to manage files and connect to a remote site.

promoted after being uploaded to a server. In addition, many Websites need to constantly evolve, right along with the changing needs and desires of their audiences, to remain effective and continue to draw new and repeat visitors. The ongoing process of making changes, updating and adding new content, and constantly optimizing a Website is known as *site maintenance*. The transition from the production phase to the maintenance phase of a Website involves setting the site up on a server, thoroughly testing the site, going through the process of launching the site, and preparing for ongoing management and maintenance.

Site management, which is a vital part of Web development, is important for the continued use of a site. Dreamweaver provides extensive management tools that enable you to easily update and control your Website, maintaining site files that are located in the local root folder as well as on the remote server. Dreamweaver uses site definitions to keep track of your files, allowing updates to be made automatically when you use site tools to perform maintenance tasks including moving, adding, and deleting files and folders. Managing the workflow of a team can be done through a variety of tools that are geared toward coordinating teamwork and collaborative efforts. Through Dreamweaver, you can manage multiple Websites, import and export site settings, and even perform quick transfers by creating connections to servers without having to go through the process of setting up a site.

Note *There might be an overlap between the planning, production, and maintenance phases; and the specifics of what is done in each phase can vary from site to site. For example, testing should occur regularly before and after the launch (basic testing by previewing pages in the browser was covered in Lesson 1; more in-depth testing is covered in Lesson 15).*

What You Will Learn

In this lesson, you will:

- Learn about the purposes and uses of the Files panel
- Perform site-management functions within the Files panel
- Understand the difference between a local site and a remote site
- Set up a connection to a remote site
- Copy files to and from a remote site
- Enabling Contribute compatibility
- Administer a site with Contribute

Approximate Time

This lesson should take about one hour to complete.

Lesson Files

Media Files:

Lesson_14_Sites/Images/...(all files)

Starting Files:

Lesson_14_Sites/...(all files)

Using the Files Panel

The Files panel, which displays the file and folder structure of your site, can be viewed either as a docked panel or in an expanded mode as a larger window. You can use the Files panel in either the collapsed or expanded views to perform a wide variety of maintenance tasks such as adding, deleting, renaming, and moving files and folders. Doing all file maintenance within a Dreamweaver site ensures that the paths to links, images, and other elements are automatically updated if necessary—Dreamweaver tracks your changes and updates your files based on any changes that you make within a defined site. Conversely, if you make file or folder changes in the Finder (Macintosh), in My Computer (Windows), or in Windows Explorer File Manager (Windows), Dreamweaver doesn't recognize the changes and cannot keep the paths correct unless you are careful to use the Refresh button to update Dreamweaver's information about the files.

1. Open the Files panel group and select the Files tab.

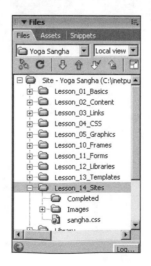

By default, the Files panel is initially accessible through the collapsed view in which the panel is docked with the Assets panel in the Files panel group, and only the local files are visible. The Files panel contains a site toolbar as well as extensive context menu options with functions specifically for site maintenance. The Show menu allows you to switch to any site that you have defined or to your computer. The View menu at the top of the panel allows you to switch between the Local view, Remote view, Testing Server, and Map view options.

Note *Macintosh users: You might see files called .DS_Store in most folders. DS_Store files contain information that is used by the Macintosh Finder to view folders. For more information on them and how to delete them, see Macromedia's Tech Note at: http://www.macromedia.com/go/tn_16831.*

2. Verify that the site Yoga Sangha is selected in the Site menu and click the Expand button on the Files panel toolbar.

Macintosh users: You should close the Start page, if it is open, by clicking the Close Window button in the upper-left corner of the window. You'll be working with the Files panel for the majority of this lesson, and the Start page might obscure the expanded Files panel at times.

Windows users: You do not need to close the Start page because the expanded Files panel expands to fill the space occupied by the Dreamweaver application.

After you click the Expand button, the Files panel opens into its own expanded window, as shown in the following figure. You'll be using the expanded Files panel throughout this lesson.

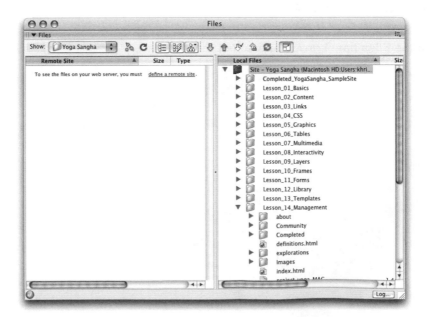

Your local files appear in the right pane of the Files panel (the Local Files pane). Any time the Files panel is expanded, you can collapse it back to the Files panel group by clicking the Expand/ Collapse button again. The local files consist of everything within the root folder,DW8_YogaSangha, which you defined in Lesson 1. In this window, that root folder is listed by the name you gave to the site in Lesson 1: Yoga Sangha.

At this point, you see help text displayed in the left pane of the Files panel window (the remote pane), which lets you know that to see the files that exist on your Web server listed in this pane, you need to define a remote site. You can adjust the size of the panes by dragging the bar that separates them.

Note *You will define a remote site later in this lesson. Clicking **Define A Remote Site** opens the Site Definition dialog box to the Remote Info category of the Advanced tab. When you connect to the remote site, the remote files appear in the left pane.*

The main Files panel tools are located on the toolbar:

- The Show menu lists all the sites that you have defined and gives you access to other files on your computer and quick connections to remote sites. To open a particular site, simply select the desired site from the menu. For this exercise, you should have Yoga Sangha selected.

- Connect/Disconnect connects to or disconnects from the remote site. Because you have not yet defined a remote site, clicking this button opens the Site Definition dialog box. By default, Dreamweaver disconnects a remote FTP site if it has been idle for more than 30 minutes.

Note *If you need to change the time limit, you should choose Edit › Preferences (while the Files panel is in the collapsed view), select the Site category, and change the number listed in the Minutes Idle text field for FTP Connection.*

- Refresh does what you would expect: It refreshes the local and remote directory lists. Any changes that were made to the file lists will be shown after a refresh. If you made changes to your site outside of Dreamweaver, in the Finder (Macintosh) or Windows Explorer (Windows), you might need to refresh Local Files to see the changes.

- The set of three buttons gives you four different view options: Site Files, Testing Server, Map Only, and Map And Files. The active view is highlighted, and the default is Site Files.

- Get File(s) copies the selected file(s) from the remote site to your local folder, overwriting any existing local copies. This option is not functional at this time because a remote site has not been defined.

- Put File(s) copies the selected file(s) from the local folder to the remote site, overwriting any existing remote copies. This option is not functional at this time because a remote site has not been defined.

- Check Out File(s) copies the selected file(s) from the remote server to your local folder, overwriting any existing copies. The file is then marked as "checked out" on the server. The Check In/Check Out feature is a great tool for collaborating on a Website. If a file is checked out, Dreamweaver prevents anyone else from editing that file. This option is not functional at this time because a remote site has not been defined, and the Check In/Check Out option has not yet been enabled for the Yoga Sangha project site.

- Check In copies the selected file(s) from your local folder to the remote server, overwriting any existing remote copies. The file that exists on the remote server is then available for editing by others. The copy of the file that exists in your local folder (usually on your computer) becomes read-only and is not editable unless you check it out. This option is not functional at this time because a remote site has not been defined, and the Check In/Check Out option has not yet been enabled for the Yoga Sangha project site.

- Synchronize synchronizes the files between the local and remote folders. This option is not functional at this time because a remote site has not been defined.

- The menu options File, Edit, View, and Site are located in the Options menu in the upper-right corner of the expanded Files panel (Macintosh) or across the upper-left of the expanded Files panel (Windows). The Options menu is also available on the upper-right of the Files panel group, providing access to the menus when the Files panel is collapsed for both Macintosh and Windows.

Accessing Files Outside a Dreamweaver Site on Your Computer

The Files panel can be used to access and work with files that are located outside of your site's root folder. At times, you might need to access files such as source files for graphics or page layouts that are not usually included in root folders.

1. Select Computer (Macintosh) or Desktop (Windows) from the Show menu on the Files panel.

Arrows (Macintosh) or plus/minus icons (Windows) allow you to expand or collapse the various drives and folders that can be accessible through your computer.

2. Click the arrow next to the Computer icon (Macintosh) or plus sign next to the Desktop icon (Windows) to browse your drives and files.

Any folder that is designated as the root folder for a Dreamweaver-defined site will be green. All other folders will be blue (Macintosh) or yellow (Windows).

Using the Files panel to drag and drop files between site folders and your computer or desktop creates copies of the files in the new location. If you drag and drop files inside a site folder, those files are moved to the new location.

Note *If you need to drag and drop files to or from a site folder and the Computer (Macintosh) or Desktop (Windows), you must do so within the Dreamweaver Files panel or in the Finder (Macintosh), in My Computer (Windows), or in Windows Explorer File Manager (Windows). You cannot drag items out of the Files panel into folders in the Finder (Macintosh), in My Computer (Windows), or in Windows Explorer File Manager (Windows), or vice-versa.*

You can open files in other programs by double-clicking them. Dreamweaver uses the program that it associates with the file you chose to open it.

Note *You can change the associated programs by choosing Edit › Preferences and selecting File Types/Editors from the category list. Select, add, or delete file extensions in the extensions list; use the editors list to define which programs to use when opening files with the selected extensions.*

Modifying Pages from the Files Panel

As you learned in Lesson 3, the Site Map displays a visual representation of a selected portion of your site. As you view pages in the site map and move the pointer over the pages, you'll see information about each page in the status area (the bottom bar) of the Files panel.

1. In the local Files panel, use the Show menu to switch back to the Yoga Sangha site. Select the index.html file that is located inside the Lesson_14_Sites folder. Click the Options menu on the Files panel (Macintosh only). Choose Site > Set As Home Page.

Because many of the Lesson folders contain a copy of the entire site for the purposes of working through the lessons in this book, you'll need to reset the home page to the index.html file that is within this lesson's folder to see the site map.

2. Switch to the Map Only view. Click the plus (+) symbol next to the file training.html. Place the pointer over the filename asana.html in the list below the training.html file.

As you learned in Lesson 3, the Site Map view uses a visual method to show you the files that the home page connects to through links. The training.html file is located in the training folder; the subsequent files listed beneath this training.html file show all the files that the training.html file links to.

The status bar at the bottom of the Files panel shows the title and size of the document as well as the date it was created. Make sure that you roll over the filename, not the file icon. The information doesn't appear in the status bar unless the pointer hovers over the name of the file. You can see by the information that appears on the status bar that the asana.html document is untitled.

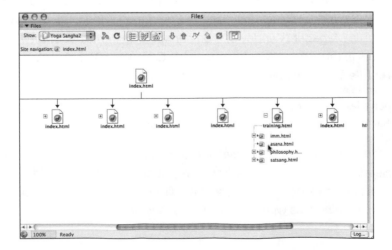

If you forgot to title a page or want to change a title, you can do so in the Files panel.

3. On the Macintosh click the Options menu; or in Windows use the menu in the Files window. Choose View > Site Map Options > Show Page Titles to see page titles instead of filenames in the site map.

The site map is regenerated to display the files by title.

4. Locate the second page titled Untitled Document in the expanded list, which is the asana.html file that you looked at in Step 2. Click the title once to select it. Pause and then click the title again.

A rectangle is placed around the title to indicate that it can be edited. Don't double-click; you don't want to open the file. You just need to select the title so you can edit it.

5. Type *Yoga Sangha: In-Depth Asana Training & Practice* as the new title and press Return (Macintosh) or Enter (Windows).

The site map shows the new title.

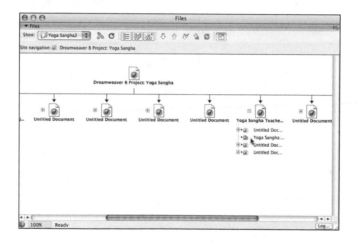

Tip *You can open a page for editing from the Files panel by double-clicking the file in either the Site Map pane or the Local Folder pane.*

6. Click the Options menu (Macintosh only); or use the menu in the File window (Windows). Choose View > Site Map Options > Show Page Titles to switch the view from titles back to filenames.

The checkmark next to the Show Page Titles option in the View > Site Map Options menu will be removed and the files switch back to displaying their filenames.

7. Click the Site Files button on the Files panel toolbar to switch to the list of files. Open the Training folder and select the imm.html file.

Note *You might want to shrink the left pane (the remote view area) by dragging the bar between the two panes to the left. This procedure will give you more room to work with in the Local Files pane, making it easier to see the files.*

When you need to change the name of one of your files, you should change the name in the Dreamweaver Files panel to preserve the link information maintained by Dreamweaver. If you change the filename outside Dreamweaver—for an HTML file, a graphics file, or any other file—Dreamweaver has no way to track your changes. By making the change within the Files panel, you give Dreamweaver the opportunity to update all pages that link to the file or contain the graphic.

8. With imm.html selected, click the filename to make it editable. Change the filename to *immersion.html* and press Return (Macintosh) or Enter (Windows).

The imm.html filename becomes highlighted at the first click, and a rectangle appears around the filename, indicating that it can be edited at the second click.

The Update Files dialog box opens, listing all the files affected by this name change.

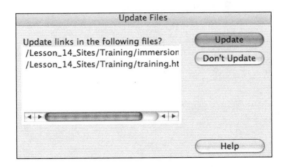

9. Click Update to update the files with the new filename.

The files list now shows the new filename.

Note *Dreamweaver makes the filename change within each file in the list that references the changed file. If a file in the list is open, Dreamweaver makes the change, but does not save or close the file. You must manually save the changes to any open files that have been changed by choosing File > Save.*

10. In Files panel, open the ysImages folder in Lesson_14_Sites.

Note *Only one image, darcy.jpg, is in the folder. If a file or folder is not in its proper place, you can move the file or folder to its correct location. Making this change in the Files panel ensures that all the link information remains correct and intact.*

11. Drag the darcy.jpg image's icon to the Images folder in Lesson_14_Sites further up in the list, near the explorations folder.

Any files that use this image will be affected by the move; you need to fix the path to the image. The Update Files dialog box opens, asking whether affected files should be updated.

12. Click Update to keep the link to this graphic correct.

The graphic moves to the Images folder. Any references to it in the HTML files are still working. If you were to move the file while working outside of Dreamweaver, the paths would not update, and this image would appear to be broken. This means that when displayed in the Document window or browser, a generic image icon would appear in its place, indicating that the file could not be found at the location specified in the HTML.

Note *Dreamweaver allows you to customize the Files panel by reordering, showing, hiding, or adding columns. To make changes to the columns in the Files panel, choose Site › Manage Sites to open the Site Definition dialog box and then select the File View Columns list. You can use the up or down arrow buttons to change the order of the columns. The Options Show checkbox controls which columns are displayed in the Files panel. You can also add or delete columns, and associate them with Design Notes. You will learn more about Design Notes later in this lesson. The rest of the book assumes that you are using the default arrangement of columns in the Files panel and have made no changes. You can use the scroll bar at the bottom of the Local Files pane to see all the columns.*

Connecting to a Remote Site

In Lesson 1, you created a local site—that is, a folder on your hard drive to store all the folders and files needed for your site. Throughout Lessons 2 through 13, you developed pages in the local site. When you create your own sites, however, you need to copy your local files to a remote site after you have completed the production phase of creating your site for visitors to see the Web pages. Typically, the remote site is on a server specified by your host, Web administrator, or client, but it can also be on a local network.

Note *It is a good idea to transfer your site to a live server—ideally the one on which the site will actually reside—and test that site to be sure that everything works as expected. Because you are transferring the site to a different location, there is always the possibility that something might not work as it did in the previous location. It is best to determine whether any such problems exist and fix the situation before launching the site—making it available to the public or other intended audience. Testing is covered in Lesson 15.*

1. Choose Site > Manage Sites.

Tip *Windows users can also use the Site menu located on the expanded view of the Files panel.*

The Manage Sites dialog box opens.

2. Select the Yoga Sangha project site and click the Edit button. The Advanced Tab should be active by default; if not, click the Advanced Tab.

The Site Definition for the Yoga Sangha dialog box opens.

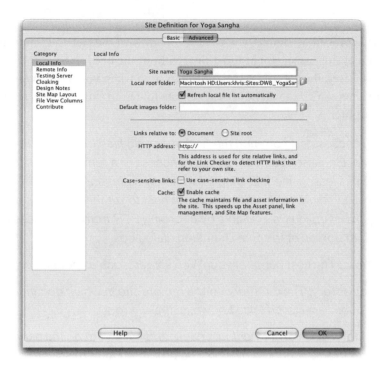

3. Choose Remote Info from the Category list on the left side of the dialog box.

The Remote Info section of the Define Sites dialog box is where you enter information to tell Dreamweaver which remote site to connect to and the attributes of that remote site.

The current selection is None, as you specified when the Yoga Sangha site was first set up in Lesson 1.

4. From the Access menu, choose Local/Network.

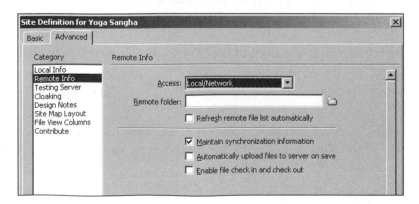

In the following steps, you will create a folder to simulate a remote File Transfer Protocol (FTP) site. This procedure enables you to experiment with the Get and Put functions, as well as additional site-management functions, without the need to have access to a remote server. In most cases, the Local/Network option is used when you have access to another computer on a network that will house the remote folder. In this instance, it will be on your own computer.

Note *FTP access is a common method of getting files from or putting files on a remote site. Because you might not have access to a remote FTP site while you complete this lesson, the following information is presented as reference material only. Consult your network administrator or host to set these options correctly. The following list of options is available by choosing FTP from the Access menu in the Remote Info portion of the Site Definition dialog box.*

- *FTP host: The host name of your Web server (such as adobe.com).*

- *Host directory: The directory on the remote site in which documents visible to the public are stored (also known as the site root).*

- *Login and Password: Your login name and password on the server. If you deselect the Save checkbox, you'll be prompted for a password each time you connect to the remote site.*

- *Use passive FTP: Used when you have a firewall between your computer and the server. This option is unchecked by default.*

- *Use firewall: Used if you are connecting to the remote server from behind a firewall. This option is unchecked by default. The Firewall settings are located in the Dreamweaver Preferences, which you can access quickly by clicking the Firewall Settings button.*

- *Use Secure FTP (SFTP): Used when you have an SFTP server, which uses encryption to create secure connections. This option is unchecked by default.*

5. Click the folder icon to the right of the Remote Folder text box to specify the remote folder.

The Choose Remote Folder For Site Yoga Sangha dialog box opens.

6. Choose a location on your hard disk that is outside your root folder, DW8_YogaSangha. Click the New Folder button, type *YogaRemote* for the folder name, and select it.

The remote folder must be outside your local root folder.

Macintosh users: Select the YogaRemote folder and click Choose.

Windows users: Select the YogaRemote folder and click Open; then click Select to use the YogaRemote folder as your remote folder.

This folder will act as a stand-in for a remote server.

7. Leave the four checkboxes for additional site options set to their defaults, click **OK** to save your site information, and click **Done** to close the **Manage Sites** dialog box.

| Note | *Dreamweaver might update the Site Cache after you click Done because you made changes to the site.* |

You can always edit your site information later by choosing Site > Manage Sites to open the Manage Sites dialog box and then selecting the site you want change. For this exercise, you left the Refresh File List Automatically box checked and the Check In/Out options unchecked, and the maintain synchronization information checked.

8. Click the Refresh button on the Files panel.

The Files panel now displays the empty remote folder in the Remote Site pane of the Files panel. The path from your hard disk to the folder is displayed next to the folder icon. You can roll over the folder name to see the full path.

In this situation, you defined a local folder, so the Connect icon button at the top of the Files panel is not active because you are already connected. The Connect button logs you on to a specified remote server when you are not automatically connected, such as when you use the FTP option.

Uploading Files

After you have a remote site defined, you need to upload any existing files to that location. You can upload an entire site all at once—doing so replaces any and all files that already exist on the server—or you can upload only those files that are new or changed.

1. In the Local Files pane of the Files panel, select the top-level folder Site—Yoga Sangha and then click the Put button on the Files panel toolbar.

| Tip | *The Put button is the blue arrow that points toward the top of the Files panel. The Get button is the green arrow that points towards the bottom of the Files panel.* |

When Dreamweaver displays a message asking if you are sure that you want to put the entire site, click OK.

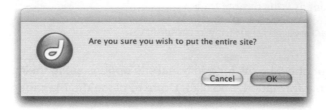

The entire site is copied to the remote folder. You can upload folders and their contents or single files by selecting the item(s) and clicking the Put button. Use Shift-click to select multiple contiguous items (those that are right next to each other), or use Cmd-click (Macintosh) or Ctrl-click (Windows) to select multiple noncontiguous items (those that are separated by other items).

The Background File Activity window will open and show the progress of the transfer. You can continue working on files in Dreamweaver while a file transfer is taking place.

2. In the Local Files pane, find and double-click the asana.html file in the Lesson_14_Sites/Training folder to open it. Open the asana.txt file in the Text folder and copy the contents to the Clipboard. Return to asana.html and paste the content over the text *info here*; then save the file. Close both files.

This file now has a newer modification date than the asana.html that exists in the remote folder.

Windows users: When you open the asana.html file, the Files panel will automatically collapse back into the Site panel in the Files panel group. Open the Files panel to the expanded version by clicking the Expand button on the Files panel when you are done working with the asana.html document.

Macintosh users: If the Start page opens when you close the asana.html files, you can close it so that it does not get in the way of the Files panel.

3. Select the local top-level folder Site—Yoga Sangha. Click the Options menu (Macintosh only). Choose Edit > Select Newer Local.

Dreamweaver compares the modification dates of all local files with the corresponding file information in the remote site and selects only the newest local files. On the Macintosh, Dreamweaver will go through a process of examining the modification dates of all files; this process is shown in the Background File Activity window. On both Macintosh and Windows, wait until Dreamweaver has completed this process—it might take several minutes to sort through all the files.

When Dreamweaver is done, the asana.html file in the Lesson_14_Sites/Training folder should be selected.

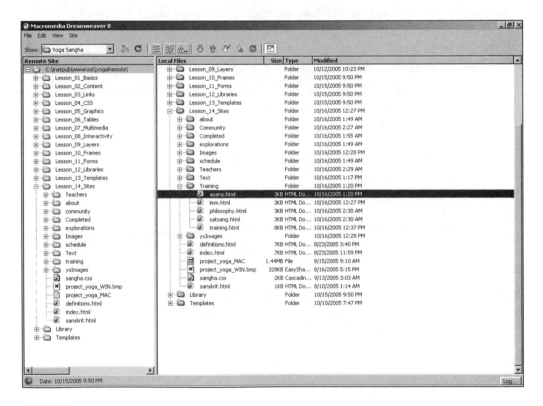

Note *There are two additional options that you can use when selecting site files that have been recently created or modified. Select Newer Remote will select the files on the remote site that are newer than the corresponding files in your local folder. Select Recently Modified will compare and select new or changed files in both locations.*

4. Click the Put File(s) button on the Files panel toolbar.

The Dependent Files dialog box opens. Your choices are Yes, No, and Cancel:

- **Yes** sends any images on the selected pages, along with the HTML pages themselves, to the server.

- **No** sends only the HTML pages. If you changed only the HTML page, and the images are already on the server, you have no reason to send the images again, so you should click No. If you have modified an image or added an image to the page, you should click Yes.

- **Cancel** prevents the transfer from occurring and closes the dialog box.

Note *The Dependent Files dialog box also contains the Don't Ask Me Again checkbox. If this option has been checked previously, you will not see the Dependent Files dialog box. If you don't see the Dependent Files dialog box, but want to have the choice, choose Dreamweaver > Preferences (Macintosh) or Edit > Preferences (Windows). Select the Site category and check the two Dependent Files boxes for the options to Prompt On Get/Check Out and Prompt On Put/Check In.*

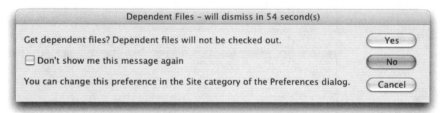

5. Click No if you see the Dependent Files dialog box.

You haven't modified any of the dependent files in this exercise, so it is not necessary to replace them in the YogaRemote remote folder.

The selected file is uploaded (copied) to the remote site.

When the upload has finished, you will see a list of files in the remote site pane that mirrors the list in the Local Folder pane.

Note *Another way to upload or download only files that have been created or changed is to synchronize your local and remote sites. Synchronizing ensures that you maintain a parallel file and folder structure between the local folder and remote site—that the files in one location are duplicates of the corresponding files in the other location.*

To synchronize your site, Dreamweaver compares the modification dates of existing files on both the local or remote site. Synchronizing enables you to update only the files that have been created or changed. To synchronize a site, choose Site › Synchronize from the context menu on the Files panel (Macintosh) or choose Site › Synchronize in the expanded Files panel (Windows). You can choose how to synchronize by selecting a direction from the Direction menu. Put newer files to remote uploads files only if Dreamweaver finds any files in your local folder that are newer than those on the remote site. Get newer files from remote downloads files only if Dreamweaver finds any files on the remote site that are newer than those contained in your local folder. Get and Put newer files transfers files in both directions. To start the process, click the Preview button. Dreamweaver scans the files located in both the local and remote folders and compares the modification dates. After Dreamweaver is done scanning the local and remote folders, it opens a list of the files that it determines are necessary to transfer. This dialog box lists the action (Put or Get), the filename, and the status. For each file, you have the option to uncheck the action box, which causes Dreamweaver to skip the transfer of that file. The number of files to be updated is listed at the bottom of this dialog box.

Use the synchronize function cautiously if you are using Check In/Out because synchronizing Gets and Puts files—even if you are using Check In/Out. It does not check files in or out; it merely replaces them. You'll learn more about Check In/Out in the later in this lesson. When the transfer is done, the list of site files informs you how many files were updated. You can click Save Log to create a log of the file transfer if you need to keep track of when files were transferred.

Cloaking Files and Folders

While you are developing your Website, you might want to prevent certain files from being uploaded or downloaded. For example, if you have a large number of Flash and QuickTime movies embedded in your pages, you might not want to replace those Flash and QuickTime files in your local folder or on the remote server every time you get or put files—but you might want other dependent files to be automatically uploaded. You might also have source files for graphics in your local folder—source files are typically not uploaded to remote servers because they are not necessary for visitors to view the Web pages and they can take up a great deal of space.

You can cloak folders or file types to exclude them from site transfer functions including Synchronize, Get and Put, and Check In/Out. Cloaked folders and file types are also excluded from site-wide operations such as select newer local and newer remote, checking links, search/replace, reports, and library/template updating. Cloaked folder and file types do not appear in the Assets or Files panels.

Note *Cloaking, like many Dreamweaver site functions, is not recognized by other FTP programs. The data needed by Dreamweaver to maintain information on the folders you will cloak in this exercise will be contained in the Library folder. This folder takes up very little space and should not be deleted from either the local or remote locations.*

1. In the Local Files pane of the Files panel, select the PNG folder that is located in the Lesson_14_Sites folder.

This folder contains a PNG file.

You cannot cloak individual files; you must cloak either entire folders or all files of a certain file type.

Tip *A good way to organize your site is to keep all your media files together in the same folder. For instance, if your site has a large number of Portable Document Format (PDF) files, creating a folder solely for PDF files will help keep your site organized and make it easier to maintain.*

2. Click the Options menu and choose Site > Cloaking > Cloak (Macintosh only) or right-click and choose Cloaking > Cloak.

Note *Cloaking should be turned on by default, but if the Cloak option is grayed-out, you should click the context menu and choose Site > Cloaking > Enable Cloaking (Macintosh) or choose Site > Cloaking > Enable Cloaking (Windows). Macintosh users can also Ctrl-click to access the context menu and cloak settings.*

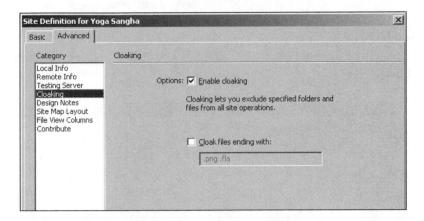

The PNG folder icon is now displayed with a diagonal red line across it in both the Local Files and Remote Site panes of the Files panel. The diagonal red line indicates that the file has been cloaked and will be excluded from site operations. If you open the folder, you will see that the Yoga-Sangha.png file also has a diagonal red line through its file icon.

Tip *You can uncloak the folder to include it in site operations by right-clicking or Ctrl-clicking (Macintosh single button mice) the folder and choosing Cloaking › Uncloak.*

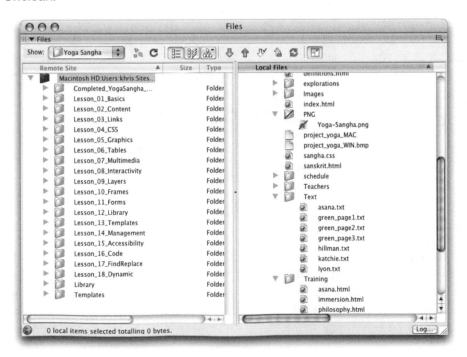

3. Right-click or Ctrl-click (Macintosh single button mice) the PNG folder and choose Cloaking > Settings.

The Advanced tab of the Site Definition dialog box will open with the Cloaking category selected.

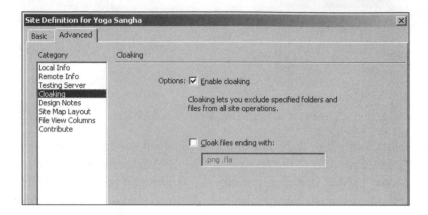

4. Check the Cloak Files Ending With: checkbox. Click in the text field at the end of the list of default file extensions already in the text field. Press the Spacebar and type *.pdf* into the text field.

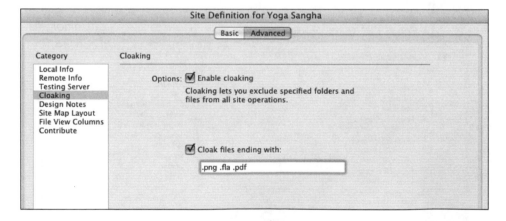

You can insert additional file extensions into the text field to cloak more than one kind of file. To cloak multiple file types, the extensions must be separated by a space, as demonstrated by the default .png .fla extensions that were originally listed in the text field. Fireworks source files use the .png extension; Flash source files use the .fla extension. You can also insert extensions for other common source files, such as the .psd Adobe Photoshop file extension.

5. Click OK to close the Site Definition dialog box and click OK when Dreamweaver tells you that the cache will be re-created. Click the Refresh button on the Files panel when the process is complete.

All PDF files contained in the Yoga Sangha project site are now cloaked. There is a PDF file in the Lesson_14_Sites folder that is now displayed with diagonal red lines through its file icon: ysSchedule.pdf. All PDF files are now excluded from site operations.

Note *To uncloak file types, click the context menu on the Assets panel group (Macintosh) or the Files panel group (Windows) and choose Site › Cloaking › Settings. In the Site Definition dialog box, either remove the specific extension from the text field for the file type that you want to uncloak or uncheck the Cloak Files Ending With: checkbox to uncloak all file types.*

6. Right-click or Ctrl-click (Macintosh single button mice) anywhere within the Local Files pane of the Files panel and choose Cloaking › Enable Cloaking.

The checkmark is removed from the Enable Cloaking option to indicate that cloaking is now disabled for the Yoga Sangha project site. This is an easy way to temporarily remove cloaking from your site's folders and files. If you choose Site > Cloaking > Enable Cloaking again, cloaking will become re-enabled, and all previously cloaked folders and files will be recloaked. Cloaking is enabled on all sites by default. You must have cloaking enabled to cloak folders and file types.

Note *You can also choose the Cloaking category from the Site Definition dialog box and uncheck the Enable Cloaking checkbox to disable cloaking for the site. You can also uncloak all folders and file types simultaneously by choosing Cloaking › Uncloak All. This option leaves cloaking enabled and removes cloaking from all folders and files in your site. You cannot automatically re-cloak folders and files if you have used the Uncloak All function. If you want to suspend cloaking only temporarily, you should disable cloaking, as demonstrated in Step 6. Cloaking options are also located under the Site menu on the Files (or Assets) panel group context menu (Macintosh and collapsed File panel on Windows) or in the Site menu (expanded files panel on Windows).*

Checking In and Checking Out

If you are working on a team, the Check In/Out options can make collaborating on a Website much easier. When this feature is activated, if a team member checks out a file for editing, Dreamweaver locks the checked-out file on the remote server so that no one else on the team can edit the file until it is checked back in. As long as the entire team is using

Dreamweaver and all team members enable Check In/Out, use the Files panel, and are connected to the remote server, the Check In/Out feature lets your group know when someone else is working on a specific file, preventing accidental overwriting of material or duplicate efforts.

1. Choose Site > Manage Sites.

The Manage Sites dialog box opens.

2. Choose the Yoga Sangha project site in the list and click the Edit button.

The Site Definition For Yoga Sangha dialog box opens.

3. Choose Remote Info in the Category list in the Advanced portion of the dialog box.

The remote-site information is displayed.

4. In the Check In/Out area, check the Enable File Check In And Check Out box.

One additional checkbox and two additional text boxes appear. Files become checked out automatically as you open them if Check Out Files When Opening is checked. You must be connected to the remote site for this feature to function properly; if you are not connected, Dreamweaver connects to the remote site automatically.

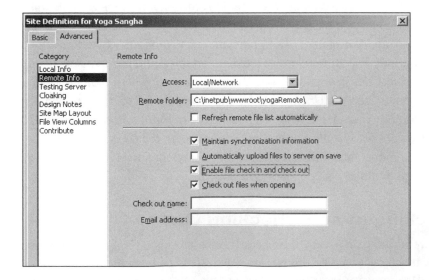

The additional text boxes are Check Out Name and Email Address.

5. Type a checkout name and your e-mail address in the appropriate text fields. Click **OK** in the Site Definition dialog box and then click **Done** in the Manage Sites dialog box.

Your checkout name is only for group reference; it can be your full name or simply a user name. This name will display in the Checked Out By column of the Files panel when you check out a file. Your e-mail address is available to allow team members to contact you with questions.

6. In the Local Files list view of the Files panel, select the index.html page in the Lesson_14_Sites Folder and click the Check In button at the top of the window. Do the same for the sanskrit.html page. Click **No** if asked whether you want to include dependent files.

Check In Button

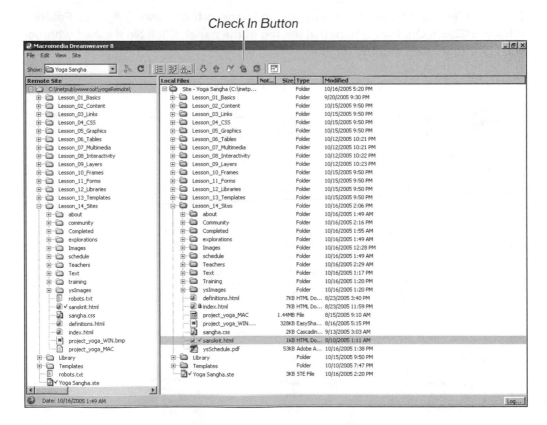

Dreamweaver uploads the selected files to the remote folder. In the Local Folder pane of the Files panel, the files are marked with a small lock icon to let you know the files have been checked in and will need to be checked out for you to edit them locally.

When you work with a group of people and use the Check In/Out feature, it is important for everyone to use the Check In and Check Out File(s) icons instead of the Get File(s) and Put File(s) icons to upload and download files.

If you already have a local copy of your remote site, you must check in each local file for the Check In/Out feature to work properly. When you enable Check In/Out, keep in mind that your files are not automatically checked into the remote server. The check and lock icons indicate the status of a file. A check indicates that a file is checked out; a lock indicates that a file is checked in. If a file has neither a check nor a lock, it has no Check In/Out status. Such an unmarked file is available to open or edit. If you are working with team members and using Check In/Out, it is a good idea to check out and check in your entire site after you enable Check In/Out so that no unmarked files are opened and edited accidentally.

7. In the Files panel, select the sanskrit.html page in the Lesson_14_Sites Folder. Click the Check Out File(s) button at the top of the panel. Click No if asked whether you want to include dependent files.

Check Out Files button

To ensure that you will be working with the most recent version, the file is downloaded to your local site. The file is marked in both the local and remote panes with a small green checkmark next to the file icon, indicating that the file has been checked out by you. The Checked Out By columns in both the local and remote panes show your checkout name in the form of a clickable link to your email address. Files checked out by other members of your team are displayed with a red checkmark, indicating that you cannot check those files out until they have been checked back in.

If you attempt to open a file that someone else has checked out, Dreamweaver informs you that the file is already checked out and gives you several options: You can cancel opening the file, open the file to view it, or override the checkout.

Note *If you receive a warning that the file is checked out by someone else during this exercise, choose to override the checkout.*

For the Check In/Out feature to work properly, everyone on your team should be using Dreamweaver. Other FTP programs don't recognize the Check In/Out feature. Other programs will be able to overwrite files, negating the purpose of checking files in and out. When you use the Check In/Out feature, FTP programs can see the files that Dreamweaver creates: For each file that is checked out, an LCK file is created on the server, letting Dreamweaver know that the file is checked out. For this exercise, you might be able to see the sanskrit.html.lck file in the Finder (Macintosh) or Windows Explorer (Windows). Don't delete these files! They are required for the functionality of the Check In/Out feature and take up very little space.

In addition, all files that are used by the team must initially be checked in on all users' workstations so that Dreamweaver will apply the Check In/Out restrictions. If a file has never been checked in or out, that file will still be editable—bypassing the Check In/Out feature.

8. In the Files panel, select the sanskrit.html page in the local panel. Click the Check In button at the top of the window. Click No if asked whether you want to include dependent files.

This file is now checked in and cannot be edited until it is checked out again. You should leave the Check In/Out feature enabled for now—it is necessary for an exercise later in this lesson.

Note *If Check In/Out is disabled and you want to unlock files, you can click the Options menu on the Files (or Assets) panel group and choose File > Turn Off Read Only. You can also access this option by right-clicking or Ctrl-clicking (Macintosh single button mouse) the file and choosing Unlock.*

Using Design Notes

Design notes are useful for keeping track of information related to your files. These notes are for your information only; they are hidden text files that cannot be accessed or displayed in browsers by the users of your site. You can share information with your co-workers easily by uploading design notes to the remote server. These notes can be used with all files in your site.

1. Choose Site > Manage Sites. Select the Yoga Sangha site and click Edit. Select the File View Columns category and select the Notes item in the list of File View Columns. Check the Show box in the options section. Click OK to apply the changes to the Site and click Done on the Manage Sites dialog box.

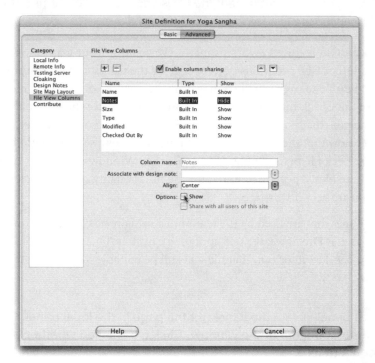

The Notes column must be enabled for you to see the design note that you will create in the Files panel.

2. In the Files panel, select the AboutGreen.html file in the Lesson_14_Sites/Community folder. Click the Options menu on the Files panel and choose File > Design Notes (Macintosh only) or right-click the AboutGreen.html file and choose Design Notes.

Note *You can also attach a design note from the Files panel by double-clicking the Notes column for the selected file or by choosing the option from the context menu, which you can access by right-clicking or Ctrl-clicking (Macintosh single button mouse) the file.*

The Design Notes dialog box appears. You can use the method used in this step to attach a design note to a file when it is selected in the Files panel or when the file is open in the Document window. The Basic Info tab displays information about the file to which the note will be attached and the path of that file in the site. You can change the status of the file by making a choice from the Status menu.

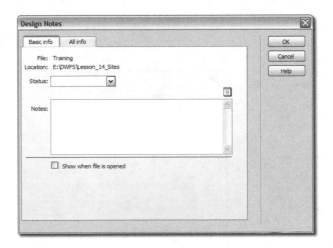

Note *The Design Notes category in the Site Definition dialog box allows you to turn design notes on or off. By default, both the Maintain Design Notes and the Upload Design Notes For Sharing boxes are checked. Dreamweaver automatically uploads or downloads the design notes for any file you get, put, check in, or check out from the remote server when the Upload Design Notes For Sharing checkbox is checked.*

3. Click the Date icon above the right corner of the Notes text box. Select revision1 from the Status menu and check the Show When File Is Opened box. Click OK.

Note *When using file Check In/Out, you will need to ensure that the file is checked out to create a design note. In this case, the file has not previously been checked in, so you can add the design note without checking out the file.*

The date is inserted into the first line of the Notes text box. Use this area to enter any important information about your files.

The Show When File Is Opened box at the bottom of this window allows you have this note displayed when the file is opened—a good way to be sure your team members take notice of your notes.

The Design Notes dialog box closes, and the note is attached to the AboutGreen.html file with the information you added.

4. In the Local Files pane of the Files panel, scroll to the right until you see the Notes column.

The Design Notes icon is displayed as a yellow text bubble in the Notes column, located to the right of the filename, indicating that a note is attached to the file.

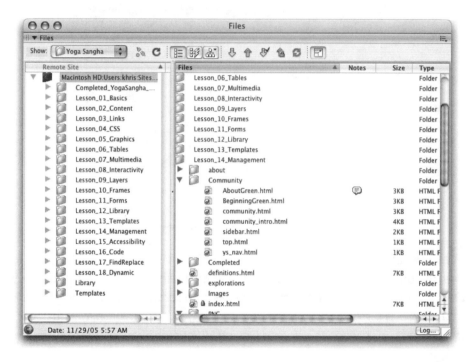

Tip   *To edit the note, double-click the Design Notes icon (the yellow bubble) to reopen the Design Notes dialog box.*

Exporting Site Definitions

The Site Export function allows you to select a site from your list of sites and move it to another computer. This function is useful for many situations, including sharing sites with other team members or when you need to switch computers. Sites are saved as XML files, and all settings from the Site Definition dialog box are retained.

1. Choose Site > Manage Sites and select the Yoga Sangha site in the Manage Sites dialog box. Click the Export button.

> **Tip** *To export the current site, you can click the context menu on the Files panel (Macintosh) and choose Site > Export.*

The Export Site dialog box opens, in which you can name the file and specify the location to save the exported site.

2. Save the Exported Site file in a location outside of your Yoga Sangha site root folder.

The site is saved with the .ste extension. Do not delete or change this extension.

Conversely, you can use the Site Import function to import a site into Dreamweaver. To do so, choose Site > Import; then use the Import Site dialog box to find and select the site. You will be prompted to select a Local Root Folder. You can only import sites that have been exported from Dreamweaver as XML files with the .ste extension. The Export and Import features transfer settings from the Site Definition only; files are not transferred along with the site settings. To keep or include files in the transfer, you need to transfer your root folder with all your files to the new location in addition to exporting the site. If you are using the Local/Network remote access option, you might need to update the path to the remote folder in the imported site.

Creating Server Connections

You can set up quick connections to remote servers to transfer files without going through the process of defining a site. Using a Dreamweaver site, such as the one that you initially set up in Lesson 1 and have been working with throughout this lesson, gives you access to a large number of site-management features. Server connections using FTP or Remote Development Services (RDS) do not provide access to the Dreamweaver site-management features that have been covered in this lesson.

1. Choose Computer (Macintosh) or Desktop (Windows) from the Show menu on the Files panel. Collapse Macintosh HD (or whatever you have named your hard drive–Macintosh) or My Computer (Windows) if it is open. Right-click or Ctrl-click (Macintosh single button mouse) the FTP & RDS Servers item in the Files panel list and select Add FTP Server.

The Configure Server dialog box opens.

Note *You can also access the Configure Server dialog box by choosing Site ›
Manage Sites, clicking the New button, and choosing FTP & RDS Server from
the menu that appears.*

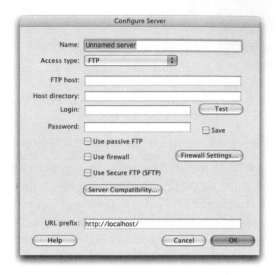

Many of the options available here are similar to those that are available in the Remote
category of the Site Definition dialog box.

2. If you do not have access to an FTP server, you can click the Cancel button.

Because you might not have access to a remote server while you complete this lesson, the
following information is presented as reference material only:

- **Description:** A name or brief description of the server to which you are creating
  a connection.

- **Access type:** You can choose FTP or RDS. FTP is most common and is the one
  described here. The RDS option should be selected only when you are connecting
  to a server that is running ColdFusion.

- **FTP host:** The host name of your Web server (such as adobe.com).

- **Host directory:** The directory on the remote site in which documents visible to the
  public are stored (also known as the site root).

- **Login:** Your login name on the server.

- **Password:** Your password on the server. If you deselect the Save checkbox, you are
  prompted for a password when you connect to the remote site.

Enabling Contribute Compatibility

Macromedia Contribute is a program (included with Macromedia Studio 8) that is used primarily by nontechnical users, such as content editors who might have little or no experience creating, editing, or managing Websites. Contribute gives Web developers the ability to share the responsibility for editing and updating your site with a team while maintaining control over the design, style, code, and structure of the site. As the administrator of a Website, you can set a variety of options to control the site, including setting user access to specific sections of the site on an individual basis and specifying style sheets (covered in Lesson 4) and templates (covered in Lesson 13) for content editors to use.

1. Choose Site › Manage Sites, select the Yoga Sangha project site and click the Edit button.

The Site Definition for Yoga Sangha dialog box opens.

2. Click the Advanced tab if it is not already selected. Choose Contribute in the Category list and click the Enable Contribute compatibility box.

Note   *If Design Notes and Check In/Out are not both enabled prior to enabling Contribute, a message appears to inform you that working with Contribute requires the Design Notes and Check In/Out features of Dreamweaver to be enabled. Click OK to enable both.*

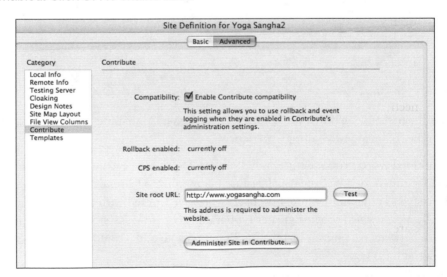

After enabling, there are several other settings that display:

- **Site root URL:** The full URL of the Website that you are setting up to administer should be typed in this text field in the Contribute section of the Site Definition dialog box. (The Advanced tab of the Site Definition dialog box should be active.) After typing in the URL, click the Test button to verify that Dreamweaver can connect to the site you specified.

- **Administration:** The Administer Site In Contribute button opens Contribute and allows you to set the administrative settings, such as controlling access to the site. For this to function, the Macromedia Contribute program must be installed on your computer.

All other settings and options for administering a Contribute site are set in Contribute. If you do not have Contribute installed on your computer, you will not be able to proceed with the rest of this exercise—you can click Cancel to close the Site Definition dialog box and click Done to close the Manage Sites dialog box.

3. Click the Administer Site in Contribute button. Click the radio button on Dreamweaver-style editing and click Yes.

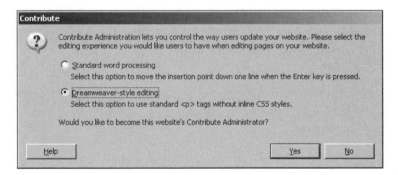

If this is the first time that this site is administered using Contribute, you have to decide between the following two editing experiences:

- **Standard word processing:** Applies inline CSS styles to each new p tag. The CSS styles defined for a Website usually cause paragraphs to be rendered closer together. This style is often more familiar to users who have worked with desktop-publishing applications, which provide greater typographic control. Users can include more space between paragraphs by pressing Enter twice to add a standard HTML paragraph (p) tag.

- **Dreamweaver-style editing:** As with Web page editors, adds standard HTML paragraphs using p tags. When a user presses the Enter key, Contribute adds the HTML p tag; browsers display a blank line between paragraphs that use the p tag.

Note *A drawback of using inline CSS styles causes more complex markup tags to be added to the page. This can make the HTML structure of the page less clear to Web designers who view the HTML tags.*

After choosing, you will see the Administer Websites dialog box with yourself added in the Administrator role.

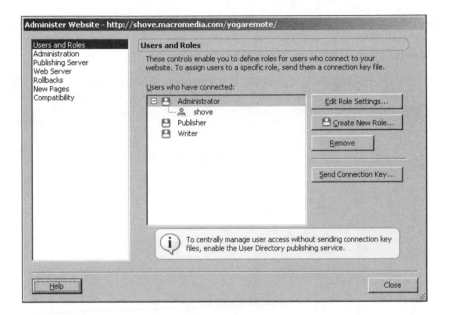

4. Click Close to close the Administer Websites dialog box. A dialog box will appear asking if you want to leave the Administrator password empty. Click No to change the Administer Websites dialog box to the Administration category and to set the Administrator password. In the Administration dialog box, click the Set Administrator Passsword button. Set the password as *password*. You will need to enter the password a second time to confirm, then click OK. Click Close to close the Administer Websites dialog box.

5. Select the Remote Info category and uncheck the Enable File Check In And Check Out box. Click OK in the Site Definition dialog box and Done in the Manage Sites dialog box.

Because you are not creating the Yoga Sangha project site with a team, the Check In/Out feature is not necessary. The rest of this book assumes that you have Check In/Out disabled.

Creating a Connection in Contribute

If you have a well-designed Website using templates and CSS, you can easily have end users create and modify pages without being able to change or harm the underlying design of your pages.

These steps can be performed only if you have Contribute installed on your computer.

1) Launch Contribute. Within the Address bar type the URL to the Yoga Sangha site represented in the Lesson_14_Sites folder by using this URL: `http://localhost/ yogaRemote/Lesson_14_Sites/index.html`.

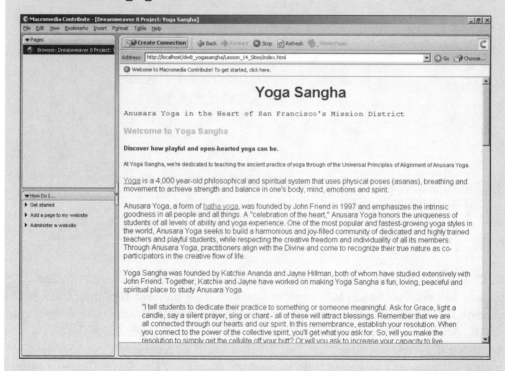

You will view the Yoga Sangha home page. Above the home page will be a note that you have not yet created a connection to this Website.

Creating a Connection in Contribute *(continued)*

2) Click the Create Connection button. Click Next to begin the Connection Wizard.

The Connection Wizard allows you to create a connection to the Website. Once created, you can then begin to create and maintain pages in your Website using Contribute.

End users usually will not create their own connections because you do. As an Administrator you will usually set up users and send out connection keys, so end users do not have to know the inner workings of the connection.

3) Click Next because the URL to the Website is already filled in for you. Select Local/Network as your connection method. Click the Choose button and select the remote folder: `C:\inetpub\wwwroot\yogaRemote\Lesson_14_Sites`. Click Next.

You can connect to a Website that uses Contribute by using FTP, Secure FTP, Local/Network or WebDAV.

4) On the User Information step of the Connection Wizard, fill in your name and e-mail address. Click Next and then click Done to finish the wizard.

If you have multiple copies of Contribute, use a different user name for each machine that has a copy. For example, Bob(laptop), and Bob(Mac). Using the same user name can cause problems because you can override checkouts you make on the other computer.

You are now ready to maintain the Web pages in the Yoga Sangha site.

What You Have Learned

In this lesson, you have:

- Performed site-management functions within the Files panel, including creating new files, renaming files, and moving files (pages 461–470)

- Used the Update Files dialog box to ensure that your paths and links stay correct when you moved files (pages 468–479)

- Customized the Files panel and edited the columns (page 469)

- Created a site map, viewed it horizontally and vertically, used it to manage your files, and learned how to save the site map as an image (page 470)

- Learned the difference between a local site and a remote site, how to use local/network and FTP to connect to servers, and how to define and edit both kinds of sites (pages 470–473)

- Copied files to and from a remote site using the Select Newer Local command to save time (pages 473–477)

- Enabled cloaking to prevent certain file types from being uploaded or downloaded (pages 477–481)

- Used the Check In/Out options for collaboration (pages 481–485)

- Attached a design note to a file, edited design notes, and learned to use them to share information with team members and keep track of file status and versions (pages 486–488)

- Learned how to export a Dreamweaver site and how to import the site definition to transfer site settings from one computer to another (pages 488–489)

- Learned how to create quick server connections to transfer files without setting up a Dreamweaver site (pages 489–490)

- Learned how to administrate Macromedia's Contribute to work for people who might not know Dreamweaver, such as content editors (pages 491–495)

15 Accessibility and Testing

Up to this point in the lessons, you have tested Web pages by previewing them in a browser, usually when you completed an exercise. As you built individual pages or sections, you had a chance to see how those pages looked and make modifications as needed. Before making a site available to the public or to your intended audience, however, you should go further and test your entire site. Take the extra time to be sure that you've worked out all the potential problems. If you have access to a testing server—a remote server on which you can test your site without making it publicly available—it's a good idea to load the site onto that server and access the pages from all computer types and from as many versions of browsers as you can find. Test the pages under real user conditions. If you think a majority of your users will be using a dial-up modem, make sure that you use a dial-up modem to test the speed at which the pages load. If you are the primary Web developer, have others test your pages. Watch how other people try to navigate your site and then consider the usability: Is the site intuitive and functional? Make sure to test every link and fix any broken ones. Remember that not all users think alike—try to prepare for the unexpected as you check the entire site. Analyze which possible paths a visitor might take. Make a list of potential tasks

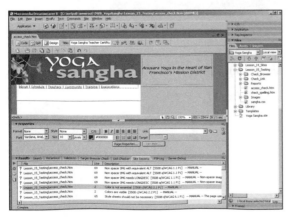

In this project, you will use Dreamweaver to test Web pages for accessibility. You will also test the links in your project site and use reports to determine how your site is functioning and what browsers, if any, might have problems accessing your site.

your viewers might perform (searching for and buying an item, looking for contact information, and so on) and go step-by-step through what those visitors will need to do to complete the task.

Ideally, you should not wait to begin the testing process until the Website is finished. By starting the testing process early and incorporating it as a part of the production process, you can catch and solve problems quickly. If you wait until the end, after you've put hours or weeks of work into your site, it is possible that you might catch an error that will require a great deal of time to fix throughout the site. If you can discover such problems early on, you can address them and save yourself and your Web team a great deal of time.

On any site, large or small, the task of thorough testing can be daunting. You worked hard on the content and the design, but if users get frustrated because of broken links, pages that don't work in their browsers, or pages that are large and very slow to load, you've lost them. In this lesson, you will learn how to use Macromedia Dreamweaver in your testing process by running reports on your site to find out whether the pages are compatible with certain browsers. You'll also learn how to check links throughout the site and test for accessibility.

What You Will Learn

In this lesson, you will:

- Test your site for accessibility
- Test your site for browser compatibility
- Test the links in your site
- Create site reports
- Check for orphaned files
- Check spelling

Approximate Time

This lesson should take about one half hour to complete.

Lesson Files

Media Files:

Lesson_15_Testing/Images/…(all files)

Starting Files:

Lesson_15_Testing/…(all files)

Testing for Accessibility

You can run reports on pages within your sites to determine how well they stack up in terms of compliance with accessibility standards.

1. Open access_check.html from the Lesson_15_Testing folder. Choose Site > Reports.

The Reports dialog box opens.

2. Select Current Document from the Report on menu. Click to check the Accessibility box in the HTML Reports section. Leave all other options unchecked and click the Run button.

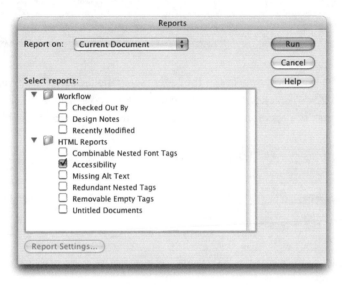

A list of results displays in the Site Reports tab of the Results panel. Each item indicates the filename of the document in which it was found—which in this case is the current document, access_check.html—along with the line number where the item can be found in the code and a brief description of the item.

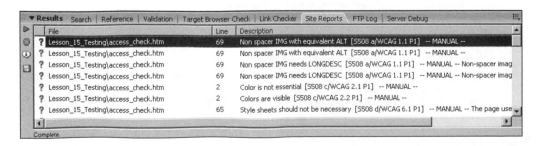

3. Select the fifth item in the list, which begins with Color is not essential. Click the More Info icon on the left side of the Results window.

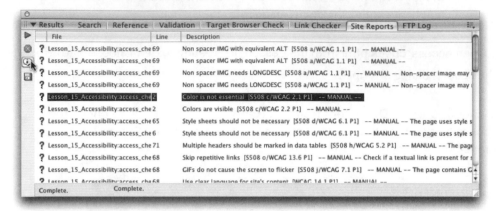

A more detailed description appears in the Reference panel, located in the Results panel. This description gives you specifics about the particular accessibility rule in question, as well as suggestions about methods that can make your pages more accessible.

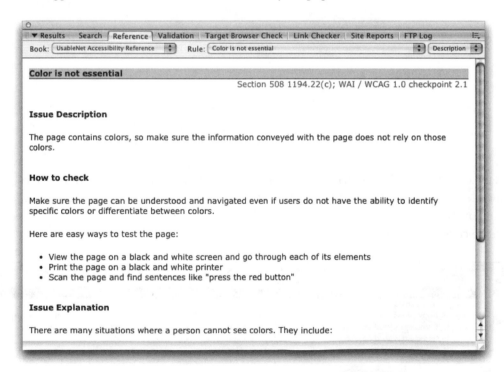

Note *Color, brightness, and contrast are important elements to consider when building your Website. Monitor displays often vary dramatically; typically, Windows screens tend to be considerably darker than Macintosh screens. You can test your pages by using different settings to calibrate your monitor. Using a variety of monitors to test your page is also helpful.*

Dreamweaver provides you with a number of books in the Reference panel through which you can learn more about the code used to create Web pages. The UsableNet Accessibility Reference provides you with a quick way to get a thorough explanation of the many standards required by Section 508, which you learned about in Lesson 5.

Tip *As with all panels, you can resize the Reference panel. Enlarging it might help you to read the content. When the panel is reduced, it can be hard to read the information it contains.*

4. Verify that UsableNet Accessibility Reference is selected on the Book drop-down menu at the top of the Reference panel. From the Rule menu on the Reference panel, choose Spacer IMG with Valid ALT.

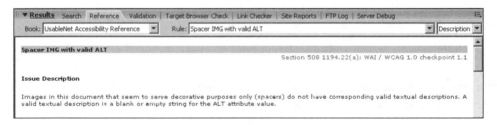

The description of the selected accessibility standard appears in the Reference panel. Displayed in green just above the text description is the specific location of this accessibility standard in Section 508. The description gives you information about the necessity of using the proper alternative text for all spacer and decorative (non-essential) images used. You learned to specify the alternative attribute of images in Lesson 5; in the same lesson you used the <empty> option available in the Alt menu on the Property inspector for spacer images and other similar images that serve only a graphical, aesthetic purpose—that is, they do not convey vital information to the visitor.

5. Close (Macintosh) or collapse (Windows) the Results panel and the access_check.html file.

The Reference panel will be particularly helpful for developing accessible Websites after you start working directly in the code, as you will learn in Lesson 16.

Checking Browser Compatibility

Many of the elements that you can add to your Web pages work only in the later versions of browsers. Cascading Style Sheets (CSS) and layers, for example, are supported only in 4.0 or later browsers. Before making a site available to the public, you should test your pages so you have a chance to fix any errors and be sure that your audience can view the pages as you intend them to be seen. To develop an accessible site, you can identify target browsers and design your pages with those browsers in mind. If your pages are geared toward people who might be using hand-held devices, readers, or ways other than standard browsers to access your pages, you should test your site with those devices and software applications.

In this exercise, you will use Dreamweaver to test the HTML in your pages against a browser profile and determine whether or not that browser supports the code in your page. You can run a browser check on a saved file, a folder, or the entire site. Dreamweaver only reports the errors—it does not make any changes to your files. To make your site compatible, you need to take into account the errors reported by Dreamweaver and modify the pages in your site accordingly until you come to an acceptable solution. What is acceptable might vary from site to site and depends on your intended audience.

1. Open the check_browser.html file from the Lesson_15_Testing/Check_Browser folder.

In the following steps, you will run a target browser check on this file.

2. Click the Check Target Browser menu on the Document toolbar and choose Show All Errors. Make sure the option Auto-check on Open is active.

Tip   *You can also choose File > Check Page > Check Target Browsers.*

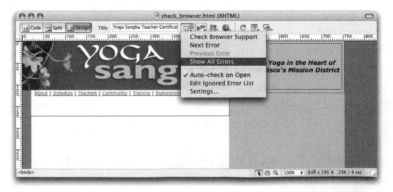

Whenever you open a document, Dreamweaver automatically scans the page, checking for browser errors. The Check Target Browser icon on the Document toolbar changes depending on whether any errors have been detected: If there are no errors but possibly warnings and informational messages, it displays a green checkmark. If errors are found, it displays a yellow warning icon.

The Target Browser Check tab of the Results panel opens.

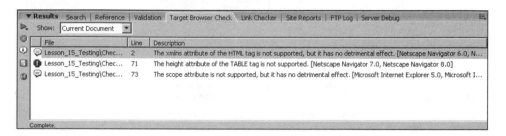

In the Results panel, errors are indicated by red octagons with exclamation marks in white. Warnings are represented by yellow triangles with exclamation marks in black. Errors are signals that there is something wrong with the code that will cause browser errors or other serious viewing problems. Warnings also signal potential display problems, although they are of a less-serious nature and generally do not affect the display or functionality of a page as much as an error might. You might also see informational messages appear in the Results panel—they generally alert you to code that although it might not be supported in a particular browser, it is simply ignored.

In this case, one error and two warnings were found in the check_browser.html document.

You can close the Results panel, or simply move it to the side.

3. Choose Settings from the Check Target Browser menu on the Document toolbar and choose 3.0 from the Netscape Navigator version menu to check that browser against the page; then click OK.

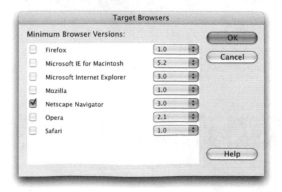

The Check Target Browser icon on the document toolbar now displays the yellow triangle, warning you that portions of the document are incompatible with one of the browsers Dreamweaver is set to check the page against.

The Results panel refreshes and displays the error(s) associated with the document.

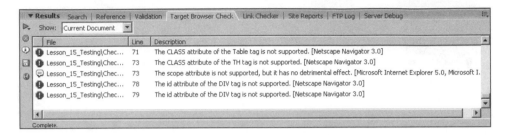

Tip *If the Results panel does not refresh, close it and choose Show All Errors from the Check Target Browser menu on the Document toolbar.*

4. Double-click the Style tag error that is displayed third from the top of the Results panel.

Tip *You might have to scroll up in the Results panel to find the Style tag error, which is the third error.*

When you double-click an error, Dreamweaver lets you know exactly where that error occurs. The Document window switches to Split view, and the <style> tag is highlighted in the code. The problematic code is also underlined with red squiggly lines (it can be hard to see the color when the code is selected). Only errors are indicated in the code by these red lines—warnings and informational messages appear only in reports and the results panel. This option can be extremely helpful when you are trying to correct errors in your documents.

In this case, you do not need to make any modifications because the 3.0 version of Netscape simply ignores this tag. This item is considered an error and not a warning because even though the tag will be ignored, the lack of support can potentially cause display problems, or unexpected results. When developing your Web pages, it is best to test your pages to be sure that any code or elements that are not supported in certain browsers degrade or fail gracefully. When a behavior "fails gracefully" it will not produce any errors or warning in the browser (although you might still see errors and warnings in Dreamweaver); the browsers will simply ignore those elements that they do not support. If an error does appear in the browser, you might want to modify your page accordingly, to develop an alternative that does not produce a visible error.

5. Choose Settings from the Check Target Browser menu on the Document toolbar and check the Opera box to include the Opera browser in the Browser check. Click OK.

The Results panel now displays several additional errors that can be found in various versions of Opera, a popular alternative browser.

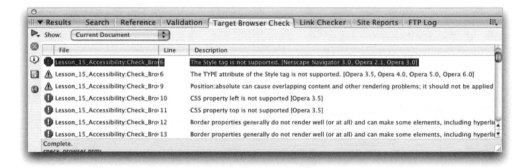

Note *Dreamweaver uses browser profiles to check your document for errors. Information on supported tags, attributes, and elements—as well as warnings, error messages, and tag substitute suggestions—can be included in browser profiles. You can create or add profiles for browsers that are not included in this list (such as WebTV and mobile phone browsers) by using a browser profile that has already been developed or by creating one yourself. You can find additional browser profiles on the Dreamweaver Exchange Website: http://www.macromedia.com/go/dreamweaver_exchange/.*

6. Click the Browse Report icon on the left side of the Results dialog box. Review the information presented in the browser; then switch back to Dreamweaver.

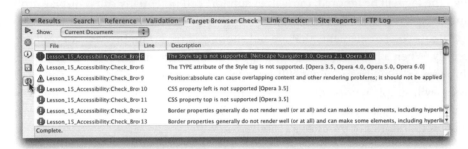

A detailed report is now displayed in a browser window. A list of target browsers indicates the number of errors and warnings that are found for each browser version in the list.

The Check Target Browser feature runs when you open a document and when you manually run the test by choosing Show All Errors from the Check Target Browser menu. The icon on the Document toolbar is not continuously updated as you work.

7. Use the Files panel to select the Check_Browser folder in Lesson_15_Testing. On the Results panel, click the Check Target Browser menu, indicated by the green arrow in the upper-left corner of the Target Browser Check tab, and choose Check Target Browsers For Selected Files/Folders In Site.

On the Macintosh, the Check Target Browser menu/button will appear to be highlighted after you select the Check Target Browsers For Selected Files/Folders In Site option—you will need to click the button to run the check. On Windows, the check is automatically run after you make your selection—you do not need to click it again.

Note *You do not have to make a selection from the Show menu on the Results panel—Dreamweaver automatically switches to Site Report when you choose Check Target Browsers For Selected Files/Folders In Site.*

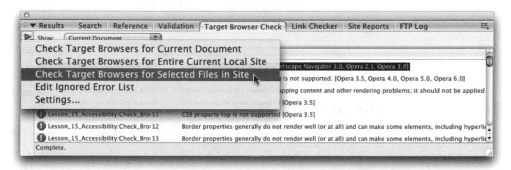

The test runs, and a report displays in the Target Browser Check Tab of the Results dialog box.

There are differences in the way your site displays in every browser version. You might have to make trade-offs in the way the pages appear. Certain JavaScript routines, for example, produce error messages in browsers that do not support them; other JavaScript routines simply do not work, and the visitor might never know it. To reach the widest audience possible, you want to create a Website that is error-free for older browsers. It is far better for visitors to miss certain features than to have error messages appear. If your audience uses a wide variety of browsers, you might want to make sure that the navigation of your pages does not rely on features that might not be supported in older browsers (or provide alternative pages for those who are either not using the latest versions or who might be using drastically different Internet applications).

8. Choose Settings from the Check Target Browser menu on the Document toolbar. Return the setting to the defaults by choosing 4.0 from the Netscape Navigator version menu, checking the Microsoft Internet Explorer box and choosing 5.0 from the menu, and unchecking the Opera box. Click OK to close the dialog box.

Tip *You can also select Settings from the Check Target Browser menu on the Results panel.*

The Check Target Browser settings are now returned to the original Dreamweaver default settings. When deciding which browsers to target, consider the latest browser trends and your target audience. After your site is available to the public, you can continue to assess what your target browsers are by using Website statistics and programs that gather and evaluate that information to find out what browsers your visitors are using the most. You might need to talk with your Web host, service provider, or system administrator for more information.

Many Web designers test their pages in multiple versions of Netscape, Explorer, and other browsers. It is a good idea to have multiple versions of browsers on your computer for this reason.

You can close any open files.

Checking Links in Your Site

It is not uncommon for a Web designer to add, delete, or change the filenames of pages in a site during the development process. It can be easy to overlook pages that link to deleted or renamed files and that have not been updated. It can be very frustrating for visitors to receive the "404: File Not Found" error message, indicating that a page is missing when they click a link.

In this exercise, you will use the Check Link feature to find those missing links. Dreamweaver can verify links only to files within the site. External links are listed, but it is up to you to test those links and make sure that the external links are valid URLs.

1. Open links.html from the Check_Link folder in the Lesson_15_Testing folder. Choose File > Check Page > Check Links.

The Link Checker tab of the Results dialog box opens. Broken Links should be selected by default when you run Check Links; any broken links are displayed in the Broken Links column. If Broken Links is not selected, choose it from the Show menu.

In this exercise, only one broken link is displayed in the list.

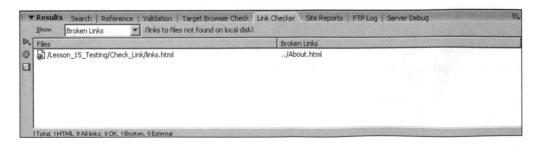

Tip *You can also use the keyboard shortcut Shift+F8 to open the Link Checker report window.*

2. Click the name of the file to which the broken link points: ../About.html.

The filename highlights, and a folder icon appears to the right of the broken link.

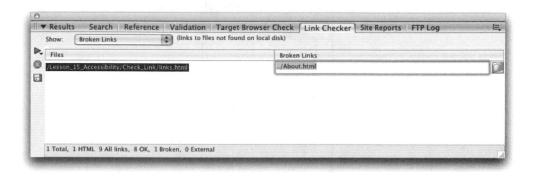

3. Replace ../About.html by typing *About.html* in its place; then press Return (Macintosh) or Enter (Windows).

You can also click the folder icon and browse to the correct file to link to.

If there were any other broken references to the same file, a dialog box would open, asking if you want to fix the other references as well. Clicking Yes will fix all the references to the file.

Note *You can also check files or folders by selecting them in the Files panel and clicking the Files panel group context menu, and choosing File › Check Links. If you want to view the document or fix the links by using the Property inspector, double-click the filename in the Link Checker window to open the file. You used the context menu with the Files panel in Lesson 14.*

You can save and close this file and leave the Results panel open.

Checking for Orphaned Files

In the process of creating a Website, you build new files as well as revise and replace old ones. Throughout the development phase, you might develop multiple versions of certain files or end up disregarding other files entirely. An orphaned file is one that is included with the site files, but is not used on your site. These files might be HTML files that have no links pointing to them, or images that haven't been used on any pages.

1. In the Files panel, select the local root folder for your project Website, Site - Yoga Sangha.

To run an Orphaned files report, you must first run a link check on the entire site.

2. Click the Link Checker tab of the Results dialog box and verify that Broken Links is selected in the Show drop-down menu. Click the Check Links icon (the green arrow) and choose Check Links For Entire Current Local Site from the Check Links menu.

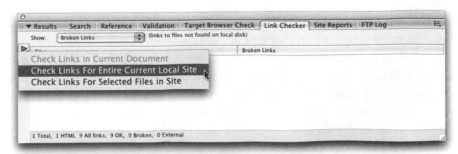

Macintosh users need to click the now-highlighted Check Links menu/button to start the link checking process. The process will start on Windows immediately after the Check Links For Entire Site option is selected.

The Results panel status bar indicates that Dreamweaver is checking the site. When the process is done, a large list appears in the dialog box. The Results panel status bar displays a summary of the report.

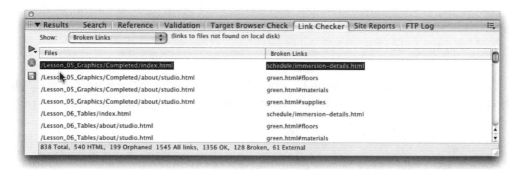

3. From the Show menu, choose Orphaned Files.

A list of orphaned files appears in the dialog box.

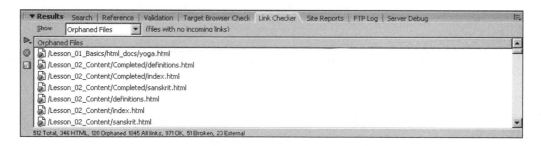

4. Close (Macintosh) or Collapse (Windows) the Results panel.

Deleting orphaned files can reduce the amount of disk space used by your site. It is particularly helpful to perform regular maintenance on large sites. Identifying and removing all orphaned files can have a great impact on the size of your site.

When deleting orphaned files, be sure to thoroughly review the list of files. There might be necessary files that are needed on your site that are not linked to or used in any other file.

For this exercise, do not delete any of the orphaned files listed. The files in the Yoga Sangha project site are needed for completion of this book's lessons. There are a number of broken links and orphaned files in the list of results because this project site is geared towards providing files to accompany the lessons and is not an actual site.

Generating Reports for a Site

While testing your site, you can compile and generate reports on several HTML attributes by using the Reports command, which lets you check several options, including searching for untitled documents and redundant nested tags. You can run reports on a single document, a folder, or the entire site to help you troubleshoot and find potential problems before publishing your site.

1. Select the Reports folder in the Lesson_15_Testing folder in the Files panel. Click the Files panel group Options menu (Macintosh only) and choose Site > Reports.

The Reports dialog box opens.

2. Choose Selected Files In Site from the Report On menu. Leave all the options in the Workflow area unchecked. Check all the options in the HTML Reports area except for Accessibility.

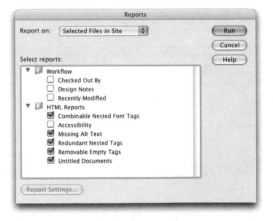

The Workflow options are most useful when you are collaborating with a Web team and need to quickly see who has checked files out and what design notes have been created. The Check In/Out and Design Notes features were covered in Lesson 14.

The HTML Reports options check for combinable nested font tags, accessibility, missing alt text, redundant nested tags, removable empty tags, and untitled documents.

You can choose to run reports on the current document, an entire local site, selected files in a site, and a specific folder.

3. Click Run to create the report.

A list of results displays in the Results panel. In this case, Dreamweaver alerts you that the About.html document has not been given a title.

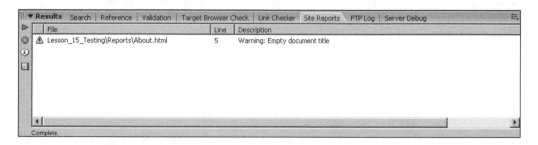

4. Click Save Report on the lower-left corner of the Results panel and save the report in the Lesson_15_Testing folder.

All reports are saved as XML files with the .xml file extension.

The Reports command lists problems in your pages, but does not fix them.

> **Note** *After running the reports, you can use Clean Up HTML on any open documents by choosing Commands › Clean Up HTML. This command fixes many, but not all, of the problems found in the site report. A dialog box appears with a number of items you can choose to have Dreamweaver remove: empty tags, redundant nested tags, non-Dreamweaver HTML comments, Dreamweaver HTML comments, and specific tags. You can also choose to combine nested <font> tags when possible (if <font> tags are used in your pages) and to show the log upon completion. The log gives you a detailed list of the changes that were made to the document. More information about this feature will be given in Lesson 16 when you work with the code.*

Checking Spelling

Correct spelling is an important aspect of the appearance of your Website. Dreamweaver can check the spelling of text in your Web pages, much like a word processor such as Microsoft Word.

1. Open the check_spelling.html file in the Lesson_15_Testing folder. Choose Text › Check Spelling.

The Check Spelling dialog box opens with the word Sangha selected.

2. Click the Ignore button to bypass the word **Sangha** and click it a second time to bypass the word **Anusara.**

The word Trainning should now be selected. A list of suggested words with similar spellings appears. Select Training from the list and click the Change button.

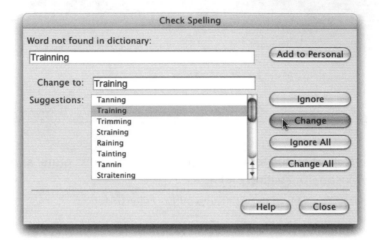

You can save and close the check_spelling.html document and close the Results panel by clicking the Results panel context menu and choosing Close panel group.

What You Have Learned

In this lesson, you have:

- Discovered how Dreamweaver can help build accessible Web pages (pages 499–502)

- Used browser profiles to test individual pages, folders, or an entire site for browser compatibility and find out whether there are any errors or unsupported tags (pages 502–508)

- Tested the links in your pages to quickly find any broken links within your site (pages 508–509)

- Checked for and viewed a list of orphaned files (pages 509–511)

- Created site reports to find common problems in your site, such as redundant nested tags and untitled documents (pages 511–513)

- Checked and fixed the spelling in a document (pages 513–514)

16 Editing the Code

You can gain more control over many of the elements on your Web pages after you become familiar with the code used to create those pages and how to edit that code or even write it from scratch (otherwise known as *hand coding*). Macromedia Dreamweaver does a great deal of work for you, saving you time by creating the code in the background while you visually design your pages. However, Dreamweaver is a great deal more than just a visual editor. It provides an extensive array of tools and resources for hand coding and code editing. These features enable advanced programmers to make precise modifications, troubleshoot their documents, and make use of the most recent progress in code development—even if those advances go beyond what is available in Dreamweaver.

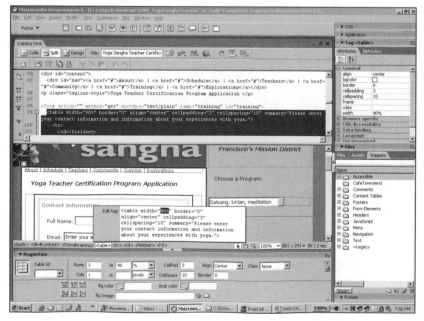

In this lesson you will work directly with the code, using features such as snippets and the Quick Tag Editor to speed up the process.

The ability to introduce items that Dreamweaver might not recognize and the level of control that you have over the code makes for a very flexible program that you can use while staying up-to-date in the rapidly changing world of Web development. Even as a beginner, you can make use of these code features and use Dreamweaver's code tools and resources to learn about the code. You can use Dreamweaver to work with a variety of different programming languages including JavaScript, ColdFusion, ASP, JSP, XML, and more. In this lesson, you will work with Hypertext Markup Language (HTML).

In this lesson, you will learn to edit the code and make use of many of the tools that will enable you to create code by hand. This lesson is intended to give you a basic introduction to the extensive code-editing features available in Dreamweaver—a thorough and advanced exploration of these tools is outside the scope of this book.

To see examples of the finished pages for this chapter, open training.html and asana.html from the Lesson_16_Code/Completed/Training folder.

What You Will Learn

In this lesson, you will:

- Learn to switch document views
- Use the Code view to edit HTML
- Use the Code toolbar
- Create meta tags and HTML comments
- Use the Tag inspector
- Use the Quick Tag Editor
- Use snippets
- Clean up HTML
- Clean up Word HTML
- Extend Dreamweaver

Approximate Time

This lesson should take approximately one hour to complete.

Lesson Files

Media Files:

Lesson_16_Code/Images/…(all files)

Starting Files:

Lesson_16_Code/Training/training.html
Lesson_16_Code/Training/asana.html

Completed Project:

Lesson_16_Code/Completed/Training/training.html
Lesson_16_Code/Completed/Training/asana.html

Switching Document Views

As you develop your pages, you might need to view the source code generated by Dreamweaver. Perhaps a stray line break or other unseen character is ruining the effect you are trying to achieve, but you can't locate it in the Document window. By looking at the HTML source code, however, you can find and remove the line break easily.

Dreamweaver gives you three options for viewing your documents: Design view, which shows all the objects (text, images, tables, and so on) that you have added to your page; Code view, which shows only the HTML source code; and Split view, a combination of both Code and Design views. In the following exercise, you'll look at each of these views.

1. Open the training.html document from the Lesson_16_Code/Training folder.

The document toolbar is displayed at the top of the Document window on the Macintosh and above the Document window as its own panel in Windows.

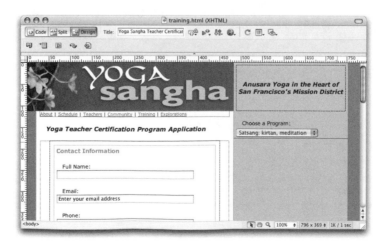

Tip *If the document toolbar is not visible, choose View > Toolbars > Document.*

2. Click the Code button on the document toolbar.

Tip *You can also choose View > Code to switch to Code view.*

In Code view, you don't see the visual elements of the Web page as they would appear in a browser window. Instead, you see the HTML code in a text editor. The document toolbar contains the following code-related controls:

- **Refresh Design View:** This feature updates the Design view (the visual representation of your page) to reflect any changes you make in Code view while using Split view.

- **View Options:** This menu provides options that adjust the display of Code view. You can add line numbers for each line of code, enable wrapping to eliminate horizontal scrolling and make the code easier to view, and so on. You can customize any of these options by choosing Dreamweaver > Preferences (Macintosh) or Edit > Preferences (Windows) and selecting the Code Format category.

*Refresh Design   View Options
View button   button*

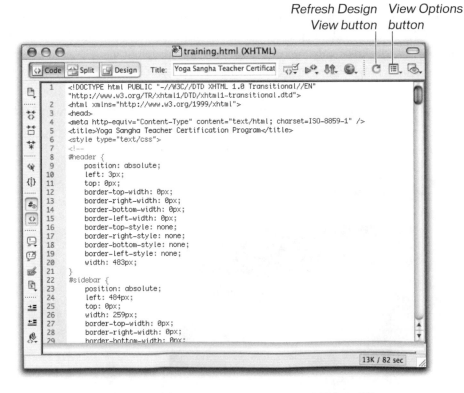

Note *You can also open the Code inspector, which gives you the same options and controls as Code view. The difference is that the inspector opens in a separate window. Some developers use two monitors and place the Code inspector on one screen to simultaneously view the code as they work in the Design view of the Document window. This serves a function similar to the Split view, while giving more room for each view. To open the Code inspector, choose Window > Code Inspector or press the F10 key.*

3. Click the Split button in the document toolbar.

Tip *You can also switch to Split view by choosing View > Code and Design.*

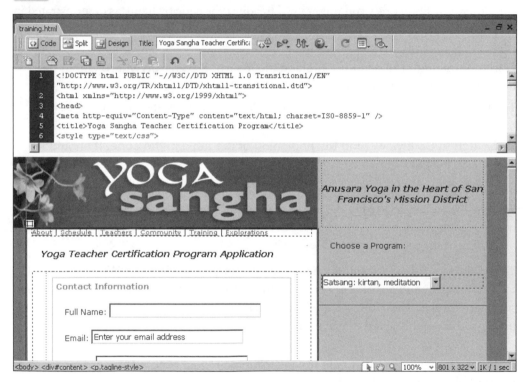

In this view, you can see both the design and the code that creates the page. You can resize the HTML pane by dragging the border between the design and HTML panes. To change the location of the HTML pane, click the View Options button in the toolbar and choose Design View On Top from the menu. This menu also contains other options for adjusting the view, including rulers, visual aids, and the grid.

4. Click the Design button in the toolbar.

Tip *You can also choose View > Design to switch to Design view.*

Your Document window changes to Design view, which shows you all the visual elements of your page approximately as they will appear in the browser. As in the other document views, you can access several view options through the toolbar.

Editing HTML in Code View

You can edit code by hand, and Dreamweaver does not overwrite those changes. If a change is made that appears to be wrong, however, Dreamweaver highlights it to call the code to your attention. Sometimes you might need to adjust the code by hand, as demonstrated in the following steps.

1. In the training.html document, place the insertion point anywhere within the form and click the **<table>** tag in the Tag selector.

The nested table is now outlined with a thick black line to indicate that it is selected.

2. Switch to Split view. Find the beginning of the table in the code. It should appear as follows:

```
<table width="90%" border="0" align="center" cellpadding="0" cellspacing="10">
```

Because the table is selected in the Design view of the Document window, the corresponding code in the Code view is also highlighted. To find the opening table tag, look at the beginning of the selection in the Code view.

This table doesn't have a summary describing the purpose of the table. When you insert a table, there are a number of accessibility features available, including the option to create a summary for the table. However, after a table has been inserted, you can't add a summary unless you do so through the code or the Tag inspector.

3. In the Code view pane, place the insertion point just before the > character at the end of the opening table tag.

Note *The Code view pane displays with a heavy line around the edges of the pane (Macintosh) or a highlighted margin (Windows) to indicate that it is active.*

To learn more about any of the HTML tags that you see in Code view, place your insertion point anywhere inside a tag and press Shift + F1. The Results window's Reference tab opens, which automatically displays information on a currently selected attribute—that is cellspacing because it is the last attribute defined in the opening table tag where the insertion point is. You can choose other tags from the Tag menu at the top of the Reference panel. For example, selecting TABLE from the Tag menu presents you with information about the `<table>` tag. An additional menu, located to the right of the Tag menu, enables you to select a specific attribute of the `<table>` tag or to read a detailed description of the `<table>` tag itself by choosing Description. For instance, you could choose Summary from this menu to learn more about the summary attribute that you will be creating in the following steps.

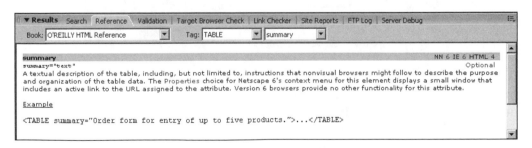

Note *You can read introductory information about the O'REILLY HTML Reference by using the Book menu at the top of the Reference panel to select a different book. Then use the Book menu to select the O'REILLY HTML Reference again, which causes the HTML reference material to open up to the introductory information, without any tags selected.*

4. In the Code view pane, press the Spacebar and you will see a list of attributes for the `<table>` tag.

When you are using Code view Dreamweaver provides a feature known as Code Hinting. Code Hints display attributes of a tag as you are typing. You can type in letters and it will match your typed string until you find the attribute you desire.

5. Type *su* and it will match your keystrokes with the summary attribute. After the summary attribute is selected, press Enter (Windows) or Return (Macintosh). The `summary=""` string is added to the tag, and your insertion point will be left between the double quotes. Type *"Please enter your contact information and information about your experiences with yoga"* within the double quotes. Click in the Design view pane to refresh the document.

> **Tip** *You can also click the Refresh button that appears on the Property inspector after you make a change to the code.*

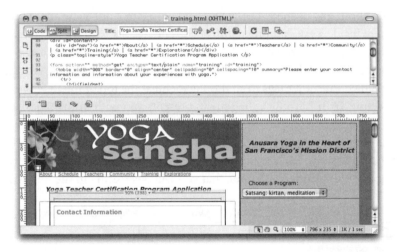

If you make a mistake while editing HTML code, Dreamweaver does not correct the mistake. Dreamweaver does have a feature called Highlight Invalid HTML (which is off by default) that highlights the code that appears to be invalid in bright yellow. You have to make the corrections yourself. This feature is one of Dreamweaver's advantages, known as *RoundTrip HTML*. The fact that Dreamweaver does not change the code is important because sometimes Dreamweaver comes across code that appears to be invalid that you used for a reason. For instance, you can add special tags that your Web server recognizes but are not standard HTML. Dreamweaver leaves them alone. The Invalid Markup highlight appears only in Dreamweaver and does not affect what is seen in the browser. The Property inspector informs you that the selection is Invalid Markup and lists the problematic tag, along with additional information concerning why the code is invalid and a suggestion for how to remedy the problem.

You can turn the Invalid Markup highlight on or off in the Code view by choosing View > Code View Options > Highlight Invalid HTML. You cannot turn the Design view highlight of Invalid Markup off.

Although you won't see any outward sign of the change that you made, the page is now more accessible. You can add summary tags or otherwise edit code when you need to make a change that is not provided for within Dreamweaver's visual interface.

Note *You can also right-click or Ctrl-click (Macintosh single button mouse) on a tag in the Code view pane to pull up the context menu and then choose Edit Tag. The Tag Editor dialog box will open and give you a number of categories and options for editing the tag. The number of categories and options depends on the tag selected.*

Using the Code Toolbar

Dreamweaver 8 includes a Code toolbar full of conveniences for coding.

1. In the Design view portion of the training.html page that you are viewing in Split view, place your insertion point within the table and select the **<table>** tag in the tag selector. On the Code toolbar in the Code view portion of the document, click the Collapse Full Tag toolbar icon.

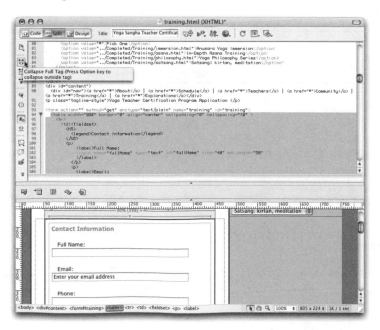

The Code toolbar enables you to collapse full tags, a selection, or everything outside of the selected tag or selection (by holding down the Alt/Option key). This enables you to close code that you are not working with so that you can view more of the code that you want to work with.

2. On the Code toolbar, click the Expand All toolbar option.

Dreamweaver never disturbs the code; it only hides portions for easier viewing. You can expand the code at any time.

3. Place your insertion point within any table row (<tr>) tag. Click the Select Parent Tag button on the Code toolbar.

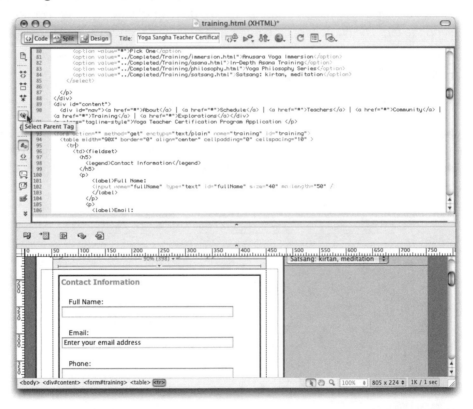

Dreamweaver selects the parent tag—in this case, the <table> tag.

4. With the <table> tag still selected, click the Apply Comment button on the Code toolbar. From the resulting menu select Apply HTML Comment.

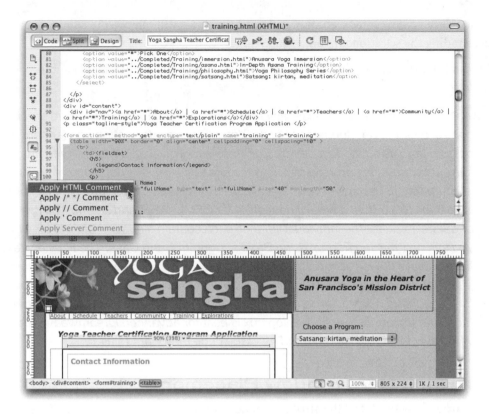

HTML *comments* are used to make notes in the code, to indicate or explain the use of a particular section of code, or to disable a portion of the document without actually deleting the code. Using the Code toolbar's Apply Comment option makes it quicker to comment out a section of code.

Dreamweaver surrounds the table with the HTML comments tags (<!-- -->), thus removing the table from view while browsing the page.

5. With the commented **<table>** tag still selected, click the **Remove Comment** button on the Code toolbar.

Note | *Cascading Style Sheet (CSS) comments are different from standard HTML comments. A CSS comment appears as /*Comment*/ in a style sheet. You can insert CSS comments by selecting Apply /* */ Comment from the menu after clicking the Apply Comment button.*

If you select a commented section of code, Dreamweaver will remove the comments surrounding the selection for you.

You can leave the training.html document open—you'll work with it again later in this lesson.

Note *Dreamweaver includes many tools for code editing that give users precise control over the development of code. You can store information on standard and custom tags using the Tag Library Editor. This tool gives you the ability to modify current tags and import new tags into the already extensive database of tags that is integrated in Dreamweaver. Tags are set up in a system of libraries; each library is specific to a different type of code (HTML, CFML, ASP, and so on). You can add or delete libraries. The individual libraries each contain a number of tags for which you can edit the Tag Format: Line Breaks, Contents, and Case. The Preview text field displays the tag according to the options you set. Each tag contains a number of attributes that can be customized as well. Choose Edit > Tag Libraries to open the Tag Library Editor. Use caution when adding, modifying, or deleting tag libraries, tags, and tag attributes. This dialog box is best for advanced Dreamweaver users who have a thorough understanding of the code they want to alter.*

Adjusting New Window Placement

You learned how to control the attributes of new windows in Lesson 8 with the Open Browser Window behavior. By editing the HTML in Code view, you can also control the placement of those windows.

1. Preview the explorations/poses.html document in your primary browser. Click the Uttanasana link in the first column.

A new browser window opens with a photograph of the yoga pose. You created a new window like this one using the Open Browser window behavior to select the fwd-fold.jpg file, but you had no control over the exact placement of the window. You can control the placement by adding certain parameters to the JavaScript code to place the window in an exact location on the visitor's screen.

2. In the poses.html document, look in the Code view pane for the code that opens the new browser when the visitor clicks the link.

You can find the code by placing the insertion point in the linked "Uttanasana" text in the Design view pane. The corresponding code in the Code view pane will automatically become selected. It should be on line 106 in the Code view pane.

You'll see some code like this:

```
<a href="#" onclick="MM_openBrWindow('images/fwd-fold.jpg','','width=405, ¬
height=605')">Uttanasana</a>
```

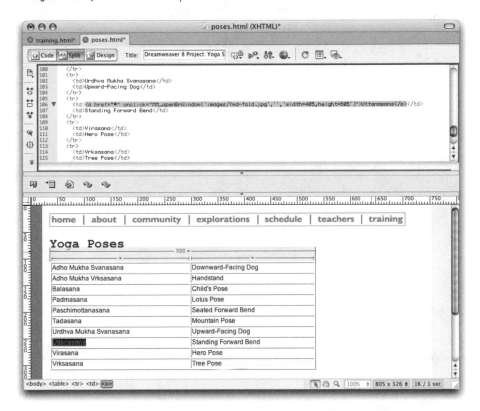

3. **After the value of the height parameter, type a comma and the following code:**
top=0,left=0

Be sure to type the comma and code after the numeric value of 605 and before the single apostrophe. Do not include any spaces.

The top and left parameters position the window at the top and left side of the screen. Using a parameter of 0 places the new window at those coordinates—in the top-left corner of the screen.

The resulting code should look like this:

```
<a href="#" onclick="MM_openBrWindow('images/fwd-fold.jpg','','width=405, ¬
  height=605,top=0,left=0')">Uttanasana</a>
```

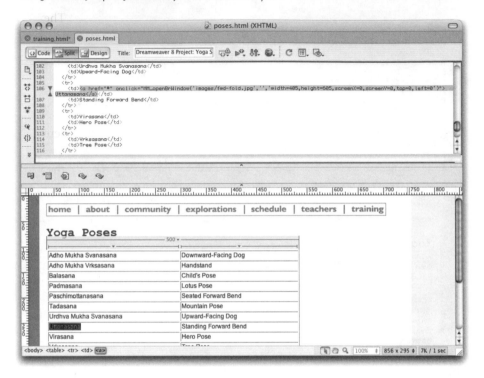

4. Save your page and test it in the browser.

The new window displays at the top and left corner of your screen.

> **Tip** The ¬ character signifies where the book needed to insert a line break so it could fit on the page—you don't actually need to have a line break in your document. And you definitely don't need to type this character into your code.

5. Change both new parameters to *200* and see the difference when you view the page in the browser.

The new window displays in a different position.

When defining the placement of a new browser window, be careful not to position the window too far down or too far to the right. Users who have smaller monitors might not be able to see your window if the coordinates place the window outside the dimension of their screen.

Meta Tags

You can insert certain elements into your code that are not displayed in a browser, but are nonetheless important to the document. Meta tags and HTML comments are two examples of these kinds of elements. **Meta tags** are used for many purposes: They identify and describe documents, provide copyright information, identify the authors or creators, redirect visitors to different pages, control the appearance of the document summary in some search engines, and affect ranking within some search engines.

1. In the training.html document, choose View > Head Content.

The head content area appears right above the Design view pane, which is where icons will appear for items that are located in the head of your document, between the <head> and </head> tags. At this point, the items contained in this area include icons for the title of the document, the <meta> tag with the http-equiv attribute, the link to the external CSS document, the internal CSS, and the portions of JavaScript that are required to appear in the head of the document.

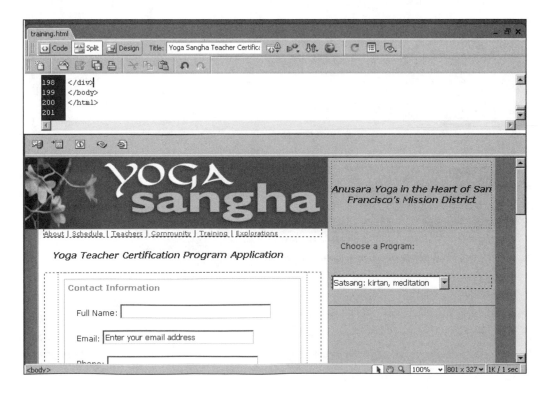

As you click the icons in the head pane, the corresponding code for those items will highlight in the Code view pane.

You must be in either Design view or Split view to view this head content area. If you are in Code view, the View > Head Content option is unavailable. For this exercise, you should use Split view.

2. Click the View Options button on the document toolbar and choose Design View On Top. From the same View Options menu, verify that the line numbers option is turned on. Place the pointer over the bar that separates the Design and Code views. When the pointer turns into a line with double arrows, click and drag the bar upward to enlarge the Code view and shrink the Design view.

Tip   *You can also use View Options menu to toggle on and off other code and design tools including code line numbers, guides, rulers, word wrap, and more. The view options are Dreamweaver tools only; they do not affect the page when viewed in a browser.*

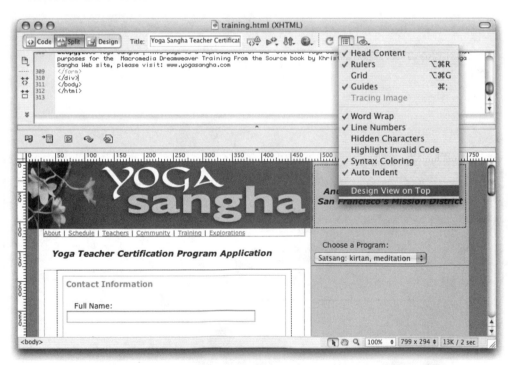

You can now see the head area content near the top of your Document window, just above the Design view pane. You also now have only a minimal amount of the Design view pane showing, and you can easily see the corresponding code in the Code view when selecting the head area icons.

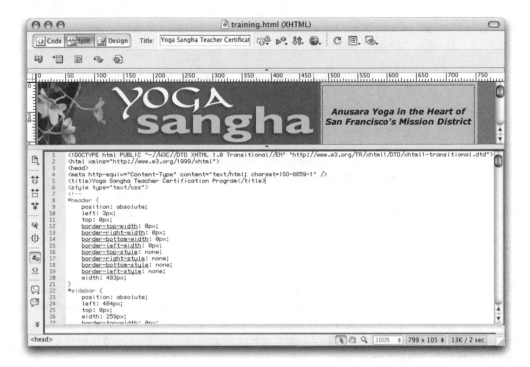

3. In the Code view pane, place the insertion point at the end of line 5, which contains the title of the document, just after the `</title>` tag, and then press Return (Macintosh) or Enter (Windows). Select the HTML category on the Insert bar; choose Description from the Head menu.

The Description dialog box opens with a text field in which you can type a description of your page. The description meta tag, used to give a brief synopsis to identify your page, is included in search results displayed by some search engines. Adding the description meta tag to your pages is an important part of site promotion.

4. Type *Submit your contact information to receive more information about Yoga Sangha training offerings.* **Click OK.**

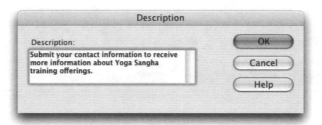

Descriptions should be short—200 characters or fewer. Most search engines have a cutoff; anything more than their limit will not be used. A good description is a very short, concise indication of the contents of the document.

5. The insertion point should now be at the end of line 6. Press Return (Macintosh) or Enter (Windows) to create a new line and choose Keywords from the Head menu in the HTML category of the Insert bar. Type *yoga, sangha, ansara, training* into the Keywords text field. Click OK to close the Keywords dialog box and insert the keywords into your document.

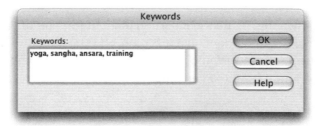

Tip *If the insertion point is already on a blank line (line 6), you do not need to press Return (Macintosh) or Enter (Windows).*

When developing a list of keywords, you can separate individual words or phrases by commas. Do not repeat the same keyword or phrase over again—using "yoga yoga yoga yoga" as a keyword list is considered spamming because of the repetition of the word "yoga." Keywords should be representative of what is on your page and also be words that are actually used on your page.

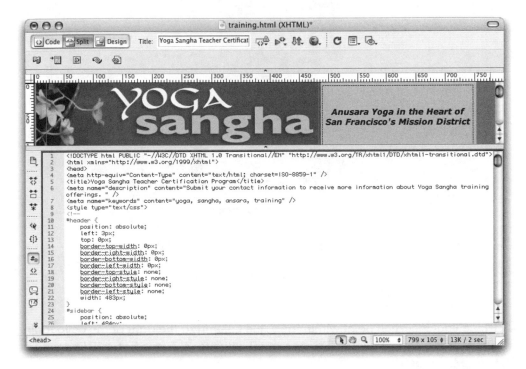

6. Choose View > Head Content to remove the checkmark next to the Head Content view option.

The head area disappears. The rest of this book assumes that you have the Head Content view option turned off.

Using the Tag Inspector

The Tag inspector is a panel group found within the panel set. You can use the Tag inspector to edit tags and objects using a property sheet similar to the ones found in other integrated development environments (IDEs).

1. Put the training.html page in Code view. Place your insertion point within the `<table>` tag on line 96. Open the Tag inspector panel group and ensure that the Attributes panel is displayed.

The Tag inspector displays all attributes of the `<table>` tag and their values.

Tip *If the Tag inspector panel is not displayed, you can choose Window > Tag Inspector or press F9.*

2. Place your insertion point within the value column to the right of the cellpadding attribute in the Tag inspector. Change the *0* value to *3*. Press Enter (Windows) or Return (Macintosh).

The Tag inspector allows you to make quick and precise changes to any attribute of any tag. Here you changed the cellpadding attribute of the `<table>` tag.

You can save the training.html page and leave it open.

Editing Code with Quick Tags

Quick Tags give you the ability to rapidly insert HTML tags. This is especially important when you are writing code by hand because it will help to speed up the process. There are three ways to edit HTML with the Quick Tag Editor. You can insert new HTML code, edit an existing tag, or wrap a new tag around the current selection.

1. Open the asana.html page in the Lesson_16_Code/Training directory. Place the insertion point between the image of the class under the "In-Depth Asana Training and Practice" header and the text beginning with "We will" in the Design view. Click the Quick Tag Editor button near the upper-right corner of the Property inspector.

QuickTag Editor button

The Quick Tag Editor opens in the Insert HTML mode because the insertion point was in the Document window, and there was nothing selected. For the Quick Tag Editor to appear in the Insert HTML mode, the cursor must be in the Design view of the Document window as if you were going to insert an object.

The Insert HTML Quick Tag Editor opens as a box with a text field and a hints menu that you can scroll through to choose a tag. You will need to pause and wait for the Code Hints menu to appear.

2. Scroll through the list of tags in the hints menu; find and double-click br. Press Return (Macintosh) or Enter (Windows).

The selection br is the break tag, and it will appear between the < and > characters in the Quick Tag text field when you double-click it. After pressing Return (Macintosh) or Enter (Windows), the break will be inserted into the Document window at the place where the insertion point was located.

The text is now on a line directly below the image.

Note *You can also perform more extensive code edits by typing directly into the text field; as you do so, Dreamweaver will automatically make corrections to the code for you.*

3. In the Design view of the Document window, select the image of the class and click the Quick Tag Editor button on the Property inspector.

The Quick Tag Editor opens in Edit Tag mode because you had an object in the document selected. Edit Tag mode allows you to edit the values of the tag attributes. The path (also known as the source) to the image is initially selected in the Quick Tag text field.

4. Press the Tab key to move from the path of the image to the next attribute. Keep pressing the Tab key until you reach the value of the Alt text, which is Training Class. Change the Alt text to read *Asana Training Class*. Press Return (Macintosh) or Enter (Windows) to apply the changes.

Each time you press Tab, the Quick Tag Editor applies the change you just made (if any) and jumps you to the next attribute.

Tip *You can move the Quick Tag Editor to a different position by clicking and dragging the left corner.*

The alt text of the image has changed.

5. With the image of the training class still selected, click the Quick Tag Editor button on the Property inspector. Press Cmd+T (Macintosh) or Ctrl+T (Windows) to cycle through the three different Quick Tag options until you get the Wrap Tag mode.

Each time you Press Cmd+T (Macintosh) or Ctrl+T (Windows), the Quick Tag Editor switches to a different mode.

Note *Depending on what you have selected in the document, the Quick Tag Editor might open in either Edit Tag mode or in Wrap Tag mode. For example, if you select text, the Quick Tag Editor will open in Wrap Tag mode. If you want a different mode, use Cmd+T (Macintosh) or Ctrl+T (Windows) to select a different option.*

6. Choose div from the Quick Tag Editor menu. Press the Spacebar and type *a*. Wait for the Code Hints menu to appear and then double-click align. When the Code Hints menu appears after `align=""` is inserted into the text field, double-click center. Press Return (Macintosh) or Enter (Windows) to apply the changes to the code.

The training class image is now centered. The tags `<div align="center">` and `</div>` have been placed around the image.

Note *If you were to select a tag in the Tag selector and press Delete (Macintosh) or Backspace (Windows), the tag and everything it contains would be deleted. However, if you want to remove just the tag while leaving the contents intact, you can right-click or Ctrl-click (Macintosh single-button mice) and choose Remove Tag.*

Using Snippets

In Dreamweaver you can store portions of code, called *snippets*, so that they can be reused easily. There are a certain number of predefined snippets provided in Dreamweaver that you can use, or you can create your own snippets from comments, JavaScript routines, portions of code, and other sources. Snippets are particularly useful for code that needs to be used repetitively throughout a site, such as an email address or a link. In this way, they are similar to library items (covered in Lesson 12); however, unlike library items, snippets do not update throughout a site when you make changes to the original snippet. You can either place a snippet directly into the code or have it wrap around a selection.

1. In the training.html document, place the insertion point after the "Phone" text field in the Contact Information section of the form and press Return (Macintosh) or Enter (Windows).

In the following steps, you will insert a predefined Dreamweaver snippet on the new paragraph line.

2. In the Files panel group select the Snippets tab. Open the Accessible folder and open the enclosed Form Elements folder. Select the Browse For File Button snippet. Click Insert at the bottom of the Snippets panel. Save the training.html document.

This snippet creates a button that the visitor can click to select a file on their hard drive to upload with the rest of their contact information.

Tip *You can also drag the snippet to the point in the document where you want it to be placed.*

3. In the asana.html document, select the div surrounding the table at the bottom of the page that contains the placeholder image and corresponding caption.

Tip *To select the div, you can click the thin dotted border surrounding the table, or you can place the insertion point anywhere inside the table and use the Tag selector at the bottom of the Document window to select the <div> tag.*

This table is an example of one that might be used throughout a Website for images and corresponding captions. By creating a snippet that contains this table, you no longer have to re-create the same code every time you want to include an image and caption combination. You can just insert the snippet quickly and easily. Another advantage is the consistency that comes from using a snippet—you can use a standard look and layout for the image and caption combinations.

4. Click the New Snippet button at the bottom of the Snippets panel.

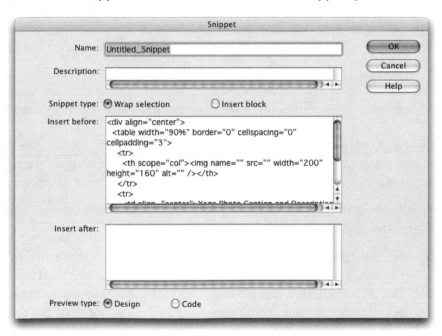

The Snippet dialog box opens.

Note *You can delete or modify snippets by selecting them and clicking the Edit Snippet or Remove buttons at the bottom of the Snippets panel. You can create folders to organize your snippets by clicking the New Snippet Folder button.*

5. Type *Image and Caption Table* in the Name text field. Type *Table layout for images needing captions* in the Description text field. Select Insert Block For Snippet Type and select Design For Preview Type. Click OK.

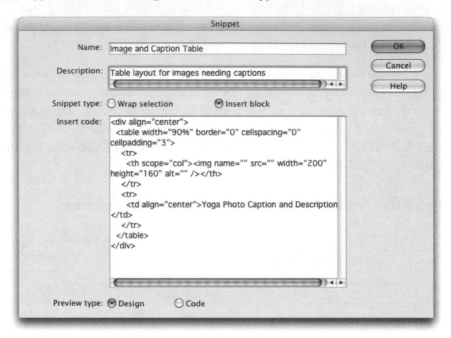

The snippet is created and now appears in the Snippets panel. You can now insert this snippet into a document whenever you need it by selecting it in the Snippets panel and either dragging it to your document or clicking the Insert button on the Snippets panel.

Because the last snippet you inserted was in the Form Elements folder in the Accessible folder, the new snippet appears inside the Form Elements folder.

Note *You can organize your snippets by dragging them into different folders, creating folders, and renaming folders—similar to working with files in the Files panel. You can also create keyboard shortcuts for your snippets. You can access the Keyboard Shortcuts dialog box from either the context menu on the Code panel group or by pressing Dreamweaver › Keyboard Shortcuts (Macintosh) or Edit › Keyboard Shortcuts (Windows). To create shortcuts for snippets, choose Snippets from the Commands menu, select a snippet from the list of snippets, click the plus (+) button to add a shortcut for the selected item (follow the Dreamweaver prompts to create a new set if necessary), and press a key combination. The combination of keys pressed will appear in the Press Key text field.*

6. Test your new snippet by deleting the original div at the bottom of asana.html and replacing it with the new snippet by selecting the Image and Caption Table snippet in the Snippets panel and clicking the Insert button.

Keep the names and descriptions of your snippets as short as possible. The first column in the Snippets panel displays the icons and names; the second column displays the descriptions. You can roll over a description to see the full description popup.

Using Clean Up XHTML

Throughout the process of creating an XHTML document, you might wind up with empty or redundant tags, unnecessary or improperly nested tags, and more problems with the XHTML code in your document. Using the Clean Up XHTML command gets rid of nearly all of these problematic instances. It is recommended that you run the Clean Up XHTML command whenever you finish a page or site.

1. In the asana.html document, choose Commands › Clean Up HTML.

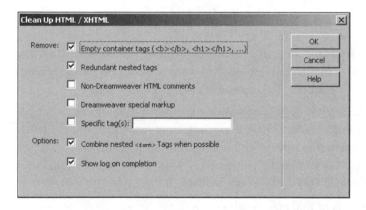

The Clean Up HTML/XHTML dialog box opens. By default, the first two options under the Remove section are checked, and both options under the Options section are checked. The choices in the dialog box are as follows:

- **Remove Empty Container Tags (<b></b>, <h1></h1>, ...):** Empty tags such as the example <b></b> (where there is nothing between the open bold and end bold tags) given in this dialog box can occur as you format text—particularly when you format, edit, reformat, and so on. The more you work on a document, the more likely it is to have these kinds of nested tags. These tags might not cause problems in the browser, but they do take up space and make it harder to read through the code if you are editing in Code view. This option is checked by default.

- **Remove Redundant Nested Tags:** When you have a duplicate set of tags inside of a set of tags that do the same thing, the inner set of tags is redundant because the outside set has already made the definition. As you work in a document, redundant nested tags can occur. If this box is checked, Dreamweaver removes all instances of a set of duplicate tags because they are unnecessary. This option is checked by default.

- **Remove Non-Dreamweaver HTML Comments:** Any comments that have not been inserted by Dreamweaver are removed if this box is checked, including comments that have been inserted while using Dreamweaver. Dreamweaver HTML Comments are those that are created by Dreamweaver to mark certain objects such as the `<!--#BeginEditable "teachers" -->` comment that signifies the editable region "teachers" in a template (refer to Lesson 13). This option is unchecked by default.

- **Remove Dreamweaver Special Markup:** Dreamweaver creates a number of tags that are not standard HTML. These tags include items (such as `<mm:libitem>`, which signifies a library item) that indicate to Dreamweaver how specific objects should be handled. Only Dreamweaver recognizes this markup; browsers ignore it. Use caution when checking this box because it causes all tags related to library items, templates, and tracing images to be removed. If this is done, you can no longer update the page using those features. This option is unchecked by default.

- **Remove Specific Tag(s):** This text field allows you to instruct Dreamweaver to remove particular tags. If you want to remove multiple tags at the same time, separate the tags with commas. This option is unchecked by default.

- **Combine Nested <font> Tags When Possible:** If your document uses `<font>` tags, these tags might become nested as you format text in your documents. For example, you might wind up with something that looks similar to this:

```
<font size="-1"><font face="Verdana, Arial, Helvetica, sans-serif"> ¬
    <font color="#336633">Yoga Sangha</font></font></font>
```

The three sets of font tags in this example can be combined into one `<font>` and `</font>` set, making the code much cleaner and leaner:

```
<font size="-1" face="Verdana, Arial, Helvetica, sans-serif" ¬
    color="#336633">Yoga Sangha</font>
```

This option is checked by default.

Note *The <font> tag is deprecated in HTML 4.0—that is, it might become obsolete in future versions of HTML. Styles sheets are recommended for text formatting instead.*

- **Show Log On Completion:** The log lets you know what items Dreamweaver was able to clean up. This option is checked by default.

2. Leave the default options selected and click OK.

Dreamweaver runs Clean Up HTML and displays a dialog box with a log of what was cleaned up. In some cases, there might not be anything to clean up.

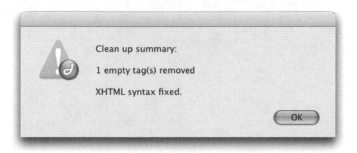

3. Click OK to close the log. Save and close the asana.html document.

Running Clean Up XHTML helps to make your code as clean and free of errors as possible. It can potentially help decrease the file size and browser loading time for your document.

> **Note** *To further optimize the code in your documents, you can run Validate Markup to examine the code for tag and syntax errors by choosing File > Check Page > Validate Markup or selecting the Validation tab in the Results window and clicking the Validate button (the green triangle on the left). Any errors found will be displayed in the Results dialog box.*

Working with Microsoft Word HTML

Web page content can come from a variety of sources. Clients or colleagues might send material in a Microsoft Word file. If the format of the Word document is fairly simple, you can use the copy-and-paste method to import your text into Dreamweaver. If the Word document has formatting such as bullets or tables, you might want to save the document as a Web page (choose File > Save As Web Page in Word 97 or later) and open the resulting HTML file in Dreamweaver. Word inserts a great number of unnecessary tags, however. You can clean up this code in Dreamweaver in one step. The tags that Dreamweaver removes are required to display the page in Word, but are not needed in HTML or a browser.

1. Open the GreenStudio.html file from the Lesson_16_Code/Word folder.

This HTML file was created by using the Save As Web Page command within Microsoft Word.

2. Choose Commands › Clean Up Word HTML.

The Clean Up Word HTML dialog box opens.

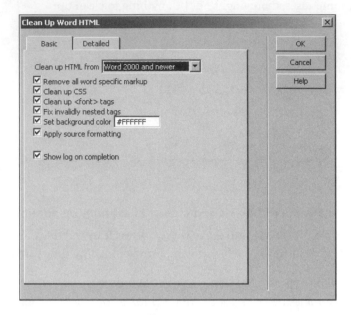

Dreamweaver attempts to determine which version of Word was used to create the HTML. If Dreamweaver cannot determine the version, you should choose Word 2000 And Newer from the menu.

The dialog box has two tabs, Basic and Detailed, with several options to check for each. For this exercise, use the default setting (all options checked).

The options on the Basic tab are as follows:

- Remove All Word-Specific Markup
- Clean Up CSS
- Clean Up <font> Tags
- Fix Invalidly Nested Tags
- Set Background Color
- Apply Source Formatting
- Show Log On Completion

The Detailed tab contains additional options to remove all Microsoft Word-specific markup and clean up CSS.

3. Make sure that all the boxes on the basic tab are checked and click OK. Click OK again to close the dialog box after reviewing the changes Dreamweaver made when cleaning up the file and then save the document.

Dreamweaver displays a dialog box listing all the changes it made.

Printing from Code View

It can often be difficult to view code on a computer screen. Dreamweaver allows you to print out the code, a useful feature that can allow you to simply work on a hard copy or share with team members. You will need to have a printer connected to your computer to complete this exercise.

1. In the training.html file, choose File > Print Code.

As long as you have a printer connected to your system you can print by clicking the Print button after specifying the printing options such as number of copies and page numbers.

> **Note** *You can't print the Design view from within Dreamweaver. If you need to have a printout of the Web page as it will look in a browser, preview the page in a browser and print it from the browser.*

You can close the training.html file.

Advanced Customization

There are a number of options available for the customization of Dreamweaver. You can work with basic program preferences to customize the setup of the program, tools, panels, and keyboard shortcuts to develop a workspace that is tailored to your needs.

Dreamweaver was designed to be extensible, so you can expand Dreamweaver's capabilities through the use of extensions—pieces of software that can be added to increase the functionality of the program. There are several different kinds of extensions, ranging from simple HTML objects to more complex JavaScript commands. The Dreamweaver Extension Manager is used to install, manage, and remove extensions.

You can create new behaviors and extensions for use in Dreamweaver yourself or you can obtain extensions created by others from the Dreamweaver Exchange Website. There are a wide range of extensions available on Macromedia's Dreamweaver Exchange, ranging from ones that you can buy to freeware-style scripts.

1. Choose Help › Manage Extensions.

Extensions are installed into Dreamweaver using the Extension Manager, a separate program that is installed along with Dreamweaver. The Macromedia Extension Manager folder is usually installed in the same folder as the Macromedia Dreamweaver 8 folder. The default installation location will be inside your Applications (Macintosh) or Program Files > Macromedia (Windows) folders.

The Extension Manager enables you to install extensions, remove extensions, find out more information about an installed extension, and prepare your own extensions. It also provides a convenient way to bring up the Dreamweaver Exchange Website, through which you can find more extensions.

The Macromedia Extension Manager displays the extension name, version number, type, and author. A description appears for the selected extension that gives details concerning what the extension does as well as the location of the extension in Dreamweaver. Older extensions might have outdated descriptions that refer to interface elements in prior versions of Dreamweaver (the Objects palette, for example, is now known as the Insert bar).

2. Quit the Extension Manager by choosing Extension Manager > Quit Extension Manager (Macintosh) or File > Exit (Windows).

Extensions listed on the Dreamweaver Exchange indicate which version of Dreamweaver they were written for. Some older extensions work fine with newer versions of the program, whereas others can cause problems. If you encounter any difficulties after installing an extension, you should remove it. If you run into a problem, you can test your extensions by turning them off. You can check the boxes in the On/Off column on the Extension Manager to temporarily disable extensions. Doing so can help determine whether errors are related to specific extensions. A checkmark in a box indicates that the corresponding extension is currently installed.

Obtaining and Installing Extensions

If you are connected to the Internet, you can obtain more extensions from the Dreamweaver Exchange by choosing File > Go To Macromedia Exchange while you are in the Extension Manager or by choosing Help > Dreamweaver Exchange while you are in Dreamweaver. The Dreamweaver Exchange will open in your default browser. You must be a member of macromedia.com to download, submit, or review extensions. (It is a free membership, and you can sign up and log in at the Dreamweaver Exchange home page). Macromedia provides the Dreamweaver Exchange Website as a repository for all kinds of extensions. When you download extensions from the Dreamweaver Exchange, the Extension Manager automatically opens and begins the installation process after the download is complete for Macintosh users. Windows users have to open the downloaded file or follow the install process described in this exercise. Macromedia creates some extensions, whereas third parties create other extensions.

To install an extension with the Extension Manager, choose File > Install Extension or double-click the extension file to automatically open the Extension Manager dialog box. The Install Extension (Macintosh) or Select Extension to Install (Windows) dialog box opens.

It is a good practice to always restart Dreamweaver after installing extensions. When you restart Dreamweaver, you can use the new extensions. Extensions might not be available until the program is restarted.

What You Have Learned

In this lesson, you have:

- Switched document views and edited the HTML in Code view (pages 517–520)
- Edited HTML code by hand using split Code and Design view (pages 520–523)
- Changed the location of a new browser window by adding x and y coordinates to the code (pages 526–529)
- Inserted keyword and description meta tags (pages 529–533)
- Used the tag Inspector to quickly edit tags (pages 533–535)
- Inserted and edited code using Quick Tags and Code Hints (pages 535–537)
- Created and inserted code using snippets (pages 537–541)
- Ran the Clean Up HTML command to streamline code (pages 541–543)
- Imported a Word HTML file and used Clean Up Word HTML to remove unnecessary tags (pages 543–545)
- Learned how to print the HTML code (page 545)
- Learned how to find and install Dreamweaver Extensions (pages 545–547)

17 Using Find and Replace

The Find and Replace feature in Macromedia Dreamweaver provides you with a powerful searching tool. You can search the current document, a specified folder, or an entire site. The extensive options enable you to search for text or HTML tags, or even limit your search to certain attributes within HTML tags. After you find what you are looking for, you can modify or replace it. The Find and Replace feature can save a lot of time when you need to make massive changes to a document or an entire site.

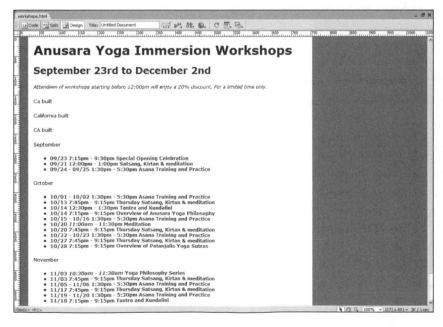

In this project, you will use Find and Replace to change words in this document. You will also adjust the formatting attributes of text by using Find and Replace to automate the process of linking to an external style sheet and applying a custom style to text.

In this lesson, you will use the Find and Replace feature to make a wide variety of changes to several documents. You will use the Find and Replace feature to apply Cascading Style Sheet (CSS) styles, and attach an external style sheet to a number of documents all at once. You'll find and replace text, change text formatting, learn to save your searches to use at a later time, find dates, and replace names.

To see examples of the finished pages for this lesson, open index.html and workshops.html from the Lesson_17_FindReplace/Completed folder.

What You Will Learn

In this lesson, you will:

- Find and replace text
- Find text within HTML tags
- Use the Find and Replace feature to apply a custom style
- Use the Find and Replace feature to attach external style sheets
- Save and reuse your search settings
- Search for patterns in text
- Find variations of a name

Approximate Time

This lesson should take about one half hour to complete.

Lesson Files

Starting Files:

Lesson_17_FindReplace/index.html
Lesson_17_FindReplace/Training/...all files
Lesson_17_FindReplace/schedule/workshops.html

Completed Project:

Lesson_17_FindReplace/Completed/...(all files)

Searching Your Document

In this exercise, you will perform a simple search to find and replace words in the text of a document.

1. Open the index.html file from the Lesson_17_FindReplace folder. Select the word *Sanga* within the header Welcome to Yoga Sanga.

This document refers to Yoga *Sanga* throughout the text, when it should actually be Yoga *Sangha*. You'll replace that text in this exercise.

2. Choose Edit › Find and Replace.

The Find and Replace dialog box opens.

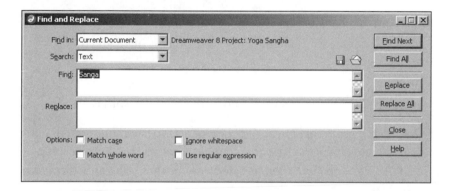

Tip *Selecting a portion of text before opening the Find and Replace dialog box automatically causes the selected text to appear in the Search For text field.*

3. In the Find In menu, choose Current Document. In the Search menu, choose Text. Ensure that the Find text field has the highlighted text of *Sanga*. In the Replace text field, type *Sangha*. Uncheck the boxes for four options (Match case, Match whole word, Ignore whitespace, Use regular expression).

Find In Current Document, which searches the entire document, can be used only from a single document while it is open. The Find In menu also has five additional options:

- **Selected Text:** Searches what you have selected in the current document.
- **Open Documents:** Searches all files that are open.
- **Folder:** Allows you to browse to select a folder and search all the contents of that folder.
- **Selected Files In Site:** Searches files you have selected in the site panel.
- **Entire Current Local Site:** Searches the active site.

There are four options at the bottom of the Find and Replace dialog box:

- **Match case:** Limits the search to the exact case of the words. If the Match Case box is checked, a search looks only for content that exactly matches the capitalization you used in the Find text field.

- **Match whole word:** Matches only complete words.

- **Ignore whitespace:** Ignores all spaces—if this is checked and you are searching for two words, Dreamweaver also finds all instances in which those two words have additional spaces between them.

- **Use regular expression:** Provides patterns to describe character combinations in the text. Use this option to select sentences that begin with "The" or attribute values that contain a number.

4. Click Find Next.

The first occurrence of the word after the insertion point is highlighted.

5. Click Replace.

The word is changed to **Sangha** and the next occurrence of the word is highlighted.

> **Note**   *When replacing text in your document, it is recommended that you click Replace first and check the new text to make sure you typed the correct information in the Replace field; then use Replace All after you verify the search criteria and results.*

6. Click Find All.

The results of the search are found and displayed in the Results panel—eight more instances of the text for which you searched. Double-clicking an item in this list highlights the instance in the Document window. Using the Find All option allows you to review all instances of the text.

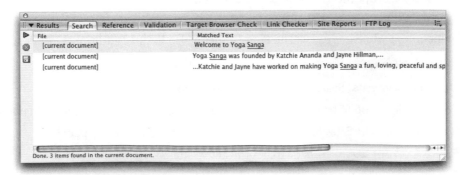

7. Click the green arrow on the left of the Results panel.

The Find and Replace dialog box opens again.

Dreamweaver remembers the settings from your most recent search. If you close and reopen the dialog box, the text and options you set the last time the dialog box was open are still there. The Find text field should contain **Sanga** and the Replace text field should contain **Sangha**.

8. Now click Replace All on the Find and Replace dialog box.

The Find and Replace dialog box automatically closes after it finishes searching for and replacing text. The status bar of the Results panel reports the number of items found and replaced in your document.

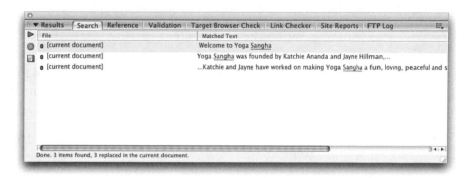

9. Click the Options menu in the upper-right corner of the Results panel and choose Clear Results; then close the Results panel (Macintosh) or collapse the Results panel (Windows). Save the index.html document.

Leave this file open for the next exercise.

Removing HTML Tags

The index.html file contains <font> tags. As explained in Lessons 2 and 4, the <font> tag has been deprecated in HTML 4.0 and it might become obsolete in the future. Although it is still supported by browsers, CSS (covered in Lesson 4) is the recommended way to style text.

You should be aware that in documents that were created using previous versions of Dreamweaver, you might not be able to access some CSS document attributes—defined through the Page Properties—if the <font> tag or deprecated <body> tag attributes exist in that document and if those attributes are not already defined for the document using CSS.

If you were to open a document that uses <font> tags and does not use any CSS, the Property inspector would list only the Appearance, Title/Encoding, and Tracing Image categories. The Links and Headings categories use CSS to set the attributes and are not available until the <font> tags are removed. The link colors and background color or images will be available in the Appearance section, although they will be set as attributes of the <body> tag.

The <font> tag is a type of local formatting. In CSS, local formatting overrides any internal or external styles—if you want to apply CSS styles, the local formatting needs to be removed. In older versions of Dreamweaver, local formatting was applied using the Property inspector to define the text attributes with <font> tags. For new documents in Dreamweaver 8, the default formatting applied with the Property inspector is CSS-based. When you open documents such as this one, which use <font> tags, the Property inspector uses the <font> tags to edit and define text formatting.

In this exercise, you will use the Find and Replace feature to remove the HTML <font> tag.

1. In the index.html document, choose Edit > Find and Replace to open the Find and Replace dialog box. The Find In menu should be set to Current Document. Change the Search menu selection to Specific Tag.

Tip *You can also use the shortcut Ctrl+F (Windows) or Cmd+F (Macintosh) to open the Find and Replace dialog box.*

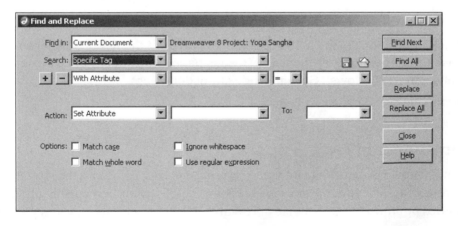

Choosing Specific Tag allows you to search Dreamweaver for a certain tag. The dialog box changes to reflect this search method. A set of options to choose from is displayed to narrow the search and look for tags with specific attributes.

2. Select font from the list of HTML tags in the Tag menu, located to the right of the Search menu.

You can also type tags (without the <> brackets) in the Search For text field instead of using the menu.

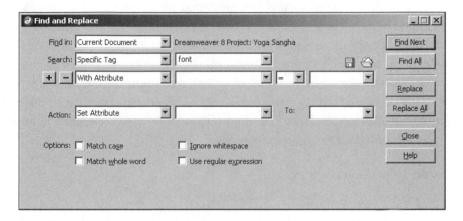

3. Click the minus (–) button to remove the tag modifier option. Choose Strip Tag from the Action menu and uncheck all four boxes in the Options area.

Because you will entirely remove the <font> tags, the modifiers are not needed.

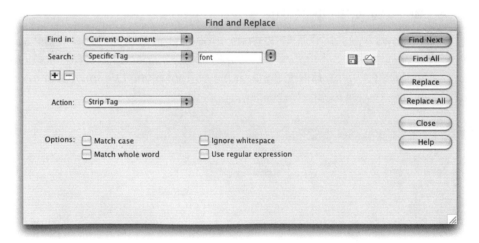

Note *You can continue to add additional modifiers by clicking the plus sign (+) button. Several menus and text fields appear that allow you to make very specific selections. You can use these menus and text fields to limit your searches and find unique occurrences of a tag or a tag with a specific attribute. The additional options here include a number of qualifiers for attributes, including the capability to search for a tag with or without a specific attribute, a tag that contains or doesn't contain a specific attribute, or an attribute that is inside or not inside of the specified tag. The tag modifiers give you the ability to choose a specific attribute that can be used with the selected tag; to select whether the attribute should be equal to (=), less than (<), greater than (>), and not equal to (!=); and to choose a place to set a value for the desired attribute. The options in the menus vary depending upon the tag and attribute that you have selected.*

4. **Click the Replace All button.**

All <font> tags within the document are removed.

The Find and Replace dialog box closes automatically. The Results panel contains details on what was replaced, or in this case deleted, from the document. If the Results panel does not open automatically, Macintosh users can choose Window > Results to open the panel that was closed in the previous exercise, and Windows users can expand the panel that was collapsed in the previous exercise. For Windows users, by default, the collapsed panel is located beneath the Property inspector.

Note *Windows users can click the white arrow on the thin bar located just above the Property inspector to reduce both the Property inspector and Results panel at the same time. Click this button again at the bottom of the Dreamweaver interface to expand the panels located in that area again.*

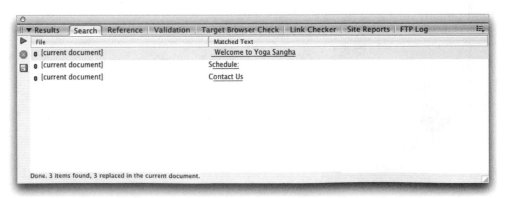

5. Click the Options menu in the upper-right corner of the Results panel and choose Clear Results. Close the Results panel (Macintosh) or collapse the Results panel (Windows). Save the index.html document.

You can close the index.html document.

Using Find and Replace to Attach External Style Sheets

In Lesson 4, you created an external style sheet and attached that style sheet to another document. The steps to add a style sheet to a document are not difficult, but they can be time-consuming if you need to attach a style sheet to multiple pages or throughout an entire site. By using the Find and Replace feature, you can accomplish that task in a matter of minutes.

In this exercise, you attach the external style sheet sangha.css to multiple pages.

1. Open the asana.html file from the Lesson_17_FindReplace/Training folder and select Design view. Choose Edit > Find and Replace.

The Find and Replace dialog box opens with the same settings that were used in the previous exercise.

2. The Find In menu should be set to Folder. Click the browse folder icon to the right of the folder text box and choose the Lesson_17_FindReplace/Training folder. Set the Search menu to Source Code. Type `</head>` in the Find text field. In the Replace text field, type the following code: `<link href="sangha.css" rel="stylesheet" type="text/css"></head>`.

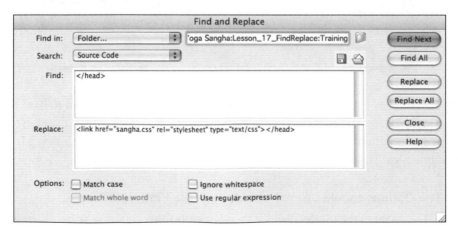

Note *The `<link>` tag specifies that the style sheet is attached by linking it to the document, which is the recommended way to attach the first style sheet (as opposed to the import method of attaching style sheets—both methods were covered in Lesson 4). The location of the style sheet is specified by href="sangha.css", the relationship between the current document and attached stylesheet is defined by rel="stylesheet", and the output header type="text/css" specifies the kind of content through the Multipurpose Internet Mail Extensions (MIME) type, allowing browsers that do not support style sheets to ignore the link tag.*

When you use the Attach Style Sheet icon, Dreamweaver adds the `<link>` tag within the `<head>` tag. You are using Find and Replace to search for the end head (`</head>`) tag and then add the `<link>` tag before it by replacing it with the `<link>` tag followed by a `</head>` tag.

Tip *To get a new line when you are within the Replace text field, press Shift+Return (Macintosh) or Shift+Enter (Windows). Using the Return or Enter key alone activates the Find Next button in the dialog box. Because the `</head>` tag is usually on a different line, you might want to place a line break in the code before the `</head>` tag—this is not a `<br>` (break); it is simply a new line in the code.*

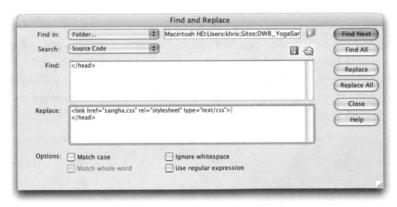

There are a total of five HTML documents in the Training folder that need to have the external style sheet attached. None of the documents in the Training folder uses `<font>` tags, so you don't need to use the Find and Replace feature to strip the `<font>` tag from the documents as you had to do with index.html in the previous exercise.

3. All The Options should be unchecked. Click the Find Next button.

The first document in the folder in which Dreamweaver finds the `</head>` tag opens in Code view; asana.html is now shown in Code view, and Dreamweaver selects the `</head>` tag.

4. Click Replace.

Dreamweaver makes the replacement, and the next document that meets the search criteria is opened automatically in Code view with the </head> tag selected.

5. Click the Replace All button. Click Yes when asked to verify whether you want to replace matches in unopened documents.

Note *For demonstration purposes of this exercise, there is a duplicate of the sangha.css file inside the Training folder. In your own sites, however, it is recommended that you not duplicate external style sheets in this manner because if you make a change in one, the documents that draw on a duplicate of that style sheet do not reflect the changes unless the duplicate is also updated. To link documents in different folders to the same CSS file, you might want to use site-root relative links, which ensure that no matter where the HTML documents are located, they still link to the correct CSS file. (Site-root relative links were covered in Lesson 4.)*

You might not see the change applied to the background in the open documents until you close the Find and Replace dialog box, and either click in the document window or click the Refresh button as you might be prompted to do by the Property inspector.

6. Click the Options menu in the upper-right corner of the Results panel and choose Clear Results. Close the Results panel (Macintosh) or collapse the Results panel (Windows).

The style sheet is now attached to all documents in the folder. You can save all open documents and close them.

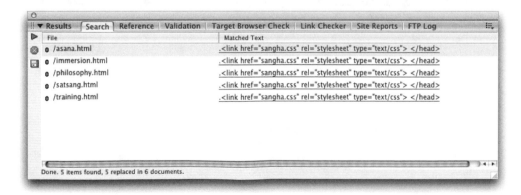

Applying Custom Styles with Find and Replace

Now that you have removed the <font> tags and attached an external style sheet, you can apply a custom CSS style to text in the index.html document. In this exercise, you will use the Find and Replace feature to locate the text in the code and apply the HTML tags for the custom style.

1. Reopen the index.html document. Select the first occurrence of the phrase "Anusara Yoga" in the body text—at the end of the sentence that begins with "At Yoga Sangha, we're dedicated..."

In the following steps, you'll use Find and Replace to style all instances of this phrase with CSS.

2. Choose Edit › Find and Replace. Select Current Document from the Find In menu and select Source Code from the Search menu. Type _Anusara Yoga_ in the Find text field.

> **Tip** _If you select text before you open the Find and Replace dialog box, that specific text appears in the Find text field._

The dialog box changes to reflect the Source Code search method.

3. Type `<span class="boldcolor">Anusara Yoga</span>` into the Replace text field. All four options should be unchecked.

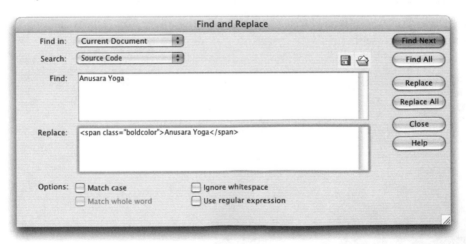

The code `<span class="boldcolor">Anusara Yoga</span>` will replace all instances of the phrase "Anusara Yoga" in the index.html document—the styled word will replace the unstyled words.

4. Click Replace All to change all occurrences in your document.

The Find and Replace dialog box closes automatically, and the Results panel lets you know which changes have been made to the code. All instances of "Anusara Yoga" are now formatted with the boldcolor CSS style. Using the Find and Replace feature to apply styles in this way can save you a lot of time. You might need to click in the Document window or click the Refresh button to see the changes appear in the Document window.

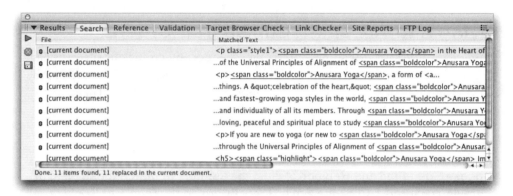

Note *When using this method, you need to be certain that there no occurrences of the exact word(s) that you are replacing (in this case, it is "Anusara Yoga") in the code anywhere but in the text. If any images used "Anusara Yoga" for its alt text or if the words you were replacing were part of a path name, you would have problems with your code. When in doubt, use the Replace button rather than the Replace All button so you can double-check each item to be replaced.*

5. On the Results panel, click the Options menu in the upper-right corner of the Results panel and choose Clear Results; then close (Macintosh) or collapse (Windows) the Results panel. Save the index.html document.

Tip *If you do not see the Results panel, you can open it and view the results of the Find and Replace function by choosing Window > Results.*

You can also apply a style to selected text and copy the corresponding code from Split or Code view to paste into the Find and Replace dialog box. However, if you do this, be sure to look back to the first occurrence of the text in which you manually applied the custom style—you will see two <span> tags applied because the Find and Replace feature added the extra tag. Although the word appears to display properly in Dreamweaver, you should remove the extra tag. You can manually remove the second set of tags in Code view or you can choose Commands > Cleanup HTML (covered in Lesson 15). When using the Cleanup HTML command, make sure that the Remove Redundant Nested Tags option is selected in the Cleanup HTML dialog box and click OK.

Note *You can close the index.html document.*

Saving and Reusing Your Search Criteria

You might want to save your search criteria for other documents in your site, especially with complex searches. Saved search criteria, known as *queries*, are usually saved in the Configuration/Queries folder inside the Dreamweaver folder by default. They can, however, be saved in different places.

In this exercise, you will save your search query in the Lesson_17_FindReplace folder.

1. Choose Edit > Find and Replace. Adjust the settings to match those used in the previous exercise. Click the Save Query button in the Find and Replace dialog box.

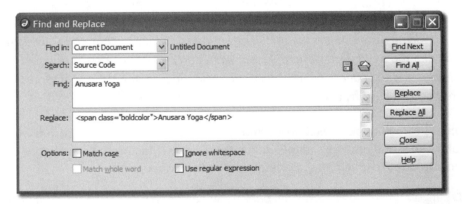

The Find and Replace dialog box has the same settings that were used in the last exercise.

The icon on the Save Query button looks like a floppy disk. This command makes it possible for you to save and reuse complex searches.

2. In the Save query to file (Macintosh) or Save Query (Windows) dialog box, locate and open the Lesson_17_FindReplace folder; then type *addStyle* in the Save As (Macintosh) or File Name (Windows) text field and click Save.

Find queries have a .dwq extension; Replace queries have a .dwr extension. The extension is automatically added for you upon saving the query.

Now that you have saved the addStyle query, it is available to you any time you need to run the same Find and Replace function in other documents.

Note *To learn how to save your own searches, set up a search of your own and test it. Then follow steps 1 and 2 in this exercise.*

3. Click the Load Query button in the Find and Replace dialog box.

The icon on the Load Query button looks like an open folder.

4. In the Load Query (Windows) or Load query from file (Macintosh) dialog box, locate and open the addstyle.dwr query in the Lesson_17_FindReplace folder.

You can open stored find and replace queries and execute them from within the Find and Replace dialog box. You can close the Find and Replace dialog box, collapse the Results panel and close any open files.

Searching and Replacing with Regular Expressions

Regular expressions are control characters that describe character combinations or patterns in text. For example, if you want to find all occurrences of years from 1700–1799, the pattern is "17" followed by any combination of two numbers from 0–9. You can use a number of special characters to define the search pattern. For example, the backslash (\), dollar sign ($), and question mark (?) are all special characters. When using regular expressions, it is important to know these characters; if you are looking for such special characters in your text, you need to precede the character with a backslash to indicate that it is part of the character search and not used as a special character.

Appendix A contains a table with all the special characters, regular expressions, and their meanings.

In this exercise, you will use patterned searches in a document.

1. Open the workshops.html file in the Lesson_17_FindReplace/schedule folder, place the insertion point at the beginning of the document and choose Edit › Find and Replace.

The Find and Replace dialog box opens.

2. Select Current Document in the Find In menu. Set the Search menu to Text. Check the Use Regular Expression option box.

Notice that Ignore Whitespace is disabled or dimmed when you select Use regular expression.

> **Note** *The Ignore Whitespace option, when selected, treats all whitespace as a single space for the purposes of matching. For example, with this option selected, "this text" matches "this text" but not "thistext." The Ignore Whitespace option is not available when the Use Regular Expression option is selected; you must explicitly write your regular expression to ignore whitespace. Note that p and br tags do not count as whitespace.*

3. In the Find text field, type \d*:\d\dam.

Be sure to type backslashes (\), not forward slashes (/), when you enter \d*:\d\dam into the text field.

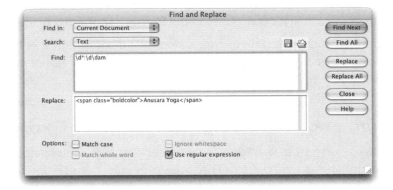

In this exercise, you will apply emphasis styling to workshops starting before 12:00 pm to draw attention to them. The search pattern you defined in Step 3 uses the special character \d, which represents any digit (0–9). An asterisk means "find zero or more of the previous character," so \d* looks for zero or more digits. Thus this pattern searches for zero or more numbers, followed by a colon, followed by exactly two digits and the text "am." This will match any time in the morning, such as 11:30 am. See Appendix A for more regular expressions to use for search patterns.

> **Note** *To distinguish decimal numbers from years—19.09 for example—when searching in the document, include a period in your search. A period is also a special character, so you need to precede it with a backslash in your search.*

4. Click the Find Next button.

Dreamweaver selects "11:00am" by the entry for October 20. You might need to move the Find and Replace dialog box to see the selection.

5. Continue to click the Find Next button several times to see what gets selected.

There are two workshops that begin before 12:00 pm.

6. In the Find and Replace dialog box, change the Search menu selection to Source Code.

In the following steps, you use the emphasis tags (<em> and </em>) to make the times bold. However, if you were to type <em>\d*:\d\dam</em> in the Replace text field, the text in the Document window would be changed to \d*:\d\dam—it would literally change the numbers in the time. Instead, you need to isolate the search as a pattern by surrounding the pattern that you are searching for in parentheses.

7. In the Find text field, insert a left parenthesis before the text and a right parenthesis after the text, like this: **(\d*:\d\dam)**.

The parentheses create the first pattern.

8. In the Replace text field, type **<em>$1</em>**.

To reference the pattern you created in the previous step, you use $1 in the Replace text field. Surrounding this symbol with emphasis tags causes the same tags to be added around the results of the first pattern search. If you were to create several patterns, the next pattern, as indicated by the parentheses, would be referenced in this text field with $2, and so on in a sequential manner.

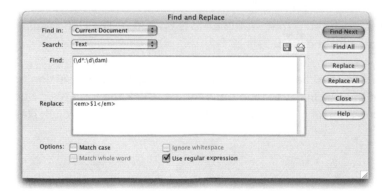

9. Click the Find Next button and then click the Replace button.

The emphasis tags are placed around the time in the Code inspector. Click in the Document window to see the results.

10. Click the Replace All button to find and replace all occurrences in the document. Save the workshops.html document. Click the context menu in the upper-right corner of the Results panel and choose Clear Results. Close (Macintosh) or collapse (Windows) the Results panel.

> **Tip** *To view and clear the results, Macintosh users need to open the Results panel if it is not already open by choosing Window › Results.*

Close the Results panel but leave the workshops.html file open for the next exercise.

Finding Variations in a Name

You can also look for variations in a name. For example, some of these workshops are Satsang, but the name of the class isn't always consistently an uppercase S. You want to make the format consistent and change it to Satsang.

1. In the workshops.html document, switch back to Design view, place the insertion point at the top of the document, and choose Edit › Find and Replace. Set the Find In menu selection to Current Document and the Search menu selection to Text. Type *[sS]?atsang, [kK]?irtan* in the Find text field.

The [sS] searches for any word that begins with a lower or capital S; the ? specifies only one character; and the atsang, is the literal string. The same pattern is used for the Kirtan string.

2. In Options, make sure that Match case is checked. The Use regular expression box should also be checked.

3. In the Replace text field, type *Satsang, Kirtan*. Place the insertion point at the beginning of the text in the Document window. Click the Find Next button to find the first occurrence of a variation of Satsang, kirtan and then click Replace to change it.

The first version of the Satsang, *kirtan* is found in this document and replaced with Satsang, *Kirtan*.

4. Click the Find Next button. Continue to replace all the remaining versions of the Satsang, kirtan. Save the workshops.html document.

You can close this document and the Results panel.

What You Have Learned

In this lesson, you have:

- Found and replaced text using detailed options to quickly modify a document (pages 551–553)

- Found text within HTML tags and learned how to change it using the Find and Replace feature (pages 553–557)

- Used the Find and Replace feature to attach external style sheets to multiple pages within a site (pages 557–559)

- Used the Find and Replace feature to quickly apply a custom style to a document (pages 560–562)

- Saved your search settings for later use and loaded saved queries (pages 562–563)

- Searched for patterns in text using regular expressions to find specific text such as dates and names (pages 563–566)

- Found multiple variations of a name and replaced them with one version (pages 566–567)

A Regular Expressions

Regular expressions describe patterns that you can use to search code and text. Searching with regular expressions is covered in Lesson 17. The following table lists the special characters that are used in regular expressions, descriptions of their meanings, and examples of their matches.

Type	Description	Example
^	Beginning of input or line	^T matches "T" in "This good earth," but not in "Uncle Tom"
$	End of input or line	h$ matches "h" in "teach," but not in "teacher"
*	The preceding character zero or more times	um* matches "um" in "rum," "umm" in "yummy," and "u" in "huge"
+	The preceding character one or more times	um+ matches "um" in "rum" and "umm" in "yummy," but nothing in "huge"
?	The preceding character zero or one time	st?on matches "son" in "Johnson" and "ston" in "Johnston" but nothing in "Appleton" or "tension"
.	Any single character except newline	.an matches "ran," "can," and "and" in the phrase "bran muffins can be tasty and healthy"
x|y	Either x or y	FF0000|0000FF matches "FF0000"in bgcolor="#FF0000" and "0000FF" in font color="#0000FF"
{n}	Exactly n occurrences of the preceding character	o{2} matches "oo" in "loom" and the first two o's in "mooooo," but nothing in "money"
{n,m}	At least n and at most m occurrences of the preceding character	F{2,4} matches "FF"in "#FF0000" and the first four Fs in "#FFFFFF"

Type	Description	Example
[abc]	Any one of the characters enclosed in the brackets. Specify a range of characters with a hyphen (for example, [a-f] is equivalent to [abcdef].	[e-g] matches "e" in "bed," "f" in "folly," and "g" in "guard"
[^abc]	Any character not enclosed in the brackets. Specify a range of characters with a hyphen (for example, [a-f] is equivalent to [abcdef].	[^aeiou] initially matches "r" in "orange," "b" in "book," and "k" in "eek!"
\b	A word boundary (such as a space or carriage return).	\bb matches "b" in "the book," but nothing in "goober" or "snob"
\B	Anything other than a word boundary.	\Bb matches "b" in "goober," but nothing in "the book"
\d	Any digit character. Equivalent to [0-9].	\d matches "3" in "C3PO" and "2" in "apartment 2G"
\D	Any nondigit character. Equivalent to [^0-9].	\D matches "S" in "900S" and "Q" in "Q45"
\f	Form feed	
\n	Line feed	
\r	Carriage return	
\s	Any single white-space character, including space, tab, form feed, or line feed.	\sbook matches "book" in "blue book," but nothing in "notebook"
\t	A tab.	
\w	Any alphanumeric character, including underscore. Equivalent to [A-Za-z0-9_].	b\w* matches "barking" in "the barking dog" and both "big" and "black" in "the big black dog"
\W	Any non-alphanumeric character. Equivalent to [^A-Za-z0-9_].	\W matches "&" in "Jake & Mattie" and "%" in "100%"

B Macintosh Shortcuts

Keyboard shortcuts can speed up the process of developing your site, making it quicker and easier to work with design and code elements as well as site management functions. You can add, remove, or modify Dreamweaver's keyboard shortcuts by choosing Dreamweaver > Keyboard Shortcuts to open the Keyboard Shortcuts dialog box.

Menu Shortcuts

Dreamweaver Menu

Command	Shortcut
Preferences	Command+U
Hide Dreamweaver	Command+H
Quit Dreamweaver	Command+Q

File Menu

Command	Shortcut
New	Command+N
Open	Command+O
Open in Frame	Shift+Command+O
Close	Command+W
Close All	Shift+Command+W
Save	Command+S
Save As	Shift+Command+S
Print Code	Command+P
Preview in Primary Browser	Option+F12
Preview in Secondary Browser	Command+F12, Shift+F12
Check Links	Shift+F8
Validate Markup	Shift+F6

Edit Menu

Command	Shortcut
Undo	Command+Z or Option+Delete
Redo	Command+Y or Shift+Command+Z
Cut	Command+X or Shift+Delete
Copy	Command+C
Paste	Command+V
Paste Special	Shift+Command+V
Clear	Delete
Select All	Command+A
Select Parent Tag	Command+[
Select Child	Command+]
Find and Replace	Command+F
Find Again	Command+G
Go to Line	Command+,
Show Code Hints	Control+Space
Indent Code	Shift+Command+>
Outdent Code	Shift+Command+<
Balance Braces	Command+'
Code Collapse > Collapse Selection	Shift+Command+C
Code Collapse > Collapse Outside Selection	Command+Option+C

Edit Menu (continued)

Command	Shortcut
Code Collapse > Expand Selection	Shift+Command+E
Code Collapse > Collapse Full Tag	Shift+Command+J
Code Collapse > Collapse Outside Full Tag	Command+Option+J
Code Collapse > Expand All	Command+Option+ E

View Menu

Command	Shortcut
Zoom In	Command+=
Zoom Out	Command+-
Magnification > 50%	Command+Option+5
Magnification > 100%	Command+Option+1
Magnification > 200%	Command+Option+2
Magnification > 300%	Command+Option+3
Magnification > 400%	Command+Option+4
Magnification > 800%	Command+Option+8
Magnification > 1600%	Command+Option+6
Fit Selection	Command+Option+0
Fit All	Shift+Command+0
Fit Width	Shift+Command+Option+0
Switch Views	Control+`
Refresh Design View	F5
Live Data*	Shift+Command+R
Head Content	Shift+Command+H
Table Mode > Expanded Tables Mode	F6
Table Mode > Layout Mode	Command+F6
Visual Aids > Hide All	Shift+Command+I
Rulers > Show	Option+Command+R
Grid > Show	Option+Command+G
Grid > Snap to Grid	Option+Shift+Command+G
Guides > Show	Command+;
Guides > Lock Guides	Command+Opt+;
Guides > Snap to Guides	Command+Shift+;
Guides > Guides Snap to Elements	Command+Shift+/
Plugins > Play	Option+Command+P
Plugins > Stop	Option+Command+X
Plugins > Play All	Option+Shift+Command+P
Plugins > Stop All	Option+Shift+Command+X
Hide/Show Panels	F4

*Command is not included in the View Menu.

Insert Menu

Command	Shortcut
Tag	Command+E
Image	Option+Command+I
Media > Flash	Option+Command+F
Media > Shockwave	Option+Command+D
Table	Option+Command+T
Named Anchor	Option+Command+A
HTML > Special Characters > Line Break	Shift+Return
HTML > Special Characters > Non-Breaking Space	Shift+Command+Space
Copyright Character (©)*	Option+G
Template Objects > Editable Region	Option+Command+V

*Command is not included in the Insert Menu.

Modify Menu

Command	Shortcut
Page Properties	Command+J
Quick Tag Editor	Command+T
Make Link	Command+L
Remove Link	Shift+Command+L
Table > Select Table	Command+A
Move to the Next Cell*	Tab
Move to the Previous Cell*	Shift+Tab
Table > Merge Cells	Option+Command+M
Table > Split Cell	Option+Command+S
Table > Insert Row	Command+M
Table > Insert Column	Shift+Command+A
Table > Delete Row	Shift+Command+M
Table > Delete Column	Shift+Command+-
Table > Increase Column Span	Shift+Command+]
Table > Decrease Column Span	Shift+Command+[
Arrange > Align Left	Shift+Command+1
Arrange > Align Right	Shift+Command+3
Arrange > Align Top	Shift+Command+4
Arrange > Align Bottom	Shift+Command+6
Arrange > Make Same Width	Shift+Command+7
Arrange > Make Same Height	Shift+Command+9
Timeline > Add Object to Timeline	Ctrl+Opt+Shift+T

*Command is not included in the Modify Menu.

Text Menu

Command	Shortcut
Indent	Option+Command+]
Outdent	Option+Command+[
Paragraph Format > None	Command+0
Paragraph Format > Paragraph	Shift+Command+P
Paragraph Format > Heading 1	Command+1
Paragraph Format > Heading 2	Command+2
Paragraph Format > Heading 3	Command+3
Paragraph Format > Heading 4	Command+4
Paragraph Format > Heading 5	Command+5
Paragraph Format > Heading 6	Command+6
Align > Left	Option+Shift+Command+L
Align > Center	Option+Shift+Command+C
Align > Right	Option+Shift+Command+R
Align > Justify	Option+Shift+Command+J
Style > Bold	Command+B
Style > Italic	Command+I
Check Spelling	Shift+F7

Commands Menu

Command	Shortcut
Start Recording	Shift+Command+X

Site Menu

Command	Shortcut
Get	Shift+Command+D
Check Out	Option+Shift+Command+D
Put	Shift+Command+U
Check In	Option+Shift+Command+U
Check Links Sitewide	Command+F8

Window Menu

Command	Shortcut
Insert	Command+F2
Properties	Command+F3
Layers	F2
Behaviors	Shift+F4
Databases	Shift+Command+F10
Bindings	Command+F10
Server Behaviors	Command+F9
Components	Command+F7
Files	F8
Assets	Option+F11
Tag Inspector	Option+Shift+F9
Results	F7
Reference	Shift+F1
Frames	Shift+F2
Code Inspector	Option+F10
Timelines	Option+F9
Hide/Show Panels	F4
Next Document	Command+`
Previous Document	Shift+Command+`

Help Menu

Command	Shortcut
Using Dreamweaver	F1
Using ColdFusion	Command+F1
Reference	Shift+F1

Code Shortcuts

Command	Shortcut
Select Parent Tag	Command+[
Select Child	Command+]
Balance Braces	Command+'
Select All	Command+A
Bold	Command+B
Italic	Command+I
Copy	Command+C
Find and Replace	Command+F
Find Selection	Command+Shift+G
Find Next	Command+G
Paste	Command+V
Cut	Command+X
Redo	Command+Y
Undo	Command+Z
Print Code	Command+P
Next Document	Command+`
Surround with #	Command+Shift+3
Delete Word Left	Command+Delete
Select Line Up	Shift+Up
Select Line Down	Shift+Down
Character Select Left	Shift+Left
Character Select Right	Shift+Right
Select to Page Up	Shift+PgUp
Select to Page Down	Shift+PgDn
Move Word Left	Command+Left
Move Word Right	Command+Right
Select Word Left	Command+Shift+Left
Select Word Right	Command+Shift+Right
Move to Start of Line	Home
Move to End of Line	End
Select to Start of Line	Shift+Home
Select to End of Line	Shift+End
Move to Top of File	Command+Home
Move to End of File	Command+End
Select to Start of File	Command+Shift+Home
Select to Start of File	Command+Shift+End

Files Panel Menus

File Menu

Command	Shortcut
New File	Shift+Command+N
New Folder	Option+Shift+Command+N
Rename	F2
Preview in Primary Browser	Option+F12
Preview in Secondary Browser	Command+F12
Check Links	Shift+F8

Edit Menu

Command	Shortcut
Cut	Command+X
Copy	Command+C
Paste	Command+V
Duplicate	Command+D
Select All	Command+A

View Menu

Command	Shortcut
Refresh	F5
Show/Hide Link	Shift+Command+Y
View as Root	Shift+Command+R
Show Page Titles	Shift+Command+T
Site Map	Option+F8

Site

Command	Shortcut
Get	Shift+Command+D
Check Out	Option+Shift+Command+D
Put	Shift+Command+U
Check In	Option+Shift+Command+U
Check Links Sitewide	Command+F8
Link to New File	Shift+Command+N
Link to Existing File	Shift+Command+K
Change Link	Command+L
Remove Link	Shift+Command+L

C Windows Shortcuts

Keyboard shortcuts can speed up the process of developing your site, making it quicker and easier to work with design and code elements as well as site management functions. You can add, remove, or modify Dreamweaver's keyboard shortcuts by choosing Edit > Keyboard Shortcuts to open the Keyboard Shortcuts dialog box.

Menu Shortcuts

File Menu

Command	Shortcut
New	Ctrl+N
Open	Ctrl+O
Open in Frame	Ctrl+Shift+O
Close	Ctrl+W
Close All	Ctrl+Shift+W
Save	Ctrl+S
Save As	Ctrl+Shift+S
Print Code	Ctrl+P
Preview in Primary Browser	F12
Preview in Secondary Browser	Ctrl+F12
Check Links	Shift+F8
Validate Markup	Shift+F6
Exit	Ctrl+Q

Edit Menu

Command	Shortcut
Undo	Ctrl+Z
Redo	Ctrl+Y
Cut	Ctrl+X
Copy	Ctrl+C
Paste	Ctrl+V
Paste Special	Ctrl+Shift+V
Select All	Ctrl+A
Select Parent Tag	Ctrl+[
Select Child	Ctrl+]
Find and Replace	Ctrl+F
Find Next	F3
Find Selection	Shift+F3
Go to Line	Ctrl+G
Show Code Hints	Ctrl+Space
Indent Code	Ctrl+Shift+>
Outdent Code	Ctrl+Shift+<
Balance Braces	Ctrl+'
Preferences	Ctrl+U

View Menu

Command	Shortcut
Switch Views	Ctrl+'
Refresh Design View	F5
Live Data*	Ctrl+Shift+R
Head Content	Ctrl+Shift+H
Table Mode > Expanded Tables Mode	F6
Table Mode > Layout Mode	Ctrl+F6
Visual Aids > Hide All	Ctrl+Shift+I
Rulers > Show	Ctrl+Alt+R
Grid > Show Grid	Ctrl+Alt+G
Grid > Snap to Grid	Ctrl+Shift+Alt+G
Plugins > Play	Ctrl+Alt+P
Plugins > Stop	Ctrl+Alt+X
Plugins > Play All	Ctrl+Shift+Alt+P
Plugins > Stop All	Ctrl+Shift+Alt+X
Hide/Show Panels	F4

*Command is not included in the Modify menu.

Insert Menu

Command	Shortcut
Tag	Ctrl+E
Image	Ctrl+Alt+I
Media > Flash	Ctrl+Alt+F
Media > Shockwave	Ctrl+Alt+D
Table	Ctrl+Alt+T
Named Anchor	Ctrl+Alt+A
Special Characters > Line Break	Shift+Enter
Special Characters > Non-Breaking Space	Ctrl+Shift+Space
Template Object > Editable Region	Crtl+Alt+V

Modify Menu

Command	Shortcut
Page Properties	Ctrl+J
CSS Styles	Shift+F11
Quick Tag Editor	Ctrl+T
Make Link	Ctrl+L
Remove Link	Ctrl+Shift+L
Table > Select Table	Ctrl+A
Move to the Next Cell*	Tab
Move to the Previous Cell*	Shift+Tab
Table > Merge Cells	Ctrl+Alt+M
Table > Split Cell	Ctrl+Alt+S
Table > Insert Row	Ctrl+M
Table > Insert Column	Ctrl+Shift+A
Table > Delete Row	Ctrl+Shift+M
Table > Delete Column	Ctrl+Shift+-
Table > Increase Column Span	Ctrl+Shift+]
Table > Decrease Column Span	Ctrl+Shift+[
Align > Left	Ctrl+Shift+1
Align > Right	Ctrl+Shift+3
Align > Top	Ctrl+Shift+4
Align > Bottom	Ctrl+Shift+6
Align > Make Same Width	Ctrl+Shift+7
Align > Make Same Height	Ctrl+Shift+9
Timeline > Add Object to Timeline	Ctrl+Alt+Shift+T

*Command is not included in the Modify menu.

Text Menu

Command	Shortcut
Indent	Ctrl+Alt+]
Outdent	Ctrl+Alt+[
Paragraph Format > None	Ctrl+0
Paragraph Format > Paragraph	Ctrl+Shift+P
Paragraph Format > Heading 1	Ctrl+1
Paragraph Format > Heading 2	Ctrl+2
Paragraph Format > Heading 3	Ctrl+3
Paragraph Format > Heading 4	Ctrl+4
Paragraph Format > Heading 5	Ctrl+5
Paragraph Format > Heading 6	Ctrl+6
Align > Left	Ctrl+Shift+Alt+L
Align > Center	Ctrl+Shift+Alt+C
Align > Right	Ctrl+Shift+Alt+R
Align > Justify	Crt+Shift+Alt+J
Bold	Ctrl+B
Italic	Ctrl+I
Check Spelling	Shift+F7

Commands Menu

Command	Shortcut
Start Recording	Ctrl+Shift+X

Site Menu

Command	Shortcut
Get	Ctrl+Shift+D
Check Out	Ctrl+Shift+Alt+D
Put	Ctrl+Shift+U
Check In	Ctrl+Shift+Alt+U
Check Links Sitewide	Ctrl+F8

Window Menu

Command	Shortcut
Insert	Ctrl+F2
Properties	Ctrl+F3
CSS Styles	Shift+F11
Layers	F2
Behaviors	Shift+F4
Snippets	Shift+F9
Reference	Shift+F1
Databases	Ctrl+Shift+F10
Bindings	Ctrl+F10
Server Behaviors	Ctrl+F9
Components	Ctrl+F7
Files	F8
Assets	F11
Tag Inspector	F9
Results	F7
History	Shift+F10
Frames	Shift+F2
Code Inspector	F10
Timelines	Alt+F9
Hide/Show Panels	F4
Next Document	Ctrl+`
Previous Document	Ctrl+Shift+`

Help Menu

Command	Shortcut
Using Dreamweaver	F1
Using ColdFusion	Ctrl+F1
Reference	Shift+F1

Code Shortcuts

Code Editing Shortcut

Command	Shortcut
Select Parent Tag	Ctrl+[
Select Child	Ctrl+]
Balance Braces	Ctrl+'
Select All	Ctrl+A
Bold	Ctrl+B
Italic	Ctrl+I
Copy	Ctrl+C
Find and Replace	Ctrl+F
Find Selection	Shift+F3
Find Next	F3
Paste	Ctrl+V
Cut	Ctrl+X
Redo	Ctrl+Y
Undo	Ctrl+Z
Print Code	Ctrl+P
Surround with #	Ctrl+Shift+3
Switch to Document	Ctrl+`
Select Line Up	Shift+Up
Select Line Down	Shift+Down
Character Select Left	Shift+Left
Character Select Right	Shift+Right
Delete Word Left	Ctrl+Backspace
Delete Word Right	Ctrl+Del
Move to Page Up	Page Up
Move to Page Down	Page Down
Select to Page Up	Shift+Page Up
Select to Page Down	Shift+Page Down
Move Word Left	Ctrl+Left
Move Word Right	Ctrl+Right
Select Word Left	Ctrl+Shift+Left
Select Word Right	Ctrl+Shift+Right
Move to Start of Line	Home
Move to End of Line	End
Select to Start of Line	Shift+Home
Select to End of Line	Shift+End
Move to Top of File	Ctrl+Home
Move to End of File	Ctrl+End
Select to Start of File	Ctrl+Shift+Home
Select to End of File	Ctrl+Shift+End
Snippets	Shift+F9

Files Panel Menus

File Menu

Command	Shortcut
New File	Ctrl+Shift+N
New Folder	Ctrl+Shift+Alt+N
Rename	F2
Delete	Del
Check Links	Shift+F8
Exit	Ctrl+Q

Edit Menu

Command	Shortcut
Cut	Ctrl+X
Copy	Ctrl+C
Paste	Ctrl+V
Duplicate	Ctrl+D
Select All	Ctrl+A

View Menu

Command	Shortcut
Refresh	F5
Show/Hide Link	Ctrl+Shift+Y
View as Root	Ctrl+Shift+R
Show Page Titles	Ctrl+Shift+T
Site Files	F8
Site Map	Alt+F8

Site Menu

Command	Shortcut
Get	Ctrl+Shift+D
Checkout	Ctrl+Shift+Alt+D
Put	Ctrl+Shift+U
Check In	Ctrl+Shift+Alt+U
Check Links Sitewide	Ctrl+F8
Link to New File	Ctrl+Shift+N
Link to Existing File	Ctrl+Shift+K
Change Link	Ctrl+L
Remove Link	Ctrl+Shift+L

Index

Bg Image background (layers), 320
BGCOLOR attribute, 453
block-level elements, 43
blockquotes, 50–51
Bold button, 59
Bold command (Text menu), 59
Book menu, O'Reilly HTML
    Reference, 521
BORDER attribute, 453
Border attribute, 225
Border Thickness option (Table
    dialog box), 212
borders, graphics, 184–185
Bottom option, alignment, 183

 tag, 47
breadcrumb navigation, 95
Brightness and Contrast tool, 198
Brightness/Contrast dialog box, 198
Browse For File button, 78, 538
Browse For File Folder icon, 181
browsers
    compatability, testing accessibility,
        502–508
    Internet Explorer preferences, 152
    preview specification, 33–35
    user interactivity
        Check Browser behavior, 294–297
        open new browser, 297–300
bulleted lists, 52–56
Button command (Insert menu), 401
Button Name text field, 402

C

carriage returns (CR), 41
Cascade option, 31
Cascading Style Sheets. *See* CSS
Cell Padding option (Table dialog
    box), 212
Cell Spacing option (Table dialog
    box), 212
CELLPADDING attribute, 453
cells, tables
    copying and pasting, 217–219
    formatting, 220–225, 249–250
CELLSPACING attribute, 453
CGI (Common Gateway Interface),
    378
Char Width text field, 387–388
characters
    adding to content, 61–62
    formatting inline text, 59–61
    naming files, 23
Check Box command (Insert menu),
    393
Check Browser behavior, user
    interactivity, 294–297
Check Browser dialog box, 295

Check In button, 483
Check In/Out options, site
    management, 481–485
Check In tool (Files panel), 464
Check Link feature, 508–509
Check Links command (File menu),
    508
Check Out Files button, 484
Check Out File(s) tool (Files panel),
    464
Check Page command (File menu),
    502, 508, 543
Check Spelling command (Text
    menu), 513
Check Spelling dialog box, 513
Check Target Browser menu, 502
Check Target Browsers command
    (File menu), 502
Checkbox button, 393
checkboxes, forms, 393–395
Checked Value text field, 393
checking spelling, 513–514
Choose Remote Folder For Site Yoga
    Sangha dialog box, 472
Choose Spacer Image dialog box, 250
cite attribute, 51
Class selectors, 124
Clean Up HTML command
    (Commands menu), 513,
    541–543
Clean Up HTML/XHTML dialog
    box, 541
Clean Up Word HTML command
    (Commands menu), 544
Clean Up Word HTML dialog box,
    544
Clear command (Edit menu), 219,
    328
Client Questionnaire, 5
client-side scripting, 402
clipping area (layers), 318
Cloak Files Ending With: checkbox,
    480
cloaking, site management, 477–481
Cloaking command (Site menu),
    478–481
Code and Design command (View
    menu), 519
Code command (View menu), 518
Code inspector, 519
Code Inspector command (Window
    menu), 519
Code toolbar, 523–526
Code view, 517–523
Code view button, 24
Code View Options command (View
    menu), 523

Coder workspace, 3
codes
    editing, 515–548
        adjusting new window
            placement, 526–528
        advanced customization,
            545–547
        Clean Up HTML command,
            541–543
        Code toolbar, 523–526
        HTML in Code view, 520–523
        Meta tags, 529–533
        Microsoft Word HTML, 543–545
        printing from Code view, 545
        Quick Tags, 535–537
        snippets, 537–541
        switching document views,
            517–520
        Tag inspector, 533–535
    keyboard shortcuts
        Macintosh, 574
        Windows, 578
Collapse Full Tag toolbar icon, 523
colors
    CSS (Cascading Style Sheets),
        backgrounds, 110–111
    fonts, 118–120
    hexadecimal codes, 76
    links, 73–77
Colors dialog box, 119
Colors icon, 120
Columns option (Table dialog box),
    211
Combine As Tabs option, 31
Commands menu commands
    Add/Remove Netscape Resize Fix,
        340
    Clean Up HTML, 513, 541–543
    Clean Up Word HTML, 544
    keyboard shortcuts, 573, 577
    Snippets, 540
comments (HTML), 524–525
Common Gateway Interface (CGI),
    378
communication goals, project sites, 7
Configure Server dialog box, 489
Connect/Disconnect tool (Files
    panel), 463
Connection Wizard (Contribute),
    495
connections, Contribute, 494–495
content, 39–40
    adding special characters, 61–62
    automatically adding dates, 66–68
    blockquotes, 50–51
    forms, grouping, 381–382

site management, 459–496
    accessing files outside
        Dreamweaver site, 464–465
    Check In/Out options, 481–485
    cloaking files and folders, 477–481
    Contribute compatability, 491–495
    design notes, 486–488
    Files panel, 461–469
    remote site connection, 470–473
    server connections, 489–490
    Site Export function, 488–489
    uploading files, 473–477
Site Map button, 90
Site Map Options command (View
    menu), 90, 467
Site Map view, links, 91–94
Site Map View command (Site
    menu), 92
site maps
    creating, 89–90
    saving, 96
    working with links, 91–94
Site menu commands
    Cloaking, 478–481
    Export, 489
    keyboard shortcuts, 573, 577
    Manage Sites, 11, 468
    New Site, 11
    Reports, 499
    Set As Home Page, 89, 466
    Site Map View, 92
    Synchronize, 477
site root-relative paths, 79
sites
    development plans
        design, 8–9
        maintenance, 9
        research, 5–7
        structure, 7–8
        testing, 9
    links, 71–72
        adding files, 82–88
        colors, 73–77
        e-mail, 104–105
        file structure, 80–81
        hypertext, 77–80
        named anchors, 98–103
        site map, 89–94
        Site Map view, 91–94
        targeting, 96–97
        viewing subsets, 94–96
    local, defining, 10–18
    multilingual documents, 63–65
    new page, 18–23
    structure, links, 80–81
Sites And Servers button, 177
size, layers, 348

Snap to Grid command (View
    menu), 328
Snippet dialog box, 539
snippets, editing code, 537–541
Snippets command (Commands
    menu), 540
Sort Table dialog box, 226
sorting tables, 226–227
spaces, naming files, 23
<span> tag, 127
special characters
    adding to content, 61–62
    formatting inline text, 59–61
    naming files, 23
    regular expressions, 569–570
Special Characters command (Insert
    menu), 47
speech synthesizers, 178
spell check, 513–514
Split attribute, 225
Split button, 121, 519
Split Cell button, 228
Split Cell command (Modify menu),
    228
Split Cell Into Rows Or Columns
    button, 238
Split view, 517
Split view button, 24
spreadsheets, importing data,
    215–217
Src option (Property inspector), 419
stacking order, layers, 322–324
Standard command (View menu), 23
Start pages, 4
status bars
    creating messages, user
        interactivity, 293–294
    window attributes, 298
<strong> tag, 59
structural markup, 43
structures, content, 43–46
Style command (Text menu), 59
style sheets. See CSS
<style> tag, 130
styles, 122
Submit button, 401
Swap Image command (Actions
    menu), 283
Swap Image dialog box, 284
switching document views, editing
    code, 517–520
Synchronize command (Site menu),
    477
Synchronize tool (Files panel), 464
synchronizing local and remote sites,
    477
system requirements, xviii

T

Tab Index (accessibility attribute),
    386
Table button, 211
Table command
    File menu, 230
    Insert menu, 211, 381
    Modify menu, 219, 228
Table dialog box, 211
Table menu commands, Insert Rows
    Or Columns, 229
Table Mode command (View menu),
    210, 233
Table Objects command (Insert
    menu), 216
<table> tag, 219
Table Width option (Table dialog
    box), 212
Table Widths command (View
    menu), 214, 245
tables, 207–208
    cells
        copying and pasting, 217–219
        formatting, 220–225, 249–250
        checking layout with window size,
            242–243
        converting tables to, 336–340
        creating, 209–215
    versus CSS (Cascading Style
        Sheets), 210
    designing for monitor types,
        241–242
    exporting, 229–230
    graphics, 230–237
    importing spreadsheet data,
        215–217
    layout
        modification, 247–249
        width, 250–252
    Layout view, 243–246
    modifying, 227–229
    nesting, 237–241
    selecting, 219–220
    sorting, 226–227
    tracing image, 252–254
Tabular Data button, 216
Tag Accessibility Attributes dialog
    box, 189
Tag inspector, editing code, 533–535
Tag Inspector command (Window
    menu), 212, 534
Tag inspector (Image Viewer),
    266–270
Tag Libraries command (Edit menu),
    526
Tag Library Editor, 526
Tag selectors, 124